2500 ANECDOTES FOR ALL OCCASIONS

ORIGINALLY PUBLISHED AS
THESAURUS OF ANECDOTES

A NEW CLASSIFIED COLLECTION
OF THE BEST ANECDOTES
FROM ANCIENT TIMES TO THE PRESENT DAY

EDITED BY

EDMUND FULLER

Editor of THESAURUS OF QUOTATIONS

Dolphin Books
Doubleday & Company, Inc.
Garden City, New York

2500 Anecdotes for All Occasions was originally published as *Thesaurus of Anecdotes* by Crown Publishers in 1943. The Dolphin Books edition is published by arrangement with Crown Publishers.

Dolphin Books edition: 1961

INTRODUCTION

ABRAHAM LINCOLN speaking:

"They say I tell a great many stories; I reckon I do, but I have found in the course of a long experience that common people, take them as they run, are more easily informed through the medium of a broad illustration than in any other way, and as to what the hypercritical few may think, I don't care."

Anecdotes are stories with points. They are tools—nail-sinkers to drive home arguments firmly. The recognition of their usefulness goes back centuries from Lincoln, America's greatest anecdotist. They are the origin of all teaching.

In their old form they were known as parables. By means of them Jesus Christ taught. The prophets and sages of all ancient religion and wisdom employed the simple, effective parable. "I will like him unto a wise man, which built his house upon a rock——." "Hearken; Behold, there went out a sower to sow——." "A certain man had two sons——." Thus, stories with points were made to embody profound teachings. So the Greek slave, Aesop, sagely propounded his fables.

Today the true anecdote is still the counterpart of the parable and fable. Time has tended to shorten it somewhat and, as an attribute of our temperament, we have made it often funny. The majority of the anecdotes in this book are humorous. Many are serious and thoughtful. All prove something. The thing to remember is, many jokes are anecdotes but not all anecdotes are jokes.

To see best how to use the wealth of anecdotes in this book for your own needs, for speaking, teaching, preaching, lecturing, arguing or writing, read the rest of this introduction carefully. Study it before you proceed to the selection and adapting of your material. It will tell you:

1. How to select anecdotes.
2. How to write and tell them.
3. How to vary and adapt them.

HOW TO SELECT YOUR MATERIAL

THE Table of Contents will show you the general plan of the book. The anecdotes are classified in ten basic divisions. These are divided and subdivided by logical association. The association of ideas is not only the basis of much humor, it is the key by which stories to drive home your idea may be located. In each main division every story bears a general relation to those immediately before and after it.

A simple and complete system of cross reference is provided. This counteracts the slightly arbitrary trend unavoidable in any method of classification. Many of the subject headings are related to subjects in other parts of the book. These are listed as RELATED SUBJECTS at the end of each group of anecdotes. You will also find, in each case, a list of SEE ALSOS. These refer you to individual stories listed under other headings yet bearing on the subject at hand.

As an example turn to Judges, 2486-2497. Here are 12 anecdotes. If no one of them quite fills the bill try:
1. The preceding subjects, Courts, Trials.
2. The RELATED SUBJECTS at the end.
3. The SEE ALSOS at the end.
4. The following subjects, Witnesses, Juries, etc.

Continue this process until you find the anecdotes you want and as many as you need.

The Index is alphabetical and naturally is much more comprehensive and detailed than the Table of Contents. It is better to look first in the Index when searching for a topic. The numbers are anecdote numbers, not page numbers. If by any chance your topic is not listed try a synonym, a related word, and more general or more specific words.

HOW TO WRITE AND TELL ANECDOTES

IN using the written anecdote, if you wish to open with it, begin at once, just as the Lincoln statement is used to open this Introduction. So used, it may serve as the ideal presentation of the subject you are about to discuss and the point which you plan to stress in connection with it.

In making a speech, the telling of a well-chosen anecdote may serve as an attention fixer. Witness the story of the ass and his shadow (No. 776):

An Athenian crowd demonstrated impatience at a public assembly one day and hissed the orator Demosthenes, refusing to hear him. He said he had but a short story to tell them and began, "A certain youth hired an ass, in the summer time, to go from his home to Megara. At noon, when the sun was very hot, both he who had hired the ass and the owner of the animal were desirous of sitting in the shade of the ass, and fell to thrusting one another away. The owner insisted that he had hired out only the ass and not the shadow. The other insisted that as he had hired the ass, all that belonged to the ass was his." Turning away, Demosthenes made as though to depart, but the mob, which had been piqued by the story, would not allow him to leave and insisted that he continue. He then turned upon them and demanded, "How is it that you insist upon hearing the story of the shadow of the ass, and will not give an ear to matters of great moment?" He was permitted to deliver the speech for which he had come. And the fine point of the ass and his shadow remains unsettled to this day.

The telling of an anecdote in a speech or conversation requires a certain amount of "build-up," serving first to settle upon the speaker any wandering attention, then to maintain this attention and keep it at a maximum for the climax of the story. By an extension of this principle, the anecdote itself is the "build-up" for the message which is to follow. In addition to this, in speech making, you should use a few generalized opening remarks before beginning the "build-up" for the story. Your remarks to the Chairman, a statement of the pleasure it gives you to be present, or any other such matters will serve. Your first few words are seldom clearly heard. The function of these preliminary remarks is to permit your audience to focus itself upon the sound and pitch of your voice.

The anecdote may be brought into your speech or article at any point. When you have a good story, tell it. It doesn't need an introduction. If you feel that some preface is necessary you can avoid the hackneyed "That reminds me of a story" by simply letting it arise naturally from the association of ideas and subject matter. You need say no more than, "This is like Mark Twain's long-winded missionary," in the case of a story such as that below.

Don't be afraid even to entrust the meat of your message to an adecdote upon occasion. To use a story shrewdly and briefly in this fashion is far wiser than to drift into the pitfall of long-windedness, which may well undo everything for which you have striven.

Mark Twain, after enduring a series of intolerably long drawn out speeches, told a little parable of his own.

"Some years ago in Hartford, we all went to church one hot sweltering night to hear the annual report of Mr. Hawley, a city missionary who went around finding people who needed help and didn't want to ask for it. He told of the life in cellars, where poverty resided; he gave instances of the heroism and devotion of the poor. 'When a man with millions gives,' he said, 'we make a great deal of noise. It's noise in the wrong place, for it's the widow's mite that counts.' Well, Hawley worked me up to a great pitch. I could hardly wait for him to get through. I had $400 in my pocket. I wanted to give that and borrow more to give. You could see greenbacks in every eye. But instead of passing the plate then, he kept on talking and talking, and as he talked it grew hotter and hotter, and we grew sleepier and sleepier. My enthusiasm went down, down, down—$100 at a clip—until finally, when the plate did come around, I stole ten cents out of it. It all goes to show how a little thing like this can lead to crime." (No. 344)

HOW TO ADAPT ANECDOTES TO YOUR OWN PURPOSE

If names make news, still more do they make anecdotes. The "anecdotal" quality as against the "joke" quality in a story is primarily its seeming authenticity or its factual nature. Most of the anecdotes in this book are about specific people. Every reader will encounter one or two stories, attributed in the present version to certain persons, which will be familiar to him by other names. This is where skill may be brought into the use of anecdotes.

In the compiling of this book, anecdote No. 1325 came to hand in three versions:

When the American composer, George Gershwin, died, a man of sentiment combined with musical aspirations wrote an elegy in his honor. He sought out Oscar Levant. Reluctantly Levant granted him a hearing. Eagerly the man rendered the piece with his own hands and then turned expectantly toward Levant, seeking approbation.

"I think it would have been better," Levant said, "if you had died and Gershwin had written the elegy."

To all listeners to *Information Please* this story will have an authentic ring. Yet it exists currently in a version about Liszt bringing to Rossini an elegy on the death of Meyerbeer, and a version about a lady composer approaching Josef Hofmann with an elegy on the death of MacDowell.

Countless other instances could be cited of one anecdote attributed to a lot of people. In this book all choices have been made favoring names of current interest. As you use the book you must be ingenious for in these stories, with the endless simple variations possible to them, you have the raw material of endless anecdotes on any possible subject. Change names to bring them up to date, add names where none are given, change names for the sake of local reference, change place names and scenes for the same purpose. A story about Napoleon and one of his soldiers may serve you as a story about an employee and his boss. A story about a musician may serve for a writer. In each case your need will be served by the *point* of the story. You must be clever in manipulating its framework.

Even the details of subject matter can be changed endlessly to suit occasions, with the effect of creating, for every practical purpose, a brand new story. The story of the shadow of the ass could be placed anywhere and told about anyone. Instead of the ass and its shadow it could be about a dog and its fleas. It could be about a house and its smell; the point could be neatly reversed and made into a pretext for lease-breaking, "I rented the house but I didn't rent the smell." Also the story is precisely the shrewd device of Portia for the confounding of Shylock.

"This bond doth give thee here no jot of blood;
Take then thy bond, take thou thy pound of flesh;
But, in the cutting, if thou dost shed
One drop of Christian blood, thy lands and goods
Are, by the laws of Venice, confiscate. . . ."

Thus, any story in this book has latent in it a dozen more.

Anecdotes are no one's property. They are common stock.

x

They are an aspect of folk-lore. They are yours to use as you wish. No matter how shiny the trimmings of modernism it is hard to prove novelty or originality. That story about the man and woman and the automobile was probably told in Athens about a chariot.

Nicholas Murray Butler and Brander Matthews were discussing stories. Said Matthews, "In the case of the first man to use an anecdote there is originality, in the case of the second there is plagiarism; with the third, it is lack of originality; and with the fourth it is drawing from a common stock."

"Yes," broke in Butler, "and in the case of the fifth it is research." (No. 1168)

Your judgment should tell you when it is wise to vary an anecdote and when to let it stand. Where the original name and locale are not closely involved with the point, or where the names may be largely forgotten, change often improves the story. Most Lincoln stories, on the other hand, derive a unique value from being Lincoln stories and would be much weakened by omitting or changing this magic name.

Nationalities and dialects, however, are a rich field for variation. No. 332 opportunely makes a brand new Japanese story out of a venerable classic about two merchants of Pinsk.

It is said that the Japanese inspire no more confidence one in the other than they do in the citizens of the rest of the world. Two merchants of Tokyo once met in the railway station.

"Where are you going?" asked the first one.

His friend hesitated, then said, "To Kobe."

"Oh, you liar!" said the first one angrily. "You tell me you are going to Kobe to make me think you're going to Osaka, but I have made inquiries and I *know* you are going to Kobe!"

Again the *point* is the thing. You can ring these changes for yourself with almost any story in this book. The whole wide world of nationalities, dialects, and localisms is open to you.

A note is necessary on the numbering of the anecdotes. These numbers are not for the purpose of counting but of locating. They are reference numbers. In order to keep the book from becoming frozen by numbers it was necessary to break their numerical sequence, leaving "expansion joints." The practice has been followed, at the end of each subject, of advancing the numbers to begin the next unit of five—thus a 4 to 6, a 16 to 21, a 42 to 46. This has made it editorially practical to readjust and expand this book up to the last minute. It will permit the expansion of further editions without disrupting the entire editorial organization. It is suggested that the constant user may also avail himself of the opportunity to add his own supplementary stories, using the blank numbers to correlate them with the material in this book.

TABLE OF CONTENTS

NOTE: *In order to know how to use this book properly, it is important to read the introduction.*

ANECDOTES

(For alphabetical list of subjects, see *Index* page xxxiv)

Numbers below are anecdote numbers, not page numbers.

CHARACTER AND MANNERS

LOVE—MARRIAGE—FAMILY

LEARNING AND THE ARTS

RELIGION AND MORALS

MEDICINE AND HEALTH

RECREATION AND SPORTS

GOVERNMENT AND RULERS

BUSINESS, INDUSTRY AND POSSESSIONS

WAR AND THE MILITARY

LAW AND JUSTICE

CHARACTER AND MANNERS

BEHAVIOR

1 George Cheyne, a Scotch physician, when a person was talking about the excellence of human nature, exclaimed:

"Hoot, hoot, man! human nature is a rogue and a scoundrel, or why should it perpetually stand in need of laws and of religion?"

RELATED SUBJECTS: *Prohibitions and Restrictions* 1641-1642; *Sin and Sinners* 1646-1647; *Chiseling and Swindling* 2121-2132; *Criminals* 2571

EATING

6 At a certain dinner party Daniel Webster found himself preyed upon by that type of hostess who endlessly and mercilessly worries her guests with the insistence that they are not eating enough, that possibly they do not like this or that, will not have more, is there anything else they would prefer, and so forth.

"You're hardly eating a thing, Mr. Webster," she protested for the umpteenth time.

"Madam," said Webster solemnly, "permit me to assure you that I sometimes eat more than at other times but never less."

7 Bishop Davidson of Winchester was once one of a party of ecclesiastics who went into dinner after a religious conference. One of the others observed in a tone of pompous self-righteousness, "This is the time to put a bridle on our appetites."

"No," returned the Bishop, "this is the time to put a bit in our mouths."

8 One of the chief reasons for Thackeray's visit to America was his great desire to eat some Massachusetts oysters. The publisher James T. Fields knew of the novelist's secret longing, and as soon as he could get Thackeray in his possession he carried him off to get a magnificent oyster spread.

Thackeray gazed in delight at the six colossal specimens set before him. Not knowing how to begin the attack he asked his companion in a troubled voice, "How do I do it?" "This way," said Fields promptly, and proceeded to dispatch his first oyster. Then in the midst of a profound silence Thackeray did likewise. After a moment Fields anxiously asked him how he felt. Drawing a deep breath, Thackeray replied: "As if I swallowed a baby."

9 Swift, in travelling, called at a hospitable house. The lady of the mansion, rejoiced to have so distinguished a guest, with great eagerness and flippancy asked him what he would have for dinner. "Will you have an apple-pie, sir? Will you have a gooseberry-pie, sir? Will you have a cherry-pie, sir? Will you have a currant-pie, sir? Will you have a plum-pie, sir? Will you have a pigeon-pie, sir?"—

"Any pie, madam, but a mag-pie!"

10 "Why did I come to Africa?" Cecil Rhodes once remarked to a friend. "Well, they will tell you that I came on account of my health, or from love of adventure—and to some extent that may be true, but the real fact is that I could no longer stand their eternal cold mutton."

11 In his early boarding-house days in Kansas City, Eugene Field was invited to dine at a hospitable house where the best of everything was to be found. Some delicious strawberries were passed. Field gazed at them longingly but shook his head.

"Why, Mr. Field," said his host in surprise, "don't you like strawberries?"

"I dote on them."

"Then why don't you take some?"

"I'm afraid," said the poet sadly, "that if I did, they'd spoil my appetite for prunes."

12 Thomas Hood, tempting Charles Lamb to dine with him, said, "We have a hare."

"And how many friends," anxiously inquired Lamb.

13 John Randolph, the American statesman, said to a waiter, at the same time handing him his cup and saucer: "Take that away—change it."

"What do you want, Mr. Randolph?" asked the waiter, "Do you want coffee or tea?"

"If that stuff is tea," said he, "bring me coffee, if it's coffee, bring me tea. I want a change."

14 Alfred Hitchcock is a man notably fond of food. He is said to have once been a guest at a rather sparsely furnished dinner table, which had yielded him no more than a small portion of one thing or another amounting to a totally unsatisfactory sum. As the coffee was being brought in, his host said, "I do hope that you will soon dine here again."

"By all means," said Hitchcock. "Let's start now."

15 Shelley had "for all the sensualities of the table . . . an ineffable contempt, and, like Newton, used sometimes to inquire if he had dined." He was vegetarian, believing that "abstinence from animal food subtilizes and clears the intellect." Bread was his staff of life. When he felt hungry he would rush into a bake shop, emerge with a loaf under his arm, and stride on—rapidly breaking off pieces and swallowing them greedily. While visiting Shelley, his friend Hogg once ventured to say something about a pudding. "A pudding," said Shelley, "is a prejudice." He did sometimes permit Harriet or Mary to supply a "murdered chicken" for a guest.

16 Will Rogers, invited to dinner by a friend, replied, "No thanks, I've already et."

"You should say 'have eaten,'" his friend corrected.

"Well," drawled Rogers, "I know a lot of fellers who say 'have eaten' who ain't et!"

17 At the boarding house in Kansas City where he once lived, Eugene Field, the humorist, found the table-fare uninteresting. One day, when hash was served for dinner, he asked his neighbor to, "Kindly pass the Review of Reviews."

18 George Bernard Shaw is noted as a vegetarian. One time, at a dinner party in London, he had before him on his plate the special concoction which was always provided for him, consisting of some greens with a mixture of salad oils.

Sir James Barrie, who was Shaw's neighbor at the table, bent over to him and, in a confidential tone, asked, "Tell me one thing, Shaw, have you eaten that or are you going to?"

19 Mark Twain habitually bemoaned the poor quality of French coffee. It was his insistence that the concoction was brewed by, "rubbing a chicory bean against a coffee bean and dropping the chicory bean in the water."

20 At a Sunday night tea which the author Hamlin Garland attended he was served some fresh mushrooms.

"Are you sure, Madam," he asked his hostess with great concern, "that these are not a poisonous variety of mushrooms?"

The hostess assured him they were harmless and edible. As he still hesitated, looking speculatively into space, his hostess asked him if he was still afraid.

"No," mused Mr. Garland, "I was just thinkng of the effect on American letters should you be wrong."

21 The wonderful Madame Ernestine Schumann-Heink, greatest contralto of her time, was seated in a restaurant near the Metropolitan Opera House with an enormous steak before her. Enrico Caruso came in and joined her at the table.

"Stena," he said in mock astonishment, "you're not going to eat that alone?"

"No," said the portly contralto, "no, not alone; with potatoes."

22 Sir Richard Jebb, the famous doctor, was a liberal eater, a high liver. He believed the digestive organs were made to be used, not nursed. The question frequently asked by his patients, "What may I eat, doctor?" was exceedingly annoying to him. On one occasion he gave this answer: "My directions, sir, are simple. You must not eat the poker, shovel, or tongs, for they are hard of digestion; nor the bellows, for they will produce wind in your stomack; but you may eat anything else you please."

23 The old saying that many great inventions are the products of accidents seems to hold true in the culinary field.

There is a tradition surrounding the origin of Melba toast, which was supposedly a creation of the great French master chef, Escoffier. At the Savoy in London, César Ritz was maitre d'hotel and Escoffier was chef. Nellie Melba, celebrated prima donna, was staying there and was strenuously dieting, living largely on toast.

It chanced one day, while the master was preoccupied, that an underling prepared the great lady's toast. It was bungled and was served to her in a thin dried-up state resembling parchment. Ritz beheld with horror his celebrated guest crunching this aborted toast, and hastened over to apologize. Before he could utter a word Madame Melba burst out joyfully, saying, "César, how clever of Escoffier. I have never eaten such lovely toast."

RELATED SUBJECTS: *Drinking* 36-55; *Banquets and Dinners* 751-753; *Hotels and Restaurants* 2296-2302; *Waiters* 2306-2308; *K. P.* 2466

SEE ALSO: *Eccentricity* 198; *Imagination* 306; *Rudeness* 511; *Tact* 589; *Fatness* 684, 687; *Parties* 745; *Talking* 816; *Learned Men* 1083; *Concerts* 1345; *Sermons* 1543; *Believers* 1594; *Psychiatrists* 1686; *Longevity* 1781; *Advertising* 2108; *Hotels* 2299

SLEEPING

26 Stephen Leacock says, "I often think this 'insomnia' business is about 90% nonsense. When I was a young man living in a boarding house in Toronto, my brother George came to visit me, and since there was no spare room, we had to share my bed. In the morning, after daylight, I said to George, 'Did you get much sleep?'

" 'Not a damn minute,' said he.

" 'Neither did I,' I rejoined. 'I could hear every sound all night.'

"Then we put our heads up from the bedclothes and saw that the bed was covered with plaster. The ceiling had fallen on us in the night. But we hadn't noticed it. We had 'insomnia.' "

27 The old lighthouse-keeper had been at his post continuously for thirty years. During that entire period he had been accustomed to a gun going off, practically under his nose, every six minutes, day and night. This was the method for warning the ships. Naturally, he grew hardened to this periodic explosion, and paid no attention to it. Then, one night, in his 31st year at this post, the gun failed to go off. The old man awoke from a sound slumber. "What was that?" he cried in alarm.

> RELATED SUBJECTS: *Laziness* 326-327; *Hotels and Restaurants* 2296-2302

> SEE ALSO: *Dullness* 193; *Gratitude* 261; *Introductions* 790; *Small Children* 975; *Authors* 1194; *Sermons* 1550, 1557; *Doctors* 1667; *Debt* 2157

HABITS

31 In reply to an invitation to lunch with Lady Randolph, George Bernard Shaw wired: "Certainly not; what have I done to provoke such an attack on my well known habits?"

Lady Randolph sent another telegram:

"Know nothing of your habits; hope they are not as bad as your manners."

> RELATED SUBJECTS: *Prohibitions and Restrictions* 1641-1642; *Sin and Sinners* 1646-1647

> SEE ALSO: *Sleeping* 27; *Fatness* 690

DRINKING

36 One day Dr. Johnson was conversing with Mrs. Williams, a blind friend of his. She was telling him where she had dined the day before. "There were several gentlemen there," said she, "and I found that there had been a good deal of hard drinking." She closed this observation with a trite moral reflection: "I wonder what pleasure men can take in making beasts of themselves!"

Dr. Johnson replied, "I wonder madam that you have not the penetration to see that he who makes a beast of himself gets rid of the pain of being a man."

37 A lady once asked Secretary of State Evarts if drinking so many different wines did not make him feel seedy the next day.

"— madam," he replied, "it's the indifferent wines that pro— at result."

38 All teetotallers should be as gracious in their excuses as the Irish poet, George Russell, better known as A. E.

When declining a drink, he would murmur, "No thank you. You see . . . I was born intoxicated."

39 Sir Campbell Bannerman M.P. was once asked his opinion on the liquor traffic. He replied: "The liquor traffic is a large subject, and I can hardly enter on it here. There is an old story of a Highlander who was asked if whiskey was not a bad thing. 'Yes,' said he, 'very bad—especially bad whiskey.'"

40 "I see you're drinking coffee, Judge," someone remarked to Ben Lindsey on a hot summer's day. "Why don't you try something cooling? Did you ever try gin and ginger ale?"

"No," said Judge Lindsey, "but I've tried several fellows who have."

41 The story is told about Arthur Sullivan, the composer, that the one faculty which never forsook him was his tonal sense. It is said that he returned one night to his flat in a state of inebriation sufficient to render the row of identical houses in which he lived a difficult problem in identification. Sullivan ambled down the row pausing from time to time and kicking at the metal shoe scrapers by the side of the steps of the houses. Coming to one, he paused, kicked it again, murmured to himself, "That's right. E flat," and entered the door.

42 While Sir Wilfred Lawson was pushing anti-liquor agitation in the House of Lords, some of his waggish enemies passed this story about: During Sir Wilfred's university days he was accused of breaking rules, and the head of his college called him upon the carpet. "Sir," said the dignitary, "I am told you have a barrel of beer in your room, which you should know is contrary to orders."

"Well, sir," the delinquent admitted, "that is true; but the fact is, I am of a weak constitution, and the doctors told me that if I drank this beer I should get stronger."

"And are you stronger?" the head asked sarcastically.

"Oh, yes, sir; indeed I am. When the barrel came I could scarcely move it; but it was not long before I could easily roll it around the room."

43 W. C. Fields was suffering from one of his daily hangovers. "May I fix you a Bromo-Seltzer?" suggested the waiter.

"Ye gods, no!" moaned Fields, "I couldn't stand the noise."

44   In Texas they like their liquor straight, as witness the case of one old-timer who, upon taking in his hand a small tumbler of whiskey, said, "Blindfold me and hold my nose—'cause if I see it or smell it, my mouth will water and dilute it!"

45   In one of our Southwestern proverbially dry states a couple of strangers in town asked a man on the street where they could get a drink. "Well," said the man, "in this town they only use whiskey for snake bite. There's only one snake in town, and it's gettin' kind of late. You'd better hurry down and git in line before it gits exhausted."

46   A question of perspective was raised by the case of the drunk, who, while unconscious, had some Limburger cheese rubbed on his mustache. Coming to later, staggering feebly along, he began to say, "Ain't it awful!"
   "What is the trouble?" someone asked.
   "Ain't it awful!" said the drunk. "The whole world smells."

47   An inebriated gentleman was weaving gently down the street carrying in his hand a box with perforations in the lid and sides. An acquaintance stopped him and said, "My word, what have you got in the box?"
   "Shh," said the drunk. "It's a mongoose."
   "What on earth for?" asked his friend.
   "Well," he said, "you know how it is with me. I'm not very drunk now, but I'll be soon, and when I am I see snakes and I'm scared of 'em, and that's what I got the mongoose for; to protect me."
   "But, good heavens," said his friend, "those are imaginary snakes!"
   "That's all right," said the drunk reassuringly. "That's all right; this is an imaginary mongoose."

48   The young fellow, slightly green in the ways of the smart set, apologized to his hostess, explaining, "Though I may be slightly under the affluence of incohol, I'm not so think as you drunk I am."

49   At a fashionable bar the main decorations were mounted game and fish. A drunk, fascinated by them, carefully walked

from one to the other, mumbling as he went. Suddenly he came upon an enormous stuffed tarpon. Swaying precariously he stared at it for a full minute, then burst forth, "The fella who caught that fish is a liar!"

50 A clergyman told an Indian he should love his enemies. "I do," said the latter, "for I love rum and cider."

51 William Penn was exhorting a drunkard to cast off his habit. The drunkard lamented that this was impossible.

"No," said Penn, "it is as easy as opening thy hand, friend."

"Tell me how this is and I will do as you say," said the drunkard.

"Friend, when thee finds any vessel of intoxicating liquor in thy hand, open the hand that contains it before it reaches thy mouth and thee will never be drunk again."

52 The temperance lecturer, having exhorted the audience with the full force of his eloquence, having demonstrated all the familiar tricks, such as the emersion of an angleworm in a glass of whiskey with its consequent agonies, decided to cap the climax with a homely object lesson: "If I put a pail of whiskey and a pail of water in front of a hard-working donkey toiling in the fields, which would he drink?"

"The water," bellowed a lusty voice in the audience.

"That's true, my friend," said the lecturer. "And why would he drink the water?"

"Because he's a jackass," was the immediate reply.

53 No durance vile could be more pathetic than that suffered by the drunk who was found wandering agonizedly around and around on the sidewalk outside the fence which encloses Gramercy Park, beating upon the bars and screaming, "Let me out!"

54 In the days when Nevada was a territory Bill Nye, the humorist, was appointed Governor. As he journeyed to Carson City to take over his duties in this wild and wide-open silver country, Mark Twain accompanied him.

Word of the new Governor's arrival had reached Carson City, and the boys had gotten together and decided to put the Easterner and his friend in their place by giving them a big banquet and drinking them under the table in short order. The night of the banquet drinks and speeches flowed unceasingly for hours. One by one those present slipped gracefully under their chairs and slumbered noisily beneath the tablecloths.

At a small hour of the night only two men were left in a state of consciousness and seated upright—Bill Nye and Mark Twain.

"Well, Bill," said Twain, stretching and getting up from his chair, "let's go out of here somewhere and get a drink."

55   The representative of an auction house was sent to a home to take an inventory of the goods therein in preparation for a sale. The inventory had progressed in an orderly manner through many large items, such as, one walnut bedroom suite, then listed in detail, one walnut dining room suite, likewise listed in detail, and similar items of household furnishings, until at last came the individual items of miscellany.

At the top of this list was "One quart Scotch whiskey, full"; the list continued, then appeared the item, "One quart whiskey, partially full." The list continued; then appeared the item, "One whiskey bottle, empty."

The final item on the list was, "Two revolving Turkish rugs."

> RELATED SUBJECTS: *Eating* 6-23; *Parties* 741-746; *Banquets and Dinners* 751-753; *Prohibitions and Restrictions* 1641-1642; *Hotels and Restaurants* 2296-2302; *Law Enforcement* 2546-2548

> SEE ALSO: *Accuracy* 92; *Boastfulness* 103; *Liars* 333; *Quick Thinking* 492; *Rough and Ready* 500; *Stinginess* 560, 561; *Zanies* 642; *Prejudice* 682; *Speeches* 759; *Husband* 918; *Hollywood* 1446; *Evangelists* 1515; *Conversions* 1622, 1625; *Doctors* 1666; *Medicines* 1731; *Billiards* 1827; *Miscellaneous Contests* 1882; *Bosses* 2232; *Servants* 2283; *Officers* 2416

SMOKING

61   Charles Steinmetz, "the electrical wizard," was an inveterate smoker. When a notice forbidding smoking was posted in the General Electric plant where he worked, Steinmetz ignored it until an executive asked if he was not aware of the rule. The answer was a cold indifferent stare. The next day Steinmetz didn't show up, and for two days no one heard from him, while

important work remained untouched. Then began a serious search which ended in the lobby of a Buffalo hotel where he was found sitting at ease in a huge chair and puffing a cigar.

Told that the whole company was looking for him, and asked why he had left so unceremoniously, he calmly replied, "I came up here to have a smoke." After that the smoking rule was never applied to him.

62 Thomas Edison was telling Mr. Cary a story one day about the way his friends, when they came into his office, would help themselves to his pure Havana cigars. "They just take 'em by the handful," he said.

"Why don't you lock them up?" asked Mr. Cary.

"Never could remember to do it," returned Edison. "Then Johnson, my secretary you know, did a clever trick. He had a friend in the cigar business and promised to get him to make me some entirely of cabbage leaves and brown paper. I thought that was a fine scheme. But the cigars didn't come, so I asked him one day about it when I noticed my Havanas disappearing again.

" 'Why, I sent them to you,' he said. 'I left them with your manager.'

"I called the manager in and asked him where those cigars were. 'Why,' he said, 'I put them in your valise when you went to California last month. I didn't know what they were.'

"Do you know, Cary," continued Edison, "I smoked every-one of those damned cigars myself!"

63 This story is told by Max Mueller:

"Tennyson's pipe was almost indispensable to him, and I re-member one time when I and several friends were staying at his house, the question of tobacco turned up. Some of his friends taunted Tennyson that he could never give up tobacco. 'Anybody can do that,' he said, 'if he chooses to do it.' When his friends still continued to doubt and to tease him, 'Well,' he said, 'I shall give up smoking from tonight.' The very same evening I was told that he threw his tobacco and his pipes out of the window of his bedroom. The next day he was most charming, though somewhat self-righteous. The second day he became very moody and captious, the third day no one knew what to do with him. But after a disturbed night I was told that he got out of bed in the morning, went quietly into the garden, picked up one of his broken pipes, stuffed it with the remains of the tobacco scattered about, and then having had a few puffs, came to breakfast, all right again."

64 A minister was deeply impressed by an address on the evils of smoking given at a synod. He arose from his seat, went over to a fellow minister, and said: "Brother, this morning I received a present of 100 good cigars. I have smoked one of them, but now I'm going home to burn the rest in the fire."

The other minister arose and said it was his intention to accompany his reverend brother.

"I mean to rescue the ninety-nine," he added.

65 When Dr. Creighton was Bishop of London he rode on a train one day with a small, meek curate. Dr. Creighton, an ardent lover of tobacco, soon took out his cigar case and with a smile, said: "You don't mind my smoking, I suppose?"

The meek curate bowed and answered humbly: "Not if your lordship doesn't mind my being sick."

> RELATED SUBJECTS: *Will Power* 631; *Prohibitions and Restrictions* 1641-1642

> SEE ALSO: *Longevity* 1782; *Advertising* 2102

PROFANITY

66 Mark Twain's habit of swearing was revolting to his wife, who tried her best to cure him of it. One day, while shaving, he cut himself. He recited his entire vocabulary and when he was finished, his wife repeated every word he had said. Mark Twain stunned her by saying calmly:

"You have the words, dear, but you don't know the tune."

67 A minister on a fishing trip was delighted to find that his guide was once hired by Bishop Phillips Brooks. They immediately began talking about him, recalling many noble traits and characteristics.

"Yes," said the guide, "he was a fine man 'cept for his swearing."

"What," exclaimed the minister, "Bishop Brooks swear? Impossible!"

"Oh, but he did, sir. Once he hooked a fine big bass. Just

as he hoisted him into the boat, the fish slipped and went clean off the hook. So I said to the Bishop, 'That's a damned shame,' and the Bishop come back and said, 'Yes, it is.' But that's the only time I ever heard him use such language."

68   A certain Elector of Cologne, who was at the same time archbishop, had one day made use of profane words and then said to a farmer who could not conceal his astonishment:

"Why do you look so surprised?"

The farmer replied: "Because an archbishop can be so profane."

"I do not swear as an archbishop," replied that person, "but as a prince."

"But Your Highness," answered the farmer, "when the prince goes to hell what will become of the archbishop?"

The Elector's reply was not reported.

> RELATED SUBJECTS: *Rough and Ready* 496-507; *Rudeness* 511-524; *Temper* 596-598; *Prohibitions and Restrictions* 1641-1642

> SEE ALSO: *Golf* 1864; *Witnesses* 2504; *Ministers* 2607

GAMBLING

71   At a large party, Mrs. Henry Clay, chaperoning a young lady, passed through a room where gentlemen were playing cards, Mr. Clay among them. "Is this a common practise?" inquired the young lady.

"Yes," said Mrs. Clay; "they always play when they get together."

"Doesn't it distress you to have Mr. Clay gamble?"

"No, my dear," said the old lady composedly, "he 'most always wins."

72   An ailing bookmaker sent his son to summon the doctor. Instead of the expected man, a stranger arrived. Later, the bookmaker asked for an explanation. "Well," said the boy, "there were a lot of brass plates on the doors, and when I got to the one you told me to go to, it said, 'Consultations, 11 to 12.' The one next to it said, '10 to 1.' And I knew you'd like the one who gave the best odds."

73 The British comedienne, Beatrice Lillie, once won a hundred and fifty thousand francs at Chemin de fer through having the hiccoughs. Her repeated convulsions and noises were interpreted by the croupier as cries of "Banquo."

74 Grandmother was bitterly opposed to gambling games—especially poker—but gave her sanction to the playing of authors. So the grandchildren engaged her interests in the game of her choice. Her enthusiasm increased as the game progressed, and while she knew that the cards used were a deck of authors, she didn't know that the game she was playing was poker, and that grandmother was enthusiastically playing Whittiers wild.

> RELATED SUBJECTS: *Extravagance* 231-232; *Prohibitions and Restrictions* 1641-1642; *Card Playing* 1836-1840

> SEE ALSO: *Liars* 333; *Natural Death* 1756; *Deathbed Scenes* 1771; *Card Playing* 1836; *Bargaining* 2081; *Chiseling* 2130

REPUTATION

76 One of the powerful figures in Wall Street fell in love with an actress and for many months danced constant attendance upon her and squired her about in the fashionable circles of town. Deciding to marry her, he first prudently put a private detective to the job of looking into her antecedents in order to guard himself against any rash mistake. At last he received his agent's report. "Miss Blank enjoys an excellent reputation. Her past is spotless. Her associates have been irreproachable. The only breath of scandal is that, in recent months, she has been seen in the company of a business man of doubtful reputation."

77 It is humbling, to all men of note to find themselves at some time outside of the spheres in which their talent and fame are known, and to see themselves as lesser individuals. The great Enrico Caruso once stopped at a farm during a drive through the country. He obtained water and something to eat, and while he was talking in a friendly way with the farmer, the latter chanced to inquire his name. He said his name was

Caruso. Instantly the farmer was transfixed. "What an honor," he said, "what an honor to have in my own house that great traveler, Robinson Crusoe."

78   An Irishman was charged with a petty offense. "Have you anybody here who can vouch for your character?" said the judge. "Yes, Your Honor, the sheriff there can."

"Why, I do not even know this man," exclaimed the sheriff.

"Observe, Your Honor," said the Irishman triumphantly, "that I've lived twelve years in this county and the sheriff doesn't even know me."

> RELATED SUBJECTS: *Behavior* 1; *Discretion* 181-182; *Modesty* 376-390; *Gossip* 821-826; *Credit* 2166-2167

> SEE ALSO: *Authors* 1212; *Politics* 1899

TRAITS

ABSENT-MINDEDNESS

81   The late Dwight Morrow, who was very absent-minded, was once reading earnestly on a train when the conductor asked for his ticket. Frantically Mr. Morrow searched for it.

"Never mind, Mr. Morrow," the conductor said. "When you find it, mail it to the company. I'm certain you have it."

"I know I have it," exploded Mr. Morrow. "But what I want to know is, where in the world am I going?"

82   In his old age, Lessing, the German author became very absent-minded. Coming home one night with his mind on some work he intended to finish, he found the door locked, and discovered that he had not taken his key with him. In answer to his knock, a servant looked out of an upstairs window, and mistaking his master for a stranger, called out, "The professor is not at home."

"Very well," Lessing answered meekly as he turned away. "Tell him that I'll call another time."

83   J. David Stern, former publisher of the New York Post, was sometimes accused of absent-mindedness. Once, as he hastened down the street, he was accosted by a friend who said, "Come, have lunch with me."

"All right," said Stern, "if we go to some place nearby. I am already late."

They entered a restaurant close at hand, and as he ordered, Stern wondered what could be the matter with him for he said, "I am not a bit hungry."

"I beg pardon, sir," the waiter said, "but you just finished lunch five minutes ago."

84 When her daughters were very small girls, Mrs. Dwight Morrow gave a high tea at which one of the guests was to be the senior J. P. Morgan. The girls were to be brought in, introduced and ushered out. Mrs. Morrow's great fear was the possibility that Anne, the most outspoken of them, might comment audibly upon Mr. Morgan's celebrated and conspicuous nose. She therefore took pains to explain to Anne that personal observations were impolite, and to caution her especially against making any comment upon Mr. Morgan's nose, no matter what she might think of it. When the moment came and the children were brought in, Mrs. Morrow held her breath as she saw Anne's gaze unfalteringly fix upon this objective and remain there. Nonetheless, the introduction was made, the little girls curtsied and were sent on their way. With a sigh of relief Mrs. Morrow turned back to her duties as hostess and said to her chief guest, "And now, Mr. Morgan, will you have cream or lemon in your nose?"

85 "That absent-minded Professor Schmaltz has left his umbrella again. He'd leave his head if it were loose," observed the waiter.

"That's true," said the manager, "I just heard him say he was going to Switzerland for his lungs."

86 The professor was very absent-minded. "Did you see this?" his wife asked as he came in. "There's a report in the paper of your death."

"Dear me," said the professor, "We must remember to send a wreath."

87 Another story about Dwight Morrow's notorious absent-mindedness. Getting off the train in New York, he hastened

into the telegraph office and wired to his secretary: "Why am I in New York? What am I supposed to do?"

He received a prompt answer; that he was on his way to Princeton to deliver a lecture.

88 It is said that the late dictator of Greece, General Georges Metaxas, during an inspection of a Mediterranean air base, was invited to try out a new flying boat. He undertook to pilot it himself, and all went well until the commander, his host, observed that they were about to make a landing on the airdrome. "Excuse me, General, but it would be better to come down on the sea; this is a flying boat."

"Of course, Commander, what was I thinking of!" said Metaxas, suddenly recollecting himself, and making a safe landing on the water. Rising from the wheel he said, "Commander, I greatly appreciate the tact with which you drew my attention to the incredible blunder which I nearly made." Saying which, he opened the door and stepped into the sea.

89 "You mean to say," asked the Judge of the defendant, "that you threw your wife out of the second story window through forgetfulness?"

"Yes, sir," replied the defendant. "We used to live on the ground floor and I plumb forgot we moved."

90 Thomas Henry Huxley once arrived late in a town in which he was to deliver an important lecture. Jumping into a cab, he cried to the driver, "Top speed!" In a hurry the cabby whipped his horse into action and the vehicle went bumping along the streets at a wild clip. The lack of dignity and organization in the proceedings then dawned upon Huxley, and above the clatter of the wheels he shouted to the driver, "Here, here, do you know where I want to go?"

"No, Your Honor," called the cabby, cracking his whip the while, "but I'm driving as fast as I can."

RELATED SUBJECTS: *Eccentricity* 196-209; *Memory* 371-375; *Professors* 1026-1032

SEE ALSO: *Smoking* 62; *Books* 1223; *Churches* 1527; *Death* 1749

ACCURACY

91 Cordell Hull was an extremely cautious speaker, striving always for scientific accuracy. One day on a train, a friend pointed to a fine flock of sheep grazing in a field. "Look, those sheep have just been sheared," he said.

Hull studied the flock. "Sheared on this side, anyway," he admitted.

92 The captain of a certain freighter was a martinet who, although technically just, was noted far and wide for the strictness of his interpretation of facts.

On a certain voyage he had a new first mate, an able and conscientious man. Following an occasion of shipboard revelry, the captain entered in the log the note, "The first mate was drunk last night."

Seeing this the mate was greatly distressed and pled with the captain to strike it off the record. He had never been drunk before, he insisted, would not be drunk again; was conscientious in the performance of his duties and had been off duty at the time of the offense anyway. He begged for leniency, pointing out what an unduly detrimental effect on his record such an entry on the log might have.

The captain remained adamant, "You were drunk last night and I can't change the fact. The record will stand."

Much wounded by this the first mate resumed his duties. That night it fell to his lot to make the next entry in the log for the period of his watch. This he did, with what may be called a malicious scrupulousness of accuracy. Accordingly the captain next day found on the log the innocently damning statement, "The captain was sober last night."

> RELATED SUBJECTS: *Carelessness* 136; *Diligence* 176-177; *Liars* 331-336; *Memory* 371-375; *Scientists* 1116-1122; *Mathematicians* 1146-1154; *Statistics* 2221-2222; *Evidence* 2521-2523

AMBITION

96 Some of Mr. Lincoln's intimate friends once called his attention to a certain member of his Cabinet who was quietly working to secure a nomination for the Presidency, although knowing that Mr. Lincoln was to be a candidate for reëlection. His friends insisted that the Cabinet officer ought to be made to give up his Presidential aspirations or be removed from office. The situation reminded Mr. Lincoln of a story:

"My brother and I," he said, "were once plowing corn, I driving the horse and he holding the plow. The horse was lazy, but on one occasion he rushed across the field so that I, with my long legs, could scarcely keep pace with him. On reaching the end of the furrow, I found an enormous chin-fly fastened upon him, and knocked him off. My brother asked me what I did that for. I told him I didn't want the old horse bitten in that way. 'Why,' said my brother, 'that's all that made him go.'

"Now," said Mr. Lincoln, "if Mr. —— has a Presidential chin-fly biting him, I'm not going to knock it off, if it will only make his department go."

97 Oliver Herford, the well known humorist, attended a dinner at which he was seated next to a very serious and soulful young lady.

"Tell me, Mr. Herford," she asked, "have you no other ambition beyond making people laugh?"

In the same serious vein, Herford replied, "Yes, I have. And some day I hope to gratify it."

Eagerly the girl asked, "Please tell me. What is it?"

"I want to throw an egg into an electric fan," replied Herford simply.

> RELATED SUBJECTS: *Diligence* 176-177; *Laziness* 326-327; *Campaigning* 1911-1920; *Office Seekers* 1966-1970; *Salesmen* 2091-2097; *Competition* 2116

> SEE ALSO: *Patriotism* 399; *Conductor* 1332; *Efficiency* 2269

BOASTFULNESS

101 Mark Twain, whenever feats of heroism or ingenuity were being bragged about, would come forth with a little story of his own which usually climaxed the discussion.

"There was a fire in Hannibal one night, and old man Hankinson got caught in the fourth story of the burning house. It looked as if he was a goner. None of the ladders was long enough to reach him. The crowd stared at one another, nobody could think of anything to do.

"Then, all of a sudden, boys, an idea occurred to me. 'Fetch a rope,' I yelled, 'somebody fetch a rope,' and, with great presence of mind, I flung the end of it up to old man Hankinson; 'Tie it around your waist,' I yelled. The old man did so, and I pulled him down."

102   An over-patriotic American gazed at the superb masses of a European cathedral with its marvelous statues and ornaments, and asked the guide how long it had taken to build. "Five hundred years," replied the guide.

The American sniffed, "Five hundred years. Why, we would build a structure like that and have it fall to pieces on our hands all inside of two or three years."

103   A group of men in a bar-room were exchanging wild boasts about their feats of courage and bravery. When the tall tales had almost stretched themselves to the limit, a quiet old Swede who had been silently drinking and listening, spoke up, "I myself never do anything so very brave," said he. "But my brudder, he call Yessie Yames a big s-o-b." The others were appalled.

"What," they cried, "he called Jessie James an s-o-b? Tell us about it."

"My brudder he vas drinking and he get pretty drunk. Yessie Yames in same bar-room. My brudder he go over and say, 'Yessie Yames, you are one great big s-o-b.' "

"What did Jessie James do?" demanded his listeners.

"He shoot my brudder!"

> RELATED SUBJECTS: *Exaggeration* 221-226; *Liars* 331-336; *Long-Windedness* 341-363; *Modesty* 376-390; *Pompousness* 421-427; *Pride* 456-457; *Vanity* 606-628

> SEE ALSO: *Exaggeration* 226; *Baseball* 1824; *Fishing* 1846, 1853; *Hunting* 1877; *Miscellaneous Contests* 1883

BONERS

106   While shown the sights of Chicago by the Mayor of that city, M. Cambon, the French Ambassador of another genera-

tion, expressed his thanks for the Mayor's kindness. "But," he added, "I am sorry so to cockroach on your time."

"Oh," answered the Mayor, "don't think of that. But you don't mean cockroach Mr. Cambon; it is encroach, you mean."

"Oh, is it? I see—a difference in gender."

107 As is usual, during public events of any kind, the newspapers hurriedly set up their front pages to describe the inauguration of Theodore Roosevelt.

The evidence of this haste was shown by a New York paper which described the event as follows:

"It was a scene never to be forgotten when Roosevelt, before the Chief Justice of the Supreme Court and a few witnesses, took his simple bath."

108 There is a Congressional legend about the newly elected Congressman who, in his maiden speech on the floor of the House, said, "As Daniel Webster makes clear in his famous dictionary . . ."

He was interrupted from the floor by a cry of, "Noah Webster wrote the dictionary."

"Noah nothing," replied the speaker, "Noah built the ark!"

109 Every newspaper makes its more or less amusing or more or less disastrous typographical errors in headlines or stories. Usually, when these occur, they must be corrected, if caught, in subsequent editions. It is said that recently one of the most important newspapers in Washington reported on its front page a mild indisposition of President Roosevelt with the headline, "President Kept to Rooms by Coed." Most of the run had been printed and had to be destroyed. The President, however, heard of the matter and procured from the paper in question several copies to distribute to his friends.

110 A man stopped at the shop of a Cockney bookseller and asked for Omar Khayyam. "Sorry, sir," said the Cockney, "we 'ave 'is Hilliad and 'is Hodessey but not 'is Khayyam."

111 Benjamin Franklin, being present at the meeting of some literary society in Paris, where many pieces were read, and not well understanding the French when declaimed, but wishing to appear polite, resolved to applaud when he should see a lady of his acquaintance, Mme. de Boufflers, express satisfaction.

After the reading was over, his little boy said to him, "But grand-papa, you always applauded, and louder than anybody else, when they were praising you."

112　When Julia Ward Howe died, memorial services were held at San Francisco. The local literary colony attended practically en masse to pay their final tribute. The Mayor was asked to preside. Advancing to the edge of the platform he said:

"Your attendance here, ladies and gents, in such great numbers, shows San Francisco's appreciation of good literature. This meeting is a great testimonial to the immortal author of "Uncle Tom's Cabin"—the late Julia Ward Howard!"

113　"Marse" Henry Watterson used to tell with pleasure of his favorite typographical boner in newspapers. It happened that a New York journal transposed, one day, the headings of its obituary column and the marine and shipping news which had chanced to fall on the same page. As a result a number of respected and deceased citizens were listed under the disconcerting heading, "Passed through Hell Gate today."

114　This was one of Cardinal Gibbons' favorite jokes: Patrick Gilmore, the bandmaster, famous for his rendition of Mozart's "Twelfth Mass," once presented his favorite number in a small North Carolina town. The reporter of the one newspaper in town, who was assigned to "cover" the performance evidently thought that the occasion was one that called upon him to avoid any undignified abbreviations in his write-up of the concert. He began with this statement: "Gilmore's band rendered with great effect Mozart's 'Twelfth Massachusetts.' "

115　A young lady, who had recently acquired a large fortune, invited Paderewski to give a private concert at her home. Her knowledge of music was by no means as large as her newly found wealth.

Commenting on one of his selections, she exclaimed, "What a beautiful piece. Who composed it?"

"Beethoven, Madam," was the reply.

"Ah, yes," she said knowingly, "and is he composing now?"

"No," replied Paderewski gravely, "he is decomposing."

116　A woman whose husband had entered the Navy, gave the pastor of her church a note just as he was mounting to the pulpit one Sunday morning. The note said, "John Anderson, having gone to sea, his wife desires the prayers of the congregation for his safety." The minister in haste picked up the slip and read aloud, "John Anderson, having gone to see his wife, desires the prayers of the congregation for his safety."

117 In the early days of his career the famous writer of short stories, Bret Harte, was editor of a newspaper in a California mining town. It was his painful duty one time to write an obituary for the highly respected wife of a leading citizen. Harte concluded his remarks with the sentence, "She was distinguished for charity above all the other ladies in this town."

When the proof of this was handed to him he found that the compositor had rendered his statement, "She was distinguished for chastity above all the other ladies of this town." Carefully, Harte corrected the matter thinking it sufficient to refer the compositor back to the original copy by a large query in the margin. To his horror, the following day the paper appeared with the statement: "She was distinguished for chastity (?) above all the other ladies in this town."

118 A freight agent on the Delaware, Lackawanna and Western received a shipment including a donkey, which was itemized on the freight bill as, "1 Burro."

He checked over his shipment carefully and then filed his report, concluding with, "short, 1 bureau; over, 1 jackass."

119 A cub reporter was sent to cover the annual class play of the local high school. Being new to his job he described the event in glowing terms, instead of the scant few lines used by a more experienced newspaperman for such an event, and concluded with the words:

"And the auditorium was filled with expectant mothers, eagerly awaiting their offspring."

RELATED SUBJECTS: *Absent-Mindedness* 81-90; *Carelessness* 136; *Stupidity* 576-583; *Tact* 586-591

SEE ALSO: *Practical Joking* 436; *Speeches* 772; *Introductions* 789, 791; *Marriage* 877; *Father* 990; *Learned Men* 1089; *Producers* 1393; *Collections* 1567; *Billiards* 1827; *Dancing* 1841; *Fishing* 1852; *Rationing* 2358; *Officers* 2425

BORROWING

121 Mark Twain once went to borrow a certain book from a neighbor.

"Why, yes, Mr. Clemens, you're more than welcome to it," the neighbor told him. "But I must ask you to read it here. You know I make it a rule never to let any book go out of my library."

Some days later the neighbor wished to borrow Twain's lawn mower.

"Why, certainly," the humorist genially assured him. "You're more than welcome to it. But I must ask you to use it here. You know I make it a rule."

122 Charles Lamb meeting an acquaintance, asked him to lend him five shillings; but the friend had only half-a-crown about him, which he handed to Lamb.

Some time after, the acquaintance meeting Lamb, said, "Ah by-the-bye you owe me half-a-crown."

"N-n-not at all," replied Lamb, "y-you owe me h-half-a-crown; f-for d-don't you recollect, I asked y-you for f-five sh-shillings and you only g-g-gave me t-two-and-six-p-pence?"

123 The first time Jerrold saw Tom Dibdin, the song-writer said to him, "Youngster, have you sufficient confidence in me to lend me a guinea?"

"Oh, yes," was the reply, "I've all the confidence—but I haven't the guinea."

124 Mr. Temple Stangan borrowed a sum of money from Joseph Addison the English author and statesman, who soon remarked that his debtor ceased to converse with him on equal terms, and yielded tamely to whatever Addison said. The change displeased Addison and one day when Mr. Stangan had expressed perfect agreement on some topic which had frequently been the subject of keen dispute between them, he exclaimed, heatedly: "Either contradict me, sir, or pay me my money."

125 A visitor in the home of Mark Twain remarked upon the great number of books, many of which were piled about without any adequate provision for them.

"You see," Twain explained, "it is so very difficult to borrow shelves."

126 "I visit my friends occasionally," remarked Hazlitt bitterly, "just to look over my library."

RELATED SUBJECTS: *Economy* 211-213; *Extravagance* 231-232; *Banks* 2151-2158; *Loans* 2161-2164; *Credit* 2166-2167; *Debt* 2171-2174

SEE ALSO: *Playwrights* 1380, 1385

BREVITY

131 The editor of a small Missouri paper sent a notice to one Bill Jenkins that his subscription had expired. The note came back with the laconic scrawl, "So's Bill."

132 During his administration, President Coolidge was one time taken on a tour of inspection through the fabulously magnificent and variegated horticultural conservatories on the estate of Pierre S. DuPont at Longwood, Pennsylvania.

The marvelous beauties of the spring flowers, the exotically cultivated special fruits, the weird and unreal forms of cacti, the beautiful ferns, the orchids; all these things elicited from the President no word of comment. Stepping into the close and humid atmosphere of the room devoted to tropical trees, the President looked about for a moment and remarked with interest, "Bananas."

133 At one of the White House press conferences various reporters were vainly firing their questions at Calvin Coolidge.

"Have you anything to say about Prohibition?"

"No."

"Have you anything to say about the World Court?"

"No."

"About the farm situation?"

"No."

"About the forthcoming senatorial campaign?"

"No."

The meeting broke up and the reporters began to file out of the room.

"And," called the President, "don't quote me."

134 Bob Burns, the local-boy-who-made-good from Arkansas, is well-known for his stories about his large and amusing fam-

ily. One day, when chided for his loquaciousness, he explained that not all members of his family were as given to the gift of gab as himself.

"Now take my cousin Wilfred. He was eleven years old before he so much as said one word. One day he was sittin' on a fence, watching his father plow a field. A bull broke through into the pasture and made straight for Wilfred's Pa. All of a sudden, Wilfred's mouth opened and he yelled, 'Hey, Pa! Hey! Look out fer the bull!'

"Soon as his Pa got out of the field he went straight for Wilfred and said, 'Wilfred, you shore done me a right smart favor that time. But how come you're speakin' all of a suddent? You ain't never said nothin' afore.'

" 'Well, Pa,' was Wilfred's reply, 'I jest ain't never had nothin' t' say before.' "

RELATED SUBJECTS: *Long-Windedness* 341-363; *Quick Thinking* 471-492; *Rough and Ready* 496-507

SEE ALSO: *Authors* 1167

CARELESSNESS

136 Heywood Broun was noted for the general carelessness and disarray of his dress and personal appearance. One story has it, that on the occasion when Broun and a number of other war correspondents were presented to General Pershing, the General eyed the journalist with some concern and said, "Have you fallen down, Mr. Broun?"

RELATED SUBJECTS: *Gambling* 71-74; *Extravagance* 231-232; *Procrastination* 461; *Laziness* 326-327

CHEERFULNESS

141 When they reached Bolt Court Edwards said to Dr. Johnson:

"You are a philosopher, Dr. Johnson. I have tried, too, in my time, to be a philosopher; but, I don't know how, cheerfulness was always breaking in."

142 "Uncle Joe," said Albert Edward Wiggam, the author, meeting an old Negro who was always cheerful in spite of having had more than his share of life's troubles, "how have you managed to remain so cheerful and calm?"

"Well, I'll tell yo," replied Uncle Joe. "I'se jus' learned to cooperate wid de inevitable."

143 When Thomas Hart Benton's house in Washington was burned Benton left Congress and came to the ruin of his house. As he looked at it he said, "It makes dying easier. There is so much less to leave."

RELATED SUBJECTS: *Courage* 151-153; *Melancholy* 366-368; *Pessimism* 411

SEE ALSO: *Cheerfulness* 677

CONSCIENCE

146 There is a tradition to the effect that Noel Coward once sent identical notes to the twenty most prominent men in London, saying, "All is discovered. Escape while you can."

All twenty abruptly left town.

147 To a friend who defended the behavior of the upper chamber, saying, "At least you find consciences there," Talleyrand replied: "Ah yes, many, many consciences. Semonville, for example, has at least two."

RELATED SUBJECTS: *Honesty* 286-294; *Honor* 296-298; *Hypocrisy* 301-303; *Devout Persons* 1601-1602; *Prohibitions and Restrictions* 1641-1642; *Sin and Sinners* 1646-1647; *Chiseling and Swindling* 2121-2132; *Criminals* 2571

COURAGE

151 An Athenian, who was lame in one foot, was laughed at by the soldiers on account of his lameness.

"I am here to fight," said he, "not to run."

152 Brasidas, that famous Lacedemonian general, caught a mouse. It bit him, and by that means made its escape.

"Oh!" said he. "What creature so contemptible but may have its liberty if it will fight for it!"

153 As Hugh Latimer and Nicholas Ridley, the English reformers were led to the stake, Latimer said to Ridley:

"Play the man, Master Ridley; we shall this day light such a candle, by God's grace, in England, as I trust shall never be put out."

> RELATED SUBJECTS: *Cheerfulness* 141-143; *Cowardice* 156-160; *Endurance* 216; *Battles* 2371-2385
>
> SEE ALSO: *Newspapers* 1247; *Civilians in War* 2336; *Battles* 2380, 2382; *Strategy* 2389; *Soldiers* 2430, 2431

COWARDICE

156 A French colonel had one day punished a young officer, just arrived from Saint-Cyr, for showing fear during his first battle. Marshal Foch to whose notice it came, severely reprimanded the disciplinarian. "Colonel!" said he, "none but a coward dares to boast that he has never known fear!"

157 When Caesar was advised by his friends to be more cautious as to the security of his person, and not to walk among the people without arms or anyone to protect him, he replied: "He who lives in the fear of death, every moment feels its tortures; I will die but once."

158 When a certain politician was spoken of as capable of assassinating anyone, Talleyrand remarked: "Assassinating, no! Poisoning, yes!"

159 The evening before a battle an officer came to ask Marshal Toiras for permission to go and see his father who was at the point of death.

"Go!" said the general who saw through his pretext—"Honor thy father and thy mother, that thy days may be long on earth."

160 Lincoln was often the despair of his generals because of his lenient treatment of cases where soldiers were absent without leave.

"If the good Lord has given a man a cowardly pair of legs," Lincoln reasoned, "it is hard to keep them from running away with him."

RELATED SUBJECTS: *Courage* 151-153; *Battles* 2371-2385

SEE ALSO: *Officers* 2422

CURIOSITY

161   "What made the deepest impression upon you?" inquired a friend one day, of Abraham Lincoln, "when you stood in the presence of the Falls of Niagara, the greatest of natural wonders?"

"The thing that struck me most forcibly when I saw the Falls," Lincoln responded with characteristic deliberation, "was where in the world did all that water come from?"

RELATED SUBJECTS: *Imagination* 306; *Inventors* 1126-1131; *Experimenters* 1136-1138

CYNICISM

166   Dr. Johnson was told that a certain cynic of his acquaintance maintained that there was no distinction between virtue and vice. "If he does really think there is no distinction between virtue and vice," answered Dr. Johnson, "why, sir, when he leaves our houses let us count our spoons."

167   Someone once asked the former Prince of Wales, "What is your idea of civilization?"

"It's a good idea," replied the Prince, "somebody ought to start it."

168   When it was remarked that Fouché, an associate of Talleyrand under Napoleon, had a profound contempt for human nature, Talleyrand replied, "To be sure; he has made a careful study of himself."

169   In one of his travels Mungo Park, the African explorer, traversed a wide extent of uncultivated regions, but at last he chanced upon a gibbet, "The sight of which," said he, "gave me infinite pleasure, as it proved that I was in a civilized society."

170   When the motto of the Hanover Club of Göttingen, to which as a student he had belonged, was quoted to him as applicable to his own life, Bismarck reflected: "Yes, 'No Steps Backwards,' but a good many zig-zags."

> RELATED SUBJECTS: *Hypocrisy* 301-303; *Atheists and Agnostics* 1651-1659

> SEE ALSO: *Gratitude* 265; *Speeches* 782; *Husband* 916; *Authors* 1216; *Sermons* 1547; *Politics* 1896; *Chiseling* 2131

DEVOTION

171   R. L. Stevenson won the devotion of the Samoans. When the European powers imprisoned Mataafa, one of their chiefs, Stevenson visited him and other political prisoners, bringing them tobacco and other gifts. When they were released they voluntarily built a wide road up to Stevenson's house; and they made him a chief of one of their tribes. Once when Sosimo, his body-servant, had been unusually thoughtful, Stevenson complimented him, "Great is the wisdom." "No," Sosimo replied, "great is the love."

When Stevenson died a group of picked natives bore the coffin to the place of interment on the mountain top. A stranger had appeared at the funeral, to which only close personal friends were invited, a Scotchman who explained that some years before Stevenson had met him on the road as a stranger on a day when he was contemplating suicide, but that Stevenson had dissuaded him. The Samoan chiefs tabooed the use of firearms on the hill of his grave, that the birds might sing there undisturbed.

172   It is said that a great French actress—reproved for wearing bright colors the day after her lover's funeral—replied: "Ah, you should have seen me yesterday; then you would have known what true sorrow is!"

173 Mrs. Isadore Strauss was one of the few women who went down on the Titanic in 1912, and she went down because she could not bear to leave her husband. Both he and she were calm throughout the excitement of loading the lifeboats. Both aided frightened women and children to find places aboard them. Finally, Mr. Strauss, who had been urging his wife again and again to seek safety in a lifeboat, forced her to enter one. She was no more seated, however, than she sprang up and got to the deck before her husband could stop her. There, she caught his arm, snuggling it against her side, exclaiming, "We have been long together through a great many years. We are old now. Where you go, I will go."

> RELATED SUBJECTS: *Generosity* 241-248; *Kindness* 311-316; *Patriotism* 396-407; *Love* 846-850; *Friendship* 866-867; *Devout Persons* 1601-1602

> SEE ALSO: *Kindness* 313

DILIGENCE

176 Abe Lincoln's father was never at a loss for an answer. An old neighbor of Thomas Lincoln was passing the Lincoln farm one day when he saw Abe's father grubbing up some hazelnut bushes and said to him:
"Why, Grandpop, I thought you wanted to sell your farm?"
"And so I do," he replied, "but I ain't goin' to let my farm know it."
"Abe's jes' like his father," the old ones would say.

177 Clarence Darrow was a hard working and energetic man. His clothes were often disheveled. Once he was ragged about this by a group of reporters. He silenced them by saying, "I go to a better tailor than any of you and pay more money for my clothes. The only difference between us is that you probably don't sleep in yours."

> RELATED SUBJECTS: *Ambition* 96-97; *Patience* 391; *Procrastination* 461; *Stubbornness* 571-572; *Will Power* 631

> SEE ALSO: *Instrumentalists* 1351, 1356; *Hiring* 2249

DISCRETION

181   "Pray," said a facetious lady, "Mr. Pitt, as you know everything that is moving in the political world tell me some news."

"I am sorry madam," said the discreet premier, "I have not read the newspaper of the day."

182   Secretary of the Navy Knox, was asked by an old friend some casual question about the movement of certain ships in Atlantic waters. The question was thoughtless and Knox leaned over with an air of confidence and said, "Look here, can you keep a secret?"

"Of course, of course," replied the friend eagerly.

"Well," said Knox, "so can I!"

> RELATED SUBJECTS: *Carelessness* 136; *Modesty* 376-390;
> *Tact* 586-591

> SEE ALSO: *Father* 989

DULLNESS

186   Lincoln was told of a profound historian, "It may be doubted whether any man of our generation has plunged more deeply into the sacred fount of learning."

"Yes, or come up drier," said Lincoln.

187   One day one of the greatest bores of the Players Club said to Oliver Herford, "Oliver, I have been grossly insulted. Just as I passed that group over there I overheard someone say he would give me $50 to resign from the club."

"Hold out for a hundred," counseled Mr. Herford, "you'll get it."

188   A gentleman who introduced his brother to Dr. Johnson was desirous of recommending him to his notice; which he did by saying, "When we have sat together some time, you'll find my brother growing very interesting."

"Sir," said Dr. Johnson, "I can wait."

189   To a very thin man who had been boring him, Douglas Jerrold said:

"Sir, you are like a pin, but without either its head or its point."

190   Douglas Jerrold, 19th Century wit, was approached one day by a chatty bore. "Well, well, Jerrold," he said. "What's going on?"

"I am," said Jerrold, and did.

191   An impertinent chatterbox, entertaining Aristotle, the philosopher, with a tedious discourse, and observing that he did not much regard him, made an apology, that he was afraid he had interrupted him.

"No, really," replied the philosopher, "you have not interrupted me at all, for I have not minded one word you said."

192   Talleyrand was asked if a certain authoress whom he had long since known, but who had belonged rather to the last age, was not, "a little tiresome." "Not at all," said he, "she was perfectly tiresome."

193   Sir Walter Scott's faithful servant Tom said to him one day, "Them are fine novels of yours; they are invaluable to me. When I come home very tired, and take up one of them, I'm asleep directly."

194   Speaking of a dull, tiresome fellow whom he chanced to meet, Dr. Johnson said: "That fellow seems to possess but one idea, and that is a wrong one."

195   The modest Joseph Addison was accused by a lady of being dull and heavy in conversation. "Madam," he replied with great dignity, "I have only ninepence in my pocket, but I can draw for a thousand pounds."

RELATED SUBJECTS: *Long-Windedness* 341-363; *Stupidity* 576-583

SEE ALSO: *Practical Joking* 432; *Snobbishness* 547; *Parties* 686, 742; *Authors* 1179; *Bull Fighting* 1831

ECCENTRICITY

196 There was a tale current in Park Row—how Richard Harding Davis, finding a stranger at his favorite table at Delmonico's, was supposed to have remarked: "I beg your pardon. My name is Richard Harding Davis and you are in my chair."

"Do not mind," replied the usurper. "My name is Jove. Many swear by me. If you are one, sit down."

197 A story of Isadora Duncan's: At the Hotel Trianon D'Annunzio had a gold-fish which he loved. It was in a wonderful crystal bowl and D'Annunzio used to feed it and talk to it. The gold-fish would agitate its fins and open and shut its mouth as though to answer him.

One day when I was staying at the Trianon, I said to the maitre d'hotel:

"Where is the gold-fish of D'Annunzio?"

"Ah, madame, sorrowful story! D'Annunzio went to Italy and told us to take care of it. 'This gold-fish,' he said, 'is so near to my heart. It is a symbol of all my happiness!' And he kept telegraphing: 'How is my beloved Adolphus?' One day Adolphus swam a little more slowly round the bowl and ceased to ask for D'Annunzio. I took it and threw it out of the window. But there came a telegram from D'Annunzio: 'Feel Adolphus is not well.' I wired back: 'Adolphus dead. Died last night.' D'Annunzio replied: 'Bury him in the garden. Arrange his grave.' So I took a sardine and wrapped it in silver paper and buried it in the garden and I put a cross: 'Here lies Adolphus!' D'Annunzio returned: 'Where is the grave of my Adolphus?'

"I showed him the grave in the garden and he brought many flowers to it and stood for a long time weeping tears upon it."

198 Edward W. Bok told how, "I was asked to come to a breakfast at Oscar Wilde's house, and noticed as I sat down that next to me, at my left, had been placed a man instead of the usual rotation. I turned to my left to find my neighbor had pushed his chair back from the table about three feet, and buried his chin in his shirt-bosom and was reaching forth for his eatables, and practically eating them from his lap, his cup resting on his knee. There was something familiar about the features of my neighbor who was eating in the most grotesque fashion I ever saw, and yet I could not place him. I looked for his place-card, but I could see none. So I shoved back my chair and tried to engage him in conversation. But I was not rewarded by even a glance. When I asked a question I received either no answer at all or a grunt. After a few heroic efforts, I gave up the struggle.

"At the close of the breakfast, I asked Wilde: 'Who in the world was that chap at my left?'

" 'I know,' returned Wilde. 'I saw your valiant struggle. He gets that way once in a while, and this morning happened to be one of those whiles. That was Whistler!' "

199 "My rubber," said Nat Goodwin, describing a Turkish bath that he once had in Mexico, "was a very strong man. He laid me on a slab and kneaded me and punched me and banged me in a most emphatic way. When it was over and I had gotten up, he came up behind me before my sheet was adjusted, and gave me three resounding slaps on the bare back with the palm of his enormous hand.

"What in blazes are you doing?" I gasped, staggering.

"No offense, sir," said the man. "It was only to let the office know that I was ready for the next bath. You see, sir, the bell's out of order in this room."

200 Alexander Pope said, "Dean Swift has an odd blunt way that is mistaken by strangers for ill-nature: it is so odd that there is no describing it but by facts. I'll tell you one that first comes into my head. One evening (John) Gay and I went to see him: you know how intimately we were all acquainted. On our coming in, 'Heyday, gentlemen,' (says the doctor), 'what's the meaning of this visit? How come you two to leave all the great lads that you are so fond of, to come hither to see a poor dean?' 'Because we would rather see you than any of them.'

" 'Ay, anyone that did not know you so well as I do might believe you. But since you have come, I must get some supper for you, I suppose?'

" 'No, doctor, we have supped already.'

" 'Supped already? Why it is not eight o'clock yet. That's very strange, but if you had not supped, I must have got something for you. Let me see, what should I have had? A couple of lobsters? Ay, that would have done very well, two shillings; tarts, a shilling. But you will drink a glass of wine with me, though you supped so much before your usual time, only to spare my pocket.'

" 'No, we had rather talk with you than drink with you.'

" 'But if you had supped with me, as in all reason you ought to have done, you must then have drank with me. A bottle of wine, two shillings. Two and two is four, and one is five; just two and six-pence apiece. There Pope, there's half a crown for you; and there's another for you (Gay) Sir; for I won't save anything by you I am determined.'

"This was all said and done with his usual seriousness on such occasions: and in spite of everything we could say to the contrary, he actually obliged us to take the money."

201 Into the bakery shop, the most famous and costly of its kind in New York, came a customer with an order for a cake to be baked in the shape of the letter "s". He insisted on various details of its decoration and specified that it must be ready by a certain date. The day before the deadline the customer dropped around and found that his cake was finished and being decorated. "Oh, this is all wrong," he said, flying into a rage. "You've baked it in the shape of a capital "S". I wanted it especially to be a small "s". The whole thing will have to be done over, and you'll have to have it by tomorrow anyway."

He created such a fuss that the apologetic manager said that they would make every effort to satisfy him; would make it over; felt that it had been a natural mistake; but were willing to accommodate him, and so and so forth.

The following day the customer returned and found his lower case cake decorated in its final details as he desired. "That's fine," he said, much mollified. "That's just right." He drew out his wallet and paid for the cake.

"Now, sir," said the proprietor, "where shall it be sent or do you wish to take it with you?"

"Oh, that's all right," said the customer, with a wave of his hand, "I'll eat it here."

202 The Italians thought Landor the ideally mad Englishman. On one occasion he threw his cook out of the kitchen window and immediately stuck his own head out after him exclaiming, "Good God, I forgot the violets!"

203 In 1766 David Hume, the philosopher and historian, carried off Rousseau to England and tried to get a pension for him from George III. Rousseau was beginning to suffer from the persecution obsession that afflicted his later years, but at first he was purring and grateful. Then his old suspicions, his old hatred of being under obligation, came back upon him and he began to explode nervously. At such times Hume could only pat him on the back, exclaiming:

"What, my dear sir? . . . Eh, my dear sir! . . . What now, my dear sir?"

204 In one of his lodgings Francis Thompson, the poet, habitually walked around the table all night and went to bed at dawn. Finally he wore out the carpet in a perfect circle round his table. He habitually stayed in bed most of the day and never kept appointments. Wherever he was he always sought the fire and stood against it forever getting his trousers and his coat afire. Once, in his lodging, he set the curtains afire and tipped over the lamp in trying to extinguish it. His hands were badly burned and he walked the streets all night, for, as he later remarked, "The room was quite burned out."

205 Alfred Steiglitz has always been a highly arbitrary and erratic dealer in paintings. Once, at a show of the work of Georgia O'Keeffe, a wealthy woman expressed, with a slightly patronising attitude, a desire to purchase a certain picture. Repelled subtly by the woman's manner, Steiglitz snapped, "Why do you want that painting? Give me some reason why you want it."

The prospective purchaser could think of no satisfactory reason and was refused the picture.

206 A traffic cop will signal Pop Gershwin to stop. Pop has been exceeding the speed limit, perhaps in the unconscious belief that the father of the jazz king has rights that even the police force must respect. "Don't you know who I am?" he asks the officer. "I'm the father of George Gershwin." At the same time, being a New Yorker, he pronounces the first name to rhyme with "judge." (The Jewish-American pronunciations of "George" and "judge" are surprisingly similar.) The officer scratches his head. He doesn't know every judge in Gotham. Perhaps this Judge Gershwin is a big gun up in the Bronx. Better to be safe than sorry. A salute and he lets Pa Gershwin pass. Who now can tell Pa that Gershwin isn't king?

207 In 1874, Sarah Bernhardt was advised to give up acting if she wished to live, but she returned to the theatre as soon as she was able to leave her bed. When she was asked by an admirer what gift he could send her, she replied, "They say I am to die, so you may send me a coffin."

A week later, she was notified by a famous coffin maker that an order had been received for a coffin, to be constructed according to her wishes. Sarah was most particular about its design, finally agreeing that it should be made of rosewood, with handles of solid silver—later changed to gold.

For the remainder of her life this coffin never left her side, even during her travels. She had a trestle made on which it stood at the end of her bed, so she could see it without effort, on awakening.

"To remind me that my body will soon be dust and that my glory alone will live forever," she explained.

208 Gray, the English poet, had an abnormal terror of fire and when he was living at Peterhouse got Wharton to supply him with a sixty-five-foot rope ladder with strong hooks which he fastened to a bar across his window—which bar remains there to this day.

One chill February night some undergraduates, aware of his pyrophobia, shouted, "Fire!" on his staircase. The timid Gray hastily threw out his rope ladder and descended through the darkness and cold in his night-clothes, only to drop into a carefully placed tub of water. He fell to shivering. A night-watchman discovered him and helped him back, up the stairs, to his rooms.

209 A woman visitor to the London Zoo asked a keeper whether the hippopotamus was a male or a female.

"Madam," replied the keeper sternly, "that is a question that should be of interest only to another hippopotamus."

ECONOMY

211 Shortly before sailing back to England, foreign correspondent Quentin Reynolds was received by President Roosevelt in his office at the White House. While he was there the President put through a transatlantic call to another eminent statesman, Winston Churchill. Mr. Reynolds was slightly startled when, after a conversation, the President said: "I'll have to hang up now. My three minutes are up!"

212 A visitor to the White House during the Coolidge administration said to the President that he would greatly apprecite the gift of a cigar, not for himself but for a friend who had the eccentricity of collecting cigar bands from famous smokers all over the world. President Coolidge thought the matter over for a few seconds, then reached for a box of cigars. Taking one out, he carefully removed the band, replaced the cigar in the box, and handed the band to his visitor.

213 At Lobb's, the famous English bootmaker, one day, I saw on the floor a heap of 20 or 30 boots, all needing cobbling badly. "Oh, sir," Lobb explained, "these belong to the best customer I ever had. He used to come in here and order 15 or 20 pairs of boots. But when his father died he left him some £3,000,000. Well sir, since then he has not ordered a single pair of new boots, but sends the old ones to be repaired."

"Who is he, Lobb?" I asked.

"An American, sir . . . his name is Pierpont Morgan."

> RELATED SUBJECTS: *Carelessness* 136; *Extravagance* 231-232; *Stinginess* 556-566

> SEE ALSO: *Stinginess* 559; *Poverty* 2205; *Soldiers* 2432

ENDURANCE

216 In the days of the homestead law a prospective settler sought out a lawyer friend and asked him to explain the law and its operations.

"I don't know the exact text of the law," said his friend, "but I can give you the drift of it. The Government is willing to bet you 160 acres of land against $14 that you can't live on it five years without starving to death."

EXAGGERATION

221 Mark Twain once asked a baggage handler in the railroad station in Washington, "Is that satchel strong enough to go in the baggage car?"

The baggage man lifted the grip high above his head and smashed it to the ground with all his might. "That," said he, "is what it will get in Philadelphia." He picked it up and bashed it against the side of the car four or five times. "That is what it will get in Chicago," he continued. He next threw it high in the air and when it had landed, jumped on it vigorously. It split open and scattered its contents over the platform. "And that is what it will get in Sioux City," he said, according to Twain. "So if you are going any farther than Sioux City, you'd better take it in the Pullman with you."

222 The Chase National Bank, operating all over the world, receives from its clients some very strange letters.

A short time ago, a furrier in Australia wrote in the following: "Dear Sirs:

"Am sending draft for a thousand pounds, with which please credit my account. Last year I crossed a kangaroo with a raccoon, and now I'm raising fur coats with pockets."

223 Colonel Cody (Buffalo Bill) used to tell the story of an English visitor to the West. While riding through a Rocky Mountain canyon one day, a tremendous gust of wind swooped down and actually carried the Englishman off the wagon-seat. After he had picked himself up and combed the sand and gravel out of his whiskers, he said, "I say! I think you overdo ventilation in this country!"

224 Bill Nye, the humorist, was not given to mild statements. He had the following to say about liars:

"We have nothing more to say of the editor of the Sweetwater Gazette. Aside from the fact that he is a squint-eyed, consumptive liar, with a breath like a buzzard and a record like a convict, we don't know anything against him. He means well enough, and if he can evade the penitentiary and the vigilance committee for a few more years, there is a chance for him to end his life in a natural way. If he don't tell the truth a little more plentifully, however, the Green River people will rise as one man and churn him up till there won't be anything left of him but a pair of suspenders and a wart."

225 Bear stories are the stock in trade of the Alaskan sourdoughs.

One of them told of his encounter with a giant Kadiak monster. "He was all of two tons and he riz up and come at me. I didn't manage to wound him but just enough to make him mad. But then my rifle jammed. I headed for the nearest tree, but it only had one limb and that was thirty feet off the ground. I got there not more than a foot ahead of the bear and he took a swat at me as I gathered for the leap. He tore my britches but didn't quite get me. But he scairt me so badly I missed the limb."

"What happened?"

"I caught it on my way down."

226 Col. John Cremony was a famous Western figure and known as a yarn spinner. He told one story of a desperate flight from pursuing Indians. "I had a fine horse and managed to keep far enough ahead so their arrows couldn't reach me. I picked 'em off until my last cartridge was gone. Then I headed up a canyon and I'll be doggoned if it didn't end in a sheer wall. I was trapped like a rat with a dozen Apaches closing in on me. And me without as much as a penknife to defend myself."

"What happened, Colonel?" someone in his audience would invariably ask.

"Why, they killed me! Damn them, sir, they killed me!"

> RELATED SUBJECTS: *Boastfulness* 101-103; *Imagination* 306; *Liars* 331-336

> SEE ALSO: *Baseball* 1824; *Fishing* 1846, 1851

EXTRAVAGANCE

231 After 150 years the truth is out about Benjamin Franklin. "The name 'Poor Richard' might easily have derived from his bank account rather than from his almanac," said William Fulton Kurtz after reading early records of the Bank of North America, where Franklin and many of his illustrious compatriots kept their money. "He was overdrawn at least three days out of every week."

232 When E. H. Harriman, the railroad magnate and millionaire, was dying, reporters were on the spot for the story. The reporter of one of the metropolitan dailies was notorious for his enormous expense accounts. After the millionaire's death, the reporter's expense account, carefully itemized but out of all just proportions, was handed to the city editor. He looked it over and handed it back, saying, "If this is the will, it's worth a story."

RELATED SUBJECTS: *Boastfulness* 101-103; *Imagination* 306; *Liars* 331-336

SEE ALSO: *Wife* 927

FLATTERY

236 The politic philosopher Aristippus, by paying court to the tyrant Denys, had acquired a comfortable living and looked down upon his less prosperous fellow sages with no small degree of contempt. Seeing Diogenes washing some vegetables, he said to him disdainfully: "If you would only learn to flatter King Denys you would not have to be washing lentils."

"And you," retorted Diogenes in the same tone, "if you had only learned to live on lentils, would not have to flatter King Denys."

237 A friend once remarked to the famous cartoonist, Ding, "You must get a great deal of praise from all sides."

"No more than I need," he replied.

RELATED SUBJECTS: *Hypocrisy* 301-303; *Liars* 331-336; *Vanity* 606-628

SEE ALSO: *Borrowing* 124; *Salesmen* 2097

GENEROSITY

241 Aristotle, on being censured for giving alms to a bad man, answered: "I did not give it to the man, I gave it to humanity."

242 Lafcadio Hearn tells the story of a hero of the Chinese ricefields during an earthquake. From his hill-top farm he saw the ocean swiftly withdrawn, like some prodigious animal crouching for the leap, and knew the leap would be the tidal wave. He saw also that his neighbors working in low fields must be gathered to his hill or swept away. Without a second thought he set fire to his rice-ricks and furiously rang the temple-bell.

His neighbors thought his farm on fire and rushed to help him. Then, from that safe hill they saw the swirl of waters over fields just forsaken—and knew their salvation and its cost. Afterwards the people of these rice-fields used to go to the temple to worship their neighbor's spirit while he was still alive.

243 On his deathbed Governor Hogg of Texas requested that no monument be placed at his grave; but that instead, there be planted, "at my head a pecan tree, and at my feet an old fashioned walnut and when these trees shall bear, let the pecans and walnuts be given out among the Plains people of Texas, so that they may plant them and make Texas a land of trees."

His wishes were carried out. The first nuts were saved in 1926 and planted in nursery rows. And the same thing has been done each year since. When the saplings are large enough to transplant they are distributed to schools and county boards.

244 When Frederick the Great was seized with his mortal illness, he asked whether "it was necessary to forgive all his enemies." On receiving the proper answer, he said to the queen, "Dorothy, write to your brother that I forgive him all the evil he has done me; but wait till I am dead first."

245 Abe Lincoln was a simple man with honest generous impulses. When he was a candidate for the legislature, it was the practice at that date in Illinois for two rival candidates to travel over the district together. The custom led to much good-natured raillery between them.

On one occasion he had driven out from Springfield in company with a political opponent to engage in joint debate. The carriage, it seems, belonged to his opponent. In addressing the gathering of farmers that met them, Lincoln was lavish in praise of the generosity of his friend.

"I am too poor to own a carriage," he said, "but my friend has generously invited me to ride with him. I want you to vote for me if you will but if not then vote for my opponent, for he is a fine man."

246   "I am rich enough," said Pope to Swift, "and can afford to give away a hundred pounds a year. I would not crawl upon the earth without doing good. I will enjoy the pleasure of what I give by giving it alive and seeing another enjoy it. When I die I should be ashamed to leave enough for a monument if a wanting friend was above ground."

247   An English lover of Brahms' music willed him £1,000. When Joachim sent the news Brahms replied:

"One can experience nothing more beautiful, nothing that does one more good, than what you have just told me. That a perfect stranger, who has, as far as I know, never even written me, should remember me thus, touches me most deeply and intimately. Once before I have had the inestimable joy of experiencing the like. All exterior honors are nothing in comparison.

"As I do not need to 'invest' the money, I am enjoying it in the most agreeable manner, by taking pleasure in its distribution . . ."

248   The despised and rejected often found in this great-hearted man (Brahms) a ready ally. Widmann tells how, one night under the arcades of Bologna, Brahms enthusiastically admired a deaf-and-dumb sidewalk artist who had drawn in the flags a portrait of Cavour. "A plate stood nearby into which one could throw the soldo which one might feel like offering to such art of the highways. But there was a new surprise when the coin, ringing on the hard stone, showed that the plate was not a real one but a well and truly drawn imitation. Brahms could not find words enough to praise this fine idea of the poor artist. And his offering showed how deeply he was moved by learning that in this gifted race, even the street beggar knew how to cover his nakedness with a corner of the hem of Art's sumptuous robe."

GENTLEMANLINESS

251 Sir Walter Raleigh would have devised different techniques had he lived today. An authentic descendant of his turned up in Philadelphia as told in the story of the three girls who were marooned on the curb, after a violent cloudburst had left a deep puddle in the poorly drained street stretching nearly all the way between themselves and the car which they wished to board. Two of them had jumped for it only to go in over their ankles. The third was still standing in despair when a sedan rolled up and stopped directly in front of her. With a flourish its driver opened the rear door on her side, then opened the other. Catching the idea, the young lady proceeded to walk through the car and on to the trolley. Tipping his hat, the driver closed his doors and proceeded to drive away.

252 One night a Negro was walking along Forty-second Street in New York, from the terminal to the hotel, carrying a heavy suitcase and a heavier valise. Suddenly a hand took hold of the valise and a pleasant voice said: "Pretty heavy, brother! Suppose you let me take one. I am going your way."

The Negro resisted, but finally allowed the young white man to assist him in carrying his burden, and for several blocks they walked along, chatting like old cronies.

"And that," said Booker T. Washington years afterward, "was the first time I ever saw Theodore Roosevelt."

253 Charles Lamb once said:

"Don't introduce me to that man! I want to go on hating him, and I can't hate a man whom I know."

254 It was late at night and the young lady was taking a taxi home. Checking in her handbag, she was mildly horrified to discover that she would not have enough money for the full fare. When the meter had reached the sum which she had, she called to the driver and told him to let her out, explaining the situation.

"Listen, lady," said he, "money isn't everything. There's still what you call chivalry. You just sit still."

255   In 1803 the American Congress granted to General Lafayette, 11,520 acres of land, in what was then called the Territory of Orleans; but by some inadvertency, a portion of the same land was afterwards granted to the Corporation of New Orleans. Lafayette was advised to bring forward his claim; and eminent lawyers assured him it was perfectly legal. To which the gallant Frenchman replied:

"I cannot consent even to inquire into the validity of my title. It was gratuitously bestowed by Congress, and it is for them to say what was given. I cannot for a moment think of entering into litigation with any public body in the United States."

On this tract that Lafayette relinquished was built the City of New Orleans.

256   Edmund Waller had a tremendous, international reputation for wit, in spite of his "obstinate sobriety." Being shown the Duchess of Newcastle's verses on the death of a stag, he declared that he would give all his compositions to have written them; and being charged with the exorbitance of his adulation answered that "nothing was too much to be given, that a lady might be saved from the disgrace of such a vile performance."

RELATED SUBJECTS: *Politeness* 416-420; *Tact* 586-591

SEE ALSO: *Quarrelsomeness* 466; *Beauty* 661; *Ministers* 1471; *Doctors* 1668; *Credit* 2166

GRATITUDE AND INGRATITUDE

261   An old deacon, having occasion to spend a night at a hotel, was assigned a room containing three single beds, two of which already had occupants. Soon after the light was extinguished one of these began to snore so loudly as to prevent the deacon from getting to sleep. The tumult increased as the night wore away, until it became absolutely fearful. Some two or three hours after midnight the snorer turned himself in bed, gave a hideous groan, and became silent. The deacon had supposed the third gentleman asleep, but at this juncture he heard him exclaim, "He's dead! Thank God. He's dead!"

262   Dr. Walter Adams, astronomer at Mount Wilson Observatory told a story of gratitude:

"A hunter in the jungle came across an elephant limping. The hunter followed it. Finally it toppled over. The hunter examined its feet. In one there was a large thorn. This he removed.

"Years passed and the hunter was in a cheap seat at a circus. A turn was given by a troupe of performing elephants. One of these elephants reached in its trunk, encircled his waist, and lifted him from his cheap seat and set him down in a seat in a private box."

263   "While fishing one day," said the old-timer, "I ran short of bait and was temporarily at loss as to what to do. Upon looking down near my feet, I noticed a small snake which held a frog in its mouth. I removed the frog and cut it up for bait, feeling very fortunate that my eyes had lighted on the snake at that moment.

"I did, however, feel a bit guilty at relieving the poor reptile of his meal, and in order to give him a slight recompense for my supply of bait, I poured a few drops of whiskey into its mouth. Fortunately for my conscience, the snake seemed to leave in a contented mood, and I turned and went on fishing.

"Some time had passed when I felt something hitting against the leg of my boot. Looking down, I saw the identical snake, laden with three more frogs!"

264   "Are you fond of lobster salad?" asked the hostess of the doctor.

"No," he replied, "I'm not fond of it but I'm grateful to it."

265   "You have much to be grateful for," said the clergyman to the old farmer. "Providence cares for us all. Even the birds of the air are fed each day."

"Yeah," growled the farmer, "off my corn."

266   When told that somebody had spoken something against him, had indeed systematically abused him, Jerrold quietly observed:

"Ah! I suppose I have done him a good turn."

267   In some parts of Mexico hot springs and cold springs are found side by side. The women often boil their clothes in the hot springs and rinse them in the cold springs. A tourist, who had been watching this procedure, remarked to his Mexican friend, "I guess they think old Mother Nature is pretty generous."

"No, señor," the other replied. "There is much grumbling because she supplies no soap."

268 Notwithstanding his long career of snatching killers out of the clutches of the law, Samuel Leibowitz is not an admirer of the class. He considers them unlovable natures and born ingrates. Demonstrating this, he notes that no single one of the 78 men whom he has saved from the chair ever sent him a Christmas card.

> RELATED SUBJECTS: *Generosity* 241-248; *Helpfulness* 281; *Kindness* 311-316; *Stinginess* 556-566

> SEE ALSO: *Generosity* 242

GREED

271 One evening Rachel, the famous French actress, dined at the house of Comte Duchâtel. The table was loaded with the most magnificent flowers; but Rachel's keen eyes presently spied out the great silver centerpiece. Immediately she began to admire it. The Count, fascinated by her manners, said that he would be glad to present it to her. Being greedy, she accepted it at once, but was rather fearful lest he should change his mind. She had come to dinner in a cab, and mentioned the fact. The Count offered to send her home in his carriage.

"Yes, that will do admirably," said she. "There will be no danger of my being robbed of your present, which I had better take with me."

"With pleasure, Mademoiselle," replied the Count. "But you will send me back my carriage, won't you?"

272 Roland Diller who was one of Lincoln's neighbors in Springfield, tells the following story:

"I was called to the door one day by the cries of children in the street, and there was Mr. Lincoln, striding by with two of his boys, both of whom were wailing aloud. 'Why, Mr. Lincoln, what's the matter with the boys?' I asked. 'Just what's the matter with the whole world,' Lincoln replied. 'I've got three walnuts, and each wants two.' "

273 Rachel, the celebrated 19th Century French actress, was notorious for her avarice. The younger Dumas once received a ring from her. Immediately he bowed low and returned it to her finger, saying:

"Permit me, Mademoiselle, to present it to you in my turn so as to save you the embarrassment of asking for it."

274 The Mexican War was not a popular one with the American people. Abraham Lincoln, then a member of Congress, opposed it, declaring that those who said that the war was not one of aggression made him think of the Illinois farmer who said: "I ain't greedy 'bout land. I only want what jines mine."

275 Rachel, the famous French actress, had a curious way of asking everyone she met for presents and knickknacks, whether they were valuable or not. She knew how to make them valuable.

Once in a studio she noticed a guitar hanging on the wall. She begged for it very earnestly. As it was an old and almost worthless instrument, it was given her. A little later it was reported that the dilapidated guitar had been purchased by a well-known gentleman for a thousand francs. The explanation soon followed. Rachel had declared that it was the very guitar with which she used to earn her living as a child in the streets of Paris.

276 On one occasion P. D. Armour, the meat packer, made a present of a suit of clothes to each of his employes in a certain department. Each man was told that he might order his own suit, and send the bill to Mr. Armour, no restriction being made as to price. In order to avail himself fully of this liberality, one young man ordered evening clothes costing $80. When the bill was sent in, Mr. Armour sent for the clerk to vouch for its accuracy, and finding it right, assured the man it would be paid. As the clerk was leaving, however, Mr. Armour said to him:

"I wish to say to you that I have packed a great many hogs in my time, but I never dressed one before."

RELATED SUBJECTS: *Ambition* 96-97; *Competition* 2116; *Chiseling and Swindling* 2121-2132

SEE ALSO: *Wealth*, 2181; *Laws* 2596

HELPFULNESS

281   There is a story that tells of a rabbit being chased by a dog, and the people following and telling the rabbit to run hard and escape.
  "Thank you for your kind encouragement," said the rabbit, "but for goodness' sake shoot the dog."

> RELATED SUBJECTS: *Generosity* 241-248; *Kindness* 311-316

HONESTY

286   A beggar asking Dr. Smollett for alms, he gave him, through mistake, a guinea. The poor fellow on perceiving it, hobbled after him to return it; upon which Smollett returned it to him with another guinea as a reward for his honesty, exclaiming at the same time, "What a lodging Honesty has taken up with!"

287   Mirabeau was seldom sincere; Robespierre, nearly always. Once, when Robespierre was speaking, Mirabeau, who had listened attentively, bent his leonine head over to his neighbor and remarked:
  "That man will go far; he believes all he says."

288   Pace, jester to Queen Elizabeth, was so bitter in his retorts to her, that she forbade him her royal presence. After he had been absent for some time, a few of his friends interceded for him, assuring the Queen that he would be more guarded in his remarks in the future.
  The very first time Pace was as bad as ever. "Come on, Pace," said the Queen in a gracious humor, "now, we shall hear of our faults."
  "No, Madam," said Pace, "I never talk of what is discoursed by all the world."

289   A young man, starting out on a business career, was being given some advice by his father, himself a very successful and wealthy man.
  "And, remember, son," said the older man, "always keep in mind that honesty always has been and always will be the best policy."

"Oh, yes indeed," agreed the son.

"Oh, and incidentally," were the parting words of his father, "you might read up a bit on corporation law. It's really surprising how many things can be done in a business way, and still be honest."

290 A little boy asked his father, "Papa, what does it mean, business ethics?"

"Well," exclaimed the merchant, "it's like this. Comes into the store a man and makes a purchase. He gives me a bright, new five-dollar bill, which is just the right amount, and he starts out. I'm turning to the cash register when I discover that it's not one, it's two five-dollar bills stuck together. Now comes it in the business ethics—should I tell mine partner?"

291 One day Senator George W. Norris sat taking stock of the situation and puffing a cigar. A visitor came in looking rather smug. He had called because Norris was on the committee on public buildings and grounds. Washington was still in the mushroom stage with land developments in progress. The man wanted to see him about "a little matter" and as soon as he promised to show "appreciation" Norris jumped up and grabbed him, vigorously pushing him out of the room.

292 President Wilson was scrupulous to the degree of fanaticism on the point of avoiding any personal or family favoritism in appointments or the awarding of war contracts.

A caller at the White House quite casually mentioned that the firm headed by a distant relative of the President had received a building contract. Although this might readily have been accepted as a legitimate and purely coincidental transaction, the President said in great agitation, "It must be stopped at once."

The nation could well have used, in his successor's administration, so high a degree of integrity, yet the action created a family breach that was never healed.

293 While visiting his prison at Potsdam, Frederick William I listened to a number of pleas for pardon from prisoners who had grievances against the law's injustice. All said they had suffered imprisonment on account of prejudiced judges, perjured witnesses, unscrupulous lawyers. From cell to cell the tale of wronged innocence continued, until the King stopped at the door of one cell inhabited by a surly inmate who said nothing. Surprised at his silence Frederick said jocosely, "Well I suppose you are innocent too."

"No, your Majesty," was the startling response; "I am guilty and richly deserve all that I get."

"Here, turnkey," thundered Frederick; "come and get rid of this rascal quick, before he corrupts this fine lot of innocent people that you are responsible for."

---

294 All clients knew that, with Old Abe as their lawyer, they would win their case—if it was fair; if not, that it was a waste of time to take it to him. After listening some time one day to a would-be client's statement, with his eyes on the ceiling, he swung around in his chair and exclaimed:

"Well, you have a pretty good case in technical law, but a pretty bad one in equity and justice. You'll have to get some other fellow to win this case for you. I couldn't do it. All the time while standing talking to that jury I'd be thinking, 'Lincoln, you're a liar,' and I believe I should forget myself and say it out loud."

> RELATED SUBJECTS: *Conscience* 146-147; *Honor* 296-298; *Hypocrisy* 301-303; *Liars* 331-336; *Chiseling and Swindling* 2121-2132; *Stealing* 2581-2590
>
> SEE ALSO: *Cynicism* 166; *Books* 1224; *Atheists* 1652; *Advertising* 2103; *Credit* 2166; *Partnerships* 2242; *Judges* 2486; *Lawyers* 2527

HONOR

296 "Why is it," asked a Frenchman of a Swiss, "that you Swiss always fight for money, while we French only fight for honor?"

"I suppose," said the Swiss, "that each fight for what they most lack."

---

297 A German officer, talking to a senior member of the British Embassy in Berlin in 1933, made the odd remark that the British are gentlemen, but the French are not. Asked what he meant, he explained: "One day in 1920, some of the Military Control Commission under a French and a British officer, came to the barracks of which I had charge. They said they had reason to believe that I had a store of rifles concealed behind a brick wall, contrary to the terms of the Peace Treaty. I denied this. 'I give you my word of honor as a German officer,' I said, 'that I have no rifles concealed in the barracks.'

"Well, your British officer was a gentleman. He accepted my word of honor and went away. But the French officer was not a gentleman. He would not accept my word of honor. He pulled down the brick wall. And he took away my rifles."

298 An officious informer came to tell Cardinal Richelieu of certain free expressions that some persons had used in speaking of him. "Why how now!" said the Cardinal, "do you dare to come and call me all these names to my face, under the pretense of their having been said by honest gentlemen?"

Ringing his bell, he said to the page in waiting, "Kick that fellow down stairs."

RELATED SUBJECTS: *Conscience* 146-147; *Honesty* 286-294; *Pride* 456-457; *Stool Pigeons* 2591-2592

SEE ALSO: *Presidents* 1931; *Soldiers* 2433

HYPOCRISY

301 The Bishop of Hereford was once being patronized by a great lord who talked very insolently.

"I never go to church," boasted the lord. "Perhaps you have noticed that, Bishop?"

"Yes, I have noticed it," answered the Bishop gravely.

"Well, the reason I don't go is that there are so many hypocrites there."

"Oh, don't let that keep you away," said the Bishop smiling blandly. "There is always room for one more, you know."

302 An eminent banker from the West End, Boston, once visited Father Taylor's church during a warm revival, and somewhat varied the usual character of the prayer meeting, by an address setting forth the beneficence of the merchant princes, the goodness of the Port Society, and above all the duty of seamen to show their gratitude to the merchants. He was somewhat taken aback when Father Taylor arose, at the close of this rather presumptuous exhortation, and simply inquired:

"Is there any other old sinner from up-town that would like to say a word?"

303 Julius Streicher, Hitler's No. 1 Jew persecutor, complained recently to foreign correspondents about the way the foreign press portrays him as a depraved brute. "Of course," he explained, "I do fight the Jews in every way I can, but in private life I'm far from heartless. For example, I have two pet canaries, and whenever I am late coming home I stumble around in the dark rather than turn the light on and wake them up."

RELATED SUBJECTS: *Flattery* 236-237; *Honesty* 286-294; *Liars* 331-336; *Believers* 1591-1596

SEE ALSO: *Rabbis* 1486; *Equality* 2046

IMAGINATION

306 Professor Buckland, the distinguished biologist of the early 19th Century, gave a dinner one day, after dissecting a Mississippi alligator.

"How do you like the soup?" asked the doctor, after having finished his own plate, addressing a famous gourmand of the day.

"Very good, indeed," answered the other; "turtle, is it not? I only ask because I do not find any green fat."

The doctor shook his head.

"I think it has somewhat of a musky taste," said another, "not unpleasant but peculiar."

"All alligators have," replied Dr. Buckland; "the fellow I dissected this morning, and whom you have just been eating—"

There was a general rout of guests. Everyone turned pale. Half a dozen started up from the table and hurriedly left the room.

"See, what imagination is!" exclaimed Dr. Buckland. "If I had told them it was turtle or terrapin, or bird's nest soup, they would have pronounced it excellent."

"Tell me, doctor, was it really an alligator?"

"Alligator!" laughed the doctor. "Stuff and nonsense—it was nothing but a good calf's head."

KINDNESS

311 A kindly passer-by assisted a small boy in pushing a heavily loaded cart up a long, steep hill. Reaching the top, and at last getting his wind back, he said indignantly, "Only a scoundrel would expect a youngster to do a job like that! Your employer should have known it was too heavy for you."

"He did," replied the boy, "but he said, 'Go on, you're sure to find some old fool who'll help you up the hill.' "

312 The sentiment of "Woodman, spare that tree," is carried out on an extensive scale by the screen actor, Edward Everett Horton. He has a large ranch which he has converted into an "Old Trees Home." Whenever he discovers a beautiful oak, maple, or elm condemned to be cut down to make way for highways or buildings, he purchases it and has it removed to his sanctuary for unwanted trees.

313 Archibald Rutledge tells this story: "When I was a boy in Carolina, I was cured forever of caging wild things. Not content with hearing mocking-birds sing from the cedars, I determined to cage a young one, and thus have a young musician all my own. On the second day in the cage, he saw his mother fly to him with food in her bill. This attention pleased me for surely the mother knew how to feed her child better than I did. The following morning my pathetic little captive was dead. When I recounted this experience to Arthur Wayne, the renowned ornithologist, he said, 'A mother mocking-bird, finding her young in a cage, will sometimes take it poison berries. She thinks it better for one she loves to die rather than to live in captivity.' "

314 When Grant, knowing Lincoln's attitude of leniency and desiring to be prepared for all eventualities, inquired whether he was to "try to capture Jeff Davis or let him escape from the country if he would," Lincoln explained his stand: "About that I told him the story of an Irishman who had taken the pledge of Father Matthew. He became terribly thirsty, applied to a bartender for a lemonade, and while it was being prepared whispered to him, 'And couldn't ye put a little brandy in it all unbeknown to meself?' I told Grant if he could let Jeff Davis escape all unbeknown to himself, to let him go. I didn't want him."

315   President Lincoln once dropped a few kind words about the Confederates. A woman flashed forth a question of how he could speak kindly of his enemies when he should rather destroy them.

"What, Madam, do I not destroy them when I make them my friends?"

316   Never was a famous composer kinder than Brahms to his young colleagues—where he found genuine talent. With might and main he urged Simrock to publish the works of Knorr, Roentgen, Fuchs, and Novak. He rescued Dvorak from the direst poverty, made Simrock bring out the Slavonic Dances, and helped them to their wide success. Twice he begged Dvorak, with all his heart, to consider the Brahmsian fortune as his own. And when he learned that the Bohemian was a most incompetent proofreader, he himself actually assumed the drudgery of correcting all his friend's proofs.

> RELATED SUBJECTS: *Generosity* 241-248; *Gratitude and Ingratitude* 261-268; *Helpfulness* 281

> SEE ALSO: *Hypocrisy* 303; *Homeliness* 652; *Friendship* 867; *Babies* 957; *Horse Racing* 1872; *Discipline* 2441

LATENESS

321   At the East India House the head of the office once reproved Charles Lamb for the excessive irregularity of his attendance.

"Really, Mr. Lamb, you come very late!"

"Y-yes," replied Lamb with his habitual stammer, "b-but consi-sider how ear-early I go!"

322   On one occasion, when Lincoln was going to attend a political convention, one of his rivals, a liveryman, provided him with a slow horse, hoping that he would not reach his destination in time. Lincoln got there, however, and when he returned with the horse he said:

"You keep this horse for funerals, don't you?"

"Oh no!" replied the liveryman.

"Well, I'm glad of that, for if you did you'd never get a corpse to the grave in time for the resurrection."

323   A gentleman, having an appointment with another who was habitually unpunctual, to his great surprise found him waiting. He thus addressed him: "Why, I see you are here first at last. You were always behind before, but I am glad to see you have become early of late."

324   On his way to Gettysburg, where he delivered his immortal address, Lincoln was urged by General Fry to hurry in order not to hold up the train. To this Lincoln replied:

"I feel about this as the convict in one of our Illinois towns felt when he was going to the gallows. As he passed along the road in custody of the sheriff the people, eager to see the execution, kept crowding and pushing past him. At last he called out: 'Boys, you needn't be in such a hurry to get ahead. There won't be any fun till I get there.'"

RELATED SUBJECTS: *Procrastination* 461

SEE ALSO: *Trains* 1801

LAZINESS

326   Lincoln admitted that he was not particularly energetic when it came to real hard work.

"My father," said he one day, "taught me how to work, but not to love it. I never did like to work and I don't deny it. I'd rather read, tell stories, crack jokes, talk, laugh—anything but work."

327   Judge Davis was going through the docket and came across a long bill in chancery, drawn by an excellent but somewhat indolent lawyer. He exclaimed: "Why Brother Snap, how did you rake up energy enough to get up such a long bill?"

"Dunno, Judge," replied the party addressed. The Judge

held up the bill. "Astonishing, ain't it? Brother Snap did it. Wonderful—eh Lincoln?"

This amounted to an order on Lincoln for a joke at this point. He was ready. "It's like the lazy preacher," drawled he, "that used to write long sermons, and the explanation was, he got to writing and was too lazy to stop."

RELATED SUBJECTS: *Sleeping* 26-27; *Carelessness* 136; *Diligence* 176-177; *Lateness* 321-324; *Procrastination* 461

SEE ALSO: *Sickness* 1705; *Longevity* 1782

LIARS

331 Lord Chatham said of an approaching debate: "If I cannot speak standing I will speak sitting, and if I cannot speak sitting I will speak lying."

"Which he will do in whatever position he speaks," remarked Lord North.

332 It is said that the Japanese inspire no more confidence one in the other than they do in the citizens of the rest of the world. Two merchants of Tokyo once met in the railway station.

"Where are you going?" asked the first one.

His friend hesitated, then said, "To Kobe."

"Oh, you liar!" said the first one angrily. "You tell me you are going to Kobe to make me think you're going to Osaka, but I have made inquiries and I know you are going to Kobe!"

333 Speaker Reed, Ambassador Choate and Senator Westcott were chatting together one evening. Mr. Choate said with great solemnity: "Well, gentlemen, I have not drunk whiskey, played cards for money, or attended a horse race in twenty-eight years."

"My gracious!" exclaimed Senator Westcott admiringly. "I wish I could say that."

"Why don't you?" blandly inquired Mr. Reed. "Choate did."

334 A generation ago, when Prime Minister Winston Churchill was still a member of the Liberal Party, he rose in Commons to defend his party against the charge that they had deliberately misrepresented the Conservative Party. The Liberals had accused the Conservatives of practising slavery in South Africa because they kept Negro laborers behind barbed-wire compounds under severe restrictions.

Churchill remarked: "I admit the term 'slavery' might be a terminological inexactitude."

At this Joseph Chamberlain, father of the late Prime Minister Neville Chamberlain, interrupted:

"I prefer the ugly little English three letter word—l-i-e."

335 A minister wound up the services one morning by saying, "Next Sunday I am going to preach on the subject of liars. And in this connection, as a preparation for my discourse, I should like you all to read the 17th Chapter of Mark." On the following Sunday, the preacher rose to begin, and said, "Now then, all of you who have done as I requested and read the 17th Chapter of Mark, please raise your hands." Nearly every hand in the congregation went up. Then said the preacher, "You are the very people I want to talk to. There is no 17th Chapter of Mark!"

336 A certain young California politician, notorious for lying, had once been unwittingly led into speaking the truth. Noah Brooks was explaining the situation to President Lincoln, who immediately reminded himself of a story, saying that he recalled a similar circumstance about a Negro barber in Illinois, who was a great liar. A crowd in front of a barber shop stood one evening gazing with admiration at the planet Jupiter. "Sho," said the barber, "I've seen that star before. I seen him 'way down in Georgy."

Said Lincoln: "Like your California friend, he told the truth, but thought he was lying."

RELATED SUBJECTS: *Boastfulness* 101-103; *Exaggeration* 221-226; *Honesty* 286-294; *Hypocrisy* 301-303

SEE ALSO: *Drinking* 49; *Honesty* 294; *Fishing* 1848; *Golf* 1866; *Campaigning* 1915; *Chiseling* 2127; *Statistics* 2222; *Censors* 2351; *Juries* 2517

LONG-WINDEDNESS

341 One of the executives of RKO, Leon J. Bamberger, once spoke at a convention, "I'm having such a good time that I'd just as soon go on speaking all afternoon, but I remember another Monday on which I was addressing a convention. I had hardly begun when I heard someone in the first row lean over and ask his friend, 'Say, what follows Bamberger?' And the answer was, 'Wednesday.'"

342 Sir Josiah Stamp, in a speech at the Chicago Club, expressed a hope that he wasn't talking too long. "I wouldn't like to be in the position of the parson," he explained, "who in the midst of an interminable sermon, suddenly stopped to chide: 'You know I don't mind a bit having you look at your watches to see what time it is, but it really annoys me when you put them up to your ears to see if they are still running.'"

343 At a banquet, a speaker was ranting on about a subject which held very little interest for most of the audience. Unable to stand it any longer, one of them slipped quietly out. Just outside the door he bumped into another sufferer who had gone out just before him.

"Has he finished yet?" he was asked.

"Yes," said the man who had just escaped, "long ago, but he won't stop."

344 The following remarks of Mark Twain may well be taken to heart by the various after-dinner speakers who inflict their long drawn out speeches upon suffering diners.

"Some years ago in Hartford, we all went to church one hot sweltering night to hear the annual report of Mr. Hawley, a city missionary who went around finding people who needed help and didn't want to ask for it. He told of the life in cellars, where poverty resided; he gave instances of the heroism and devotion of the poor. 'When a man with millions gives,' he said, 'we make a great deal of noise. It's noise in the wrong place, for it's the widow's mite that counts.' Well, Hawley worked me up to a great pitch. I could hardly wait for him to get through. I had $400 in my pocket. I wanted to give that and borrow more to give. You could see greenbacks in every eye. But instead of passing the plate then, he kept on talking and talking, and as he talked it grew hotter and hotter, and we grew sleepier and sleepier. My enthusiasm went down, down, down—$100 at a clip—until finally, when the plate did come around, I stole ten cents out of it. It all goes to show how a little thing like this can lead to crime."

345 Burke and Mr. David Hartley of the Ministry arose simultaneously on the floor of the House of Commons. As the speaker granted recognition to Mr. Hartley, Burke settled down for a long wait, as Hartley's speeches were notorious for their length. In the dreary course of three hours' argument, nearly everyone in the House managed to make his escape. At one pause in his speech, Mr. Hartley demanded that the Riot Act be read to illustrate one of the points he was making. "The Riot Act, my dear sir!" Burke exclaimed. "Look at these empty benches. Do you not see that the mob is completely dispersed?"

346 The late "Kingfish" Huey Long had been speaking on a bill in the U. S. Senate for more than two hours, when he called for a glass of water.

"Mr. Speaker, I rise to a point of order," said Senator Johnson of California.

"State your point of order."

"Mr. Speaker," continued Sen. Johnson with a straight face. "I would like to draw the attention of the Senator from Louisiana that it is out of order to run a windmill with water."

347 On one occasion Judge Olin of New York was speaking and in his excitement he walked up and down the aisle passing Thaddeus Stevens' seat. At length Stevens said: "Olin, do you expect to get mileage for that speech?"

348 Much as he hated to give long-winded speeches King Frederick William IV hated even more to have to listen to them. Once after a long and tiresome trip he arrived at a small town in Prussia where the natives had thronged the streets since daybreak waiting for his arrival. As the royal carriage pulled into town the bands began to play, the people shouted and the fat burgomaster, perspiring in a new red coat, came forward, and with a dramatic gesture opened his speech of welcome thus: "Most high and powerful lord! When Hannibal stood before the gates of Carthage—" "He was probably just as hungry as I am." Frederick broke in, putting his hand on the speaker's shoulder, "Come, my friend, let's go and have dinner together."

349 Lord North, once Prime Minister of England, was accustomed to sleep during the parliamentary harangues of his adversaries, leaving Sir Grey Cooper to note down anything remarkable. During a debate on ship-building, some tedious speaker entered on a historical detail, in which, commencing with Noah's ark, he traced the progress of the art regularly downwards. When he came to building the Spanish Armada, Sir Grey inadvertently awoke the slumbering Prime Minister, who inquired at what era the honorable gentleman had arrived. Being answered, "We are now in the reign of Queen Elizabeth."

"Dear me, Sir Grey," said he, "why not let me sleep a century or two more?"

350 An Ambassador having come to Sparta from Perinthus, spoke at great length.

"What answer shall I return to the Perinthians?" he asked.

"Say," said the king, "that you talked a great deal, and that I did not utter a word."

351 General Alexander Smyth of Virginia, a man of ability, was an excessively tedious speaker, worrying the House, and prolonging his speeches by numerous quotations. On one occasion when he had been more than ordinarily tiresome he turned to Henry Clay who was sitting near him. "You, sir, speak for the present generation; but I speak for posterity," he said.

"Yes," said Mr. Clay, "and you seem resolved to speak until the arrival of your audience."

352 On one occasion a person who was present at a sitting of the Court of Sessions in England, returned late in the afternoon and found the same case still on and the same advocate talking. He remarked to Lord Cockburn, "Surely he is wasting a great deal of time."

"Time," the jurist replied, "long ago has he exhausted time. Now he is encroaching upon eternity."

353 The late Gilman Marston of New Hampshire was arguing a complicated case, and had looked up authorities back to Julius Caesar. At the end of an hour and a half, in the most intricate part of his plea, he was pained to see what looked like inattention. The judge was unable to appreciate the nice points of his argument.

"Your honor," he said. "I beg your pardon, but do you follow me?"

"I have so far," answered the judge shifting wearily about in his chair, "but I'll say frankly that if I thought I could find my way back, I'd quit right here."

354 And then there was the case of that other counsel, this was an Irishman, who also developed an inexhaustible argument upon an exhaustible case. After he had gone on for four hours the President of the Court said to him, "Mr. Murphy, is it any good for you to continue? Everything you say goes in at one ear and comes out of the other."

"Why not," said the counsel, "there is little enough to stop it."

355 When President Franklin D. Roosevelt was a young lawyer just getting started in New York he was retained to handle a difficult civil case. The opposing lawyer was a very effective jury pleader and completely outshone his youthful rival in the argument to the jury. However, he made one fatal mistake: he orated for several hours. As he thundered on Roosevelt noticed that the jury wasn't paying much attention. So, playing a hunch when his turn came, he rose and said: "Gentlemen you have heard the evidence. You also have listened to my distinguished colleague, a brilliant orator. If you believe him, and disbelieve the evidence you will have to decide in his favor. That's all I have to say."

The jury was out only five minutes and brought in a verdict for Roosevelt's client.

356 Speaking of a lawyer Lincoln said, "He can compress the most words into the smallest ideas better than any man I ever met."

357 When Sheridan was making one of his great displays in Westminster Hall, he observed Gibbon among the auditors, and complimented him by some allusion to his "luminous pen." An acquaintance afterward reproached Sheridan with the sincerity of his compliment, and wondered how he could have used the word "luminous."

"O, it was a mistake," said Sheridan, "I meant voluminous."

358 When Diderot came to visit Voltaire he spoke so much and at such great length that Voltaire couldn't get a word in. When Diderot left, Voltaire chirped, "That man is a great wit, but nature has denied him one great gift—that of dialogue."

359 Elizabeth Barrett, meeting Wordsworth for the first time, wrote ironically, "He was very kind to me and let me hear his conversation."

360 They tell the story of Wilton Lackaye who was scheduled to speak late on the program at a banquet at which all the speakers had been brutally long-winded.

The chairman introduced Lackaye, saying, "Wilton Lackaye, the famous actor, will now give you his address."

Lackaye faced the haggard audience and said, "Mr. Chairman, Ladies and Gentlemen, my address is the Lambs' Club, New York."

He sat down and received a tremendous ovation.

361 A very pretty woman, who was tediously loquacious, complained one day to Madame de Sévigné that she was sadly tormented by her lovers.

"Oh, madam," said Madame de Sévigné to her, with a smile, "it is very easy to get rid of them, you have only to speak."

362 A talkative lady patient came to Dr. Abernathy, the eccentric English physician of another day, and talked tirelessly and tiresomely about her complaint.

"Put out your tongue, madam," barked Dr. Abernathy. The lady complied. "Now keep it there till I've done talking."

363 Sheridan, the playwright, on seeing a Member of the House of Commons, who had already bored everyone with a lengthy speech, stop to drink a glass of water, rose to a point of order.

"What is it?" asked the Speaker.

"Why I think, sir," said Sheridan, "that it is out of order for a wind-mill to go by water."

RELATED SUBJECTS: *Boastfulness* 101-103; *Pompousness* 421-427; *Vanity* 606-628; *Speeches* 756-782; *Lectures* 1106-1111; *Sermons* 1541-1559

MELANCHOLY

366 A patient suffering from profound melancholy one day presented himself to Abernathy; after careful examination the celebrated practitioner said, "You need amusement; go and hear the comedian Grimaldi; he will make you laugh, and that will be better for you than any drugs."

"My God," exclaimed the invalid, "I am Grimaldi!"

367 Dr. Goldsmith, having been requested by a woman to visit her husband who was melancholy, called upon the patient and told him he would send some pills which he had no doubt would prove efficacious. He immediately went home, put ten guineas into a chip, and sent them to the sick man. The remedy had the desired effect.

368 Philip of Spain was in such a deplorable state of despondency from ill-health, that he refused to be shaved. On the arrival of the famous singer Farinelli, the Queen ordered a concert in a room adjoining the King's chamber. Farinelli sang one of his best airs, which so overcame the King that he desired he might be brought into his presence, when he promised to grant him any reasonable request he might make. The performer, in the most respectful manner, then begged of the king to allow himself to be shaved to which request Philip graciously consented.

MEMORY

371 In the days before modern court reporting and our generally efficient and systematized courtroom procedure, an elderly Southern lawyer was the proud owner of a Negro slave named Sam, who was endowed with a phenomenal memory.

Sam was able to sit in court and, at any point in the process of a trial, he could reel off every word of testimony that had transpired before. Sam's reputation was so great that his evidence "on the record" was accepted in any court in the State. One day the old lawyer was in his study when the Devil appeared.

"What do you want?" demanded the lawyer.

"I've come for Sam," was the answer. "His time is up and he's got to go."

"Now, look here," said the lawyer, "I can't spare Sam."

"Can't help it," said the Devil.

"Come now," said the lawyer, "you're a sporting man. I'll make a little bet with you. If Sam's memory is failing he's no good to me and you can take him. You go out and test him, and if you can fool him, he's yours. But if you can't, he's mine."

"It's a bet," the Devil said, and disappeared.

Sam was then engaged in plowing up his little patch of ground with a mule. The Devil suddenly appeared before him and said, "Do you like eggs?"

"Yassah," said Sam. And the Devil vanished.

In less than a year the Civil War broke out. Sam served first with his master on the Confederate side, was captured and forced to fight on the Northern side, and was then captured again by the Confederates. He survived the War with only a minor wound, and after the Emancipation was willingly liberated by his old master, who presented him with the patch of land which he had been accustomed to work for so many years. One day as Sam was cultivating the little plot that was now his own, the Devil appeared before him. "How?" said the Devil.

"Fried!" said Sam. Whereupon the Devil vanished and left him in peace.

372 Memory training by association became a fad in a certain school. "For instance," the English teacher was explaining, "if you want to remember the name of a poet, Bobbie Burns, you might conjure up in your eye a picture of a London policeman in flames. You see, 'Bobbie Burns.' "

"I see," said one of his pupils, "but how is one to be sure that it doesn't represent 'Robert Browning?' "

373 In order to play in "Rosemary," John Drew shaved off his mustache, thereby greatly changing his appearance. Shortly afterward he met Max Beerbohm in the lobby of a London theatre, but could not just then recall who the latter was. Mr.

Beerbohm's memory was better.

"Oh, Mr. Drew," he said, "I'm afraid you don't recognize me without your mustache."

374 Archbishop Ryan was once accosted on the streets of Baltimore by a man who knew the Archbishop's face, but could not quite place it.

"Now, where in hell have I seen you?" he asked perplexedly.

"From where in hell do you come, sir?"

375 The woman's club was listening, entranced, to the lecture being given by a world-famous traveller. He concluded his remarks with, "And there are some spectacles that one never forgets . . ."

At this point a timid old lady in the audience spoke up shyly, "Pardon me, sir, would you tell me where I could get a pair? I am always forgetting mine."

RELATED SUBJECTS: *Absent-Mindedness* 81-90; *Accuracy* 91-92

SEE ALSO: *Composers* 1323; *Conductors* 1331, 1339

MODESTY

376 F. W. Wile tells how, "Once when a group of Washington newspapermen wanted Secretary of State Hughes to attend a dinner at which a number of first rank foreign statesmen were to be present, I was a committee of one to ask him where he wanted to be seated at table. That was long before Dollie Gann and Alice Longworth all but caused social civil war in Washington over dinner-table precedence. 'You need never worry about that in my case,' Hughes said. 'The only place I ever want to be first is at a fire!' "

377 A characteristic story is told of the great Principal Cairns, one of the most simple-minded and humble of men. Attending a great public meeting on one occasion in Edinburgh, which was densely crowded, his appearance on the platform was received with loud cheers. Never imagining that this was for himself, he turned and saw following him a man of diminutive stature, and totally unknown. Taking him to be the object of popular applause, he stepped aside to let him pass, and as he did so began enthusiastically to join in the clapping. The act, so characteristic of the man, was received with uproarious delight, and fairly brought down the house.

378 In the Netherlands, a few years ago, a publisher decided that his country should follow the lead of other nations and have a Dutch "Who's Who." Immediately he encountered the national feeling that publicity is a state of exposure that the Hollander shuns rather than seeks. The men and women approached for the contemplated book found something positively indecent in the inquisitive request of a publisher that one should write his own life-story. Finally sufficient cooperation was secured to publish such a book but it was obviously incomplete as a record. Then, the Dutch public would not buy it, and the experiment was dropped.

379 When conversation in a company in which Dr. Johnson was present had fallen upon rather a delicate topic, one of the ladies, with an expression of great displeasure, rose and left the room. "That woman," said the doctor, "is the most immodest of all the company."

380 Madame de Genlis carried her purity of manners to such an extent, that she reprimanded the bookseller who had the arrangement of her library, for having placed books written by male and female authors on the same shelf.

381 A man came upon Lincoln blacking his boots in the basement of the White House. He expressed astonishment that the President of the United States should be at such a menial task.
"What! Mr. President," he exclaimed, "are you blacking your own boots?"
"Whose else should I be blacking?" came Lincoln's laconic reply.

382 Cato, the Roman, on observing that statues were being set up in honor of many, remarked: "I would rather people would ask, why is there not a statue to Cato, than why there is."

383 Abraham Lincoln was free from the usual official vanity. He rather shrank from than courted the official title of Mr. President, and generally referred to his office as "this place,"

"since I have been in this place," or, "since I came here." Referring at one time to the apartment reserved in the Capitol for the Chief Magistrate, he called it "the room, you know, that they call the President's room."

Once he pleaded with some old Illinois friends who addressed him as Mr. President, "Now call me Lincoln, and I'll promise not to tell of the breach of etiquette."

384 Salmon P. Chase, when Secretary of the Treasury, had a disagreement with other members of the Cabinet, and resigned.

The President was urged not to accept it as "Secretary Chase is today a national necessity," his advisers said.

"How mistaken you are!" Lincoln quietly observed. "Yet, it is not strange; I used to have similar notions. No! If we should all be turned out tomorrow and could came back here in a week, we should find our places filled by a lot of fellows doing just as well as we did, and in many instances better.

"Now, this reminds me of what the Irishman said. His verdict was that 'in this country one man is as good as another; and, for the matter of that, very often a great deal better.' No, this government does not depend upon the life of any man."

385 At the Lyons assizes, in France, before the trial of a certain case, the presiding judge remarked on seeing the court crowded with ladies: "The persons composing the audience are probably not aware of the nature of the case about to be tried. I therefore feel it incumbent on me to request all respectable women to withdraw."

Not one of the ladies stirred from her place.

"Usher," the judge continued, "now that all the respectable women have left, turn the others out."

386 Two ladies, encountering Dr. Johnson soon after the publication of his "Dictionary," complimented him for having omitted gross, indelicate, and objectionable words.

"What, my dears!" said Dr. Johnson, "have you been searching for them?"

387 Plato tells a fable of how spirits of the other world came back to find bodies and places to work. One took the body of a poet and did his work. Finally, Ulysses came and said, "All the fine bodies have been taken and all the grand work done. There is nothing for me."

"Yes," said a voice, "the best has been left for you—the body of a common man, doing a common work for a common reward."

388 Thomas Mann was once introduced to a successful American writer who grovelled abjectly before the eminent novelist, explaining humbly that he was a simple hack who should hardly call himself a writer in the presence of so great an artist. Mann was courteous, but later said to his host, "That man has no right to make himself so small. He is not that big."

389 In Bonn, the home of Beethoven has been converted into a memorial museum. In one of the rooms, roped off from curious hands, is the piano upon which Beethoven composed many of his great works. A Vassar girl, visiting the shrine with a party of American students, looked upon the instrument with awe and asked the guard, with the additional persuader of a generous tip, if she might play upon it for a moment. The permission was granted and she sat at the piano and strummed out a few bars of the "Moonlight Sonata." Departing she remarked to the guard, "I suppose all the great pianists who have come here at one time or another have played on it." The guard said, "No, Miss, Paderewski was here two years ago but said he was not worthy to touch it."

390 Vasari relates that when Leonardo da Vinci lay on his death-bed the King came to visit and cheer him. He raised himself as far up as he could in the royal presence and lamented "that he had offended God and man in that he had not labored in art as he ought to have done."

RELATED SUBJECTS: *Discretion* 181-182; *Tact* 586-591

SEE ALSO: *Scientists* 1120; *Inventors* 1130; *Painting* 1271, 1277; *Presidents* 1933

PATIENCE

391 In the reign of Queen Elizabeth, Dr. Thomas Cooper edited a learned dictionary with the addition of thirty-three thousand words, and many other improvements. He had already been eight years in collecting materials for his edition,

when his wife, who was a worthless and malignant woman, going one day into his library, burnt every note he had prepared under the pretense of fearing that he would kill himself with study.

The doctor shortly after came in, and seeing the destruction, inquired who was the author of it. His wife boldly avowed that it was the work of her mischievous hands. The patient man heaved a deep sigh and said, "Oh Dinah, Dinah, thou hast given me a world of trouble!"

Then he quietly sat down to another eight years of hard labor, to replace the notes which she had destroyed.

> RELATED SUBJECTS: *Cheerfulness* 141-143; *Diligence* 176-177; *Endurance* 216; *Tact* 586-591; *Tolerance* 601-603

PATRIOTISM

396 Some time after the conclusion of the revolution, a young American was present in a British playhouse, where an interlude was performed in ridicule of his countrymen. A number of American officers being introduced in tattered uniforms, and barefoot, the question was put to them severally: "What was your trade before you entered the army?" One answered a tailor, another a cobbler, etc. The wit of the piece was to banter them for not keeping themselves in clothes and shoes, but before that could be expressed, the American exclaimed from the gallery: "Great Britain beaten by tailors and cobblers! Hurrah!" Even the Prime Minister, who was present, could not help smiling, amidst a general peal of laughter.

397 I once heard an Irishman say, "Every man loves his native land, whether he was born there or not."

398 In the early part of the Civil War an elderly lady who attended a meeting of the First Vermont Regiment, arose, full of enthusiasm, and said she thanked God that she was able to do something for her country; her two sons, all she possessed in the world, were in the regiment; and the only thing she had to regret was that she could not have known twenty years before that the war was coming—she would have furnished more.

399   When Lieutenant-Governor Patterson was Speaker of the legislature of one of our States, some dozen boys presented themselves for the place of messenger, as is usual at the opening of the House. He inquired their names and into their condition, in order that he might make the proper selection. He came, in the course of his examination, to a small boy about ten years old, a bright-looking lad. "Well, sir," said he, "what is your name?" "John Hancock," was the answer. "What!" said the Speaker, "you are not the one that signed the Declaration of Independence, are you?" "No, sir," replied the lad, stretching himself to his utmost proportions, "but I would be if I had been there." "You can be one of the messengers," said the Speaker.

400   When the Emperor Vespasian commanded a Roman senator to give his voice against the interests of his country and threatened him with immediate death if he spoke on the other side, the Roman, conscious that the attempt to serve a people was in his power, though the event was ever so uncertain, answered with a smile: "Did I ever tell you that I was immortal? My virtue is in my own disposal, my life in yours; you do what you will, I shall do what I ought; and if I fall in the service of my country, I shall have more triumph in my death than you in all your laurels."

401   It was a little boy in an American Sunday-school, who, in reply to his teacher's question, "Who was the first man?" answered, "George Washington," and upon being informed that it was Adam, exclaimed: "Ah, well! If you are speaking of foreigners, perhaps he was."

402   Gladstone remarked that the best example of wit he could recall in the House of Commons was Lord John Russell's reply to Sir Francis Burdett who had changed his political affiliations from Radical to Tory.

Addressing the House one day Burdett declared that there was nothing more odious than the cant of patriotism. To which Lord Russell replied that the cant of patriotism was no doubt very odious, but there was something even more odious and that was the recant of patriotism.

403   Californians are famous for their loyalty to their native state. One of its native sons was once visiting his wife's relatives in the East. While there he had occasion to attend the funeral of a man who was little liked in the community. At the services the minister, who was new to the parish, called upon someone to say a few words about the deceased. A long and significant silence ensued. Finally, the true son of California stood up and said, "Well, since there's no one present who has anything to say about our departed brother, I'd like a few minutes to tell you something about California."

404 Bismarck told a story of an Alpine host who, after pointing out the glories of his native land, asked a Berlin youth if they had any such mountains in Berlin. "No," he replied, "we have not got such mountains, but, if we had, they would be much finer than these."

405 Jerrold was in France, and with a Frenchman who was enthusiastic on the subject of the Anglo-French alliance. He said that he was proud to see the English and French such good friends at last, when Jerrold promptly answered, "Tut! The best thing I know between France and England—is the sea."

406 The leading nobles of Poland addressed a petition to Marie Walewska to accept Napoleon as her lover. They quoted Scripture to reinforce their argument:

"Did Esther, do you think, give herself to Ahasueros out of the fullness of her love for him? So great was the terror with which he inspired her that she fainted at the sight of him. We may therefore conclude that affection had but little to do with her resolve. She sacrificed her own inclinations to the salvation of her country and that salvation it was her glory to achieve. May we be enabled to say the same to you, to your glory and our own happiness!"

407 General Pershing was on a tour of inspection on the Western Front. Stopping at one of the camps that housed the wounded, he happened to notice a very bedraggled looking soldier sitting outside one of the tents. The General was just about to remark sympathetically about his condition, having noticed that he had one arm in a sling and a huge bandage about his head, when he heard the man muttering to himself.

"I love my country," Pershing heard the man say, "I'd fight for my country. I'd starve and go thirsty for my country. I'd die for my country. But if ever this damn war is over, I'll never love another country again!"

RELATED SUBJECTS: *United States* 2031-2032; *Freedom* 2036-2042; *Equality* 2046; *Civilians in War* 2331-2346; *Soldiers and Sailors* 2430-2437

SEE ALSO: *Boastfulness* 102; *Quick Thinking* 476; *Births* 1012; *Campaigning* 1914; *Civilians in War* 2339; *Battles* 2382; *Soldiers* 2430, 2437

PESSIMISM

411 On the subject of calamity howlers, the story is told of the gala crowd that had assembled for the test run of Robert Fulton's outlandish steamboat contraption "The Clermont." For some hours, in the presence of a mass of spectators, the strange craft belched smoke and sparks from its tall, thin stack as his engineers attempted to get up the necessary head of steam. When the time to cast off had come and the engines were being limbered up, the boat quivered and vibrated violently and made a loud racket. A group of doubting Thomases in the crowd had been shouting loudly and scornfully, "She'll never start! She'll never start!" But notwithstanding this, the boat pulled itself together and actually started to move up the river. After a moment of astonished silence, the voices of the scoffers resumed their shouts; this time crying with all the scorn they could muster, "She'll never stop! She'll never stop!"

RELATED SUBJECTS: *Cheerfulness* 141-143; *Melancholy* 366-368; *Worrying* 636

POLITENESS

416 When in this country on a mission during World War I Marshal Foch was buttonholed by a noisy Westerner who launched into a tirade against French politeness.

"There is nothing in it but wind," he sneered.

"There is nothing but wind in a tire," politely countered the Marshal, "but it makes riding in a car very smooth and pleasant."

417 A governor of Virginia, being saluted by a Negro, immediately returned the compliment.

"Can you demean yourself so far," said a slaveholder, "as to raise your hat to a Negro?"

"Undoubtedly," said the governor. "I should be sorry for him to exceed me in politeness."

418 It happens to everybody some time or other. The man and the woman were hastening down the street in opposite directions. They met head on, both veered abruptly to one side, and then to the other confronting each other in a vain effort to untangle themselves and pass. When the difficulty was at last solved, the man tipped his hat and said, "Good-bye, it's nice to have known you."

419 Expressing himself somewhat bitterly on the subject of storytellers who persistently interrupt themselves to ask if one has heard the story, Mark Twain told of an encounter with Henry Irving. The actor asked him if he had heard a certain story and Twain politely said, "No." Irving proceeded and later made the same query. Proceeding almost to the climax of his story, Irving again asked if he had heard it. Twain said, "I can lie once, I can lie twice for courtesy's sake, but I draw the line there. I can't lie the third time at any price. I not only heard the story, I invented it."

420 Henry Clay and John Randolph had had a violet quarrel in the Senate. For a long time they did not speak when they encountered one another outside.

It chanced one day that they found themselves confronted by one another at a very narrow point created by repairs underway on the sidewalk. They stood silently for a moment, faced by the question of which was to step aside and let the other pass. At last Randolph said haughtily, "I never turn out for scoundrels."

"I always do," said Clay, stepping politely out into the mud, giving Randolph the right of way.

RELATED SUBJECTS: *Flattery* 236-237; *Gentlemanliness* 251-256; *Kindness* 311-316; *Tact* 586-591

SEE ALSO: *Critics* 1102

POMPOUSNESS

421   To a young speaker Thomas Corwin, the Congressman, gave this advice:

"Never make people laugh. If you would succeed in life, you must be solemn, solemn as an ass. All the great monuments are built over solemn asses."

422   A peddler with a hand-cart full of shrimps was ordered out of the way by a member of Parliament, who was trying to park his limousine.

"Look out yourself," said the coster.

"Do you realize," demanded the other, "that I have an M.P. at the end of my name?"

"So 'as every blarsted shrimp in this 'ere cart!"

423   A pompous young man called on Joseph Choate the prominent lawyer and statesman. The lawyer was busy and asked the young man to take a chair. But the youth was impatient and again interrupted the lawyer with the remark, "I am Bishop Blank's son." "Please take two chairs," said Mr. Choate.

424   When Victor Hugo was an aspirant for the honors of the Academy, and called on M. Royer Collard to ask his vote, the sturdy veteran professed an entire ignorance of his name.

"I am the author of 'Notre Dame de Paris'; 'Les derniers Jours d'un Condamne'; 'Marion Delorme,' etc."

"I have never heard of any of them."

"Will you do me the honor of accepting a copy of my works?"

"I never read new books."

425   To Boston is attributed the credit of having retorted to the superciliousness of Oscar Wilde in kind. "You're Philistines," Wilde accused his Boston audience, "who have invaded the sacred sanctum of Art."

A voice in the audience called out, "And you're driving us forth with the jawbone of an ass."

426   Widmann relates that "when the school-masterish music director of a very small Swiss town graciously assured Brahms that he was familiar with every one of his compositions, the Master motioned him with his hand to be still and listen atten-

tively, as the festival orchestra was just then playing something of his own. It was, however, a military march by Gungl. I can still see the good man before me, how with open mouth and reverent contorted eyes he listened to the rather commonplace fanfares, which he now really held to be a Brahms composition while Brahms, in outrageous glee over his successful trick, whispered to the rest of us: 'Just look at the Basilio!' (the hypocritical dupe in Rossini's 'Barber of Seville')."

427 A Congressman said to Horace Greeley one day: "I am a self-made man."

"That sir," said Greeley, "relieves the Almighty of a great responsibility."

> RELATED SUBJECTS: *Boastfulness* 101-103; *Dullness* 186-195; *Long-Windedness* 341-363; *Snobbishness* 546-551; *Vanity* 606-628

> SEE ALSO: *Eating* 7; *Universities* 1019; *Music* 1306; *Public Offices* 1926

PRACTICAL JOKING

431 Mark Twain once encountered a friend at the races who said, "I'm broke. I wish you'd buy me a ticket back to town."

Twain said, "Well, I'm pretty broke myself but, I'll tell you what to do. You hide under my seat and I'll cover you with my legs." It was agreed and Twain then went to the ticket office and bought two tickets. When the train was under way and the supposed stowaway was snug under the seat, the conductor came by and Twain gave him the two tickets.

"Where is the other passenger?" asked the conductor.

Twain tapped on his forehead and said in a loud voice, "That is my friend's ticket. He is a little eccentric and likes to ride under the seat."

432 It is said that Dr. Clyde Miller of Columbia University has his way of disposing of dull books occasionally sent to him by publishers. He sends them on to friends with a note, ostensibly from the author, saying, "I hope you will be pleased by the references made to you in this volume, and hope that you will not have any objection to this use of your name."

Dr. Miller takes pleasure in the vision of his friends searching vainly through the books for the allusions to them.

433 George Bernard Shaw was poring over a second-hand bookstall of volumes much marked down, when he came across a volume containing his own plays. The book was inscribed, moreover, to a friend, beneath whose name on the fly-leaf, G.B.S. saw, written in his own hand, "With the compliments of George Bernard Shaw." Buying the book, Mr. Shaw wrote under the inscription: "With renewed compliments. G. B. S.," and sent it back to the early recipient.

434 In the days of Kipling's most popular vogue, his literary works yielded him great sums.

An American wit once wrote to him, "I hear that you are retailing literature for $1.00 a word. I enclose $1.00, for which please send me a sample."

Keeping the dollar, Kipling wrote, "Thanks."

Shortly afterward, he received another letter from his correspondent, saying, "Sold the 'Thanks' anecdote for $2.00. Enclosed please find 45¢ in stamps, being half the profits on the transaction, less postage."

435 A miserly old nobleman wanted Hogarth to paint on his staircase a picture of the destruction of Pharoah's hosts in the Red Sea. He did so much haggling over the price that Hogarth finally agreed to do the work for about half what it was worth. After two days' work, to the surprise of the nobleman, Hogarth said the picture was ready. When the curtain was removed there was nothing to be seen but the canvas painted red all over. "Zounds!" cried the miser. "What have you here? I ordered a scene of the Red Sea!"

"The Red Sea you have," replied the artist.

"But where are the Israelites?"

"They are all gone over."

"And where are the Egyptians?"

"They are all drowned."

436 Turner, the famous British painter, was much irritated by the fashionable ladies who talked pretentiously about "the masters." One day, when such a woman was gushing ignorantly about Cimabue, Turner interrupted, "Do you seriously think, your ladyship, that any of his works can compare with those of the great Florentine, Mortadella da Bologna?"

Nothing daunted the lady replied, "But how much better is Cimabue's color!"

"Not if you are a connoisseur of Italian sausages, Madame," politely purred the painter to the general hilarity.

437 Brahms once took the most elaborate pains to hoax Gustav Nottebohm, the famous Beethoven scholar. The poverty-stricken scholar often strolled with him in the Prater, and habitually bought his cold supper there from a certain cheese and sausage peddler. Kalbeck amusingly reports how "one evening he received his victuals wrapped in old music paper covered with crabbed notes, apparently in Beethoven's handwriting. Fighting down his excitement, he marched to the next lamppost, unfolded the paper, examined it carefully through his spectacles, smoothed it, and without a word shoved it into his pocket. The cheese he kept in his hand and ate as he walked, assuring the others that he was unusually hungry that day. And never did he drop a syllable about his find—to the huge disappointment of the company who had been let by Brahms into the secret. For the mysterious sheet contained a variation of the latest popular song-hit. That rascal Brahms had fabricated it in masterly imitation of Beethoven's hen scratches, and enjoined the peddler to wrap it around the professor's cheese."

RELATED SUBJECTS: *Rough and Ready* 496-507; *Zanies* 641-643; *Parties* 741-746

SEE ALSO: *Speeches* 777; *Authors* 1204; *Sermons* 1542

PREJUDICE

441 This is the remark William H. Seward made in reply to Douglas, who had been indulging, on the floor of the Senate, in a tirade against "nigger-worshippers." After the debate they walked home together from the capitol, and Mr. Seward, having in view Mr. Douglas's expectation of a nomination from the Democratic party for the Presidency, said: "Douglas, no man will ever be president of the United States who spells Negro with two g's."

442 He was a red-faced, middle-aged Irishman, who had taken just enough to make him officious. He kept a wary eye on the conductor, and a sympathetic one on the unsteady entering passenger; to each "step lively," he would rejoin, "shtiddy, shtiddy, give them toime, give them toime." Opposite the Irishman sat a young man of the most pronounced Hebrew type. He watched Pat with a humorous twinkle in his black eyes.

A good-natured Negro got in, and took the seat next to the Irishman. Pat threw one haughty look at the black man; then, rising with great dignity, he said in terms of unutterable scorn: "a nager!" and sat down next to the young Hebrew. Quick as a flash his new neighbor, with an exact imitation of Pat's tone and manner, said "an Irishman!" and took the vacant seat next to the Negro. A titter went round the car, and one Irishman looked foolish.

443 "You're a Jew, ain't you?" said the bigoted and prejudiced Yankee to the little man he found seated next to him on the train.

"Yes, I'm a Jew," he replied.

"Well, I'm not," said the Yankee arrogantly, "and I'm glad to say that in the little village in Maine where I come from, there ain't a single Jew."

His neighbor replied quietly, "Dot's why it's a village."

444 Meeting Margaret Fuller one day full-gloved in the street, Mrs. Horace Greeley, who had an antipathy to kid coverings, touched Miss Fuller's hand with a shudder and snapped out: "Skin of a beast!"

"Why, what do you wear?" asked Margaret.

"Silk," responded Mrs. Greeley.

Miss Fuller gave a comic shudder and came back with: "Entrails of a worm!"

445 "One day," related Booker T. Washington, the Negro educator, "a poor, ignorant white man came to the polls to vote.

" 'I wish you'd oblige me by voting this ticket,' said a bright mulatto, who was standing near the polls.

" 'What kind of a ticket is it?' asked the poor white man.

" 'Why,' said the mulatto, 'you can see for yourself.'

" 'But I can't read!'

" 'What, can't you read the ballot you have there in your hand and which you are about to vote?' exclaimed the colored man.

" 'No,' said he, 'I can't read at all.'

" 'Well,' said the colored man, 'this ballot means that you are in favor of giving equal franchise to both white and colored citizens.'

" 'It means to let the niggers vote, does it?'

" 'Yes, sir.'

" 'Then I don't want it. Niggers don't know enough to vote.' "

446   Pauline Bonaparte engaged a huge Negro to bathe her every morning. When some one protested, she answered innocently:

"What? Do you call that thing a man?"

She then ordered the Negro to go out and marry at once in order that she might not be compromised.

447   Theodore Roosevelt once said, "While I was Police Commissioner of New York City, an anti-Semitic preacher from Berlin, Rector Ahlwardt, came to New York to preach a crusade against the Jews. Many Jews were much excited, and asked me to prevent him from speaking and not to give him police protection. This, I told them, was impossible; and if possible would have been undesirable because it would make him a martyr. The proper thing to do was to make him ridiculous. Accordingly, I sent a detail of police under a Jewish sergeant, and the Jew-baiter made his harangue under the active protection of some 40 police, every one of them a Jew."

448   One day Jack Johnson (the Negro heavyweight champion) went alone into Bradcock's (in Mexico City), a very fashionable restaurant run by an American Southerner.

Jack had been told that there was no color line in Mexico, but in Bradcock's restaurant, after a long wait on his part, a waitress informed him she had orders never to serve a Negro.

He went over to El Globo. Two generals at once insisted on returning with him to Bradcock's. The three of them seated themselves at a table and asked to see Bradcock personally.

Bradcock appeared, rubbing his hands ingratiatingly as though about to present someone with a loving-cup.

"What can we do for you?" he asked solicitously, noticing the insignia on the uniforms.

"We want four coffees."

"Certainly, certainly." One was never impolite to a Mexican general. "You have another friend coming?"

"No," snorted one of the generals. "We are asking you to do us the honor of taking coffee with us." He laid his gun on the table.

Mr. Bradcock, proud Southerner that he was, tamely sat down.

Afterwards the generals called a policeman, and Bradcock was fined a hundred pesos for discrimination.

449   In the days of the great Abolition furore, Wendell Phillips was accosted on a lecture tour by a minister who hailed from the state of Kentucky, a place with very different views concerning the ideas of the Abolitionists. The clergyman, who was more militant on behalf of his prejudices than on behalf of his creed, said, "You're Wendell Phillips, I believe."

"Yes, I am."

"You want to free the niggers, don't you?"

"Yes, I do."

"Well, why do you preach your doctrines up North? Why don't you try coming down to Kentucky?"

Phillips began to counter-question the man. "You're a preacher, are you not?"

"Yes, I am, sir."

"Are you trying to save souls from Hell?"

"Why yes, sir. That is my business."

"Why don't you go there then?" suggested Mr. Phillips.

450   A man who was once talking with Sir Moses Montefiore at a reception, found the conversation so entertaining that he completely forgot the race of his companion and made some uncomplimentary remark about the Jewish features of a lady who was passing by. The mistake was no sooner made than it was perceived. The unhappy man began to apologize profusely. "I ask a thousand pardons. It was so stupid of me to forget. You look angry enough to eat me. I beg you not to devour me."

"Sir," replied Sir Moses, "it is impossible. My religion forbids."

451   Innocently unaware of the prejudices held against him, an old colored man, staunchly religious, applied for membership in an exclusive church. The pastor attempted to put him

off with all sorts of evasive remarks. The old Negro, instinctively becoming aware that he was not wanted, said finally that he would sleep on it and perhaps the Lord would tell him just what to do.

Several days later he returned.

"Well," asked the minister, "did the Lord send you a message?"

"Yessuh, he did," was the answer. "He told me it wan't no use. He said, 'Ah been tryin' to get in that same church myself for ten yeahs an' Ah still can't make it.'"

452 Frederick Douglass, noted Negro author and champion of the rights of his people, was once invited to have tea with President Lincoln at the White House.

Whenever Douglass spoke of this occasion he always said, "Lincoln is the first white man I ever spent an hour with who did not remind me that I am a Negro."

RELATED SUBJECTS: *Snobbishness* 546-551; *Tolerance* 601-603; *Equality* 2046

SEE ALSO: *Hypocrisy* 303; *Politeness* 417; *Prisoners* 2366

PRIDE

456 Diogenes visited Plato one day and perceiving that the floors were beautifully covered with carpets of the richest wool and finest dye, stamped his foot in scorn exclaiming:

"Thus do I tread on the pride of Plato!"

"With greater pride," mildly added Plato.

457 Ned Shuter, the 18th Century comedian, was often very poor, and being more negligent than poor, was careless about his dress. A friend overtaking him one day in the street said to him, "Why, Ned, are you not ashamed to walk the streets with twenty holes in your stockings? Why don't you get them mended?"

"No, my friend," said Ned, "I'm above it: and if you have the pride of a gentleman you will act like me, and walk with twenty holes, rather than have one darn."

"How," replied the other, "how do you make that out?"

"Why," replied Ned, "a hole is the accident of the day, but a darn is premeditated poverty."

> RELATED SUBJECTS: *Boastfulness* 101-103; *Flattery* 236-237; *Honor* 296-298; *Pompousness* 421-427; *Snobbishness* 546-551; *Vanity* 606-628

> SEE ALSO: *Soldiers* 2430, 2436

PROCRASTINATION

461 Napoleon instructed his secretary, Bourrienne, to leave all his letters unopened for three weeks, and then observed with satisfaction how large a part of the correspondence thus disposed of itself and no longer required an answer.

> RELATED SUBJECTS: *Lateness* 321-324; *Laziness* 326-327; *Efficiency* 2266-2270

> SEE ALSO: *Parliament* 2000

QUARRELSOMENESS

466 Keats was a famous little fighter, less in truculent self-assertiveness than by way of high chivalry and defense of the right. According to his schoolfellow, E. Holmes, "He would fight anyone—morning, noon and night, his brother among the rest. It was meat and drink for him."

> RELATED SUBJECTS: *Profanity* 66-68; *Boastfulness* 101-103; *Rudeness* 511-524; *Stubbornness* 571-572; *Temper* 596-598; *Dueling* 801-803

> SEE ALSO: *Banquets* 752

QUICK THINKING

471 When Champ Clark was Speaker of the House, Congressman Johnson of Indiana interrupted the speech of an Ohio representative, calling him a jackass. The expression was ruled to be unparliamentary and Johnson apologized.

"I withdraw the unfortunate word, Mr. Speaker, but I insist that the gentleman from Ohio is out of order."

"How am I out of order?" angrily shouted the other.

"Probably a veterinary could tell you," answered Johnson. And this was allowed to enter the record.

472 As Mark Hanna was walking through his office one day he overheard one of his employees remark that he wished that he had Hanna's money and Hanna was in the poor-house.

Immediately upon reaching his office Hanna sent for the young man.

He told him he had overheard his statement, and then added, "Supposing you had your wish. And you had my money and I was in the poor-house, then what would you do?"

Quickly the boy replied, "Well, I guess the first thing I'd do would be to get you out of that poor-house."

The boy got a raise in salary.

473 Anxious to avoid the clutches of a delegate from a charitable institution, the businessman instructed his secretary to say that he was ill.

Deciding to make the illness a serious and telling factor, the secretary informed the caller, "I'm sorry, but Mr. Johnson cannot see you today. He has a sprained back."

The delegate seemed slightly surprised for a moment and then, looking at the secretary with a mocking gleam in his eye, said, "I didn't come here to wrestle with Mr. Johnson. I just want to talk with him."

474 When Charles (Hell-and-Maria) Dawes was ambassador to Great Britain the story was told of his buying a newspaper from a London newsboy who charged him the usual price of a penny.

"I'd have to pay double the price for this paper in America," Dawes remarked.

"Well, guv'nor," said the newsboy, "you can pay me double if it'll make you feel at 'ome."

475 The story was once current in financial circles of New York of the Negro messenger boy who attempted to deliver a message personally to J. P. Morgan and was rebuked by a receptionist who said to him, "You can't go in there, that is J. P.

Morgan of Morgan & Company." "That's all right," replied the messenger. "I'm the coon of Kuhn, Loeb & Company."

476   When Voltaire arrived in England in 1727 he found that feeling ran high against the French, that on the streets of London he was in grave peril. One day during a walk a crowd of angry citizens shouted, "Kill him! Hang the Frenchman!"

Voltaire stopped, faced the crowd and cried:

"Englishmen! You want to kill me because I am a Frenchman! Am I not punished enough in not being an Englishman?"

The crowd cheered wildly, and provided him safe conduct back to his dwelling.

477   As William Dean Howells and Mark Twain were coming out of church one morning, it commenced to rain heavily.

"Do you think it will stop?" asked Howells.

"It always has," answered Twain.

478   When Paderewski was visiting Boston some years ago he was approached by a bootblack who called, "Shine?"

The great pianist looked down at the youth whose face was streaked with grime and said, "No, my lad, but if you will wash your face I will give you a quarter."

"All right!" exclaimed the boy looking sharply at him. He ran to a nearby fountain where he made his ablutions.

When he returned, Paderewski held out the quarter. The boy took it and then returned it gravely, saying, "Here, Mister, you take it yourself and get your hair cut."

479   When Daniel Webster was a boy in the district school, he was not noted for tidiness. Finally the teacher, in despair, told him that if he appeared again with such dirty hands she would thrash him. He did appear in the same condition. "Daniel," she said, "hold out your hand." Daniel spat on his palm, rubbed it on the seat of his trousers and held it out. The teacher surveyed it in disgust. "Daniel," she said, "if you can find me another hand in this school that is dirtier than that, I will let you off."

Daniel promptly held out the other hand.

480   De Wolf Hopper was calling down a speaking tube to the janitor of his apartment in New York. Mr. Hopper, unable to get the information he desired finally blurted out:

"Say, is there a blithering idot at the end of this tube?" The reply came quickly: "Not at this end, sir."

481 Sheridan found himself trapped at a house party. A maiden lady of vinegary mien would not be deterred one day from her proposal to take a stroll with him. Hard-pressed but desperate, Sheridan begged off on the pretext of the threatening weather.

Shortly afterward, sneaking out by a back entrance to walk alone, Sheridan was accosted by his nemesis.

"So, Mr. Sheridan," said she, "it has cleared up."

"It has cleared up just a little, Madam," said Sheridan hastily, "enough for one, but hardly enough for two."

482 An astrologer foretold the death of a lady whom Louis XI passionately loved. She did, in fact, die; and the King imagined that the prediction of the astrologer was the cause of it. He sent for the man, intending to have him thrown through the window, as a punishment. "Tell me, thou pretendest to be so clever and learned a man, what thy fate will be?"

The soothsayer, who suspected the intrigues of the Prince, and knew his foibles, replied: "Sire, I foresee that I shall die three days before your Majesty."

The King believed him, and was careful of the astrologer's life.

483 When Killigrew, the celebrated Master of Revels to Charles II of England, visited Louis XIV in Paris, the French monarch showed him his pictures. He finally pointed out to him a picture of the Crucifixion between two portraits.

"That on the right," said his Majesty, "is the Pope, and that on the left is myself."

"I humbly thank you your Majesty," replied the English Court Jester, "for the information; for though I have often heard that the Lord was crucified between two thieves, I never knew who they were till now."

484 Two Massachusetts State Senators got into an angry debate and one told the other he could "go to hell." The man thus consigned called on Governor Coolidge and asked him to do something about it.

Mr. Coolidge replied:

"I've looked up the law, Senator, and you don't have to go there."

485 "What is the difference between a misfortune and a calamity?" someone asked of Disraeli.

He got the reply, "Well, if Gladstone fell into the Thames, that would be a misfortune; and if anybody pulled him out, that would be a calamity."

486 Bursting into the lawyer's office, the butcher demanded, "If a dog steals a piece of meat from my shop, is the owner liable?"

"Of course," said the lawyer.

"Well, your dog took a piece of steak worth half a dollar about 5 minutes ago."

"All right," said the lawyer, without blinking. "Give me the other half dollar and that will cover my fee."

487 A teacher of psychology, F. L. Thomason of San Francisco, was accosted by a hold-up man late one night. Thinking quickly, Thomason asked the thief for a dime, and started a rambling hard-luck story. Astonished, the bandit admitted his original intention and gave his intended victim a ten-cent piece. The professor went home with his dime and the $200 that was in his wallet.

488 Alexander Pope, sneering at the ignorance of a young man, asked him if he knew what an interrogation was?

"Yes sir," said he, " 'tis a little crooked thing that asks questions."

489 Dr. Robertson observed that Dr. Johnson's jokes were the rebukes of the righteous, described in Scripture as being like excellent oil.

"Yes," exclaimed Edmund Burke, "oil of vitriol!"

490 The Duke of Cumberland being once in company with Samuel Foote, was so delighted with the wit of the actor, that he said, "Mr. Foote, I swallow all the good things you say."

"Do you," replied Foote, "then your royal highness has an excellent digestion, for you never bring any of them up again."

491 When practicing law in Illinois, Lincoln was sent a subscription paper in behalf of the worn-out trouser-seat of his

opponent. He returned the paper with the remarks, "I refuse to subscribe to the end in view."

492 Douglas, at a gathering at which Lincoln was also present, was repeatedly making remarks about Lincoln's lowly station in life and saying that his first meeting with him had been across the counter of a general store. He finally ended his remarks by saying, "And Mr. L. was a very good bartender too."

There was a roar of laughter at this, but it quieted down considerably when Mr. Lincoln said quietly:

"What Mr. Douglas has said, gentlemen, is true enough; I did keep a grocery, and I did sell cotton, candles and cigars, and sometimes whiskey; but I remember in those days that Mr. Douglas was one of my best customers. Many a time have I stood on one side of the counter and sold whiskey to Mr. Douglas on the other side, but the difference between us now is this: I have left my side of the counter, but Mr. Douglas still sticks to his as tenaciously as ever."

RELATED SUBJECTS: *Rough and Ready* 496-507; *Shrewdness* 526-541; *Tact* 586-591; *Speeches* 756-782

SEE ALSO: *Boastfulness* 101; *Generosity* 242; *Liars* 331; *Politeness* 420; *Prejudice* 444; *Rudeness* 516; *Homeliness* 653; *Beauty* 666; *Introductions* 788; *Infidelity* 902; *Lectures* 1111; *Ministers* 1467, 1473; *Salesmen* 2092; *Banks* 2151, 2157; *Rationing* 2356; *Judges* 2490; *Lawyers* 2526, 2533; *Detectives* 2556; *Hanging* 2568; *Stealing* 2581

ROUGH AND READY

496 When Carter Glass first began to make himself heard in 1913, in caucuses of his party in the Senate, he talked rather ponderously and frigidly. On one such occasion, the subject seemed to warm him up and soon he was not only emphatic but pugnacious. At this point one of his partisans in the caucus shouted:

"Give 'em hell, Carter!"

Mr. Glass's reply has become historic.

"Hell? Why use dynamite when insect powder will do?"

497 It is said that Thomas Hart Benton one day intended to answer a speech of Calhoun's, but hearing that Calhoun was prostrated by illness and could not be present, he announced, "Benton will not speak, today, for when God Almighty lays his hands on a man Benton takes his off."

498 A legend has it that Will Rogers once walked up to the gate of Buckingham Palace and said to the guard, "I am Will Rogers and I have come to see the King." The guards drew themselves up haughtily and Rogers continued, "You tell him that when the Prince of Wales was out my way, he told me to look up his old man sometime, so here I am." Rogers was admitted, had a long chat with the King and stayed to lunch.

499 Charles M. Schwab maintained with some of his old employees in his mills a certain comradeship. Coming into the open hearth room one morning Schwab saw a brawny old laborer, naked from the waist up, glistening with sweat, shining in the lurid glow of the furnaces.

"Pete," said Schwab, "you look like an old Rembrandt."

"Hell," said his employee, "you don't look so hot yourself, Charlie."

500 A badman rushed into a saloon brandishing his guns and shooting to the right and left. He stood in the middle of the floor and shouted, "All you dirty skunks get out of here!" The bar was virtually emptied in one wild burst of confusion, but as the smoke cleared it revealed one imperturbable man calmly finishing his drink at the bar. The badman lumbered over to him. "Well?" he demanded.

"Well," said the other, "there was sure a lot of 'em, wasn't there?"

501 Charles Fox, the English statesman, once asked a tradesman for his vote. The tradesman answered, "I admire your abilities, but damn your principles," to which Fox replied, "My friend, I applaud your sincerity, but damn your manners."

502 Chief-Justice Marshall of the U. S. Supreme Court related that Governor Giles of Virginia once addressed a note to Patrick Henry:

"Sir,—I understand that you have called me a 'bobtail politician.' I wish to know if it be true, and if true, your meaning.—Wm. B. Giles."

Patrick Henry replied:

"Sir,—I do not recollect having called you a 'bobtail politician' at any time, but think it probable I have. Not recollecting the time of the occasion, I can't say what I did mean; but if you will tell me what you think I meant, I will say whether you are correct or not.—Very respectfully, Patrick Henry.

503 At that stage in his political career at which Winston Churchill switched over from the Conservative to the Liberal side of the House, many of his erstwhile adherents were sorely offended. A snippish young lady once said to him playfully, "There are two things I don't like about you, Mr. Churchill."

"Yes?" he inquired.

"Your new politics and your mustache."

"My dear Madam," said Churchill coldly, "you are not likely to come into much contact with either."

504 At a Kentucky political meeting a certain participant in the debate was shot by several of the others at the meeting. The event occurred on the open floor and created a considerable stir in the community.

A Northerner, who was in town, asked an acquaintance, who had been present, why the shooting had occurred.

"He made a motion that was out of order," explained the Kentuckian.

Horrified at this excess of parliamentarianism, "You mean to tell me they shot a man in cold blood on the floor of the meeting just for making a motion that was out of order!"

"Well," drawled his informant, "the motion was toward his hip pocket."

505 An ambitious youth once sent his first manscript to Dumas, asking the distinguished novelist to become his collaborator. The latter was astounded at the impertinence. Angrily seizing his pen he wrote, "How dare you, sir, yoke together a noble horse and a contemptible ass?"

He received the following reply: "How dare you, sir, call me a horse?"

His anger vanished and he wrote, "Send on your ms., my friend; I gladly accept your proposition."

506 Clyde Fitch tells the following story of Whistler. The artist was in Paris at the time of the coronation of King Edward, and at a reception one evening a duchess said to him: "I believe you know King Edward, Mr. Whistler."

"No, madame," replied Whistler.

"Why, that's odd," she murmured, "I met the King at a dinner-party last year, and he said that he knew you."

"Oh," said the painter, "that was just his brag."

507 Robert Benchley had been shining as the outstanding ladies' man at a certain party in Hollywood, when two matinee idols arrived. The girls began to desert the humorist, one of them exclaiming over the new-comers, "Now, that's my idea of real he-men!"

"He-men!" growled Benchley, "I'll bet the hair of their combined chests wouldn't make a wig for a grape!"

RELATED SUBJECTS: *Quick Thinking* 471-492; *Shrewdness* 526-541; *Equality* 2046

SEE ALSO: *Drinking* 44; *Pompousness* 422; *Universities* 1019; *Authors* 1173; *Actors* 1428; *Travel* 1791; *Card Playing* 1836; *Campaigning* 1911; *Trials* 2481; *Witnesses* 2504; *Law Enforcement* 2546

RUDENESS

511 The would-be wit found himself quietly put down several pegs when, at the dinner table, he held up his fork with a piece of meat upon it and asked his hostess, "Is this pig?"

"To which end of the fork do you refer?" asked one of his fellow guests.

512 At a recent gathering of Hamilton College alumni, Alexander Woollcott was interrupted in the telling of a story by a former classmate, who said, "Hello, Alex! You remember me, don't you?"

Mr. Woollcott shook his head:

"I can't remember your name, but don't tell me. . . ." He then went on with his story.

513 At a stuffy English garden party, Beatrice Lillie (Lady Peel), wearing the Peel pearls, was approached by a lady of

lineage, who said maliciously, "What lovely pearls, Beatrice. Are they genuine?"

Miss Lillie nodded.

"Of course, you can always tell by biting them," said the cat. "Here, let me see."

"Gladly," said Lady Peel, proffering her jewels, "but remember, Duchess, you can't tell real pearls with false teeth."

514 One of Dorothy Parker's more telling retorts was in answer to the snobbish young man who had been discoursing at some length at a party and had finally observed, "I simply can't bear fools."

"How odd," was Miss Parker's reply. "Apparently your mother could."

515 For deadly comments on deadly occasions Beatrice Lillie deserves some kind of accolade. "Don't think it hasn't been charming," she said to her hostess when leaving a party, "because it hasn't."

516 Robert Hall being unsuccessful in securing the hand of a Miss Steel, while smarting under his disappointment, took tea with a company of ladies, one of whom, the lady of the house, said, in bad taste, "You are dull, Mr. Hall, and we have no polished steel to brighten you."

"O, Madam," replied Mr. Hall, "that is of no consequence; you have plenty of polished brass."

517 A celebrity hound approached Groucho Marx at a party. "You remember me, Mr. Marx. We met at the Glynthwaites' some months ago."

"I never forget a face," Groucho replied, "but I'll make an exception in your case."

518 Against the charge of malice, Samuel Rogers defended himself thus:

"They tell me I say ill-natured things. I have a very weak voice; if I did not say ill-natured things no one would hear what I said."

519 When one of the town's most important movie producers had his secretary call the late John Barrymore to invite him to a party, Barrymore politely murmured into the telephone, "I

have a previous engagement which I shall make as soon as possible."

520 Hermann Goering accompanied the Fuehrer on one of his visits to Rome. On the crowded railway platform filled with dignitaries and troops, the massive Marshal roughly jostled past an Italian gentleman of aristocratic bearing, who turned and haughtily demanded an apology. Fiercely the Marshal turned upon him and snapped, "I am Hermann Goering." The Italian bowed and replied, "As an excuse that is not enough, but as an explanation it is ample."

521 When a diplomat remarked that he could not understand why he was called ill-natured, for in all his life he had never done but one ill-natured action, Talleyrand asked: "And when will it end?"

522 Oscar Wilde indulged his penchant for baiting Yankees when he met Richard Harding Davis.

"So you are from Philadelphia where Washington is buried?"

"Nonsense, he's buried in Mount Vernon," Davis answered abruptly.

Wilde, miffed, switched the talk to a new French painter. "Do let's hear what Mr. Davis thinks of him," he purred. "Americans always talk so amusingly of art."

Davis answered: "I never talk about things when I don't know the facts."

Wilde's rapier wit flashed back: "That must limit your conversation frightfully."

523 Samuel Johnson was once vexed by the presence of a man at a small dinner party who laughed inordinately and with a great and ostentatious show of appreciation at everything the good Dr. said. Finally, irritated in the extreme, Johnson turned upon the fellow and said, "Pray, sir, what is the matter? I hope I've not said anything that you can comprehend."

524 Oliver Herford was having lunch at his club one day, when a man whom he particularly disliked came up to him. Herford attempted to disregard him but the man, smiling broadly, slapped him on the back and said jovially, "Hello, Ollie, old boy, how are you?"

Herford looked at the man coldly and answered, "I don't

know your name and I don't know your face, but your manners are very familiar."

RELATED SUBJECTS: *Gentlemanliness* 251-256; *Prejudice* 441-452; *Quarrelsomeness* 466; *Snobbishness* 546-551; *Tact* 586-591; *Temper* 596-598

SEE ALSO: *Memory* 374; *Prejudice* 450; *Names* 836; *Actors* 1429

SHREWDNESS

526 A sidewalk pitch-man was disgusted by his failure to elicit any profitable response from the large crowd assembled around him. "You pikers," he said in disgust, "are too tight to offer me 50¢ for a dollar." "I will," someone spoke up. "All right," said the pitch-man, "hand over the 50¢." "I ain't taking any chances. Take it out of the buck and hand me the change."

527 Cornelia Otis Skinner declares that as a child she was so ugly that her mother used to weep. "But I did have a genius for something even then," she says. "I was good at trade and I made money from Dad. He thought I was a good correspondent. I was; for, for every letter I wrote him, I received an answer. I cut the 'Cornelia' from the address on the envelope containing his reply, and sold the 'Otis Skinner' as my father's autograph. Sometimes it brought a dime, sometimes a quarter."

528 Otto Kahn, the well-known financier, was one day driving through the lower East Side of New York when he saw a large sign reading: "Samuel Kahn, cousin of Otto Kahn." He immediately called up his lawyer, instructing him to have the sign changed, sparing no expense. A few days later, Kahn drove by the place again. The offending sign had been changed. It read: "Samuel Kahn, formerly cousin of Otto Kahn."

529 When the films were in their infancy, David Freedman claimed to have arranged a splendid contract for Francis X. Bushman by a well conceived stratagem. Bushman had been playing in Chicago at $250 a week. Freedman brought him to

New York and met him at Grand Central to take him across to Broadway to the office of Metro. Freedman carried a sack of 2,000 pennies. He strewed these along behind him in a thin trickle as they walked. First children and then curious adults began to follow. By the time they had crossed 42nd Street to Broadway and entered the office of Metro, a vast throng was surging in their wake. Looking out the window, the executives of Metro were easily induced to sign Bushman at a thousand dollars a week.

530   A boy, generally known about the village as being not too bright, was annoying the busy blacksmith. Hoping to scare him away, the blacksmith finally held a red-hot piece of iron under the boy's nose.

"If you'll give me half a dollar I'll lick it," said the simple-looking youngster.

The smith held out the coin. Without a word, the boy took the coin, licked it, dropped it in his pocket, and whistling softly, walked away.

531   Rabelais once found himself stranded in a village in southern France without a sou to get him back to Paris. He took this means to obtain quick and easy passage to the French capital. He engaged a room in the only tavern in the town and asked for a secretary to assist him in some writing. The mistress of the inn sent him her son, a sharp lad about twelve years old. Rabelais said to his "secretary":—"My boy, we are about to undertake a very serious business here. I want you to sit down here and print these labels for me,—'Poison for the King, Poison for the Queen, Poison for the Duke of Orleans,' etc. While you are doing this I shall be preparing the poison." While the terrified youngster was busy at his task of printing, Rabelais scraped up the ashes from the grate, mixed them with the contents of his snuff-box and wrapped up the concoction in several neat packages, on which he pasted his labels. He then dismissed his "secretary" with a solemn warning, and the boy at once rushed downstairs and breathlessly told his mother of the whole business. The woman summoned the gendarmes who came to the inn and caught the dangerous guest with his damning evidence. As the suspect could not give an account of himself he was bundled off to Paris. Here he was brought to court and recognized by the king who heard his "case" and of course set him free.

532 Valentine Williams says: "I was walking with Sir Herbert Tree one day when my hat blew off. I was about to hurl myself into the thick of traffic in pursuit when Tree restrained me: 'My brother Max says,' he told me gravely, 'never run after your hat. Someone is sure to bring it to you.'

"True enough a moment later, a passerby dashed up breathlessly and restored my hat to me."

533 One sunny May day in Central Park a blind man was seen tapping for attention with his cane and carrying on his chest a sign: "Help the Blind." No one paid much attention to him. A little farther on another blind beggar was doing better. Practically every passer-by put a coin in his cup, some even turning back to make their contribution. His sign said:

"It is May—and I am Blind!"

534 Triboulet was jester to Francis I. A great lord, offended at his sallies, threatened to flog him to death. Triboulet went to complain to his master.

"If he does it," said the King, "I'll hang him a quarter of an hour after."

"Thank ye, cousin," piped the jester, "but if it's all the same to you, couldn't you do it a quarter of an hour before?"

535 Once when a deputation visited Lincoln and urged emancipation before he was ready, he argued that he could not enforce it even if he proclaimed it.

"How many legs will a sheep have if you call the tail a leg?" asked Lincoln.

"Five," they answered.

"You are mistaken," said Lincoln, "for calling a tail a leg don't make it so."

536 A wastrel grandson of Queen Victoria once begged Her Highness by letter for an advance on his allowance. The severe Queen answered with a lengthy rebuke of his way of life, and a great deal of additional advice, exhorting him to thrift and diligence. Although no money had been sent, the good Queen shortly received a letter of thanks from the young man, explaining that he had followed her precepts literally by selling her letter for £25.

537 A certain motorist drove his car to work one day and parked it in front of his office. Coming out some hours later he perceived that it was covered with a number of tickets for an assortment of offenses and violations of parking and traffic rules.

He conceived an ingenious way of extricating himself from the difficulty. Calling the police from his home address, he reported his car as lost. With interest, as time went by, he passed in and out of his office watching the slow accumulation of additional penalties piling upon the forlorn automobile.

It took the police five days to find it.

538 Uncomfortably crowded once in a London bus, Edmund Gosse said to his companion, W. M. Rossetti, "I understand you are an anarchist."

"I am an atheist," replied Rossetti in a loud voice. "My daughter is an anarchist." A sufficient number of people left the bus indignantly to make Gosse and Rossetti comfortable.

539 P. T. Barnum solved the problem of overcrowding in his popular New York museum where customers were prone to linger overlong, by rigging up a corridor toward the doorway to the street and displaying above it prominently the sign, TO THE EGRESS.

540 Marshall Field, 3rd, according to a story that was going the rounds at the turn of the century, bade fair to become a very cautious business man. Approaching an old lady in a Lakewood hotel, he said:

"Can you crack nuts?"

"No, dear," the old lady replied. "I lost all my teeth ages ago."

"Then," requested Master Field, extending two hands full of pecans, "please hold these while I go and get some more."

541 Seeking to raise enough money for a volunteer fire department in Springfield, a committee approached Abraham Lincoln for a subscription. He expressed sympathy for the movement but said, "I'll tell you what, boys. I'll talk it over with Mrs. Lincoln tonight. Here's what I'll say:

"My dear, there's a subscription paper being handed around to raise money for a new hose-cart for the fire department. The committee called on me today and I told them I'd talk it over with you. Don't you think we had better subscribe $50.00?' Then she will look up quickly and say, 'Oh, Abraham, Abraham! Will you never learn? You can't afford it. Twenty-five dollars is quite enough.' "

Mr. Lincoln chuckled as he added, "Bless her dear soul, she'll never find out how I got the better of her. Come around tomorrow, boys, and get your $25.00."

RELATED SUBJECTS: *Ambition* 96-97; *Flattery* 236-237; *Quick Thinking* 471-492; *Tact* 586-591; *Bargaining* 2076-2082; *Competition* 2116; *Chiseling and Swindling* 2121-2132

SEE ALSO: *Fatness* 681; *Speeches* 776; *College Life* 1041; *Authors* 1217; *Bargaining* 2077, 2078; *Chiseling* 2123; *Bosses* 2232; *Salaries* 2251

SNOBBISHNESS

546 The Athenian general Iphicrates was the son of a shoemaker. One of his opponents in a suit at law, a descendant of the patriot Harmodius, referred insultingly to Iphicrates' humble birth. With the spirit of a true democrat, the general answered calmly: "Yes, the nobility of my family begins with me; just as that of yours ends with you."

547 A patronising young lord was once seated opposite Whistler at dinner one evening. During a lull in the conversation he adjusted his monocle and leaned toward the artist.

"Aw, y'know, Mr. Whistler," he drawled, "I pahssed your house this mawning."

"Thank you," said Whistler, "thank you very much."

548 Boston dowagers never say die. They are the most supremely right people in America. A visitor was introduced to one such person at a Boston gathering. "Where are you from?" the grand lady asked, just a trifle condescendingly.

"Idaho," replied the stranger.

The Bostonian smiled with a gentle courtesy and said, "I know, dear, that you won't take it amiss if I tell you that here we pronounce it 'Ohio.' "

549 Mount Vernon, the estate of General George Washington, is visited by many people. One day a somewhat snobbish and patronizing young Englishman remarked to Shep Wright, an old gardener employed on the estate, "I say, old man, this

hedge. Ah . . . I see that deah old George got this hedge from England."

The old gardener was more than a match for him. Looking at the young man quizzically for about a minute, he said, "Yes, reckon he did. And that ain't all. He got this whole bloomin' country from England."

550   Displaying considerable snobbishness an Englishman remarked to an American friend, "How unpleasant it must be for you Americans to be governed by people whom one would never think of asking to dinner."

With scarcely a moment's thought, the American replied coldly, "No more unpleasant than being governed by people who wouldn't ask you to dinner."

551   There came to the National Gallery in London, one day, a gentleman rather shabbily dressed, carrying a picture under his arm, who asked to see Sir William Boxall, the governor. He was peremptorily refused an audience, and only after repeated rebuffs was he granted a moment's interview. The stranger intimated that he had a picture in his possession which he wished to give to the National Gallery, and began to unbuckle the straps to show the painting within. Sir William, however, brusquely ordered him either to leave it or to take it away altogether, saying that he was too busy to look at it.

"But you had better have one glance—I ask for no more," said the stranger.

Again Sir William refused, and was just on the point of turning away when the covering fell off the picture and there was revealed one of Terborch's masterpieces which the governor himself, some time previously, had failed to gain, though he had offered for it £6,000.

"My name is Wallace," said the stranger quietly, "Sir William Wallace, and I came to offer this picture to the National Gallery."

"I almost fainted," related Boxall later.

RELATED SUBJECTS: *Flattery* 236-237; *Pompousness* 421-427; *Prejudice* 441-452; *Pride* 456-457; *Vanity* 606-628

SEE ALSO: *Rudeness* 513, 514; *Tolerance* 603; *Equality* 2046

STINGINESS

556 A poor German, a relative of John Jacob Astor, once applied to him for charity. Mr. Astor gave him a five dollar bill.

"Why," said the disconcerted relative, "your son just gave me ten dollars!"

"Well he may!" said the stingy old magnate; "the dog has a rich father."

557 Fénelon had for some time been besieging Richelieu for a contribution to a charity-fund, but all his diplomacy had failed to make the wily French minister "come across." Meeting Richelieu in the Louvre one day, Fénelon remarked, "I have just seen a portrait of you in the other room."

"And did you ask it for a subscription?" replied Richelieu with a polite smirk.

"No,—I knew it was no use," said Fénelon, passing on. "It was a perfect likeness."

558 Russell Sage, the financier, had a wide reputation as a man difficult to separate from his money. A couple of promoters approached him one day and tried to sell him on a scheme they had. Sage talked with them for a while but said he could give them no definite answer as yet. Telling them that he would communicate with them in a few days he showed them out of the office.

One of the promoters seemed quite optimistic and voiced the opinion to his partner that he thought Sage was pretty well sold on their proposition.

"I don't know," replied the other sceptically. "He seemed too suspicious to me. Didn't you notice that, after shaking hands with me, he started to count his fingers?"

559 The young journalist was sent to get a personal interview with the wealthy old Scotch merchant. His paper desired a human interest story on how he had accumulated his riches.

"Weel, it's a long story," said the old man. "And while I'm telling it we may as well save the candle." Wherewith he blew it out.

"Never mind about the story," said the reporter, "I understand."

560 A legend of doubtful authenticity has it that J. P. Morgan was once present with a group of men at a bar in the financial district. Beckoning to the waiter, he ordered a beer; at the same time, saying, "When Morgan drinks, everybody drinks." Everybody had a beer and when Morgan had finished, he slapped a dime upon the table, saying, "When Morgan pays, everybody pays."

561 Jock said to his wife one night, "Weel, Maggie, I think I will go and pay my respects to the new neighbor."

Upon his return some time later, Maggie said, "Weel, Jock, what kind of a mon is the new neighbor?"

"He's a guid mon," replied Jock, "a guid mon and verra lib'ral with his liquor. But verra bad quality. In fact, Maggie, it was that bad, I nearly left some."

562 The story is told of the hard-bitten old Quaker who had died. At the funeral service, those who had gathered were standing silently by, waiting, as was the custom, for anyone who might wish to do so, to make some tribute to the departed. At last one old man spoke up and said, "Well, I can say one good thing about William. He wasn't always as mean as he was sometimes."

563 Two friends were walking down the street. "If you could have any wish," asked one of them, "what would it be?"

"A mountain of gold," said his friend.

"And," said his questioner, "if you had your mountain of gold, surely we're such old friends, you would give me half?"

"I would not," said the other firmly, "nothing would I give."

His friend was deeply hurt. "What," he demanded, "all these years our friendship and this is what I get?"

"Look," said the other practically, "wish yourself a mountain and leave me alone."

564 When Godwin in 1822 was on the point of being sold out to his creditors and a fund was started for him, to which Lamb, Crabbe, Robinson, Byron and Scott contributed, Wordsworth refused to subscribe. The inference is that, while generous enough to inferiors who would be duly grateful, Wordsworth was indifferent to an equal, however needy, especially an arrogant equal like Godwin from whom no gratitude was to be expected.

565 One of the stories circulated about Harry Lauder, as likely as not circulated by himself, has it that he was playing

golf one bitter cold day. As he came off the course, he slipped something into the hand of the caddy, saying, "That's for a glass of hot whiskey, lad." The boy opened his hand and found a lump of sugar.

566 James Duke, founder of the tobacco fortune, was one of those eccentrically miserly characters whose accumulation of wealth is a vast storing up and no giving out. When he had already begun to earn an income of more than $50,000 a year he took pride in living in the cheapest hall bedroom in New York and eating his meals at a Bowery restaurant. At that time he would permit no one associated with the Duke tobacco business, other than himself, to earn more than $1,000 a year.

> RELATED SUBJECTS: *Economy* 211-213; *Generosity* 241-248; *Gratitude and Ingratitude* 261-268; *Greed* 271-276; *Loans* 2161-2164

> SEE ALSO: *Practical Joking* 435; *Fatness* 683; *Wife* 929; *Painting* 1276, 1282; *Collections* 1565, 1569

STUBBORNNESS

571 General Grant was known for his tenaciousness. Having once taken a place he never surrendered it. Lincoln once commented on this to General Butler, saying, "When General Grant once gets possessed of a place he seems to hang on to it as if he had inherited it."

572 A man who was extremely successful in dealing with mule teams was once asked by General Booth of the Salvation Army, how he managed the stubborn creatures. "Well General," explained the man, "when they stop and won't go on I just pick up a handful of soil and put it in their mouths. Of course they spit it out, but as a rule they start on."

"Why do you think it has that effect?" asked the General.

"Well, I don't know, but I expect it changes the current of their thoughts," the mule driver replied.

> RELATED SUBJECTS: *Prejudice* 441-452; *Pride* 456-457; *Quarrelsomeness* 466; *Rudeness* 511-524; *Will Power* 631

STUPIDITY

576   To the city of Washington come all kinds of tourists; from visiting nobility to the representatives of our smallest communities.

A lady from a small upstate New York town was a member of a touring party. Arriving at Washington Monument, the guide took them all to the very top of the structure. Overwhelmed by the many and varied sights, the woman cried in ecstatic and somewhat incoherent tones, "Why—why, there's the White House . . . and—there's the Capitol. Look over there —it's the Lincoln Memorial!" Then, looking about with a slightly bewildered and rather disappointed air, "But—but, where's the Washington Monument?"

577   They tell of the guide showing the visiting Englishman over the battlefield of Bunker Hill. "This is Bunker Hill monument. This is where Warren fell."

The English tourist looked up at the lofty shaft and observed, "Nasty fall. Killed him, of course."

578   Someone once introduced Ed Wynn to the hostess at a gathering.

"That is Ed Wynn, who's not such a fool as he looks."

"That's right," chortled the comedian. "That's right. That's the great difference between me and my friend."

579   The story is told about a wealthy man who was desirous of building a luxurious hunting lodge in the North Woods of Wisconsin. After having his plans drawn up by a famous architect, he dispatched them to a local carpenter with instructions to go ahead and build it according to the blue prints.

Scarcely a day had passed when a post card arrived at the rich man's house, saying, "The plans is all wrong. I can't do nothing till you get them straightened out."

Being in a hurry to get the house finished, the man sent a letter post haste assuring the local workman that the plans were all right and to proceed as ordered.

By return mail came the following:

"I don't aim to saw a plank until I get them plans straightened out. Why if I was to build that house the way it's laid out here you'd have two bathrooms!"

580 There are many versions of the old hill-billy looking-glass story. The oldest war horse of them all is the version in which the mountaineer, finding a mirror, peers at it and remarks, "So —that's the no-count varmint the old lady's taken up with."

Whereupon his wife, finding the mirror where he had left it, snorted in indignation, "So—that's the old hag he's running after."

A somewhat newer version is that of the mountain lad, some 24 years of age, unshaven, untrimmed and unwashed. Peering among the purchases which his father had brought back in the wagon from the settlement he came across a large wall mirror. He burst into laughter. His mother, coming out, demanded to know what he was laughing at.

"Pa's bought a wolf," chuckled the young man.

581 St. Louis, notwithstanding improvements carried out in recent years, has been in its time one of the more famous smoky cities of America.

One of its established city offices was that of Smoke Inspector. This post of such legitimate importance degenerated through the years into a political plum. At last, after one election, it fell into the hands of an appointee of utter incompetence, who shortly after taking office, was shocked to learn that he must make a monthly report.

He submitted thereupon the following:

"Have inspected the smoke of St. Louis for the month of December, 19— and have found it to be of good quality."

582 A lady visiting Stratford-on-Avon, the birthplace of Shakespeare, showed even more than the usual fervor. She had not recovered when she reached the railway station, for she remarked to a friend as they walked on the platform: "To think that it was from this very platform the immortal bard would depart whenever he journeyed to town!"

583 At a party given in honor of Thomas Mann, a noted Glamor Girl found herself dancing with the eminent writer and was duly thrilled. She smiled up at him and purred: "I just love culture, don't you?"

RELATED SUBJECTS: *Boners* 106-119; *Dullness* 186-195; *Eccentricity* 196-209; *Erudition* 1071-1076; *Common Sense* 1156-1157

TACT

586 Once Talleyrand, the French statesman, sat at dinner between Madame de Staël and Madame Récamier, the celebrated beauty. Madame de Staël, whose beauties were certainly not those of the person, jealous of his attentions to her rival, insisted upon knowing which he would save if they were both drowning. After seeking in vain to evade her, he at last turned toward her and said with his characteristic shrug, "Ah, Madame, you know how to swim."

587 When Wu Ting Fang was Minister to the United States from China, he visited Chicago. A native of the Windy City said to him at a reception:

"Mr. Wu, I see there is a movement in China to abolish the pigtails you wear. Why do you wear the foolish thing anyhow?"

"Well," countered Mr. Wu, "why do you wear your foolish mustache?"

"Oh, that's different," said the Chicago man, "you see I've got an impossible mouth."

"So I should suppose," retorted Mr. Wu, "judging from your remarks."

588 At a large party in New York Mrs. Joseph Schildkraut said good-bye to the British consul, then shook many other hands, and finally found herself shaking his hand again. "But you've already said good-bye to me once," he remonstrated.

"Oh, yes, Mr. Campbell," she replied archly, "but it's always a pleasure to say good-bye to you."

589 During the Coolidge administration, an overnight guest at the White House found himself in a hideously embarassing predicament. At the family breakfast table he was seated at the President's right hand. To his surprise he saw Coolidge take his coffee cup, pour the greater portion of its contents into the deep saucer, and leisurely add a little bit of cream and a little sugar. The guest was so disconcerted that he lost his head. With a panicky feeling that it was incumbent upon him at the White House to do as the President did, he hastily decanted his own coffee into the saucer and followed suit. He was frozen with horror, when he had accomplished this, to see Coolidge take his own saucer and place it on the floor for the cat.

590 "You do not remember my name?" a lady said one time upon meeeting Henry Clay. "No," was the prompt and gallant response, "for when we last met long ago I was sure your beauty and accomplishments would very soon compel you to change it."

591 Edmund Gosse had a good story of Browning at a men's dinner given in his honour, at which the only guest without any claim to distinction was a young gentleman whom no one had ever seen or heard of. When the party moved upstairs, it was perceived with consternation that this whipper-snapper had manoeuvred the poet into a position behind the grand pianoforte, from which there seemed no escape. How was he to be rescued? Browning himself solved the difficulty. "But I'm monopolizing you," he said, laying on the youth's shoulder a friendly hand which left him no choice but to yield the pass.

RELATED SUBJECTS: *Discretion* 181-182; *Gentlemanliness* 251-256; *Patience* 391; *Politeness* 416-420; *Quick Thinking* 471-492; *Diplomats* 2021-2027

SEE ALSO: *Names* 838; *Courtship* 855; *Kings* 1988, 1990; *Salesmen* 2097

TEMPER

596 Some officer had disobeyed or failed to comprehend an order. "I believe I'll sit down," said Secretary Stanton, "and give that man a piece of my mind."

"Do so," said Lincoln, "write him now while you have it on your mind. Make it sharp. Cut him all up." Stanton did not need a second invitation. It was a bone crusher that he read to the President.

"That's right," said Lincoln. "Why, that's a good one."

"Whom can I send it by?" mused Stanton.

"Send it!" replied Lincoln. "Why, don't send it at all. Tear it up. You have freed your mind on the subject, and that is all that is necessary. Tear it up. You never want to send such letters; I never do."

597 It being reported that Lady Caroline Lamb had, in a moment of passion, knocked down one of her pages with a stool, the poet Moore to whom this was told by Lord Strangford, observed: "Oh! nothing is more natural for a literary lady than to double down a page."

"I would rather," replied his Lordship, "advise Lady Caroline to turn over a new leaf."

598 Henderson, the actor, was seldom known to be in a passion. When at Oxford, he was one day debating with a fellow student, who, unable to keep his temper, threw a glass of wine in the actor's face. Henderson took out his handkerchief, wiped his face, and coolly said, "That, sir, was a digression; now for the argument."

> RELATED SUBJECTS: *Patience* 391; *Quarrelsomeness* 466; *Rudeness* 511-524

TOLERANCE

601 When Abe Lincoln used to be drifting around the country, practicing law in Fulton and Menard counties, Illinois, an old fellow met him going to Lewiston, riding a horse, which, while it was a serviceable enough animal, was not of the kind to be truthfully called a fine saddler. It was a weatherbeaten nag, patient and plodding, and it toiled along with Abe—and Abe's books, tucked away in saddlebags, lay heavy on the horse's flank.

"Hello, Uncle Tommy," said Abe.

"Hello, Abe," responded Uncle Tommy. "I'm powerful glad to see ye, Abe, fer I'm goin' to have sumthin' fer ye at Lewiston co't, I reckon."

"How's that, Uncle Tommy?" said Abe.

"Well, Jim Adams, his land runs 'long o' mine, he's pesterin' me a heap, an' I got to get the law on Jim, I reckon."

"Uncle Tommy, you haven't had any fights with Jim, have you?"

"No."

"He's a fair to middling neighbor isn't he?"

"Only tol'able, Abe."

"He's been a neighbor of yours for a long time, hasn't he?"

"Nigh on to fifteen year."

"Part of the time you get along all right, don't you?"

"I reckon we do Abe."

"Well, now, Uncle Tommy you see this horse of mine? He isn't as good a horse as I could straddle, and I sometimes get out of patience with him, but I know his faults. He does fairly well as horses go, and it might take me a long time to get used to some other horse's faults. For all horses have faults. You and Uncle Jimmy must put up with each other as I and my horse do with one another."

"I reckon, Abe," said Uncle Tommy, as he bit off about four ounces of Missouri plug, "I reckon you're about right."

And Abe Lincoln, with a smile on his gaunt face, rode on toward Lewiston.

602   St. Francis De Sales, being consulted by a lady on the propriety of wearing rouge, replied, "Some persons may object to it, and others may see no harm in it, but I shall take a middle course, by allowing you to rouge on one cheek."

603   Sir Walter Scott, once happening to hear his daughter Anne say of something that it was vulgar, gave the young lady the following temperate rebuke: "My love, you speak like a very young lady; do you know, after all, the meaning of this word vulgar? It is only common. Nothing that is common, except wickedness, can deserve to be spoken of in a tone of contempt."

RELATED SUBJECTS: *Generosity* 241-248; *Kindness* 311-316; *Patience* 391; *Prejudice* 441-452; *Freedom* 2036-2042; *Equality* 2046

SEE ALSO: *Drinking* 38

VANITY

606   Scrope Davies was on very intimate terms with many of the great men of the period, and he had such admiration for the author of "Don Juan" (Byron) that he could gain admission to his rooms at all hours. On one occasion he found the poet in bed with his hair "en papillote," upon which Scrope cried in great glee, "Ha, ha, Byron, I have at last caught you acting the part of the Sleeping Beauty."

Byron, in a rage, exclaimed, "No, Scrope; the part of a damned fool, you should have said."

Upon which Scrope answered: "Anything you please—but you have succeeded admirably in deceiving your friends, for it was my conviction that your hair curled naturally."

"Yes, naturally every night; but do not, my dear Scrope, let the cat out of the bag, for I am as vain of my curls as a girl of sixteen."

607 A magnificent ball was given in Paris. Pauline Bonaparte decided "to blot out every woman there." She entered the ballroom when all the guests had already assembled. At sight of her the music stopped, silence fell upon the assemblage. Her costume was of the finest muslin bordered with golden palm leaves. Four bands, spotted like a leopard's skin, were wound about her head, while these in turn were supported by little clusters of golden grapes. She had copied the headdress of a Bacchante in the Louvre. All over her person were cameos, and just beneath her breasts she wore a golden band held in place by an engraved gem. She had, indeed, "blotted out" her rivals.

Nevertheless, Mme. de Coutades, who hated her, took a sly revenge. She went up to Pauline, who was lying on a divan to set off her loveliness, and began gazing at the princess through a double eye-glass. Pauline felt flattered for a moment, and then became uneasy. The lady who was looking at her said to a companion, in a tone of compassion:

"What a pity! She really would be lovely if it weren't for that!"

"For what?" asked her escort.

"Why are you blind? It's so remarkable that you surely must see it."

Pauline was beginning to lose her self-composure. She flushed and looked wildly about, wondering what was meant. Then she heard Mme. de Coutades say:

"Why, her ears! If I had such ears as those I would cut them off!"

Pauline gasped and fainted away.

608 A young man, who had come to the city from a small rural community, had toiled diligently until at last he had attained some prominence in the banking world. Belatedly he returned for a visit to his old home town, half expecting that the greater part of the community would be marshalled out to

meet him at the station, and that some considerable fuss would be made over the local boy who had made good. To his disappointment, there was not a soul around when he alighted at the station platform. He waited doubtfully as several people came and went, none of them giving him so much as a glance. At last he was recognized by an old baggage handler who shuffled forward and looked at him with some interest. "Hello, George," he said at last, "goin' away?"

609 One of Disraeli's admirers, speaking about him to John Bright, said: "You ought to give him credit for what he has accomplished, as he is a self-made man."

"I know he is," retorted Mr. Bright, "and he adores his maker."

610 Miss Frances Keller of the Women's Municipal League of New York illustrated at a dinner party a point she wished to make in reply to a man who had said, "Women are vainer than men."

"Of course," Miss Keller answered, "I admit that women are vain and men are not. There are a thousand proofs that this is so. Why, the necktie of the handsomest man in the room is even now up the back of his collar." There were six men present and each of them put his hand gently behind his neck.

611 Henry James, the novelist, once lived near the estate of a millionaire jam manufacturer, retired. This man, having married an earl's daughter, was ashamed of the trade whereby he had piled up his fortune.

The jam manufacturer one day wrote Mr. James an insolent letter, vowing that it was outrageous the way the James' servants were trespassing on his grounds. Mr. James wrote back:

"Dear Sir: I am sorry to hear that my servants have been poaching on your preserves.

"P.S.—You'll excuse my mentioning your preserves, won't you?"

612 When Jack London was in Korea reporting the Russo-Japanese War, an official came to his hotel one day and told him that the entire population was gathered in the square below to see him. London felt enormously set up to think his fame had spread to the wilds of Korea. But when he mounted the platform that had been erected for him, the official merely asked him to take out his bridge of artificial teeth. The crowd watched closely as he did it. And then for half an hour they kept him standing there, taking out his teeth and putting them back again, to the applause of the multitude.

613   A Chicago matron was recently seated next to a Mrs. Cabot at a Boston tea party. During the crisp exchange of conversation, Mrs. Cabot advanced the information that "in Boston, we place all of our emphasis on breeding." To which the Chicago matron responded: "In Chicago, we think it's a lot of fun, but we do manage to foster a great many outside interests."

614   P. T. Barnum craved free publicity. When he was near death the "Evening Sun," of New York, asked the great showman's publicity agent if Barnum would object to having his obituary published before he died. The agent said, "The old man will be delighted." The next day Barnum read four columns about his own death, and he loved it.

615   Theodore Roosevelt, at the height of his prominence in American public life, was once approached by a man on the street who tipped his hat and said, "Mr. Brown, I believe?"
    Roosevelt looked at the man and replied bluntly, "Sir, if you believe that, you will believe anything."

616   Oscar Levant is said to have once asked George Gershwin, "Tell me, George, if you had it to do all over, would you fall in love with yourself again?"

617   When Coolidge was Governor of Massachusetts he was once host to a visiting Englishman of some prominence. The latter ostentatiously took a British coin from his pocket, saying, "My great, great grandfather was made a Lord by the King whose picture you see on this shilling."
    Coolidge laconically produced a nickel. "My great, great grandfather," he said, "was made an angel by the Indian whose picture you see on this coin."

618   An English newspaper once printed the following bit of gossip: "James McNeill Whistler and Oscar Wilde were seen yesterday at Brighton, talking as usual about themselves." Whistler sent the paragraph to Wilde with a note saying: "I wish these reporters would be accurate: If you remember, Oscar, we were talking about me."

Wilde sent him a telegram saying: "It is true, Jimmie, we were talking about you, but I was thinking of myself!"

619 "Gershwin," observed Oscar Levant, "was the happiest man on earth. He was in love with himself and didn't have a rival on earth."

620 A little fable was formerly current about Theodore Roosevelt. The great man, after his death, was supposed to have ascended to Heaven. There he bustled about and made himself a nuisance by insisting that he be entrusted with some major responsibility. At last, wearily the higher powers instructed St. Peter to authorize T. R. to organize and train a celestial choir to replace the old one, which it was felt, had gone to seed. T. R. continued to be a nuisance by the fierce persistence with which he pressed his requisitions.

"I must have 10,000 sopranos," he told the bewildered and weary St. Peter, "and 10,000 contraltos, and 10,000 tenors. And hurry—hurry! Everything is waiting on you."

"Yes," said St. Peter, "how about the basses?"

Roosevelt fixed him with a scornful glare. "I'll sing bass!" he bellowed.

621 It was one of his own sons who so aptly characterized Theodore Roosevelt, saying, "Father always had to be the center of attention. When he went to a wedding, he wanted to be the bridegroom; and when he went to a funeral, he wanted to be the corpse."

622 There is a good story told of the way Disraeli got rid of an unfortunate applicant for a baronetcy upon whom, for many reasons, it was impossible to confer the honor. "You know I cannot give you a baronetcy," said Disraeli, "but you can tell your friends I offered you a baronetcy and that you refused it. That's far better."

623 In an interview between President Lincoln and Petroleum V. Nasby, the name came up of a recently deceased politician of Illinois whose merit was blemished by great vanity. His funeral was very largely attended.

"If General —— had known how big a funeral he would have had," said Mr. Lincoln, "he would have died years ago."

624 Oscar Levant is noted for his self-esteem. Occasionally he would tell this story on himself. "Once I was saying to an old friend how remarkable was our congeniality since we had practically nothing in common."

"Oh, but we have," replied the friend, "I think you're wonderful and you agree with me."

625 Henvy IV enacted some sumptuary laws, prohibiting the use of gold and jewels in dress; but they were for some time ineffectual. He passed a supplement to them which completely answered his purpose. In this last he exempted from the prohibitions of the former after one month, all prostitutes and pickpockets. Next day there was not a jewel nor golden ornament to be seen.

626 In London D'Annunzio, the Italian poet, asked a policeman to direct him to his destination and remarked: "I am D'Annunzio!" The bobby did not understand. Whereupon the genius burst forth into oaths and commanded his secretary to present that ignorant lout with copies of all his works.

627 While D'Annunzio was living in France, a letter was addressed to him simply with the words: "To Italy's Greatest Poet." He declined to accept it, saying that he was not Italy's greatest poet—he was the world's greatest poet.

628 A young girl came to the late Father Healey of Dublin and confessed that she feared she had incurred the sin of vanity. "What makes you think that?" asked her father confessor. "Because every morning when I look into the mirror I think how beautiful I am."

"Never fear, my girl," was the reassuring reply. "That isn't a sin, it's only a mistake."

RELATED SUBJECTS: *Boastfulness* 101-103; *Flattery* 236-237; *Pompousness* 421-427; *Pride* 456-457; *Snobbishness* 546-551

SEE ALSO: *Devotion* 172; *Modesty* 388, 389; *Tolerance* 602; *Fatness* 687; *Shortness* 691; *Society* 796; *Husband* 916; *Family* 948; *Composers* 1312; *Concerts* 1342; *Directors* 1403; *Audiences* 1438; *Dictators* 2003; *Servants* 2282

WILL POWER

631 A young man, contemplating marriage, was almost shocked out of his future state by overhearing the following conversation.

Several young women, discussing their husbands, were talking of their men's vices and how they had succeeded in curing them.

"Incidentally," said one of them to a very pretty young thing standing by, "I hear that John has given up smoking. He used to smoke a great deal. That must have taken a strong will."

In contrast to her frail prettiness, the young woman was heard to say, "It certainly did. But that's the kind of will I've got."

> RELATED SUBJECTS: *Habits* 31; *Conscience* 146-147; *Diligence* 176-177; *Endurance* 216; *Stubbornness* 571-572

> SEE ALSO: Smoking 63

WORRYING

636 Secretary of the Treasury Chase happened to remark, "Oh, I am so sorry that I did not write a letter to Mr. So-and-so before I left home!"

President Lincoln promptly responded: "Chase, never regret what you don't write; it is what you do write that you are often called upon to feel sorry for."

> RELATED SUBJECTS: *Conscience* 146-147; *Cowardice* 156-160; *Melancholy* 366-368; *Handicaps and Afflictions* 701-707; *Debt* 2171-2174; *Bankruptcy* 2196-2198

ZANIES

641 Riding on the subway during a fairly crowded hour a man was startled to see sitting opposite him in the car a man reading his newspaper and paying no attention whatever to a pair of pigeons which were seated one on each of his shoulders. Many stations further on, when the crowd had thinned out somewhat, he could repress his curiosity no longer. Stepping across the aisle he accosted the man, saying, "I beg your pardon, but would you mind telling me what those pigeons are doing on your shoulders?"

The man looked up from his paper and said, "I don't know. They got on at 14th Street."

642   A man stepped briskly up to a swanky cocktail bar at the Waldorf in New York and snapped at the barkeeper, "Martini!"

He got the drink and the bartender was astounded to see him toss the contents over his left shoulder and then proceed to nibble off the rim of the glass. Having finished this crispy morsel he slapped down the remains and said, "Another."

Another was served and the performance was repeated.

"Say," said the bartender, leaning over the bar, "are you crazy?"

"No," said the man snappily. "It's simply that I like only the rim of the glass."

"But," said the barkeeper, "the stem's the best part!"

643   One day at Ebbets Field Leo Durocher was accosted by a large and well-groomed horse, who said, "I'd like to join the Dodgers if you've got any place for me."

"What can you do?" asked Durocher scornfully.

"Well, I can bat," said the horse.

"Pick out a bat and show me," said the manager.

The horse looked over the pile of bats, selected one and stepped out to the plate with the bat between its teeth. Casey was pitching. The horse hit the first ball that came over and knocked it out of the field.

"Pretty good," said Durocher. "What else can you do?"

"I'm a mighty good first baseman," said the horse.

"Get over there," said Durocher.

The horse again proved its mettle.

"I'm a pretty good shortstop," the horse next volunteered, and again demonstrated its prowess.

"All right," said Durocher, at last convinced. "Can you pitch?"

"Oh," said the horse in disgust, "who ever heard of a horse pitching!"

RELATED SUBJECTS: *Boners* 106-119; *Eccentricity* 196-209; *Exaggeration* 221-226; *Liars* 331-336; *Practical Joking* 431-437

PHYSICAL CHARACTERISTICS

646 Mark Twain often received photographs from men whose friends had made them believe that they looked like him. Discovering that his house was beginning to run over with pictures of these aspirants to fame, Mark determined to relieve himself of the burden of answering the heavy correspondence, and so had his printer strike off a few hundred copies of the following form letter: "My dear Sir: I thank you very much for your letter and your photograph. In my opinion you are more like me than any other of my numerous doubles. I may even say that you resemble me more closely than I do myself. In fact, I intend to use your picture to shave by.

Yours thankfully,
S. Clemens"

647 Lincoln once dreamed he was in some great assembly, and the people drew back to let him pass, whereupon he heard some one say, "He is a common-looking fellow." In his dream Lincoln turned to the man and said, "Friend, the Lord prefers common-looking people; that is the reason why he made so many of them."

648 A simple youth coming to Rome from the country, was observed to resemble Augustus so much that it was the subject of general conversations. The emperor ordered him to appear at court, and inquired of him if his mother had ever been in Rome.

"No," answered the innocent youth, "but my father has."

RELATED SUBJECTS: *Homeliness* 651-656; *Beauty* 661-669; *Age* 671-678; *Fatness* 681-690; *Shortness* 691-695; *Tallness* 696; *Handicaps and Afflictions* 701-707

SEE ALSO: *Dullness* 189; *Memory* 373; *Rudeness* 517; *Children* 951; *Painting* 1283; *Diplomats* 2025

HOMELINESS

651 Lincoln delighted to tell stories on himself. One of his favorites was the following:

"In the days when I used to be on the circuit (traveling on horseback from one county court to another) I was once accosted by a stranger, who said:

" 'Excuse me, sir, but I have an article which belongs to you.'

" 'How is that?' I asked, considerably astonished.

"The stranger took a jack-knife from his pocket.

" 'This knife,' said he, 'was placed in my hands some years ago, with the injunction that I was to keep it until I found a man homelier-looking than I am myself. I have carried it from that time until this; allow me to say, sir, that you are fairly entitled to the property.' "

652 Lincoln's great love for children easily won their confidence. A little girl, who had been told that the President was very homely, was taken by her father to see the President at the White House.

Lincoln took her upon his knee and chatted with her a moment in his merry way, when she turned to her father and exclaimed:

"Oh, Pa! he isn't ugly at all; he's just beautiful!"

653 An acquaintance came to Jerrold and said, indignantly, "I hear you said my nose was like the ace of clubs!"

Jerrold looked thoughtful. "No, I did not," he drawled; "but now that I look at it, I see it is—very like."

654 The day following the adjournment of the Baltimore Convention, at which President Lincoln was renominated, various political organizations called to pay their respects. While the Philadelphia delegation was being presented, the chairman of that body, in introducing one of the members said: "Mr. President this is Mr. S. of the second district of our State, a most active and earnest friend of yours and the cause. He has, among other things, been good enough to paint, and present to our league rooms a most beautiful portrait of yourself."

President Lincoln took the gentleman's hand in his, and shaking it cordially said, with a merry voice: "I presume, sir, in painting your beautiful portrait, you took your idea of me from my principles and not from my person."

655 Said the brash traveling saleman to the farmer, "My God, that's certainly a homely woman!"

"That's my wife, young man," said the farmer, "and you might remember that beauty is only skin deep."

"Then," said the salesman, "for Heaven's sake, skin her!"

656 A farmer, making his nightly rounds, saw a shadowy figure holding a lantern and standing somewhat furtively by the side of the house.

Knowing that all his family was in the house, he shouted, "Hey, there. Who are you?"

Holding the lantern head high, the figure laughed and said, "It's only me. Albert."

"Why I thought you were in bed long ago. What are you doing out so late?"

"Well," said Albert, shifting about a bit as though in embarrassment, "I'm courtin' Annie."

The farmer chuckled. "Why the lantern? Why, when I was courtin' my missus, I didn't take a lantern."

The young man hesitated for a minute, then said in all seriousness, "Yes, sir. I know. We can all see that, sir."

RELATED SUBJECTS: *Physical Characteristics* 646-648; *Beauty* 661-669

SEE ALSO: *Vanity* 628; *Tallness* 696

BEAUTY

661 As the beautiful Duchess of Devonshire was one day stepping out of her carriage, a dustman who was accidentally standing by, and was about to regale himself with his accustomed whiff of tobacco, caught a glance of her countenance, and instantly exclaimed, "Love and bless you, my lady, let me light my pipe in your eye!" It is said the Duchess was so delighted with this compliment, that she frequently afterwards checked the strain of adulation which was constantly offered to her charms, by saying, "Oh! after the dustman's compliment, all others are insipid."

662 Fontanelle, at the age of 97, after saying many amiable and gallant things to a beautiful young lady, passed before her without seeing her, to place himself at table.

"See," said the lady, "how I ought to value your gallantries, you pass without looking at me."

"Madam," replied the old man, "if I had looked at you I could not have passed."

663   Lord Chesterfield and Voltaire were attending a reception in Paris. Noticing that the Englishman was being assailed by some of the ladies, the French wit said to him, "My Lord, it is said that you possess keen discrimination; tell me now, who are the more handsome, the French women or the women of your own country?"

"As to that," replied Chesterfield, "I must admit I cannot say, as I am no connoisseur in the art of painting."

664   Curran, speaking of Madame de Staël who was by no means handsome, but a splendid conversationalist, said she "had the power of talking herself into a beauty."

665   Someone once noted to Samuel Goldwyn the beauty of his wife's hands.

"Yes," Goldwyn said, "she has such beautiful hands, I'm thinking of having a bust made of them."

666   Chesterfield and Voltaire were once attending a ball in London. A celebrated beauty was there, much berouged and painted. This lady concentrated a great deal of her attention very flatteringly upon the renowned Frenchman. Chesterfield accosted Voltaire and cautioned jokingly, "Sir, take care that you are not captivated."

"My Lord," said Voltaire, "I scorn to be taken by an English craft with French colors."

667   Lady Randolph Churchill was canvassing among the voters of Woodstock on behalf of her husband, the then chancellor of the Exchequer. Interviewing a workingman she asked for his support.

"No, certainly not," he replied. "I should never think of voting for a lazy fellow who never leaves his bed until dinnertime."

The lady assured him that he was wrongly informed, adding, "As I happen to be his wife, my evidence ought to be conclusive."

"Lor, ma'am," he at once replied, "if you were my wife I should never want to get up."

668   One of the finest compliments ever offered was the compliment by Sir Joshua Reynolds to Mrs. Siddons, the Queen of Tragedy, whose portrait he painted. When it was finished Mrs.

Siddons noticed a peculiar brocaded effect upon the corner of the robe, and found on closer examination that it was the painter's name inscribed upon it. Turning to the artist she was met with a stately bow.

"I could not resist the opportunity," Sir Joshua explained, "of sending down my name to posterity on the hem of your garment."

669 It was at one of those Selfridge election parties that Max Beerbohm was heard to make one of his delightful remarks. He and his wife had been asked to come to the party, which was attended by nearly all London. There were beautiful girls from the stage, striking ladies from the film studios and others both beautiful and striking from addresses Mayfair.

He looked gravely round at the faces near him. All were painted, not with the art that conceals art, but with the determination to gain attention. This elderly exquisite looked again and shuddered, then he turned to his wife.

"My dear," he said, "you are looking so charming tonight that I simply must talk to you."

> RELATED SUBJECTS: *Physical Characteristics* 646-648; *Homeliness* 651-656

> SEE ALSO: *Long-Windedness* 361; *Tact* 590; *Vanity* 607; *Handicaps* 703

AGE

671 Fabia Dollabella saying she was thirty years of age, Cicero answered: "It must be true, for I have heard it these twenty years."

672 When Oliver Wendell Holmes was still on the Supreme Court bench, he and Justice Brandeis took walks every afternoon. On one of these occasions Holmes, then 92, paused to gaze in frank admiration at a beautiful young girl who passed them. He even turned to look at her as she continued down the street. Then, turning to Brandeis, he sighed: "Oh! What wouldn't I give to be 70 again!"

673 A farmer called out to Colonel Thomas Hart Benton and inquired to know his age. The Colonel replied, "According to

the Calendar my age is seventy-four, but when anything is to be done I am thirty-five years old, sir."

674 "Youth," said Bernard Shaw, "is a wonderful thing. What a crime to waste it on children."

675 The opposition of Pitt to the ministry, in a short time became so annoying, that Sir Robert Walpole meanly deprived him of his commission. Horace Walpole also taunted him bitterly on account of his youth, although he was then thirty-two, and sneeringly observed, that the discovery of truth was little promoted by pompous diction and theatrical emotion. Pitt replied:

"I will not attempt to determine whether youth can be imputed to any man as a reproach, but I will affirm that the wretch, who after having seen the consequences of repeated errors continues still to blunder, and whose age has only added obstinacy to stupidity, is surely the object of either abhorrence or contempt, and deserves not that his gray head should secure him from insult. Much more is he to be abhorred, who, as he has advanced in age, has seceded from virtue, and become more wicked with less temptation; who prostitutes himself for money which he cannot enjoy, and spends the remains of his life in the ruin of his country."

676 "I do not approve of shadows in painting," said Queen Elizabeth to Daniel Meyers. "You must strike off my likeness without shadows."

The Queen was near sixty when she said this and the "shadows," as she charitably called them were wrinkles big enough to have had a straw in them.

677 In his extreme old age John Quincy Adams was slowly and feebly walking down a street in Boston. An old friend accosted him and shaking his trembling hand asked, "And how is John Quincy Adams today?"

"Thank you," said the ex-President, "John Quincy Adams is well, quite well, I thank you. But the house in which he lives at present is becoming quite dilapidated. It is tottering upon its foundations. Time and the seasons have nearly destroyed it. Its roof is pretty well worn out. Its walls are much shattered, and it trembles with every wind. The old tenement is becoming almost uninhabitable, and I think John Quincy Adams will have to move out of it soon. But he himself is quite well, quite well."

678 Stirred by the patriotic fervor that swept over the country, an Irishman of 41 tried to enlist in the army. Although the recruiting sergeant saw that this man would make a good soldier, he could not accept any man over 38.

"Listen, fella," said the sergeant, "are you sure of your age? Suppose you go home and think it over, and then come back tomorrow."

Next day the Irishman returned.

"Well, how old are you now?" asked the sergeant.

"I was wrong yesterday," said the hopeful recruit. "Sure, I'm 38; it's me old mother who's 41."

RELATED SUBJECTS: *Physical Characteristics* 646-648; *Longevity* 1781-1782

SEE ALSO: *Divorce* 907; *Authors* 1201; *Hypochondriacs* 1720; *Insurance* 2136

FATNESS

681 One night William Howard Taft, then a young law reporter, finished studying a case in Somerville, Ohio, and discovered that he could not get back to his office that night unless he could stop a through express. He wired division headquarters:

"Will you stop through express at Somerville to take on large party?"

Promptly came back the reply: "Yes."

When the train arrived, the conductor said to Mr. Taft: "Where's the large party we were to take on?"

Mr. Taft regarded his own comfortable bulk ruefully and laughed. "I'm it," he said, stepping aboard the train.

682 The celebrated Gibbon, notwithstanding his shortness and rotundity, was very gallant. One day, being tête-a-tête with Madame de Cronzas, Gibbon wished to seize the favorable moment, and suddenly dropping on his knees, he declared his love in the most passionate terms. Madame de Cronzas replied in a tone likely to prevent a repetition of such a scene. Gibbon was thunderstruck, but still remained on his knees, tho' frequently desired to get up and resume his seat.

"Sir," said Madame de Cronzas, "will you have the goodness to rise?"

"Alas! Madame!" replied the unhappy lover, "I cannot!" His size preventing him from rising without assistance. Upon this Madame de Cronzas rang the bell, saying to the servant, "Lift up Mr. Gibbon."

683   "Would you mind walking the other w'y and not passing the 'orse?" said a London cabman with exaggerated politeness to a fat lady who had just paid a minimum fare.

"Why?" she inquired.

"Because if 'e sees wot 'e's been carryin' for a shilling 'e'll 'ave a fit."

684   The English artist C. R. W. Nevinson tells, "Sisley Huddleston and I were great friends. He was a man of enormous stature. We have dined and wined together in all parts of Paris, roared with laughter, and teased 'the girls.' On one occasion Sisley, Clive Bell, and I had eaten chicken and rice and had drunk wine with it. Being a large man, Sisley had a large appetite. We took one of those tiny Parisian taxis to the Boulevard St. Germain and when we arrived outside we discovered that the rice had swelled so much inside Sisley that it was impossible for him to get out of the door. We pushed and we pulled, but he seemed to be growing larger before our eyes; and at length the driver opened the roof, and Sisley came out through that and over the back. By that time he and I and the driver were so hysterical with merriment that they refused us admission to the Brasserie Lipp's in the belief that we were drunk; and Clive Bell, who had stood by, shocked and exquisite, was furious because he had a rendezvous there with Derain."

685   Marie Dressler used to tell the story of her first trip to Paris, when her French was one step removed from nothing. She was seeking the house of a friend, and the cab driver, whom she hired to convey her there, was attempting to tell her that the address was directly behind the hotel where she was staying.

"C'est derrière l'hotel," the driver kept saying. Miss Dressler did not know the word and kept repeating, "Que signifie derrière?"

They exchanged these remarks futilely for some moments until at last, in despair, the cab driver shrugged his shoulders and said, "If Madame does not know the meaning of derrière, nobody does!"

686 "Oh, I just love nature!" gushed the dowager with more than the usual number of shoulder-straps and chins.

"That's loyalty," mused Groucho Marx, "after what nature did to her!"

687 According to his friend Trelawney, "Byron's terror of getting fat was so great that he reduced his diet to the point of absolute starvation. When he added to his weight, even standing was painful, so he resolved to keep down to eleven stone, or shoot himself. He said everything he swallowed was instantly converted into tallow and deposited on his ribs. He was the only human being I ever met with who had sufficient self-restraint and resolution to resist his proneness to fatten. As he was always hungry, his merit was the greater. Occasionally he relaxed his vigilance, when he swelled apace. I remember one of his old friends saying, 'Byron how well you are looking!' If he had stopped there it had been well, but when he added, 'You are getting fat,' Byron's brow reddened, and his eyes flashed—'Do you call getting fat looking well, as if I were a hog?' and turning to me he muttered, 'The beast, I can hardly keep my hands off him.' I don't think he had much appetite for his dinner that day, or for many days, and he never forgave the man. He would exist on biscuits and soda-water for days together, then, to allay the eternal hunger gnawing at his vitals, he would make up a horrid mess of cold potatoes, rice, fish, or greens, deluged in vinegar, and gobble it up like a famished dog. Either of these unsavoury dishes, with a biscuit and glass or two of Rhine wine, he cared not how sour, he called feasting sumptuously. Upon my observing he might as well have fresh fish and vegetables instead of stale, he laughed and answered: 'I have an advantage over you, I have no palate; one thing is as good as another to me.'"

688 President Taft was fond of telling of an occasion upon which he was enjoying the ocean at a beach in New England. "Let us go in," said one of a group of acquaintances on the sand.

"How can we?" asked a youngster who was among them, "The President is using the ocean."

689 Years ago, when one of her sons was a cadet at Culver, Madame Schumann-Heink went to visit him. She was told

where his dormitory was and, wishing to surprise him, she decided to go to his room unannounced. Arriving at the dormitory she found it to be still under construction. As she went through a doorway a sliver of wood caught on her dress and tore a small hole in it. A cadet, who happened to be passing by at the time, called out impudently, "Madame, you should have gone through that door sideways."

Without taking offense, the heavily built singer laughed heartily. "Mein Gott, child, I have no sideways."

690 Taft always relished humor at his own expense. He liked to tell of a small boy who had had the habit of biting his nails. His nursemaid, seeking to frighten him out of it, told him that if he did not stop he would swell up like a balloon. Considerably impressed, the boy desisted from his habit.

A few days thereafter Taft appeared at his home for a luncheon. Marching straight up to the President, the boy accused, "You bite your nails."

RELATED SUBJECTS: *Physical Characteristics* 646-648; *Shortness* 691-695; *Tallness* 696

SEE ALSO: *Producers* 1397; *Sermons* 1548

SHORTNESS

691 Napoleon was one day searching for a book in his library, and at last discovered it on a shelf somewhat above his reach. Marshal Moncey, one of the tallest men in the army, stepped forward, saying:

"Permit me, Sire—I am higher than your Majesty."

"You are longer, Marshal," said the Emperor with a frown.

692 Alexander H. Stevens, Senator from Georgia and, subsequently, Vice-President of the Confederate States, was short of stature and weighed less than 80 lbs. A big Congressman from the West, in a heated debate, once said, "Why, I could swallow you and never know I'd et a thing."

"In that case, you'd have more brains in your belly than you ever had in your head," snapped Stevens.

693 Dr. Busby of Westminster, who was very short, was one day accosted in a public coffee-room by an Irish baronet of colossal stature with: "May I pass to my seat, O Giant?"

When the doctor politely making way, replied: "Pass, O Pigmy!" the baronet apologized. "Oh, Sir, my expression alluded to the size of your intellect."

"And my expression, Sir," retorted the doctor coldly, "to the size of yours."

694 Archbishop Laud was a man of very short stature. Charles the First and the Archbishop sat down to dinner one day when it was agreed that Archie, the King's jester, should say the Grace for them, which he did in this fashion: "Great praise be given to God, but little Laud to the Devil!" For this sally, Archbishop Laud was weak enough to insist upon Archie's dismissal.

695 A group of men were discussing Stephen Douglas and his physical peculiarities. Abraham Lincoln happened to join the men at this point and, turning from the specific subject under discussion, one of them asked the President how long he thought a man's legs should be.

"Well," drawled Lincoln, "I should think a man's legs ought to be long enough to reach from his body to the ground."

RELATED SUBJECTS: *Physical Characteristics* 646-648; *Fatness* 681-690; *Tallness* 696

TALLNESS

696 When Lincoln heard that a general who was supporting McClellan's Presidential candidacy had been relieved of his command the President countermanded the order, saying, "Supporting General McClellan for the Presidency is no violation of army regulations, and as a question of taste in choosing between him and me—well, I'm the longest, but he's better looking."

RELATED SUBJECTS: *Physical Characteristics* 646-648; *Fatness* 681-690; *Shortness* 691-695

SEE ALSO: *Shortness* 693

HANDICAPS AND AFFLICTIONS

701   The Reverend Whitefield having remarked in a sermon that everything made by God was perfect, "What think you of me?" said a deformed man in a pew beneath who arose from his seat, and pointed at his own back.

"Think of you," reiterated the preacher. "Why sir, you are the most perfect hunchback my eyes ever beheld."

702   Madame Bernhardt had a subtle sense of humor. Shortly after recovering from the amputation of her leg, she received a cable from the manager of the Pan-American Exposition at San Francisco. He had the temerity to ask permission to exhibit her leg at the Exposition, offering her $100,000. She cabled back only two words: "Which leg?" That ended the matter.

703   During one of Hobhouse's visits to Byron—Hobhouse was a college friend—at his villa near Genoa, and whilst they were walking in the garden, his lordship suddenly turned upon his guest, and, apropos of nothing, but always having his deformity in his mind, exclaimed: "Now I know Hobhouse you are looking at my foot!"

Upon which Hobhouse kindly replied, "My dear Byron, nobody thinks of or looks at anything but your head."

704   Junius Brutus Booth, the tragedian, had a broken nose.

"You're such a wonderful actor, Mr. Booth," said a lady upon being introduced to him, "but to be perfectly frank with you, I can't get over your nose."

"There's no wonder, Madam," Booth replied, "the bridge is gone."

705   When Milton's enemies mocked his blindness, the poet with great heat replied:

"I prefer my blindness to yours, yours is sunk into your deepest senses, blinding your minds, so that you can see nothing that is sound and solid. Mine takes from me only the color and surface of things, but does not take away from the mind's contemplation what is in those things of true and constant. Moreover how many things are there which I would not see. How many which I can be debarred the sight without repining! How few left which I much desire to see! Vile men! Who mock us! The blind have a protection from the injuries of men, and we are rendered almost sacred."

706 Thomas Edison was deaf but only a few of his friends were aware that in his case deafness was more psychological than physical. Once a specialist in diseases of the ear called upon Mr. Edison and unfolded a plan of treatment which he was sure would restore his hearing. To the proposition that he submit to treatment, however, Mr. Edison opposed an emphatic negative.

"What I am afraid of," said he, "is that you would be successful. Just think what a lot of stuff I'd have to listen to that I don't want to hear! To be a little deaf and be the only one who knows just how deaf you are has its advantages. I prefer to let well enough alone."

707 A British veteran of the Boer War was discharged from the army in a hopeless condition; he had lost a leg and an arm, and one eye was gone. In his distress he was obliged to solicit alms on the London streets. One day an Irishman who spied him showered coins upon the unfortunate man with both hands.

"Why do you do that?" demanded a bystander. "Don't you see that the man is a British soldier—a foe to Ireland?"

"I do," retorted the Irishman. "But he can have all I've got. He is the first Englishman I have ever seen that was trimmed up to suit me."

RELATED SUBJECTS: *Physical Characteristics* 646-648; *Stuttering* 711-713; *Sickness* 1701-1707; *Poor Health* 1711-1712

SEE ALSO: *Wife* 931; *Church Services* 1536; *Sermons* 1547, 1554; *Insurance* 2140; *Trials* 2480

STUTTERING

711 Henry Guy Carleton, wit, journalist, and playwright, had an impediment in his speech about which he used to joke. Meeting Nat Goodwin, the comedian, one day he asked:

"G-G-Goodwin, c-c-can you g-g-give m-m-me f-f-fifteen m-m-minutes?"

"Certainly," replied the comedian, "what is it?"

"I w-want to have f-f-five minutes' c-c-conversation with you."

712 Stammering, says Coleridge, is sometimes the cause of a pun. Someone was mentioning in Lamb's presence the cold-heartedness of the Duke of Cumberland, in restraining the Duchess in rushing up to the embrace of her son, whom she had not seen for a considerable time, and insisting on her receiving him in state. "How horribly cold it was," said the narrator. "Yes," said Lamb in his stuttering way, "but you know he is the Duke of Cu-cum-ber-land."

713 A big hulk of a man, somewhat sinister in appearance, accosted a small dapper gentleman on the street, and asked, "C-c-c-can you t-t-tell me how to g-g-get to C-c-city Hall?"

The small man paled and, turning on his heels, fled down the street. Angered and exasperated, the big man pursued him. They raced for several blocks until the little man's wind gave out and he was overtaken and captured. The big man seized him by the arm and cried angrily, "W-w-what do you m-m-mean—running away w-w-when I ask you a c-c-civil question?"

The little man looked up and gasped, "D-d-do you t-t-think I w-w-wanted my block knocked off?"

RELATED SUBJECTS: *Physical Characteristics* 646-648; *Speeches* 756-782; *Talking* 806-818

SEE ALSO: *Borrowing* 122; *Lateness* 321; *Babies* 956; *Authors* 1186, 1203; *Church Services* 1533

CLOTHING

716 H. G. Wells has such a big head that he has trouble getting hats to fit. Once when he found one that balanced nicely on his head he just walked off with it, and blandly penned a note to its owner, E. S. Peck of Cambridge, Mass.

"I stole your hat," wrote the author, "I like your hat; I shall keep your hat. Whenever I look inside it I shall think of you and of your excellent sherry and of the town of Cambridge. I take off your hat to you."

717 Whistler was standing bareheaded in a London hat-shop while a clerk was looking for his size hat. A short red-faced man with a large waistline burst into the door and, mistaking Whistler for a clerk, exploded: "See here, you, this hat doesn't fit."

The artist casually eyed the man from head to foot, then drawled out: "Well, neither does your coat. What's more, if you'll pardon my saying so, I'll be hanged if I care much for the color of your trousers."

718 Sheridan made his appearance, one day, in a pair of new boots. These attracting the notice of some of his friends, "Now guess," said he, "how I came by these boots." Many probable guesses then took place. "No," said Sheridan, "no, you've not hit it, nor ever will. I bought them and paid for them."

719 A young lady on her way to business was standing in a crowded New York bus going down Fifth Avenue one morning. She was worrying over the age-old problem of whether or not her slip was showing. Unable to twist around sufficiently to see, she put the question directly to a small boy standing next to her. "No ma'am," he informed her politely. A few blocks farther she alighted and started to move briskly along crowded Fifth Avenue. Then, to her horror, she was hailed by the voice of the little boy, calling to her as the bus went by, yelling at the top of his lungs, "Your slip is showing now, lady, it's showing now!"

720 There are numerous stories of the embarrassing predicaments that have ensnared public speakers at one time or another. Probably no worse fate ever befell any of them than that of the lecturer who, with some trepidation, had finally consented to address a banquet at a nudist colony. Upon his arrival at the extensive premises, he was greeted by large numbers of men and women in their pristine natural state. He was shown into the headquarters building and it was suggested that he might like to prepare for dinner.

Upstairs in the room to which they allotted him, he felt that there was nothing he could do except face the fact that he was expected to divest himself of his garments. In extreme mental anguish he determined to be equal to the situation. At last, hearing the bell for dinner, he marched downstairs as bare as Adam, to discover, to his horror, that the colonists had all assumed formal dress in deference to the speaker.

721 When the great Duke of Argyle was one night at the theatre in a side-box a person entered the same box in boots and spurs. The Duke arose from his seat and with great ceremony, expressed his thanks to the stranger who, somewhat confused, desired to know for what reason he received those thanks. The Duke gravely replied, "For not bringing your horse into the box."

722 After the death of Nelson, English ladies were fond of wearing the Trafalgar garter, on which was inscribed the memorable signal: "England expects every man to do his duty."

723 Old Mrs. Smith of South Orange, N. J., who kept a small shop in Washington during the Civil War, said:

"Abraham Lincoln came in one day asking for socks. I said, 'What color?'

"'Color? Why, I don't know, I'm sure.'

"Finally he stooped down and took hold of the end of his pants. 'Why I guess this color is good enough for me.'

"He pulled it up. I looked for the sock—and saw—his bare skin."

724 In his early days in New York Floyd Odlum and his wife were invited to a dinner. The only pair of shoes he happened to own at the time were bright yellow. In order to render them appropriate to the occasion he and his wife painted them black on the day of the party. During dinner, their hostess, sniffing perplexedly, said to her son, "Charlie, I smell paint. Did you upset the paint in the cellar?"

A fruitless discussion ensued in which everyone spoke of the smell of paint except the Odlums who protested that they smelled nothing.

725 Mark Twain, cherishing his comfort above his appearance, was very often wont to visit his friends and neighbors without wearing either a collar or tie. His wife objected strenuously to this habit and, meeting him one day returning from a neighborly visit without any sign of a collar or tie, scolded him soundly.

Mark returned home, searched out a collar and tie, wrapped them up and sent them to the neighbor's house with the following note:

"A little while ago I visited you without my collar and tie for about half an hour. The missing articles are enclosed. Will you kindly gaze at them for 30 minutes and then return them to me?"

726 Before the birth of the son of Marie Antoinette and Louis XVI, the fashion of pregnancy spread through the court. The Queen's ladies-in-waiting wore skirts stuffed with cushions to make themselves appear enceinte; "skirts of the season" were created, with titles such as "fourth month skirt," etc., their voluminousness adjusted to the progress of the Queen.

RELATED SUBJECTS: *Physical Characteristics* 646-648

SEE ALSO: *Carelessness* 136; *Devotion* 172; *Diligence* 177; *Greed* 276; *Gossip* 826

HANDWRITING

731 Horace Greeley is another instance of a famous man noted for the illegibility of his handwriting. He once wrote the following letter:

"Mr. M. B. Castle,
Sandwich, Ill.

Dear Sir: I am overworked and growing old. I shall be 60 on next February 3rd. On the whole, it seems I must decline to lecture henceforth except in this immediate vicinity. If I go at all, I cannot promise to visit Illinois on that errand, certainly not now.

Yours truly,
Horace Greeley"

A few days later he received this answer:

"Horace Greeley,
New York Tribune.

Dear Sir: Your acceptance to lecture before our association next winter came to hand this morning. Your penmanship not being the plainest, it took some time to translate it; but we succeeded and would say your time, February 3rd, and the terms, $60, are entirely satisfactory. As you suggest, we may be able to get you other engagements.

Respectfully,
M. B. Castle"

732 John Calhoun's handwriting, though it looked neat, was almost undecipherable. Once a friend sent him back one of his letters because it was too difficult to read. Calhoun replied: "I know what I think on this subject but cannot decipher what I wrote."

733 The actor, Macready, was notorious for the illegibility of his handwriting. He frequently was called upon to scrawl a chit for the free admission of friends and acquaintances to performances. Although unrecognizable, they were familiar to the doorman and served their purpose. One day, however, a friend of the actor jestingly took one of Macready's scrawled passes to a pharmacist and gravely handed it over as a prescription to be filled. The latter unhesitatingly compounded a potion from various phials and powder boxes, and handing it across the counter to the waiting customer, observed, "A cough mixture, and a very good one. Fifty cents, please."

RELATED SUBJECTS: *Physical Characteristics* 646-648

SEE ALSO: *Marriage* 888

SOCIAL ACTIVITIES

736 Bernard Shaw one day received an invitation from a celebrity hunter: "Lady X will be at home Thursday between four and six."

The author returned the card; underneath he had written: "Mr. Bernard Shaw likewise."

737 Said Marie Antoinette, "My tastes are not the same as those of the king, who cares only for hunting and blacksmith work. You will admit that I should not show to advantage in a forge. I could not appear there as Vulcan, and the part of Venus might displease him even more than my tastes."

RELATED SUBJECTS: *Parties* 741-746; *Banquets and Dinners* 751-753; *Society* 796-797

PARTIES

741 Dorothy Parker once attended a party at which the greater number of people seemed to be the rakings of Bohemia. Her companion said to her, "Where on earth do these people come from and where do they stay the rest of the time?"

"I think," Miss Parker said thoughtfully, "that after it's over they crawl back into the woodwork."

742 "I've had a wonderful evening," said Groucho Marx to his hostess as he was leaving a dull Hollywood party, "but this wasn't it!"

743 Once, it is said, Margot Asquith gave a party in London: a big party. She received the guests with graciousness, set them spinning into the rhythm of pleasure and then retired to an upper room to play bridge.

Next day, a well-meaning, but tactless woman fluttered up to her in a restaurant and said: "Oh, Lady Asquith, I was at your party last night."

"Thank God I wasn't," answered Margot, and moved on.

744 Thomas A. Edison was once reluctantly persuaded by his wife to attend one of the brilliant social functions of the season in New York. At last the inventor managed to escape the lionizers who had crowded about him, and sat alone unnoticed in a corner. Edison kept looking at his watch with a resigned expression on his face. A friend edged near to him unnoticed and heard the inventor mutter to himself with a sigh, "If there were only a dog here!"

745 Oliver Wendell Holmes, having been at an afternoon tea, authoritatively defined such functions for all time as, "Giggle—gabble—gobble—git."

746 Dorothy Parker, completely bored by a country week-end, wired a friend: "Please send me a loaf of bread—and enclose a saw and file."

RELATED SUBJECTS: *Social Activities* 736-737; *Society* 796-797; *Hospitality* 1006-1008; *Birth, Birthdays* 1011-1015

SEE ALSO: *Rough and Ready* 507; *Rudeness* 513, 514, 515, 517, 519; *Tact* 588, 591; *Talking* 806; *Marriage* 884

BANQUETS AND DINNERS

751 At the dinner-parties which the poet Sam Rogers gave he started the custom of having no candles on the table, all the lights being attached to the walls and ceiling. This novelty created quite a buzz of comment in London society. While Sydney Smith was dining with Rogers one evening, the host asked him to say what he thought of the illumination of the table. "For my part, I don't fancy it at all, Rogers," returned the candid guest. "It's too uncomfortably like the Day of Judgment. Here we are, a flood of light on all above, and below nothing but darkness and gnashing of teeth."

752　At dinner one day Douglas Jerrold was forced to listen to a noisy argument between an admirer of the Prince of Orange and a henchman of William III. Having exhausted the political issues of the debate, they entered upon the personal phases of the question. One of the arguers finally brought his fist down on the table and exclaimed: "Bah! to you, sir; I spit upon your Prince of Orange!"

The other, determined not to be outdone, rose to his feet and screamed, "And I, sir, spit upon your King William!"

Hereupon Jerrold, unable to endure the racket longer, rang the bell and shouted to the waiter, "Here, boy—spittoons for two!"

753　It is said of Charles Fox that from infancy to manhood it was the practice of his father, Lord Holland, to show him the most unlimited indulgence. The following story is told in proof of it. Master Charles, when six or seven years of age, one day strolled into the kitchen; and while dinner was cooking, and a pig roasting at the fire, he amused himself with making water upon the unresisting porker. It was a standing order of the house to contradict him in nothing, so there was nothing to be done —but to let the pig be so basted. The cook, however, thought it fair to give the guests warning of the sauce to it, which he did by sending up the following lines upon a label in its mouth.

> If strong and savory I do taste,
> 'Tis with the liquor that did me baste,
> While at the fire I foam'd and hiss'd,
> A Fox's cub upon me ————.

RELATED SUBJECTS: *Eating* 6-23; *Social Activities* 736-737; *Parties* 741-746; *Speeches* 756-782

SPEECHES

756 At a banquet at Princeton University, the great Chinese diplomat, Dr. Wellington Koo, was the guest of honor and main speaker. As one of a number of representatives of the student body on this occasion, a burly member of the Princeton football team found himself seated next to Dr. Koo. Very embarrassed by the formality of the occasion and utterly at a loss for conversation, the young man turned to Dr. Koo during the soup course and said, "Likee soup?"

Dr. Koo urbanely bowed his head and grinned. Later he arose and delivered a polished, thoughtful and witty address. Sitting down amidst applause, Dr. Koo turned to the chagrined student and said smiling, "Likee speech?"

757 Dean Briggs was once one of the speakers at a formal banquet at Radcliffe College. In preparation for the event, among other things, the chairs had been given a new coat of varnish. The evening was hot and humid and, as the speakers rose to deliver their remarks, it was with some difficulty. The Dean was more than equal to the occasion. "Ladies and gentlemen," he said, with a rueful backward glance, "I had expected to bring you this evening a plain and unvarnished tale, but circumstances make it impossible to fulfill my intentions."

758 When J. M. Barrie addressed an audience of one thousand girls at Smith College during his American visit, a friend asked him how he had found the experience.

"Well," replied Mr. Barrie, "to tell you the truth, I'd much rather talk one thousand times to one girl, than to talk one time to a thousand girls."

759 Henry Ward Beecher was once in the midst of an address. A drunken spectator interrupted him by crowing like a rooster. Beecher was imperturbable; looking at his watch he said, "What! morning already? I would never have believed it, but the instincts of the lower animals are infallible."

760   Dr. MacNamara on one occasion, while speaking in a marquee at Bridlington, during a torrential rain, said to the audience, "I'm afraid I've kept you too long."

"Go on, sir, it's still raining," a voice in the rear replied.

761   General Sam Carey, the great Ohio orator, was finishing up an exceptionally fiery oration: "You cannot keep me down," he shouted, "Though I may be pressed below the waves I rise again; you will find that I come to the surface, gentlemen."

An old whaler, who happened to be in the audience, said, and not too quietly, "Yes, you come to the surface to blow."

762   Congressman Fred Landis of Indiana had made a reputation for himself as an orator. Speaking at the unveiling of a monument to President Lincoln, he uttered the phrase: "Abraham Lincoln—that mystic mingling of star and clod." This was loudly applauded.

After the speech a friend of Landis approached him and, repeating the phrase, said: "Fred, what in the name of heaven does that mean?"

Landis replied: "I don't know, really, but it gets 'em every time."

763   The story is told in London that God-fearing Prime Minister Stanley Baldwin was going over with the cabinet the speech he was subsequently to make in the House of Commons upon the accession of King Edward VIII. Afterward Mr. Baldwin's secretary gathered up the manuscript and observed a marginal note by the Prime Minister, "Refer again to A.G." Promptly the speech was rushed to the Attorney-General. The hour was late and in some puzzlement the A.G. and his staff scrutinized the wholly innocuous phrases, wondering what Mr. Baldwin could possibly have thought might be indiscreet or dangerous. It turned out next morning that Orator Baldwin had meant to remind himself by his marginal note to "Refer again to Almighty God."

764   Rev. Samuel J. May: Mr. Garrison, you are too excited— you are on fire!

William Lloyd Garrison: I have need to be on fire, for I have icebergs around me to melt.

765 At the laying of a cornerstone, while President, Mr. Coolidge turned a spadeful of earth and then remained silent. The gathering expected him to speak. The master of ceremonies suggested that a few words would be fitting.

Mr. Coolidge looked over the upturned earth.

"That's a fine fishworm," said he.

766 During a parliamentary discussion on curtailing debate Sir Campbell Bannerman remarked that "it was reasonable that Members should wish to let off a certain amount of intellectual steam."

"Is that a polite way of describing debate in this House?" interposed Balfour.

"I thought steam was a motive power," replied Bannerman.

"Not when it's let off," retorted Balfour amidst the laughter of the House.

767 Some years ago Winston Churchill highly amused his fellow Members in the House by distributing among them printed copies of his recent speeches. A Liberal Member for one of the Devonshire constituencies acknowledged the gift in the following manner:

"Dear Mr. Churchill, Thanks for copy of your speeches lately delivered in the House of Commons. To quote the late Lord Beaconsfield: 'I shall lose no time in reading them.'"

768 Secretary of State William Maxwell Evarts once was asked to address the guests at a Thanksgiving dinner. He began, "You have been giving your attention to a turkey stuffed with sage; you are now about to consider a sage stuffed with turkey."

769 On one occasion, when George III came out of the House of Lords after opening the session of Parliament, he addressed Lord Eldon thus: "Lord Chancellor, did I deliver the speech well?"

"Very well indeed, sir," was the enthusiastic answer.

"I am glad of that," replied the king; "for there was nothing in it."

770 Joseph Chamberlain, Prime Minister of England, told this story about himself. He was guest of honor at a banquet. The mayor of the city presided and when coffee was being served he leaned over and touched Mr. Chamberlain saying, "Shall we let them enjoy themselves a little longer or had we better have your speech now?"

771 Eamon de Valera was once arrested at Ennis in the middle of a political speech. A year later he was released. He went forthwith to Ennis, and began to speak again with the words, "As I was saying when I was interrupted—."

772 William Lyon Phelps tells, "Having to speak at a public dinner in Chicago, I found my place at the pillory of torment, the speakers' table; and there, seeing a magnificent man in evening dress, I gave him my name and grasped his hand with what cordiality I could command.

"'I'm the headwaiter, sir,' he replied.

"'Shake hands again, old man,' I cried. 'You don't know how I envy you!'"

773 When Dr. Walter Williams spoke in a Chinese university, an interpreter translated into Chinese symbols on a blackboard. Dr. Williams noted that the interpreter stopped writing during most of the speech and at the conclusion he asked why. "We only write when the speaker says something," was the blithe reply.

774 Andrew Jackson, before he became President, was once making a stump speech in a small village. Just as he was finishing, a friend who sat near him whispered, "Tip 'em a little Latin, General; they won't be contented without it." The man of iron will instantly thought upon the few phrases he knew, and in a voice of thunder wound up with "E pluribus unum, sine qua non, ne plus ultra, multum in parvo." The effect was tremendous, and the shouts of the Hoosiers could be heard for miles.

775 At a banquet in connection with the war effort, the toastmaster opened the speaking with the assurance that all the guests had promised to make brief addresses. It chanced that the first to be called upon was the heavyweight champion, Private Joe Louis, who rose to his feet and said, "The toastmaster must have known my speed," and sat down.

776 An Athenian crowd demonstrated impatience at a public assembly one day and hissed the orator Demosthenes, refusing

to hear him. He said he had but a short story to tell them and began, "A certain youth hired an ass, in the summer time, to go from his home to Megara. At noon, when the sun was very hot, both he who had hired the ass and the owner of the animal were desirous of sitting in the shade of the ass, and fell to thrusting one another away. The owner insisted that he had hired out only the ass and not the shadow. The other insisted that as he had hired the ass, all that belonged to the ass was his." Turning away, Demosthenes made as though to depart, but the mob, which had been piqued by the story, would not allow him to leave and insisted that he continue. He then turned upon them and demanded, "How is it that you insist upon hearing the story of the shadow of the ass, and will not give an ear to matters of great moment?" He was permitted to deliver the speech for which he had come. And the fine point of the ass and his shadow remains unsettled to this day.

777   Chauncey Depew once played a trick upon Mark Twain on an occasion when they were both to speak at a banquet. Twain spoke first for some 20 minutes and was received with great enthusiasm. When Depew's turn came, immediately afterwards, he said, "Mr. Toastmaster, Ladies and Gentlemen, before this dinner, Mark Twain and I made an agreement to trade speeches. He has just delivered mine and I'm grateful for the reception you have accorded it. I regret that I have lost his speech and cannot remember a thing he had to say."

He sat down with much applause.

778   The ability of various public speakers was being discussed in Sydney Smith's club. Someone said that Archbishop Whatley was gifted with unusual oratorical powers. Smith granted that there were some things he could indeed admire in the worthy doctor's discourses, remarking with emphasis of one particular speech, "There he had some splendid flashes of silence."

779   President Lincoln was attending a dinner at which many personages were asked to give speeches. Many and flowery were the phrases that were tossed about the table. At last the President was called upon to add his remarks to all that had gone before.

"I appear before you, fellow-citizens," said Lincoln, "merely to thank you for this compliment. The inference is a very fair one that you would hear me for a little while at least, were I to commence to make a speech. I do not appear before you for the purpose of doing so, and for several substantial reasons. The most substantial of these is that I have no speech to make. In my position it is somewhat important that I should not say any foolish things. (At this point a voice was heard to say, 'If you can help it.'—but the President went on without appearing to have noticed it.) It very often happens that the only way to help it is to say nothing at all. Believing that is my present condition this evening, I must beg of you to excuse me from addressing you further."

780 The distinguished Senator from Minnesota (Cushman K. Davis), a member of the Peace Commission, said in the Senate: "We stand in the vestibule of a century full of miracles, and, following the metaphor of the English orator who eloquently proclaimed, 'The British lion, whether it is roaming the deserts of India or climbing the forests of Canada, will not draw in its horns or retire into its shell,' so the American eagle will continue to guard whatever territory comes under the shadow of its wings so long as it chooses to hold it."

781 William Lloyd Garrison, the Abolitionist, had much unhappy experience with mobs and missiles. At a dinner given him by the British Anti-Slavery Society he was presented with a watch.

"Well, gentlemen," he said, "if this had been a rotten egg I should have known what to do with it, but as it is a gold watch, I have nothing to say."

782 Jules Janin, at a banquet, was given the toast, "Long live success!"

"Yes," he retorted, "it is the only thing that succeeds!"

INTRODUCTIONS

786 During one of his campaigns, William Jennings Bryan spoke in a city in one of the northwestern states. The chairman, in presenting the speaker, made an embarrassing fulsome and eulogistic introduction of Bryan, in such bad taste that many wondered how Bryan would succeed in overcoming the unfortunate effect of it. Bryan, however, was not easily dismayed: "The very kind observations of the chairman," said he, "bring to my mind the case of the man at a formal banquet table, who impulsively put into his mouth a large forkful of steaming, hot baked potato, which he instantly spat out upon his plate. Looking about at his disconcerted fellow guests and at his hostess, he remarked blandly, 'Some damn fools would have swallowed that.' "

787 "Long introductions when a man has a speech to make are a bore," said former Senator John C. Spooner, one of the great Senate leaders. "I have had all kinds, but the most satisfactory one in my career was that of a German mayor of a small town in my state, Wisconsin.

"I was to make a political address and the opera house was crowded. When it came time to begin the mayor got up.

" 'Mine friends,' said he, 'I hafe asked been to introduce Senator Spooner who is to make a speech, ja. Vell, I haf dit so, und he vill now do so.' "

788 "I had expected to find Mr. Lloyd George a big man in every sense," playfully remarked the chairman when introducing the statesman to a meeting. "But you see for yourselves he is quite small in stature."

Lloyd George was no whit abashed. "In North Wales," he remarked, "we measure a man from his chin up. You evidently measure from his chin down."

789 The lady from Arkansas, Senator Hattie Caraway, was about to address a gathering of her constituents. The chairman introduced her with a prolonged and lavish eulogy, culminating thunderously with the words, "Ladies and Gentlemen, I now present to you the most notorious woman in Arkansas!"

790 When Woodrow Wilson was President of Princeton he was called upon to be the chief speaker at an educators' ban-

quet in New York. Dr. Nicholas Murray Butler of Columbia was toastmaster. When the time came to introduce the principal speaker, Dr. Butler presented him as "A sleepy man from a sleepy little college in a sleepy little town."

Wilson rose and opened his remarks by saying, "The charge of sleepiness could never be brought against Dr. Butler, for is it not said in the Scriptures, 'Lo, he that keepeth Israel shall neither slumber nor sleep.'"

791 At a banquet in Dublin a toastmaster was delivering a eulogy of Sir Henry Irving. "Sir Henry," he said, "is not only an artist of the first rank, the first of his profession to be honored with a knighthood, but is also a man of the utmost integrity and highest honor. It would not be too much to say that his has been a life of unbroken blemish!"

> RELATED SUBJECTS: *Speeches* 756-782; *Campaigning* 1911-1920

> SEE ALSO: *Lectures* 1107

SOCIETY

796 At a fashionable salon in London appeared a young gentleman, the son of his majesty's printer who had the patent for publishing Bibles. He was dressed in green and gold. Being a new face, and extremely elegant, he attracted the attention of the whole company. A general murmur prevailed in the room, to learn who he was. Colley Cibber, the outrageous wit, who was present, instantly made reply, loud enough to be heard by everybody: "Oh, don't you know him? It is young Bible, bound in calf and gilt, but not lettered."

797 Lord Balfour was visiting friends in Scotland. One evening, while attending a dinner given in his honor, he noticed that the little daughter of his host was eyeing him covertly. He smiled to her and she, plucking up courage, asked him:

"Are you really and truly an English Lord?"

"Yes," he answered gravely, "really and truly."

"I have often thought I should like to see an English lord," she went on, "and—and—"

"And now you are satisfied?" he asked her.

"N-no," she answered slowly, "I'm not satisfied; I'm a good deal disappointed."

> RELATED SUBJECTS: *Snobbishness* 546-551; *Social Activities* 736-737

> SEE ALSO: *Newspapers* 1239; *Concerts* 1345; *Wealth* 2186

DUELING

801 On one occasion Lord Alvanley fought a duel with Morgan O'Connell on Wimbledon Common. It appears that several shots were fired without effect, and the seconds then interfered and put a stop to any further hostilities. When his hackney coach drove up to his door Alvanley gave the coachman a sovereign. Jarvey was profuse in his thanks, and said: "It's a great deal for only having taken your lordship to Wimbledon."

"No, my good man," said Alvanley, "I give it to you, not for taking me, but for bringing me back."

802 When Professor Rudolf Virchano, famous German scientist, criticized Bismarck severely in his capacity as Chancellor, Bismarck challenged him to a duel. "Well, well," said the scientist to the Iron Chancellor's seconds, "as I am the challenged party, I suppose I have the choice of weapons. Here they are." And he held up two large sausages which looked exactly alike.

"One of these," he continued, "is infected with the deadly germ of trichinosis, the other is perfectly sound. Let His Excellency do me the honor to choose whichever he wishes, and eat it. I will eat the other."

Within an hour the Iron Chancellor had decided to laugh the duel off.

803 Mirabeau the French statesman received many challenges to duels. He always answered this way: "Sir, your favor is received, and your name is on my list, but I warn you that the list is long and that I grant no preferences."

> RELATED SUBJECTS: *Quarrelsomeness* 466; *Rudeness* 511-524

> SEE ALSO: *Soldiers* 2433

TALKING

806 At a party, someone observed to Dorothy Parker that their hostess was outspoken. "By whom?" asked Miss Parker.

807 Mark Twain met Winston Churchill in 1900, when the latter was just coming into prominence as a young statesman. The occasion was a dinner in London. Churchill and Twain went out for a brief time to have a smoke. Sir William Vernon Harcourt observed, as they departed, that whichever one got the floor first would keep it. He speculated that inasmuch as Twain was an older and more experienced hand, Churchill's voice would get the first good rest that it had had in years.

When the two men returned, Harcourt asked Churchill whether he had enjoyed himself, and the young man replied, "Yes," most enthusiastically. Turning to Twain, Sir William put the same question. Twain hesitated and said, "I have had a good smoke."

808 A talkative barber was trimming the beard of King Archelaus, and asked, "How shall I cut?"

"In silence," replied the king.

809 King Archelaus, perpetrator of that ancient joke about replying, "in silence," to the barber who asked him how he should cut his hair, would be pleased to know that his tradition is being carried on in the modern era.

A man, who might well stem from this kingly line, handed the barber a coin and then climbed into the chair.

"Why, sir, thank you," said the astonished barber, "never before have I been tipped in advance."

"That is not a tip," snarled the customer. "It's hush money."

810 The need to talk to someone finds its expression in everything from friendly confidences, to the confessional, to the psychoanalyst. Recently it has been commercialized by an organization calling itself, The Southern Listening Bureau of Little Rock, Arkansas.

Their advertisement proclaims: "We offer well trained and experienced listeners who will hear you as long as you wish to talk, and without interruptions, for a nominal fee. As our listeners listen, their faces portray interest, pity, fellow feeling, understanding; where called for, they exhibit hate, hope, despair, sorrow or joy. Lawyers, politicians, club leaders, reformers can try their speeches on us. You may talk freely about your business or domestic problems without fear of having any confidence betrayed. Just let off steam into the discreet ears of our experts and feel better."

811 Dr. Johnson was one day in conversation with a very talkative lady, of whom he appeared to take very little notice. "Why, Doctor, I believe you prefer the company of men to that of the ladies."

"Madam," replied he, "I am very fond of the company of ladies; I like their beauty, I like their delicacy, I like their vivacity, and I like their silence."

812 A lady stepped into a taxicab at Grand Central. The driver swung out into traffic, and at the same time asked, "Do you want the radio, lady, or shall we just talk?"

813 A prominent Washington society woman was sitting next to President Coolidge at a smart party.

"Oh, Mr. President," she said gushingly, "you are so silent. I made a bet today that I could get more than two words out of you."

"You lose," the President replied.

814 Samuel Rogers had a reputation for quiet, venomous wit. Knight was a great talker and a bad listener. When Rogers was told that Knight was going deaf, he remarked: "It is from lack of practice."

815 It was Mark Twain, on a balmy day of Spring, who was hailed by every passing acquaintance with some observation on the state of the weather. Upon arriving at his destination and being greeted with, "Nice day, Mr. Twain," he replied drily, "Yes, I've heard it very highly spoken of."

816 When Coolidge was Vice-President, he was invited to attend many dinners. Always he was the despair of his hostess because of his utter disregard of the art of conversation. One lady felt that she had solved this problem by placing him next to Alice Roosevelt Longworth who was a most brilliant conversationalist.

Mrs. Longworth began to chat in her usual charming fashion, but failed to elicit any response from the silent Mr. Coolidge. Finally, exasperated out of her generally calm demeanor, she acidly asked, "You go to so many dinners. They must bore you a great deal."

Calmly Coolidge replied without lifting his eyes from the contemplation of the plate before him, "Well, a man has to eat somewhere."

817 A debutante went to visit her grandmother. The old lady was distressed by what she considered the girl's wild and unruly manners and speech. Not wishing to appear stern and demanding she decided nevertheless that she should reprimand her granddaughter.

One evening as they were sitting together the old lady said gently, "Dear, there are just two words I want you to refrain from using. One is 'swell' and the other is 'lousy.'"

"All right," replied the debutante agreeably, "What are they?"

818 Diderot came to Catherine the Great in 1773 and remained for five months. On certain afternoons he conversed with her from three to five. "I listened more than I talked," she said. Discoursing vehemently, he would gradually draw his chair up to her knees. In his excitement he would pound them until they were blue, compelling her to place before her a table on which he could vent his punctuation.

> RELATED SUBJECTS: *Dullness* 186-195; *Long-Windedness* 341-363; *Stuttering* 711-713; *Speeches* 756-782; *Gossip* 821-826

> SEE ALSO: *Eating* 9; *Borrowing* 124; *Brevity* 134; *Long-Windedness* 358, 359; *Rudeness* 518; *Beauty* 664; *Parties* 745; *Newspapers* 1240

GOSSIP

821 "How this world is inclined to slander," said a maiden lady to an English nobleman. "Can you believe it, sir, some of my malicious acquaintances reported that I had twins."

"Madam, I make it a rule to believe only half of what I hear!" replied his lordship.

822 Mrs. Graham Fair Vanderbilt had been displeased by a number of things which the late Maury Paul had written about her in his Cholly Knickerbocker column.

Upon meeting him one time at a night club, she said, "You're a rude, scurrilous man."

"Yes," confessed Paul, "I am. But I'd rather make a living that way than by selling bonds."

823 Once when Mme. de Staël was praising the British Constitution, Talleyrand explained in an aside: "Above all she admires the habeas corpus."

824 The society gossip purveyor, Maury H. B. Paul, had been writing a number of familiar and impertinent items about Mrs. Cornelius Vanderbilt for many years. Then one day Vincent Astor unexpectedly introduced Paul to the mighty lady. With a gasp he said, "I'm not really the disreputable person you think I am, Mrs. Vanderbilt."

Mrs. Vanderbilt replied, "My dear Mr. Paul, from what you have been writing about me, I was under the impression that you thought I was the disreputable person."

825 The late Maury H. B. Paul, better known as Cholly Knickerbocker, in the course of his career as a society columnist had frequently aroused the ire of those about whom he had written. Every so often some such individual confronted him in a public place and demanded, "Just what did you mean by what you wrote about me?"

Mr. Paul had found a standard answer to this demand. He blandly retorted, "Just what do you think I meant," which invariably silenced further discussion.

826 Due to the exigencies of his position as purveyor of tasty news items on the doings of the upper crust, Maury Paul, widely known as Cholly Knickerbocker, had incurred many enemies. Toward these he felt no rancor.

He once said, "Even when people snub me I feel like saying to them, 'Thank you for just existing. I wouldn't be wearing solid gold garter clasps if it weren't for you.'"

RELATED SUBJECTS: *Discretion* 181-182; *Talking* 806-818
SEE ALSO: *Honesty* 288; *Honor* 298

NAMES

831 John Barrymore, at the height of his fame, went into the shop of a swanky men's clothier in Hollywood. He left an order

and started to leave.

"Your name, please?" the clerk asked.

The Barrymore brows arched high, "Barrymore," he replied coldly.

"Which Barrymore, please?"

Coolness turned to solid ice. "Ethel," he said.

832　When George Burns assumed his professional name, George Jessel remarked to him, "Well, Georgie, you can change your name to Burns but you will never get the salami out of your stomach."

833　Says Walter Winchell, "Shortly before our son was born, I remarked in the newspaper that if our new baby was a boy he would be named 'Reid' Winchell, and if a girl, 'Sue' Winchell. To which a reader-heckler telegraphed, 'Boy or girl it should be called Lynch Winchell.' "

834　A stranger in town passed the grocery store bearing on its window the name of its proprietor, "A. Swindler." Amused, the stranger entered the store and asked the grocer if he did not think that his full name would make a better impression. "No," said the grocer, "it would be worse. My first name is Adam."

835　At one time both Montague Matthews and Matthew Montague were members of the British House of Commons. Mr. Matthews was a big, powerful giant of a man. Mr. Montague was thin and emaciated. The Speaker frequently confused the two.

"I can't understand it," said Montague Matthews. "There's as much difference between us as there is between a horse chestnut and a chestnut horse."

836　One time, talking with Lord Beaverbrook, Sinclair Lewis kept on saying, "What do you think, Max?" Beaverbrook grew tired of this form of address after the eighth time and suddenly snapped at him, "What do you think, Sinc?"

837　A man named Longworth was once presented to Longfellow, and remarked upon the similarity of their names. "Yes," said Longfellow, "and I believe the advantage is yours, for as Pope has said, 'Worth makes the man, the want of it, the fellow.' "

838　"I've made up my mind what we'll call the baby," the young mother announced. "We'll call her Eulalia."

The father did not care for this choice but he was shrewd. "That's fine," he said. "The first girl I loved was named Eulalia, and it will evoke pleasant memories." The wife was silent for a moment. "We'll call her Mary after my mother," she said.

RELATED SUBJECTS: *Family* 946-950

SEE ALSO: *Reputation* 77; *Rudeness* 512; *Tact* 590; *Marriage* 888; *Small Children* 966; *Debt* 2171

WOMEN

841 When Madame de Staël published her celebrated novel "Delphine," she was supposed to have painted herself in the person of the heroine, and M. Talleyrand in that of an elderly lady, who is one of the principal characters.

"They tell me," said he, the first time he met her, "that we are both of us in your novel, in the disguise of women."

842 One day at Mr. Kipling's home in Sussex he read to Edward W. Bok his latest poem, and at its conclusion said: "You can never publish that. The 'Journal' ('The Ladies Home Journal') sisters would break all your windows with the stones they would fire at you. You wouldn't have a whole pane left."

The poem was "The Female of the Species."

843 Edwin Booth was very shy about women. He tells of a harrowing experience that once befell him on a tour, when he had lain down to rest in his room and failed to lock his door. "I heard a sound and opened my eyes. The door was being stealthily opened. I felt it was a woman. I couldn't move. She came in—the most determined woman I ever saw. She was tall, and gaunt, and strange. She couldn't help seeing I was trembling. She came to the bed, looked down upon me. Without smiling she bent over me—kissed me on the mouth. She didn't say a word. She walked out of the room. I never was so frightened in my life. I bolted the door when it was too late, but I'm not over it yet. I've tried to reason it out, but I can't. She was not silly. She looked to be the last woman on earth to care for kissing. I should say she was a hard woman."

RELATED SUBJECTS: *Love* 846-850; *Old Maids* 871-873; *Wife* 921-933; *Mother* 991-993; *Woman's Suffrage* 2051-2052

LOVE—MARRIAGE—FAMILY

LOVE

846   A woman told her husband that she had read "The Art of Love" on purpose to be agreeable to him.

"I would rather have love without art," he said.

847   The witty Oliver Herford has defined a kiss as, "A course of procedure, cunningly devised, for the mutual stoppage of speech at a moment when words are superfluous."

848   When Madame de Staël was writing her memoirs a female friend asked her how she would manage to portray herself and her amours.

"Oh!" answered Madame de Staël, "I shall give only a bust of myself."

849   A French clergyman catechising the youths of his parish, put the first question from the catechism of Heidelberg to a girl: "What is your only consolation in life and in death?"

The poor wench smiled, but did not answer. The priest insisted. "Well then," said she, "since I must tell, it is the young shoemaker of Agneaux Street."

850   A group of actors, Samuel Foote among them, was discussing the marriage of a too well-known woman-about-town, whose pre-marital life had been, to say the least, adventurous.

"It is a very good match that she has made," one of the group observed. "And they say she made to her husband a full confession of all her past affairs." "What honesty she must have had," another remarked. "What courage!" "Yes," put in Foote, "and what a memory!"

RELATED SUBJECTS: *Devotion* 171-173; *Courtship* 851-855; *Engagement* 856-857; *Marriage* 876-888; *Wedding* 891-892; *Honeymoon* 896-898

SEE ALSO: *Kindness* 313; *Long-Windedness* 361; *Infidelity* 901; *Sickness* 1705

COURTSHIP

851   It is said that Edwin C. Hill, the journalist and radio commentator, encountered upon his first arrival in New York an experience that outdoes O. Henry. Looking around the city he took a sight-seeing ride on the Elevated. His eye was attracted by the charming young lady seated across the car from him. In the vicinity of Columbus Circle he had ventured to move over and strike up a conversation with her. They found an astonishing congeniality between them, and pursued the conversation intensely.

At last they reached City Hall; left the train, and, going over to the City Hall, got married.

852   One of the most unusual beginnings of a romance in the world is the well-known case of the great Wagnerian tenor, Lauritz Melchior. When the singer was a young music student he was sitting in the garden of his pension in Munich, studying a role. According to his own story, he sang the lines, "Come to me, my love, on the wings of light," when, to his utter astonishment, a young lady literally dropped out of the sky at his feet. The heavenly visitant was Maria Hacker, a Bavarian actress who had been doing a stunt for a movie thriller. She had parachuted from a plane right into his arms. They were married.

853   One day Nicholas Schenck, movie millionaire, about to board Tom Meighan's yacht, saw a slip of a girl standing on the edge of the wharf.

"For some inexplicable reason," Mr. Schenck recalls, "I had an uncontrollable impulse to push her into the water. To my horror—I did. I had no idea if she could swim. I expected an infuriated young woman. Instead, she came to the surface, blinked the water out of her eyes and smiled a brilliant smile.

"By God!" I said to myself, "that's the girl I'm going to marry!" And he did.

854   When Aaron Burr was seventy-eight Mme. Jumel attracted him. One day, as he was about to lead her in to dinner he said:

"I give you my hand, madam; my heart has long been yours."

Much fluttered and no less flattered she uttered a sort of "No" which was not likely to discourage a man like Aaron Burr.

"I shall come to you before very long," he said, "accompanied by a clergyman; and then you will give me your hand because I want it."

855 Dr. Samuel Johnson, when paying court to Mrs. Porter, confessed that his family was not without stain, as he had had an uncle who had been hanged.

Mrs. Porter, with a woman's true tact, set the good Doctor's mind at rest by assuring him that, although this was not the case with her, she had in her family at least fifty who deserved hanging.

RELATED SUBJECTS: *Love* 846-850; *Engagement* 856-857; *Flirtation* 861-863

SEE ALSO: *Reputation* 76; *Patriotism* 406; *Rudeness* 516; *Homeliness* 656; *Fatness* 682; *Stores* 2072; *Juries* 2514; *Detectives* 2557

ENGAGEMENT

856 When George IV of England went to meet his future bride, Princess Caroline of Brunswick, he kissed her hand gallantly, and then, suddenly recoiling, he whispered to one of his friends:

"For God's sake, George, give me a glass of brandy!"

857 In breaking his engagement to Agathe von Siebold, Brahms wrote her:

"I could not love thee, dear, so much if I did not love my freedom more."

RELATED SUBJECTS: *Love* 846-850; *Courtship* 851-855; *Wedding* 891-892

FLIRTATION

861 Gilbert Stuart, the early American portrait painter, once met a lady on the street in Boston who saluted him with,

"Ah! Mr. Stuart, I have just seen your miniature, and kissed it, because it was so much like you."

"And did it kiss you in return?"

"Of course not!" she answered, laughing.

"Then," said Stuart, "it was not like me."

862 Near eighty, Aaron Burr, after he was married to Mme. Jumel, engaged in flirting with the country girls near the Jumel mansion.

One day the postmaster at what was then the village of Harlem was surprised to see Mrs. Burr drive up before the post office in an open carriage. He found her in a violent temper and with an enormous horse-pistol on each cushion at her side.

"What do you wish, Madam?" said he.

"What do I wish?" she cried. "Let me get at that villain Aaron Burr!"

863 Talleyrand once said, "Mme. de Genlis, in order to avoid the scandal of coquetry, always yielded easily."

RELATED SUBJECTS: *Discretion* 181-182; *Love* 846-850; *Courtship* 851-855; *Infidelity* 901-904

SEE ALSO: *Learned Men* 1082

FRIENDSHIP

866 Anacharsis, coming to Athens, knocked at Solon's door, and told him that he, being a stranger, was come to be his guest, and contract a friendship with him; and Solon replying, "It is better to make friends at home," Anacharsis replied, "Then you that are at home make a friendship with me."

867 Thousands of appeals for pardon came to Lincoln from soldiers involved in military discipline. Each appeal was as a rule supported by letters from influential people. One day a single sheet came before him, an appeal from a soldier without any supporting documents.

"What!" exclaimed the President, "has this man no friends?"

"No, sir, not one," said the adjutant.

"Then," said Lincoln, "I will be his friend."

RELATED SUBJECTS: *Devotion* 171-173; *Love* 846-850

SEE ALSO: *Vanity* 624; *Authors* 1198

OLD MAIDS

871   At a recent dinner the Reverend Dr. Minot J. Savage told a story of a lady who was asked "Do you ever think of getting married?"

"Think?" she answered, with asperity, "I worry."

872   Maude Adams, the famous actress, was in her dressing room preparing for a performance. Her old colored maid was dressing her hair when, without warning, she said:

"When you gwine to git married, Miss Maudie?"

"Oh," replied the star laughingly, "I don't think I'll ever get married."

"Well," said the old servant, in a soothing tone as though to comfort her mistress, "they do say old maids is the happies' kind after they quits strugglin'."

873   It was the maid's day off and the lady of the house was doing her own marketing. On her way home she happened to meet the girl who was wheeling a baby carriage which contained a smiling set of twins. Stopping to pet the children she casually asked the maid, "And whose children are these?"

"Mine, ma'am."

"Yours, Sally, why I always thought you were an old maid."

"Well, ma'am, I is. But I ain't a fussy old maid."

RELATED SUBJECTS: *Gossip* 821-826; *Women* 841-843

MARRIAGE

876   When Socrates was asked whether it was better for a man to marry or remain single, he answered:

"Let him take which course he will, he will repent of it."

877   Archbishop Ryan was one time attending confirmation in a small parish. The local pastor was giving the preparatory questions to one rather frightened little girl. He asked her to define the state of matrimony. "It's a state of terrible torment which those who enter are compelled to undergo for a time to prepare them for a better world," she replied.

"No, no," chided the rector, "that's not matrimony. That's the definition of Purgatory."

"Leave her alone," said the Archbishop, "perhaps the child has been shown the light."

878   Miss Drummond, the famous preacher among the Quakers some time ago, was asked if the spirit had never inspired her with thoughts of marriage.

"No, friend," said she, "but the flesh often has."

879   Like many tourists, Lewis Cotlow, president of the Adventurers' Club, wondered why Mexican peons always ride on burros while their wives walk along behind. Finally he stopped a peasant and asked him the reason. The Mexican, looking very surprised, replied, "But Señor, my wife doesn't own a burro."

880   Lord Lansdowne was speaking to Samuel Rogers about the marriage of a friend they both knew. "She has made a good match," Lansdowne ventured to remark.

"I am not so sure about that," returned Rogers dubiously.

"No, why not? All her friends approve it."

"Then," said Rogers, "she is able to satisfy everyone. Her friends are pleased and her enemies are delighted."

881   A gentleman who had been very unhappy in marriage married a second time, immediately after his first wife died. Dr. Johnson said of him: "His conduct was the triumph of hope over experience."

882   George Ade was fond of telling the following story, "I was sitting with a little girl of eight one afternoon. She looked up from the copy of Hans Andersen she was reading, and asked innocently, 'Does m-i-r-a-g-e spell marriage, Mr. Ade?' 'Yes, my child,' said I."

883   An old gentleman, who had never attended a football game, allowed himself to be persuaded by a fan to accompany him. "Now then," said his friend, as the game was about to begin, "you're going to see more excitement here for a couple of dollars than you ever saw before." "I doubt it," said the old timer, "that's all I paid for my marriage license."

884   At a Hollywood party the guests were playing a game which required each one to write an epitaph for himself. A much married actress was sitting next to Robert Benchley and complained that she did not know what to write for herself.

Benchley said, "I'll write it for you." He did so, and passed on her slip with his to be read out. The epitaph when read was, "At last she sleeps alone."

885   A celebrated wit was asked why he did not marry a young lady to whom he was much attached. "I know not," he replied, "except the great regard we have for each other."

886   A widower in his great bereavement, expressed his feelings by having engraved on the tombstone of his wife the line, "My light has gone out." As he was about to marry again, he asked the advice of Bishop Henry C. Potter as to whether or not he should have the inscription erased, as it seemed at variance with the new conditions. "Oh, no," said the bishop, "I wouldn't have it taken off; just put underneath it, 'I have struck another match.'"

887   Socrates' marital difficulties are well known. Out of them he coined this sage advice: "By all means marry. If you get a good wife, you will become very happy; if you get a bad one you will become a philosopher—and that is good for every man."

888   Into the office came a negress to collect her weekly wages. In signing for them, she drew a circle.

"How is it, Mandy," she was asked, "that you make a circle instead of your usual cross?"

"Why," she said, "I done got married agin and changed my name."

RELATED SUBJECTS: *Courtship* 851-855; *Engagement* 856-857; *Wedding* 891-892; *Honeymoon* 896-898; *Divorce* 906-911; *Husband* 916-918; *Wife* 921-933; *Mother-in-Law* 936-937; *Polygamy* 941-943

SEE ALSO: *Devotion* 173; *Will Power* 631; *Love* 850; *Babies* 959; *Instrumentalists* 1355; *Actors* 1427; *Sunday School* 1571; *Woman's Suffrage* 2052

WEDDING

891   Bridegrooms are known for their nervousness; but here is one who managed to retain his diplomacy in the midst of all

the hurry and tension of the ceremony and the departure for the honeymoon trip.

Finally, seated in the car which was to take them to the railroad station, the bride asked if he had remembered the tickets. He reached into his pockets and pulled out—one ticket. Hurriedly gathering his thoughts, remembering his flustered feelings when he had gone to purchase the tickets, he said, "Dear me. Look, only one ticket. You see, darling, I forgot all about myself."

892   Here is Marie Antoinette's rather dreary account of her wedding and honeymoon, from her diary:

Sunday, 13—Left Versailles. Supper and slept at Compignée, at the house of M. de Saint-Florentin.

Monday, 14—Interview with Mme. la Dauphine.

Tuesday, 15—Supped at La Muette. Slept at Versailles.

Wednesday, 16—My marriage. Apartment in the gallery. Royal banquet in the Salle d' Opera.

Thursday, 17—Opera of "Perseus."

Friday, 18—Stag-hunt. Met at La Belle Image. Took one.

Saturday, 19—Dress-ball in the Salle d' Opera. Fireworks.

Thursday, 31—I had indigestion.

RELATED SUBJECTS: *Marriage* 876-888; *Honeymoon* 896-898

SEE ALSO: *Vanity* 621

HONEYMOON

896   When Cary Grant, the film actor, married Barbara Hutton, the couple did not depart for a wedding trip because it was necessary for Grant to report on the lot for the filming of "Once Upon a Honeymoon."

897   After a whirlwind courtship, the loving couple had eloped and married. After a few days of the honeymoon, the fact came out that the wife was a snake-charmer. Slightly appalled, the husband said in reproachful astonishment, "How is it that you never told me you were a snake-charmer?"

Said his wife, "You never asked me."

898　While on her honeymoon the young bride had gone out alone one afternoon to make a few purchases. Coming back to the hotel where she had been accustomed to trustfully following her husband's guidance, she got off the elevator at the wrong floor. She went down the corridor until she reached what she supposed to be the door of her room. Finding it locked and having no key with her she knocked upon it and called out softly, "Honey, oh Honey."

There was no response. After a while she knocked again, calling somewhat more loudly, "Honey, oh Honey."

When this had occurred a number of times, a blatant male voice roared out from within, saying, "Madam, this is not a beehive, it's a bathroom."

RELATED SUBJECTS: *Marriage* 876-888; *Wedding* 891-892

INFIDELITY

901　Pauline Bonaparte was in love with Fréron, a commissioner of the Convention. She wrote him:

"I love you always and most passionately. I love you forever, my beautiful idol, my heart, my appealing lover. I love you, love you, love you, the most loved of lovers, and I swear never to love any one else!"

Soon after she fell in love with Junot who became a field marshal.

902　Charles Coghlan, the actor, was known not only for his great wit and resourcefulness, but also for his fondness for the ladies. One day his wife left him to go on a week-end trip. She had scarcely left the house when Coghlan contacted a very charming young lady, inviting her to come to his home for dinner.

Mrs. Coghlan, forgetting something of importance, returned home just in time to see her husband help the girl from a cab. No whit dismayed, Coghlan blandly introduced the two women. "My dear," said he, turning to his wife, "allow me to present Miss Johnson. Miss Johnson, Mrs. Coghlan."

The two ladies glared speechlessly at each other, while Coghlan said:

"I know you two ladies have ever so many things you want

to say to each other, so I will ask to be excused."

Whereupon he lifted his hat, stepped into the cab and was driven away.

903 When Shelley was undoubtedly carrying on an affair with Jane Williams, he got his obsession of death by water mixed up with his search for the absolute in terms of women. He took Jane rowing far out to sea. Suddenly he went into a trance, then leapt forward and cried: "Now let us solve the great mystery together." Jane, who was a brilliant woman and one of the most congenial of his "sisters," had to exercise the greatest tact to keep him from upsetting the boat, and he did upset it after they were in shallow water.

904 Percy Bysshe Shelley, in a letter to his wife, telling her he had eloped with Mary Godwin, and asking her to join them:

"Please bring my flute."

RELATED SUBJECTS: *Flirtation 861-863; Divorce 906-911*

SEE ALSO: *Flirtation 862*

DIVORCE

906 "A large number of divorces indicate that America is still the land of the free," someone observed.

"Yes," said his friend, "but the steady level of the marriage rate shows that it's still the home of the brave."

907 When Mrs. Pierre Riendeau, 79 years old, asked for a legal separation from her 86-year-old husband, the judge asked how long they had been married. "Sixty years," she replied.

"Why are you seeking a separation after all this time?" the court asked.

"Enough's enough," she said.

908 After the manner of Hollywood's "civilized" social practices, Lewis Browne, the writer, and his ex-wife appeared together at a party and listened to an announcement of their divorce by a radio commentator. Leopold Stokowski was among the guests, and said to Browne, "It's very indecent of you to be having such a good time. At least when my wife and I were divorced, we quarreled."

909 Ilka Chase likes to tell a story of the aftermath of her divorce from Louis Calhern. His next wife was Julia Hoyt. Miss Chase, going through a trunk, found a box of handsome, engraved cards, bearing simply the name, Mrs. Louis Calhern. Feeling it a shame that they should go to waste, she wrapped them up and sent them to her successor, with the little note: "Dear Julia, I hope these reach you in time."

910 After the death of Jane Seymour, Henry VIII had some difficulty in getting another wife. His first offer was to the Duchess Dowager of Milan, but her answer was, "She had but one head: if she had two, one should have been at his service."

911 Hollywood is a great place. To it came a young man from a small Western town who succeeded in making himself a noted screen lover. His own town became famous as his birthplace. Tourists, passing through, would invariably remark upon its distinguished former citizen. "Tell me," one passer-by asked of the old codger who was station master, "does he ever come back?"

"Sure, sure," said the old timer, "once in a while he comes back for quite a stay. Five times he's been back."

"Is that so? Came back for a stay, did he? And did he ever bring his wife?"

"Yes, sir, each time, and five prettier girls you never see."

RELATED SUBJECTS: *Marriage* 876-888; *Infidelity* 901-904

HUSBAND

916 When General Leclerc, unloved husband of Pauline Bonaparte, died in Haiti, she had him placed in a costly coffin and cut off her beautiful hair and buried it with him.

"What a touching tribute to her dead husband!" said someone to her brother Napoleon.

The Emperor smiled cynically:

"Hm! Of course she knows that her hair will come in longer and thicker for being cropped."

917 Henry William Anglesea, a British peer and soldier who died in 1854, was angrily beating his wife. She pointed to a house maid and cried out, "How much happier is that wench than I am!"

Her husband immediately kicked the maid downstairs and then said, "Well there is at least one grievance removed."

918 Late one night a drunken husband, after spending his whole time at his club, set out for home. "Well," said he to himself, "if I find my wife up I'll scold her; what business has she to sit up, wasting fire and light, eh? And if I find her in bed, I'll scold her; what right has she to go to bed before I get home?"

RELATED SUBJECTS: *Marriage* 876-888; *Wife* 921-933; *Mother-in-Law* 936-937; *Father* 986-990

SEE ALSO: *Prayer* 1607

WIFE

921 Of a lady, more insipid than offensive, Dr. Johnson once said, "She has some softness indeed; but so has a pillow. For my part, I do not envy a fellow one of those honeysuckle wives; as they are but creepers at best, and commonly destroy the tree they so tenderly cling about."

922 When surprise was expressed at his choice of a wife, Talleyrand replied: "A clever wife often compromises her husband; a stupid one only compromises herself."

923 "Well," said Lincoln on a certain occasion, "I feel about that a good deal as a man whom I will call 'Jones' whom I once knew, did about his wife. He was one of your meek men, and had the reputation of being badly henpecked. At last one day his wife was seen switching him out of the house. A day or two afterwards, a man met him in the street, and said:

" 'Jones, I have always stood up for you, as you know; but I am not going to do it any longer. Any man who will stand quietly and take a switching from his wife deserves to be horse-whipped.'

"Jones looked up with a wink, patting his friend on the back.

" 'Now don't,' said he; 'why it didn't hurt me any; and you've no idea what a power of good it did Sarah Ann!' "

924   Loyalty sometimes proves embarrassing. A case in point is that of the wife whose husband was unusually late, who wired to five of his friends, "Jack not home. Is he spending the night with you?" The unfortunate Jack arrived home shortly afterwards, and was followed by five telegrams all saying, "Yes."

925   By mistake a letter directed to a newly married motion picture star was delivered to the house of a poor workingman. Upon being opened, it proved to contain a threat that unless a substantial sum of money was paid, his wife would be kidnapped. The workingman immediately wrote a reply, "Sir, I don't have much money, but I'm mighty interested in your proposition."

926   A man, being suspected of impotency, met a friend one day, who had railed him on it, to whom he said, "My good Sir, for all your wit, my wife was yesterday brought to bed."

"What of that," said his friend, "nobody ever suspected your wife."

927   A person told Samuel Foote he had laid out a thousand pounds upon his dear wife.

"Indeed," said Foote, "she is truly your dear wife."

928   Cato, the elder, having buried his wife, married a young woman: his son came to him and said: "Sir, in what have I offended that you have brought a step-mother into your house?"

"Nay, son," answered the old man, "quite the contrary; you please me so well that I should be glad to have more such."

929   A niggardly farmer lost his wife and scrimped as much as he could on each phase of the funeral expenses down to the bitter end, when he lingered in the graveyard after the mourners had gone, and asked the gravedigger, "How much do I owe you?"

"Ten dollars," said the gravedigger, who was just beginning to fill in the grave.

"That's overmuch for such light sandy soil," said the farmer speculatively.

"Light sandy soil or rich loamy soil, ten dollars," said the gravedigger firmly, "or up she comes."

The farmer hastily paid.

930 A French general's wife, whose tongue-lashing ability was far-famed, demanded that an old servant, who had served with her husband during the wars, be dismissed.

"Jacques," said the general, "go to your room and pack your trunk and leave—depart!" The old Frenchman clasped his hands to his head with dramatic joy. "Me—I can go!" he exclaimed in a very ecstasy of gratitude. Then suddenly his manner changed as with the utmost compassion he added: "But you, my poor general, you must stay."

931 When the poet Milton was blind he married a shrew. The Duke of Buckingham called her a rose. "I am no judge of colors," replied Milton, "and it may be so, for I feel the thorns daily."

932 A celebrated French preacher, in a sermon upon the duty of wives, said: "I see in this congregation a woman who has been guilty of the sin of disobedience to her husband, and in order to point her out to universal condemnation, I will fling my breviary at her head."

He lifted his book, and every female head instantly ducked.

933 "I have no sympathy," bellowed the judge, "for a man who beats his wife."

"That's right, your Honor," said the policeman who stood beside the culprit. "Any man who can beat his wife don't need sympathy."

RELATED SUBJECTS: *Marriage* 876-888; *Husband* 916-918; *Mother-in-Law* 936-937; *Mother* 991-993

SEE ALSO: *Profanity* 66; *Absent-Mindedness* 89; *Boners* 116; *Patience* 391; *Shrewdness* 541; *Will Power* 631; *Homeliness* 655; *Love* 846; *Authors* 1180; *Evangelists* 1516; *Doctors* 1673; *Deathbed Scenes* 1765; *Banks* 2155; *Trials* 2478

MOTHER-IN-LAW

936 One of the witticisms of Lord Russell of Killowen was his answer to a question from a distinguished counsel who asked

what the heaviest penalty for bigamy was.

"Two mothers-in-law," said Russell promptly.

937   When Marshal Foch visited the Grand Canyon, Colonel John R. White, who spoke French fluently, hung breathlessly on the Marshal's words as he turned to him after a long scrutiny of the depths below. "Now," thought the Colonel, "I shall hear something worthy of passing along to my children and my grandchildren."

Observed the Marshal, "What a beautiful place to drop one's mother-in-law!"

RELATED SUBJECTS: *Marriage* 876-888; *Husband* 916-918; *Wife* 921-933

POLYGAMY

941   A story is told about Mrs. Amos Pinchot who dreamed one night that she had written a poem more beautiful and more fundamentally profound than any ever written before. She had awakened in one of those semi-trance-like states in the middle of the night; fumbled for a pencil at her bedside table and written it down.

When she finally awoke in the morning, she had at first forgotten the matter. Suddenly all came back to her as she saw the scrawl on the table beside her. She picked it up to see the masterpiece that she had written in her semi-conscious state. It was:

> Hogamus Higamus
> Men are Polygamous
> Higamus Hogamus
> Women Monogamous.

942   A Mormon acquaintance once inveigled Mark Twain into an argument on the issue of polygamy. After he had been beaten about the ears with long and tedious expositions justifying the practice, the climax was capped by the Mormon's demand that he cite any passage of Scripture expressly forbidding polygamy.

"Nothing easier," Mark replied. " 'No man can serve two masters.' "

943   In his old age, after he quit the warpath, Quanah Parker, the famous chief of the Comanches, adopted many of the white man's ways. But in one respect he clung to the custom of his fathers. He continued to be a polygamist.

He was a friend and admirer of Theodore Roosevelt and on one occasion when Roosevelt was touring Oklahoma he drove out to Parker's camp to see him. With pride Parker pointed out that he lived in a house like a white man, that his children went to a white man's school, and he himself dressed like a white man. Whereupon Roosevelt was moved to preach him a sermon on the subject of morality. "See here chief, why don't you set your people a better example? A white man has only one wife, he's allowed only one at a time. Here you are living with five squaws. Why don't you give up four of them and remain faithful to the fifth?"

Parker stood still a moment, considering the proposition. Then he answered: "You are my great white father, and I will do as you wish—on one condition."

"What's the condition?" asked Roosevelt.

"You pick out the one I am to live with and then you go kill the other four."

RELATED SUBJECTS: *Marriage* 876-888

SEE ALSO: *Mother-in-Law* 936

FAMILY

946   Speaking of his ancestry Lincoln once humorously remarked, "I don't know who my grandfather was, but I am much more concerned to know what his grandson will be."

947   The elder Dumas was once interviewed by an enterprising reporter, who, like many other admirers of the novelist, was curious about his ancestry. "Is it true that you are a quadroon, M. Dumas?" he asked.

"I am, sir," Dumas replied.

"So your father—?"

"Was a mulatto."

"And your grandfather—?"

"Was a Negro."

Dumas' patience was running out but the reporter was a

bold man. He continued: "And may I inquire who your great-grandfather was?"

"A baboon, sir!" thundered Dumas. "A baboon! My ancestry begins where yours ends!"

948　The story is told that Mark Twain was once a guest of an Englishman who took him, with some pride, into a manorial hall hung with a huge tapestry depicting the judging of King Charles the First. The host placed his fingers with great pride upon the figure of one of the obscure clerks of the court and said, "An ancestor of mine."

Twain, always offended by such ostentation, casually put his finger upon one of the judges seated on the tribunal and remarked, "An ancestor of mine but it is no matter, I have others."

949　To a man who had proudly said, "My ancestors came over in the Mayflower," Will Rogers retorted, "My ancestors were waiting on the beach."

950　Mark Twain, whenever confronted by people who were haughty about their ancestry, was fond of saying, "My grandfather was cut down in the prime of his life. My grandmother always used to say that if he had been cut down fifteen minutes earlier, he could have been resuscitated."

> RELATED SUBJECTS: *Marriage* 876-888; *Children* 951-952; *Father* 986-990; *Mother* 991-993; *Home Life* 996-1001

> SEE ALSO: *Physical Characteristics* 648; *Kings* 1980; *Insurance* 2137; *Poverty* 2208

CHILDREN

951　There is a legend about the fervent message George Bernard Shaw received from Isadora Duncan expressing the opinion that by every eugenical principle they should have a child.

"Think what a child it would be," she said, "with my body and your brain."

Shaw sent the following response, discouraging the proposition, "Think how unfortunate it would be if the child were to have my body and your brain."

952 Two Irishmen were discussing their families. One was boasting about his seven sons, saying that he had never had any trouble with any of them:

"Yes, indade," he said, "they are just about the finest boys in the world. An' would ye believe it, I nivver laid violent hands on any one of 'em except in self-defense."

RELATED SUBJECTS: *Babies* 956-962; *Small Children* 966-977; *Adoption* 981; *Father* 986-990; *Mother* 991-993; *Births, Birthdays* 1011-1015

SEE ALSO: *Age* 674; *Mother* 993; *Battles* 2383

BABIES

956 Mrs. K., after expressing her love for her children, added tenderly, "And how do you like babies, Mr. Lamb?"

His answer, immediate, almost precipitate, was, "B-b-boiled, ma'am."

957 When a baby in a crowded Washington horse car was screaming, Walt Whitman took it from its mother into his own arms; the infant stared at him a long time, then snuggled against him and fell asleep. Presently the conductor got off the car to get his supper, and Whitman acted as conductor the rest of the trip, still holding the sleeping baby.

958 Eleanore Duse, the great actress, once offered to look after the year-old baby of some friends while the family went for a walk.

"What will you do if she cries?" they asked.

"Do? I'll sing to her," said the resourceful Duse. "I have lots of tricks to entertain babies."

When the parents returned, they found the baby sitting quietly in her carriage, her eyes fixed with a hypnotic stare upon the sofa. There lay the great actress, her head drooping, her mouth open, her eyes shut. She was snoring—regularly, sonorously snoring.

Slowly she opened he eyes. "Sh!" she said. "If I stop for a second, she'll cry."

Then she explained: "I sang for her; I danced for her; I made faces at her; I acted the whole of 'Paolo and Francesca' to her,

and she hated it all. But the snoring—from the first faint sign—
she loved it!"

---

959   Mme. de Staël (to Napoleon): General who is the woman
you would love the most?

Napoleon: My own.

Mme. de Staël: But what woman would you admire the
most?

Napoleon: The best housekeeper.

Mme. de Staël: But with you, who would be the first among
women?

Napoleon: She who has had the most babies.

---

960   During gold rush days in California, a lady took her infant to the theatre one evening and it started crying just as the
orchestra began to play.

"Stop those fiddles and let the baby cry," called a man in the
pit. "I haven't heard such a sound in ten years!"

The audience applauded the sentiment wildly, the orchestra
was stopped, and the baby continued its performance amid un-
bounded enthusiasm.

---

961   The six-year-old wandered into the room where the
brand new baby was being nursed. Because of her interest in
the process, the mother carefully explained how mother animals
furnish milk for their babies, even the human species. The child
was satisfied on all but one point. "But Mother," she demanded,
"is it pasteurized?"

---

962   Burdened with the care of a new baby the young mother
sent her little brother to the department store to get some things
for the new arrival.

He managed to get everything without too much trouble.
The last item on his list was diapers. He went to the counter
where they were sold, stated his wishes, and in the space of a
few minutes the salesgirl returned with a bundle.

"That will be sixty cents for the diapers and two cents for the
tax."

"Ah, never mind the tacks," said the youngster, "Sis puts
them on the baby with safety pins."

RELATED SUBJECTS: *Children* 951-952; *Births, Birthdays*
1011-1015

SEE ALSO: *Names* 838; *Old Maids* 873; *Actors* 1412; *Church Services* 1537

SMALL CHILDREN

966   When he was in nursery school Woody, the young son of Heywood Broun, was constantly annoyed by grown-up visitors to whom he had been pointed out, who kept coming up to him and asking in saccharine tones, "And whose little boy are you?"

To one such inquirer, when his patience was exhausted, Woody peremptorily replied, "You know damned well whose little boy I am!"

967   Themistocles had a son who was the darling of his mother. "This little fellow," said Themistocles, "is the sovereign of all Greece."

"How so?" said a friend.

"Why, he governs his mother, his mother governs me, I govern the Athenians, and the Athenians govern all Greece."

968   Napoleon the Third was practising a Spartan method of education for the little five-year-old Louis Napoleon.

One day, in pursuance of this course, at Biarritz the child was given a swimming lesson by being tossed head first into the water. He was quite terrified and was severely reproached for this. He, a corporal, who could face a loaded cannon without wincing, and yet was afraid of the water!

"Well," whimpered little Louis, "I am in command of the cannon but I am not in command of the sea."

969   Generally Byron suffered a moody and irritable childhood, between his cruel nurse whom he hated and feared, and his eccentric and tempestuous mother. In his fourth year he bit a large piece out of a china saucer "in a silent rage." Coming into the title at ten, he burst into tears when first called "dominus" at school.

970   The late Sir Josiah Stamp, the economist, was fond of a story about a Parliamentary candidate who approached a house in his constituency and saw two small children of identical size and appearance standing hand in hand before the cottage door. Jovially he asked them if they were twins.

"No, sir," they answered.

"You're brothers, aren't you?" he inquired.

"Yes," they said.

"Well, how old are you?"

"We're both five."

"Well, my goodness, if you're both five and you're brothers, you must be twins."

"Please, sir," said one of them, "we're triplets. Billie's in-doors."

971 The little young lady of the house, by way of punishment for some minor misdemeanor, was compelled to eat her dinner alone at a little table in a corner of the dining room. The rest of the family paid no attention to her presence until they heard her audibly delivering Grace over her own repast, with the words, "I thank Thee Lord for preparing a table before me in the presence of mine enemies."

972 A mother was reproving her little girl one day, in the presence of Degas, for making mistakes in spelling.

"Why do mistakes in spelling matter?" the child protested.

"Why do they matter? Because they do, and it is very naughty in a little girl to make them, isn't it Monsieur Degas?"

"Very naughty," agreed Degas.

Then when the mother had left them, Degas said to the child: "Which would you like best: to know how to spell or have a box of candy?"

"Candy!" cried the little girl without hesitation.

"Well, so would I," replied Degas.

973 "I like to hear a child cry," jocosely said the Abbé Morold. "Why?"

"Because then there is some hope of his being sent away."

974 In animated conversation, the adults of the family and their guests around the dinner table had completely forgotten for the time being the presence of four-year-old Dorothy, who had been automatically excluded. After a time she tentatively plucked at her mother's sleeve, and asked, "Remember me?"

975 A very small boy spoke at the breakfast table about a dream he had had the night before. "Johnny," asked his mother, "do you know what dreams are?"

"Sure," he said, "moving pictures that you see when you're asleep."

976 A certain small boy had tumbled into bed, leaving his room in a characteristic state of disorder. His mother, coming in to bid him Good-Night, chided gently, saying, "Now, I wonder who it was who didn't hang up his clothes before going to sleep."

"Adam," said the little boy, and promptly pulled the covers over his head.

977 Mark Twain used to tell a pathetic story of his childhood. It seems, according to the story, that Mark was born twins. He and his twin looked so much alike, that no one, not even their mother, could tell them apart. One day, while the nurse was bathing them, one of them slipped in the bathtub and was drowned. No one ever knew which twin it was that was drowned—"And therein," says Mark, "was the tragedy. Everyone thought I was the one that lived, but I wasn't. It was my brother who lived. I was the one that was drowned."

> RELATED SUBJECTS: *Children* 951-952; *Babies* 956-962; *Births, Birthdays* 1011-1015

> SEE ALSO: *Absent-Mindedness* 84; *Greed* 272; *Quick Thinking* 478, 479; *Shrewdness* 540; *Homeliness* 652; *Fatness* 690; *Marriage* 882; *Babies* 961; *Mother* 991; *Birthdays* 1014; *Schools* 1046, 1047, 1050; *School Classrooms* 1052; *Scientists* 1121; *Language* 1233; *Actors* 1407; *Kings* 1985; *Chiseling* 2124; *Lawyers* 2532

ADOPTION

981 There is the story of the Hollywood star who had a Mexican gardener. He once informed his employer that he had adopted a baby and would like to display him. He turned up forthwith with an unmistakably Jewish child.

"How is it," the surprised actor asked, "that you didn't adopt a Mexican child?"

"Not me," said José firmly, "a Jewish child for me. Jewish children take care of their parents when they are old."

> RELATED SUBJECTS: *Family* 946-950; *Children* 951-952

FATHER

986 Paul Bourget: Life can never become entirely dull to an American. When he has nothing else to do he can always spend a few years trying to discover who his grandfather was.

Mark Twain: Right, your Excellency. But I reckon a Frenchman's got his little standby for a dull time too; he can turn in and see if he can find out who his father was!

987   A father was walking with his young son. The boy said, "Daddy, what is electricity?"

"Well now, I don't really know," said the father. "I never knew much about electricity. All I know about it is that it makes things run."

A little farther on, the boy said, "Daddy, how does the gasoline make the automobiles go?"

The father replied, "Well, I don't know. I don't know much about motors."

Several more questions followed with much the same result; until at last, the boy said, "Gee, I hope you don't mind my asking so many questions?"

"Not at all, son," said his father, "you go right ahead and ask. How else will you ever learn anything!"

988   Part of Aaron Burr's reputation for profligacy was due, no doubt, to that vanity respecting women of which Davis himself speaks. He never refused to accept the parentage of a child.

"Why do you allow this woman to saddle you with her child when you know you are not the father of it?" said a friend to him a few months before his death.

"Sir," he replied, "when a lady does me the honor to name me the father of her child I trust I shall always be too gallant to show myself ungrateful for the favor."

989   In 1814 Shelley, being then twenty-two, and the father of two children by Harriet . . . visited the family at Field Place for the first time since his expulsion from Oxford. A reconciliation would then have been easy, but instead Timothy made his son feel unwelcome. Indeed, so panicky was this patriotic M.P. of being detected harboring a liberal and an atheist—albeit his son—that he compelled Bysshe to masquerade under the name of "Captain Jones," and to wear, when on the public highways, the uniform of a young officer then visiting the Shelleys.

990   Getting on a trolley car, a kindergarten teacher sat down next to a man who appeared familiar to her. Smiling pleasantly, she turned as if to speak to him. Noticing his lack of response, she realized her error, and said, "Oh, excuse me. I mistook you for someone else. I thought you were the father of two of my children."

He got out at the next corner.

> RELATED SUBJECTS: *Husband* 916-918; *Family* 946-950; *Children* 951-952; *Mother* 991-993

> SEE ALSO: *Diligence* 176; *Children* 952; *Actors* 1424; *Priests* 1483; *Chiseling* 2131

MOTHER

991 Two small boys were hesitant about approaching their mother for a permission which was almost certain to be denied. They felt that they must take the long shot, however. "You ask her," said Billy to his younger brother. "No, you." At this point the mother chanced to overhear the balance of the conversation. "Oh, go on, you ask her," urged Billy. "No, you do it," said the younger, "you've known her longer than I have."

992 John D. Rockefeller, Sr., was reared with strict discipline. Upon one occasion, while being punished, he succeeded in convincing his mother that he was not guilty of the offense for which he was being whipped.

"Very well, son," his mother replied with grim humor, "but we have gone so far that we may as well proceed. It will be credited to your account for next time."

993 A number of years ago my little girl said to her mother, in one of those bursts of confidence that children sometimes have, "Mama, I am nearer to you than I am to papa." Her mother asked, "Why, what do you mean, my dear?" "Why," she replied, "I am your own little girl, but I am only related to papa by marriage."

> RELATED SUBJECTS: *Wife* 921-933; *Family* 946-950; *Children* 951-952; *Father* 986-990

> SEE ALSO: *Civilians in War* 2346

HOME LIFE

996 When asked how she made her soft voice heard above the notorious roars of her husband and eight sons, Rider Haggard's delicate little mother replied: "That's very simple. I whisper. In the Haggard family a whisper is so unusual that everyone listens to it with profound surprise."

997 The wife of an Iowa farmer, whose place was isolated in the vastness of the prairie, suddenly went out of her mind and was carted away in a strait-jacket by an ambulance from the nearest State hospital. An attendant remained behind to get the data on the case from the puzzled and distressed husband, who lamented, "Now what do you suppose could o' went wrong with the old woman? Why, man alive, she ain't been out of the kitchen in 20 years!"

998 We are told a story of a girl of the roaring 20's who said to a real estate agent when he wanted to sell her a house: "A home? Why do I need a home? I was born in a hospital, educated in a college, courted in an automobile, and married in a church. I live out of the delicatessen and paper bags. I spend my mornings on the golf course, my afternoons at the bridge-table, and my evenings at the movies. And when I die I am going to be buried at the undertaker's. All I need is a garage."

999 In the course of his pastoral visitations, Rev. Dr. Chalmers called upon a worthy shoemaker who, in recounting his blessings, said that he and his family had lived happily together for thirty years without a single quarrel. This was too much for the doctor, who struck his cane on the floor and exclaimed:
"Terribly monotonous man! Terribly monotonous!"

1000 Two young benedicts, married about a year, were discussing their various marital problems.
"I'm the head of my house," said one, "I think I should be; after all, I earn the money."
"Well," said the other, "my wife and I have a perfect agreement. I decide all the major matters and she takes care of all minor matters."
"And how is that working out?"
Somewhat ruefully the other replied, "Well, so far, no major matters have come up."

1001 An Athenian (as was customary with that people) had caused the following inscription to be placed over the door of his house:

"Let nothing enter here but what is good."

Diogenes asked: "Then where will the master of the house go in?"

RELATED SUBJECTS: *Marriage 876-888; Family 946-950; Servants 2276-2283*

SEE ALSO: *Small Children 969*

HOSPITALITY

1006 Alice James, wife of William James, says that often during evenings her husband would exclaim, "Are we never to have an evening alone? Must we always talk to people every night?" And she would answer, "I will see that whoever calls tonight is told that you are strictly engaged." So they would settle down to their quiet evening. Presently the doorbell would ring and Alice would go to the entry, to make sure that her instructions were carried out; but close behind her would be William, exclaiming, "Come in! Come right in!"

1007 Daniel Webster was once bested by one of the farmers of his native state. He had been hunting at some distance from his Inn, and rather than make the long trip back, he approached a farmhouse some considerable time after dark and pounded on the door. An upstairs window was raised and the farmer, with head thrust out, called, "What do you want?"

"I want to spend the night here," said Webster. "All right. Stay there," said the farmer. Down went the window.

1008 Andrew Lang at one time lived in the very far reaches of a London suburb. Inviting a friend to dinner, he instructed him how to get to the house. After long and explicit explanations he wound up by saying: "Just walk right along Cromwell Road. Keep on walking until you drop dead of exhaustion, and my house is just opposite."

RELATED SUBJECTS: *Generosity 241-248; Parties 741-746; Home Life 996-1001*

SEE ALSO: *Friendship 866; Actors 1428*

BIRTHS, BIRTHDAYS

1011   One night in New York friends of Mark Twain, remembering that it was the author's birthday, decided to send him a letter of congratulation. But no one knew in what corner of the globe he happened to be, so they addressed it: "Mark Twain, God Knows Where." Several weeks later they received a note from Italy which consisted of two words: "He did."

1012   When Lincoln went to the Legislature in 1854, after an absence of 12 years from that body, he got the indorsement of the Whigs and the Know-Nothings. He rejected their support in the following manner:

"Who are the native Americans? Do they not wear the breech clout and carry the tomahawk? We pushed them from their homes, and now turn upon others not fortunate enough to come over as early as we or our forefathers. Gentlemen, your party is wrong in principle." Then he told this story: "I had an Irishman named Patrick cultivating my garden. One morning I went out to see how he was getting along. 'Mr. Lincoln, what do yez think of these Know-Nothings?' he asked. I explained what they were trying to do, and asked Pat why he had not been born in America. 'Faith,' he replied, 'I wanted to but my mother wouldn't let me.'"

1013   Voltaire (writing to Frederick the Great): Madame du Chatelet is not yet delivered; it gives her more trouble to produce a child than a book.

Frederick the Great (replying to Voltaire): Since Madame du Chatelet writes books, I do not think she will produce her child in a moment of distraction. Tell her to hurry, for I wish to see you.

1014   A young lady of 8 or 9 years was almost overcome with joy when the occasion of her birthday netted her the two gifts which she had most ardently desired, a wristwatch and a bottle of perfume. She chattered about the new possessions all day long, wearying her parents of the subject. Guests were expected for dinner and the Mother gently admonished the child in advance, saying, "Now, dear, everybody knows about your presents and everybody is very happy for you. But now we mustn't go on talking about them all the time."

The little girl held her peace at the table throughout the greater part of the meal. A lull occurred in the conversation and, unable to restrain herself any more, she burst forth, "If anyone hears anything or smells anything, it's me!"

1015 A gentleman whose wife was delivered of a boy six months after marriage, asked a physician the reason for this. "Make yourself easy," said the latter, "this often happens in the case of the first child, but never afterwards."

RELATED SUBJECTS: *Family* 946-950; *Children* 951-952; *Father* 986-990; *Mother* 991-993

SEE ALSO: *Clothing* 726; *Names* 833

LEARNING AND THE ARTS

UNIVERSITIES AND COLLEGES

1016 When Woodrow Wilson was President of Princeton University he deplored the promiscuous giving of honorary degrees.

"Our universities have learned of late," he said, "to distribute honorary degrees judiciously. But in the past—well, in the past I met an uncouth person at a dinner, and, being told by an acquaintance that he had three degrees, I asked why it was.

" 'Well,' said my friend, 'the third was given because he had two, the second because he had one, and the first because he had none.' "

1017 Dr. Charles W. Eliot, the eminent educator of Harvard whose fate has been to be dubiously immortalized by a five-foot shelf of books, was once asked how Harvard had gained its prestige as the greatest storehouse of knowledge in the nation.

"In all likelihood," said Dr. Eliot slyly, "it is because the freshmen bring us so much of it, and the seniors take away so little."

1018 Attorney-General Seymour of Virginia snorted at the establishment of William and Mary College, which was founded not only to inculcate learning but to save souls. "Souls?" he cried. "Damn your souls. Make tobacco."

1019 Sir William B——, being at a parish meeting, made certain proposals which were objected to by a farmer. Highly enraged, "Sir," said he to the farmer, "do you know, sir, that I have been at two universities, and at two colleges in each university?"

"Well, sir," said the farmer, "what o' that? I had a calf that sucked two kye, an' the observation I made was, the mair he sucked the greater calf he grew."

1020 When James A. Garfield was president of Hiram College a man brought up his son to be entered as a student. He wanted the boy to take a course shorter than the regular one.

"My son can never take all those studies," said the father. "He wants to get through more quickly. Can't you arrange it for him?"

"Oh, yes," said Mr. Garfield. "He can take a short course; it all depends on what you want to make of him. When God wants to make an oak he takes a hundred years, but he takes only two months to make a squash."

1021 A guide, new at his business, was showing a group of tourists around Oxford. Conscientiously, he pointed out all the places of interest. Coming in front of one of the buildings he paused and said, "And this is Trinity Hall, where the president of the college, the famous Benjamin Jowett, lives."

Glancing around at the upturned faces, the guide then stooped and picked up a handful of gravel and threw it at a second story window. A red-faced and furious man opened the window almost immediately and peered out.

"And that is President Jowett himself," said the guide in a tone of voice as though he had just completed a task well done.

1022 Hendrik Willem Van Loon was visiting Cambridge. "That," said someone who was showing him around the university, "is Miss Jones," pointing to a formidable looking female striding along before them. "She's the mistress of Ridsley Hall."

"Who," asked Van Loon, "is Ridsley Hall?"

RELATED SUBJECTS: *Professors* 1026-1032; *Students* 1036; *College Life* 1041; *Schools* 1046-1050; *Erudition* 1071-1076; *Learned Men* 1081-1095

SEE ALSO: *Rudeness* 512; *Speeches* 756, 757, 758, 773; *Introductions* 790; *Learned Men* 1087; *Churchmen* 1455; *Travel* 1793; *Lawyers* 2534; *Ministers* 2607

PROFESSORS

1026 William Lyon Phelps, on a pre-Christmas examination paper, found written, "God only knows the answer to this question. Merry Christmas."

He returned the paper with the notation, "God gets an A; you get an F. Happy New Year."

1027 A certain University professor was about to depart on his sabbatical and addressed a few parting words to his students. "This parting is very melancholy to me. I wish there might be a window in my breast that you might see the innermost recesses of my heart."

"Professor," called a young man from the class, "would a pane in the stomach do?"

1028 The celebrated Prof. Maclaurin, the famous mathematician of Edinburgh College and the able expounder of Newton's "Principia," always dislocated his jaw, and was unable to shut his mouth whenever he yawned. His pupils took advantage of this physical affliction. When tired of his lecture, they either began to yawn or open their mouths in imitation of that act, and the professor began to yawn, too, by unconscious imitation. He stood before them with his mouth open and could not proceed till he rang for his servant to come and shut it. In the meantime, the mischievous enemies of Euclid effected their escape.

1029 Told by John Erskine: "At the end of my university studies when I was leaving for my first professorial job, I went to say goodbye to my old teacher, William Peterfield Trent. 'I can give you no theoretical advice in pedagogy,' he said, 'but I'll tell you one thing from experience. It will frequently happen when you are holding forth that some boy of the class will disagree. He will probably shake his head violently. You will be tempted to go after him and convert him then and there. Don't do it. He is probably the only one who is listening.'"

1030 Professor Parson, in a dispute, so exasperated his opponent by the dryness of his sarcasm that the latter at length exclaimed: "Mr. Parson, I beg leave to tell you, sir, that my opinion of you is a perfectly contemptible one."

Parson replied: "I never knew any opinion of yours, sir, which was not contemptible."

1031 Harvard's famous Professor, Charles Townsend Copeland, for many years occupied a couple of cramped, dusty rooms on the top floor of Hollis Hall. He was frequently urged to move to more comfortable and fitting quarters.

"No," he always said, "I shall always live on the top floor. It is the only place in Cambridge where God alone is above me. He's busy—but he's quiet."

1032 Interrupted by the sound of the bell announcing the end of the class, the professor was annoyed to see the students noisily preparing to leave although he was in the very middle of his lecture.

"Just a moment, gentlemen," he said, "I have a few more pearls to cast."

> RELATED SUBJECTS: *Universities and Colleges* 1016-1022; *Teachers* 1056-1057; *Erudition* 1071-1076; *Learned Men* 1081-1095; *Lectures* 1106-1111

> SEE ALSO: *Quick Thinking* 487

STUDENTS

1036 In the days when Dora Russell and others were journeying about giving out student questionnaires on sex life at most of our leading colleges, the story was told of a Wellesley girl who became tired of the endless round of intimate questionnaires. Summoned one day to a personal interview with the visiting psychiatrist, she meekly answered the many questions fired at her, and upon rising to leave, guilelessly asked, "Oh, doctor, tell me. Does it mean anything that I am so passionately fond of pancakes?" The doctor laughed heartily with professional geniality. "Why, my dear girl, of course not. I'm very fond of them myself."

"Oh, I'm so glad," replied the girl, "over in my room, I've a whole bureau drawer full and I love to take them out and stroke them."

The young lady was never troubled again by questionnaires, but reported that from time to time, the housemother dropped in and quietly went through her bureau drawers.

> RELATED SUBJECTS: *Universities and Colleges* 1016-1022; *College Life* 1041

> SEE ALSO: *Speeches* 756; *Experimenters* 1137

COLLEGE LIFE

1041 A tradition of Haverford College centers around the administration of its famous President, Dr. William Wistar Comfort. On the occasion of the erecting upon the campus of a beautiful metal sign proclaiming the name of the college, an enterprising group of seniors stole the sign and concealed it. It was missing for many days, during which Dr. Comfort instituted a search, located the sign, and caused it to be removed to a place of concealment of his own. Thereupon he announced that a joke was a joke but that unless the culprits returned the sign by the following Saturday night, all privileges of the senior class would be indefinitely revoked. The dismay of the culprits was great when they were unable to find their trophy and comply with the ultimatum. Accordingly, an extremely glum and down-in-the-mouth body of seniors assembled in chapel the Sunday morning after the deadline. Dr. Comfort stepped into the pulpit, surveyed the faces before him, and opened the great Bible for the reading of the morning text, which was, "A wicked and adulterous generation seeketh for a sign and there shall be none given unto them."

> RELATED SUBJECTS: *Universities and Colleges* 1016-1022; *Professors* 1026-1032; *Students* 1036

ATHLETICS (SEE RECREATION & SPORTS)

SCHOOLS

1046 After a lecture by the late Francis Wayland Parker, great Chicago educator, a woman asked:

"How early can I begin the education of my child?"

"When will your child be born?"

"Born?" she gasped. "Why, he is already five years old!"

"My goodness, woman," he cried, "don't stand here talking to me—hurry home; already you have lost the best five years."

1047 "What are your eyes for?" the little child in kindergarten was asked.

"To see with."

"And your nose?"

"To smell with."

"And what are your ears for?" was the last question.

"To keep clean," the child replied.

1048 A little girl who was attending a progressive school had a cold one morning and her mother suggested that she remain home from school. "But I can't, Mother," the child insisted, "this is the day when we start to make a clay model of a cow and I'm chairman of the udder committee."

1049 A certain mother wished to enter her five-year old daughter in a kindergarten, the age requirement of which was six. To the disapproving teacher the mother explained, "She can easily pass the six-year-old test."

"Say some words," the teacher said rather skeptically to the child.

The child surveyed the teacher with dignity and, turning to her mother, asked, "Purely irrelevant words?"

1050 As a special treat, a teacher took her class to visit the museum of natural history. The children returned home very excitedly, and rushing into his house, one of the little boys greeted his mother exuberantly, saying, "What do you think we did today, Mother! The teacher took us to a dead circus."

RELATED SUBJECTS: *Universities and Colleges* 1016-1022; *Classrooms* 1051-1053; *Teachers* 1056-1057; *Pupils* 1061-1066

SEE ALSO: *Boners* 119; *Memory* 372; *Quick Thinking* 479; *Small Children* 966; *Wealth* 2185

CLASSROOMS

1051 The small boy had created a disturbance in kindergarten. All the methods of the teacher had failed. The child was in revolt, and determined to go home. The teacher got the child's mother on the telephone and, after explaining the situation, put the culprit himself on the line. Clearly, as evidenced by his side of the conversation and his increasingly weaker protests, he was losing his case. At last the child said in despair, "All right then. If you want me to be a damned bead-stringer!" and hung up.

1052 The day of a big snowstorm, the country school teacher felt called upon to warn her charges against playing too long in the snow. She said, "Now, children, you must be careful about colds and over-exposure. I had a darling little brother only seven years old. One day he went out in the snow with his new sled and caught cold. Pneumonia set in and three days later he died."

The room was silent and then a youngster in the back row raised his hand and asked, "Where's his sled?"

1053 A young woman named Murphy was the teacher of the kindergarten grade in a Massachusetts school. She had taught her class to repeat together the 23rd Psalm. As the little voices chorused out, she seemed somewhere to detect a false note. She heard the children one by one, until at last she came across one little boy who was concluding the Psalm with the words, "Surely good Miss Murphy shall follow me all the days of my life."

RELATED SUBJECTS: *Schools* 1046-1050; *Teachers* 1056-1057; *Pupils* 1061-1066

TEACHERS

1056 There is the story about the famous Dr. Busby, headmaster of Westminster who, while showing Charles II of England over the school, apologized to that merry monarch for keeping his hat on in the presence of royalty, "For," said he, "it would not do for my boys to suppose that there existed in the world a greater man than Dr. Busby."

1057 In the classroom the teacher was trying, without success, to quell what looked like a small riot. The principal, passing through the hall, stopped and asked what all the noise was about.

The pretty young teacher was almost in tears. "I was explaining the difference between concrete and abstract, stating that abstract is something you can't see, and concrete is something you can see. Then I asked James to give me an illustration.

" 'My pants are concrete. Yours are abstract,' he answered."

The principal, attempting to repress a smile, helped the teacher restore order to her class, and then, going into the hall, finally gave vent to the laughter he could no longer restrain.

RELATED SUBJECTS: *Schools* 1046-1050; *Classrooms* 1051-1053; *Pupils* 1061-1066

SEE ALSO: *Father* 990; *Judges* 2494

PUPILS

1061 In English class a small boy was told to write an essay about King Alfred, but was warned not to elaborate overly much on the familiar story of the cakes. The boy delivered his essay which, after summing up the chief historical facts, concluded with "There is another incident in King Alfred's life. One day he visited a house where a certain woman lived—and the less said about that, the better."

1062 For sheer lucidity of description, it is difficult to match the young lady who wrote on her examination paper the following in reply to the question, "What is a bolt and what is a nut?"
"A bolt is a thing like a stick of hard metal, such as iron, with a square bunch on one end and a lot of scratches going round and round the other end. A nut is similar to the bolt only just the opposite, being a hole in a little square of iron sawed off short with rings also around the inside of the hole."

1063 A certain young man came home with a grievously unsatisfactory report card in January. "Oh, dear," said his mother, "what is the trouble?"
"There isn't any trouble," said the youngster, "you know how it is yourself; things are always marked down after the Holidays."

1064 When the pupils were assigned the task of writing an essay on "the most beautiful thing I ever saw," the least esthetic young man in the class handed in his paper first with astonishing speed. It was short and to the point—"The most beautiful thing I ever saw was too beautiful for words."

1065 When Theodore Roosevelt was in school, he was one day called upon to deliver an assigned recitation, beginning, "When Greece, her knees in suppliance bent—."
When he essayed to deliver the recitation, he found himself

unable to get past the first few words. He said, "When Greece, her knees—" and again, "When Greece, her knees—"; and, after a few more false starts, gave up hopelessly.

His teacher said severely, "Roosevelt, grease her knees again and then perhaps she'll go."

1066 Given the assignment of writing a composition about what they would do if they had a million dollars, all of the children in the class except Willy were busily writing away.

The teacher, becoming aware of his idleness, said severely, "Willy, don't you know that you are supposed to tell what you would do if you had a million dollars?"

"Well," said the boy, lazily leaning back on his chair, "this is exactly what I would do if I had a million dollars."

RELATED SUBJECTS: *Schools* 1046-1050; *Classrooms* 1051-1053; *Teachers* 1056-1057

ERUDITION

1071 President Woodrow Wilson would sit down beside his green-shaded lamp and take up one paper after another—and so work until the small hours. Approval was designated by "Okeh, W. W." on the margin of a paper. Someone asked why he did not use the "O.K." "Because it is wrong," Mr. Wilson said. He suggested that the inquirer look up "Okeh" in a dictionary. That he did, and discovered that it is a Choctaw word meaning "It is so."

1072 Once, during the progress of Mr. Hastings' trial, Charles Fox, struck by the solemnity of Lord Thurlow's appearance, said to the speaker, "I wonder if any man is as wise as Thurlow looks."

1073 Mark Twain once observed sagely, "One should be careful to get out of an experience only the wisdom that is in it—and stop there; lest we be like the cat that sits down on the hot stove lid. She will never sit down on a hot stove lid again—and that's well; but also she will never sit down on a cold one any more."

1074 Someone once rudely taunted John Maynard, Lord Commissioner of the Great Seal of England, with having grown so old as to forget his law.

"True, Sir," he replied, "I have forgotten more law than you ever learned."

1075 When Bernardo Tasso remonstrated with his son, the immortal Torquato, on his injudicious preference of philosophy to jurisprudence, and angrily demanded: "What has philosophy done for you?" Torquato replied: "It has taught me to hear with meekness the reproofs of a father."

1076 One time when the little Louis Napoleon was racking his brains over a pile of Latin dictionaries and grammars, Napoleon the Third entered the room. He looked at him with sympathy and said, "It is a grind, translating Latin. I never could."

The tutor spoke up in astonishment, "But, your Majesty's translation of Caesar's 'Commentaries'?"

"It wasn't mine," said the Emperor, and went off.

> RELATED SUBJECTS: *Professors* 1026-1032; *Learned Men* 1081-1095; *Common Sense* 1156-1157

> SEE ALSO: *Speeches* 774; *Children* 951

LEARNED MEN

1081 Ralph Waldo Emerson had read philosophy, science, poetry and histories, but none of them had said anything about an effective and harmonious way of pushing a female calf into a barn. His son Edward grasped an ear, the father pushed diligently from behind, and together they tried to propel the animal. The heifer resisted with calm obstinacy. The pale face of the sage reddened and perspiring beads of sweat gathered on his high white forehead. And then an Irish servant girl came by. With an amused glance she thrust a finger into the animal's mouth, and the calf, seduced by this maternal imitation, at once followed her into the barn. Edward grinned, but Emerson was already absorbed in thought. After cleansing his hands of their hairy, bovine smell, he recorded this telling declaration in his journal: "I like people who can do things."

1082 It is related of Noah Webster that his wife, coming suddenly into the pantry one day, caught him in the act of embracing the chambermaid. "Mr. Webster," she said, "I'm surprised."

The great lexicographer gazed upon her in mild reproof. "No, my pet," he replied, "you are amazed. It is we who are surprised."

1083 A nobleman observing a person eminent for his philosophical talents, intent on choosing delicacies at table, said to him:

"What! do you philosophers love dainties?"

"Why not—do you think my Lord, that the good things of this world were only made for blockheads?"

1084 The Duke of Newcastle, when Prime Minister, once told the author of "Tristram Shandy," that men of wit were not fit to be employed, being incapable of business.

"They are not incapable of business, my Lord, but above it," replied Sterne. "A sprightly generous horse is able to carry a pack-saddle as well as an ass, but he is too good to be put to the drudgery."

1085 "Bury me on my face," said Diogenes, and when he was asked why, he replied, "Because in a little while everything will be turned upside down."

1086 Talleyrand, on being told that the Abbé Sieyes was a very profound man, replied:

"Profound! Yes—he is a perfect cavity."

1087 In one of the ancient academies the students had a three years' course. In the first year they were called the wise men; in the second they were called the philosophers—those who wished to be wise men; in the third they were called disciples, learners.

1088 When the mighty Alexander the Great asked the ragged philosopher Diogenes what favor he could grant him, the Cynic, who was reclining on the ground, remarked quietly:

"Now please move a little out of my sun."

1089 A committee of the French Academy employed in the preparation of the Academy Dictionary, defined the word "crab" as follows: "Crab: a small red fish which walks back-

wards." Commenting on this definition the celebrated naturalist Cuvier said: "Your definition, gentlemen, would be perfect,
only for three exceptions. The crab is not a fish, it is not red and
it does not walk backwards."

1090   When Dante was at the court of Signor della Scala, then
sovereign of Verona, that prince said to him one day:
   "I wonder, Signor Dante, that a man so learned as you should
be hated by all my court, and that this fool should be so beloved."
   Highly piqued Dante replied, "Your Excellency would wonder less if you considered that we like those best who most resemble ourselves."

1091   Noah Webster once undertook to write out a letter for
an illiterate servant. Before concluding, he asked, "Is there anything else you wish to add?"
   His serving man replied, "Well, you might just ask him to
excuse the poor scholarship and want of sense the letter shows."

1092   At a convention of teachers in Chicago several of the
learned men became heatedly involved in a discussion on a
number of abstruse points of information. They split over an
issue which could only be solved by reference to authority.
Hastening downstairs one of the savants approached the desk
clerk and said, "Is there an Encyclopedia Britannica in the
house?"
   "No, sir," said the clerk blandly, "what is it you wish to
know?"

1093   Cottle, the Bath bookseller, recorded:
   "I removed the harness . . . , but . . . could not get off the
collar. In despair I called for assistance. Mr. W. (Wordsworth)
first brought his ingenuity into exercise, but, after several unsuccessful efforts, he relinquished the achievement as altogether impracticable. Mr. Coleridge now tried his hand, but . . .
after twisting the poor horse's neck, almost to strangulation,
and the great danger of his eyes, he gave up the useless task,
pronouncing that 'the horse's head must have grown (gout or
dropsy!) since the collar was put on! for it was a downright
impossibility for such a huge os frontis to pass through so narrow a collar!' At about this juncture the servant girl appeared,
turned the collar upsidedown, and removed it."

1094 One of Emerson's rural neighbors at Concord borrowed from him a copy of Plato. "Did you enjoy the book?" asked Emerson, when it was returned.

"I did that," replied his neighbor. "This Plato has a lot of my ideas."

1095 Queen Christina of Sweden complimented the celebrated Vossius by saying that he was so well learned as not only to know whence all the words came but whither they were going.

RELATED SUBJECTS: *Professors* 1026-1032; *Erudition* 1071-1076; *Scientists* 1116-1122; *Mathematicians* 1146-1154; *Common Sense* 1156-1157

SEE ALSO: *Cheerfulness* 141; *Dullness* 186; *Pompousness* 424; *Shortness* 693; *Churchmen* 1452; *Efficiency* 2266

CRITICS

1096 According to Richard Aldington: "In the early days of Dada (predecessor of Surrealism) I received for review a book which contained the following 'poem':

A B C D E F
G H I J K L
M N O P Q R
S T U V W X
Y Z.

"On which I commented:

1 2 3 4 5
6 7 8 9 10.

"I still think that was the most snappy review I ever wrote; but unfortunately 'The Times' refused to print it."

1097 A man said he was afraid he was going to be of no use in the world because he had only one talent. "Oh, that need not discourage you," said his pastor. "What is your talent?"

"The talent of criticism."

"Well, I advise you," said his pastor, "to do with it what the man of one talent in the parable did with his. Criticism may be useful when mixed with other talents, but those whose only activity is to criticize the workers might as well be buried, talent and all."

1098 Jerrold admired Carlyle, but objected that he did not give definite suggestions for the improvement of the age which he rebuked.

"Here," said he, "is a man who beats a big drum under my windows, and when I come running downstairs, has nowhere for me to go."

1099 Richard Aldington tells that, "An American friend of mine was then editing the 'Outlook,' and asked me to write an article telling his readers about young writers and picking out those I thought would make a name. I made a choice which I modestly think wasn't bad for 1919: James Joyce, T. S. Eliot, D. H. Lawrence, Aldous Huxley, and Marcel Proust. I received a letter from the editor in these terms:

" 'For God's sake, Richard, can't you think of somebody who has been heard of or is ever likely to be heard of?'

"I protested, and my article was submitted to the judgment of that eminent expatriate, Mr. Logan Pearsall Smith, who decided that my writers never would be heard of; and the article was rejected. If I had chosen such mediocrities as Jack Squire, Hugh Walpole, Frank Swinnertown, I should have received a cheque and a crown of wild parsley."

1100 A shallow poet took Piron into his confidence and entrusted to him a long manuscript, assuring the critic that the verses contained therein were the best he had ever written. With an air of condescension he asked Piron to put a cross before each line which he thought might possibly be improved. When he asked for his manuscript a few days later Piron handed it to him without a word. Leafing hastily through it, the author exclaimed delightedly: "Why, I don't see a single cross on my paper."

"No," returned Piron dryly, "I didn't want to make a graveyard of it."

1101 When Michelangelo had completed his great sculptural work, the David, the Gonfalonière Soderini of Florence who had ordered it came to inspect his purchase. Among his other criticisms he objected to the nose, pronouncing it to be out of all due proportion to the rest of the figure, and added, that he wished some reduction should take place in its size. Angelo knew well with whom he had to deal; he mounted the scaffold for the figure upwards of twelve feet high, and giving a few sonorous but harmless blows with his hammer on the stone, let fall a handful of marble dust which he had scraped up from the floor below; and then descending from his station turned to the Gonfalonière with a look expectant of his approbation. "Ay," exclaimed the sagacious critic; "now you have given it life indeed."

Michelangelo was content, and receiving his four hundred scrudi for his tasks, wisely said no more. It would have been no gratification to a man like him, to have shown the incapacity of a presumptuous critic like Soderini.

1102 Professor Brander Matthews was a great stickler for proprieties. At an opening night he had gone to review a play. The next day he was asked for his opinion by one of his students at Columbia University.

"Well, gentlemen," said Prof. Matthews, "the play was in four acts, and I was there as the guest of the author. After the first act the audience sat silent and I applauded. After the second act I sat quiet while the audience hissed."

The Professor took a long-drawn and reminiscent pull at his cigarette, then held it at arm's length and flicked off the ashes.

"And the third act?"

"Well, gentlemen," and there was a gleam of satisfaction in the Professor's eye, "after the third act I went out and bought standing room and came back and hissed too."

1103 When Bernard Shaw wrote dramatic criticisms for the "London Saturday Review" he commented about a certain play in his column as follows:

"I am in a somewhat foolish position concerning a play at the Opera Comique, whither I was bidden this day week. For some reason I was not supplied with a program; so that I never learned the name of the play. At the end of the second act the play had advanced about as far as an ordinary dramatist would have brought it five minutes after the first rising of the curtain; or say, as far as Ibsen would have brought it ten years before that event. Taking advantage of the second interval (intermission) to stroll out into the strand for a little exercise, I unfortunately forgot all about my business, and actually reached home before it occurred to me that I had not seen the end of the play.

Under these circumstances, it would ill become me to dogmatize on the merits of the work or its performance. I can only offer the management my apologies."

1104   While he was dramatic critic on the old "Denver Post," Eugene Field was given an assignment to report on a performance of "King Lear." His review was brief but pointed:
"Last night at the Tabor Opera House, So-and-So played King Lear. He played it as though under the premonition that someone was about to play the Ace.'

1105   A friend of Dr. Johnson's, in conversation with him, was lamenting the disagreeable situation in which those persons stood who were eminent for their criticisms. As they were perpetually expected to be saying clever things, it was a heavy tax on them.
"It is, indeed," said Dr. Johnson, "a very heavy tax on them; a tax which no man can pay who does not steal."

> RELATED SUBJECTS: *Learned Men* 1081-1095; *Art* 1256; *Music* 1303-1306; *Plays* 1386-1388

> SEE ALSO: *Sculpture* 1296, 1297; *Playwrights* 1377, 1379; *Actors* 1421

LECTURES

1106   Professor Agassiz, the naturalist, had declined to deliver a lecture before some lyceum or public society, on account of the inroads which previous lectures given by him had made upon his studies and thought. The gentleman who had been deputed to invite him continued to press the invitation, assuring him that the society was ready to pay him liberally for his services.
"That is no inducement to me," replied Agassiz, "I cannot afford to waste my time in making money."

1107   Artemus Ward was once about to lecture on "American Wit and Humor," but the chairman spoke at such length on the subject that when Artemus rose, he said: "The chairman has said all that needs to be said on 'American Wit and Humor,' so instead of taking that subject, I shall lecture on 'Indian Meal.'"
And he did.

1108 The German philosopher and theologian, Friedrich Schleiermacher, once attempted to explain to a questioner the type of people who composed his audiences. "My audience is composed mainly of students, young women, and soldiers. Students come because I'm a member of the Board of Examiners. The young women come because of the students. And the soldiers come because of the young women."

1109 After a great deal of urging, Mark Twain's friends in San Francisco persuaded him to give a lecture on the interesting things he had seen in the Hawaiian Islands during his visit in the fall of 1866. In order to encourage the new lecturer they promised to place hearty laughers at strategic points among the audience. "Tell them not to investigate my jokes, but to respond at once," Clemens said. When he came out on the platform his knees were shaking so violently that his backers thought he wouldn't last long enough for the hearty laughers to get into action. But Clemens needed no support, for he won the day by his inimitable opening, "Julius Caesar is dead, Shakespeare is dead, Napoleon is dead, Abraham Lincoln is dead, and I am far from well myself." When the lecture was over, the audience had been laughing so much they were too weak to leave their seats.

1110 Mark Twain in his lecturing days, reached a small Eastern town one afternoon and went before dinner to a barber's to be shaved.

"You are a stranger in town, sir?" the barber asked.

"Yes, I am a stranger here," was the reply.

"We're having a good lecture here tonight, sir," said the barber, "a 'Mark Twain' lecture. Are you going to it?"

"Yes, I think I will," said Mr. Clemens.

"Have you got your ticket yet?" the barber asked.

"No, not yet," said the other.

"Then, sir, you'll have to stand."

"Dear me!" Mr. Clemens exclaimed. "It seems as if I always do have to stand when I hear that man Twain lecture."

1111 On the occasion of a lecture which Charles Lamb was once delivering, a loud hiss emanated from somewhere in the audience. There was an embarrassed silence. Lamb, not turning a hair, said, "There are only three things that hiss—a goose, a snake and a fool. Come forth and be identified."

RELATED SUBJECTS: *Speeches* 756-782; *Introductions* 786-791; *Professors* 1026-1032; *Learned Men* 1081-1095

SEE ALSO: *Memory* 375; *Clothing* 720; *Handwriting* 731; *Authors* 1211; *Audiences* 1438

SCIENTISTS

1116   When Gustavus III of Sweden was in Paris, a deputation of French scientists called on him. It congratulated him on the happy fortune, that had given him so great a man as Scheele, the discoverer of magnesium, as his subject and fellow countryman.

The king, who took small interest in the progress of science, felt somewhat ashamed that he should be so ignorant as never even to have heard of the renowned chemist.

He dispatched a courier at once to Sweden with the laconic order: "Scheele is to be immediately raised to the dignity of a count." "His Majesty must be obeyed," said the Prime Minister, "but who in hell is Scheele?"

A secretary was told to make inquiries. He came back with very full information. "Scheele is a good sort of fellow," said he, "a lieutenant in the artillery, a capital shot, and a first-rate hand at billiards."

The next day the lieutenant became a count, and the illustrious scientist was completely forgotten by King and court.

1117   A botanist found a beautiful plant by the wayside. He sat down to analyze it. He pulled it apart and examined every part under a microscope.

When he had finished he could tell the color of the flower, its classification, and the number of stamens and pistils and petals and bracts, but the life and the beauty and the fragrance were gone.

1118   They tell the story of a celebrated biologist who tried for months to train a monkey to play ball. As a last resort, he shut up the little creature by itself in a room with a bat and ball. After some considerable time had elapsed he finally stooped and peered through the keyhole. He was disconcerted to find himself staring into an intent brown eye.

1119   A Cambridge lecturer on the history of chemistry thus described the celebrated Mr. Boyle: "He was a great man, a very strong man; he was the father of modern chemistry, and brother of the Earl of Cork."

1120   Lord Kelvin, the great physicist, once paid an unexpected visit to an extensive electrical plant. He had not disclosed his identity and was shown through the plant by a young foreman who painstakingly explained all the rudiments of electrical science, as here manifested, to the great man.

When the tour was completed, Kelvin asked him quietly, "What then is electricity?" His guide was stumped. "No matter," Lord Kelvin said kindly, "that is the only thing about electricity which you and I do not know."

1121   The great naturalist, Charles Darwin, was once approached by two small boys of the family whose guest he was. They had caught a butterfly, a centipede, a beetle, and a grasshopper. Taking the centipede's body, the butterfly's wings, the beetle's head and the grasshopper's legs, they had glued them together to make an alarming and original insect.

"We caught this bug in the field," they said innocently. "What kind of a bug is it, Mr. Darwin?"

Darwin examined it with great solemnity. "Did you notice whether it hummed when you caught it, boys?" he asked gravely.

"Yes, sir," they answered, trying to conceal their mirth.

"Just as I thought," said Darwin. "It is a humbug."

1122   The wife of the great physicist, Robert A. Millikan, happened to pass through the hall of her home in time to hear her maid answer the telephone. "Yes," Mrs. Millikan overheard, "this is where Dr. Millikan lives, but he's not the kind of doctor that does anybody any good."

RELATED SUBJECTS: *Learned Men* 1081-1095; *Inventors* 1126-1131; *Experimenters* 1136-1138; *Explorers* 1141-1142; *Mathematicians* 1146-1154; *Doctors* 1666-1679

SEE ALSO: *Dueling* 802; *Inventors* 1127; *Common Sense* 1157; *Bigotry* 1628; *Army and Navy* 2401; *Stool Pigeon* 2592

INVENTORS

1126 One of the most interesting incidents of a business nature is that which concerns the first steamboat fare paid to Robert Fulton. The narrator of this, who was also one of the actors on the scene, says:

I chanced to be at Albany on business when Fulton arrived there, in his unheard-of craft, which everybody felt so much interest in seeing. Being ready to leave and hearing that this craft was going to return to New York, I repaired on board and inquired for Mr. Fulton; I was referred to the cabin, and there found a plain, gentlemanly man, wholly alone, and engaged in writing.

"Mr. Fulton I presume."

"Yes, sir."

"Do you return to New York with this boat?"

"We shall try to get back, sir."

"Can I have a passage down?"

"You can take your chance with us, sir." I inquired the amount to be paid, and, after a moment's hesitation, a sum, I think six dollars, was named, the amount in coin, I laid it in his open hand, and, with eye fixed upon it, he remained so long motionless, that I supposed there might be a miscount, and said to him, "Is that right, sir?"

This question roused him as from a kind of reverie, and as he looked up to me the big tear was brimming in his eye, and his voice faltered as he said:

"Excuse me sir; but memory was busy as I contemplated this, the first pecuniary reward I have ever received for all my exertions in adapting steam to navigation. I should gladly commemorate the occasion over a bottle of wine with you, but really I am too poor, even for that just now."

1127 Thomas A. Edison never forgot his role as a business man. The profit motive was an essential part of his temperament. Once he said practically to a friend, referring to a newspaper article which discussed him as a scientist, "That's wrong. I am not a scientist. I am an inventor. Faraday was a scientist. He didn't work for money, he said he hadn't time. But I do. I measure everything I do by the size of a silver dollar. If it don't come up to that standard, then I know it's no good."

1128 The late Thomas A. Edison had a very beautiful summer residence in which he took great pride. One day he was showing his guests about, pointing out all the various labor-saving devices on the premises. Turning back toward the house it was necessary to pass through a turnstile which led onto the main path. The guests soon found out that it took considerable force to get through this device.

"Mr. Edison," asked one of his guests, "how is it that with all these wonderful modern things around, you still maintain such a heavy turnstile?"

Said Mr. Edison, his eyes lighting up with laughter, "Well, you see, everyone who pushes the turnstile around, pumps eight gallons of water into the tank on my roof."

1129   "I got fired twice," said Edison. "The first time was when I was a telegraph operator. It was my fault, all right, but I got so interested in the dinged machine and its workings that I began to see how I could improve it. But I forgot all about the messages that were coming over the wire, and I left a lot of messages unsent and undelivered. Of course, they discharged me, and I didn't blame them," he added.

"Then," he laughed again, "I got a job in an office, and there were a fearful lot of rats; terribly old office, you know. I got up a thing that killed them like flies—the same with cockroaches. The floor used to be covered with dead roaches, and they fired me for that!"

1130   A step which seems obvious after it has been taken is frequently obscure before the way has been pointed out, no matter how close to it we may have been led by the slow and painful processes of learning and experimentation. Just such a step was taken by Thomas A. Edison in one of the processes of subdividing an electric current. Subsequently a patent suit arose over the matter in which the famous English physicist, Tyndall, was called upon to testify.

He mentioned that he had followed the same course taken by Edison and had hesitated before the final step which now seemed so childishly clear. One of the attorneys demanded of him, "When the next step was so obvious, why did you not take it?"

"Because," said Tyndall, "I was not Thomas A. Edison."

1131   Thomas A. Edison told, himself, about the invention of the phonograph:

"I was working on the telephone, developing the carbon button transmitter. My hearing wasn't too good and I couldn't get the sounds as clearly as I wanted to, so I fixed a short needle on the diaphragm of the receiver. When I let my finger rest lightly on this needle the pricks would show me its amplitude and that's what I wanted to find out.

"One day when I was testing this way it occurred to me that if I could indent a yielding substance with these vibrations I could reverse the process and reproduce the sounds. I sat down and made a sketch of a machine that I thought would do the trick.

"Then I called in John Kruesi, my chief mechanic. I explained the mechanism and asked him what he would charge me for making it. He said he would make it for thirty dollars, and I told him to go ahead. Then he asked me what it was for, and I told him it was going to talk. He thought I was joking and went away laughing.

"When he finished the machine and brought it back to me I put the tinfoil on, started her up, and recited 'Mary had a little lamb.' When I reversed and the words began to come back, Kruesi nearly fell over.

"That was the only one of my inventions that was perfect from the start. When we began to manufacture it we didn't have to alter a single detail."

RELATED SUBJECTS: *Scientists* 1116-1122; *Experimenters* 1136-1138

SEE ALSO: *Pessimism* 411; *Experimenters* 1136; *Devout Persons* 1601; *Bargaining* 2079; *Wealth* 2183

EXPERIMENTERS

1136 "Results!" exclaimed Edison to an assistant marveling at the bewildering total of his failures—50,000 experiments for example, before he succeeded with a new storage battery. "Results? Why, man, I have gotten a lot of results. I know fifty-thousand things that won't work."

1137 Shelley's lifelong interest in science, especially chemistry, was aroused by a quack lecturer who visited his first school, Sion House. At Eton he was forbidden to study chemistry, and so performed experiments in his room. One day his tutor, Mr.

Bethel, heard strange noises from his room, entered and found Shelley enveloped in blue flames.

"What on earth are you doing, Shelley?" asked the teacher.

"Please, sir, I am raising the devil."

The startled tutor put his hand on some apparatus which, being a leyden jar, gave him a bad shock.

1138   Edison's school of scientific experimentation was essentially empirical. Once he was seeking a solvent for hard rubber. Many scientists, seeking it through theory or formula, were yet helpless. Edison went to his impressive and remarkably complete storeroom of chemicals. He immersed a small fragment of hard rubber in a vial of each one of these many chemicals. It was an enormous number. But Edison found his solvent.

RELATED SUBJECTS: *Scientists* 1116-1122; *Inventors* 1126-1131

SEE ALSO: *Exaggeration* 222

EXPLORERS

1141   When Captain Cook discovered Australia, his sailors brought a strange animal aboard ship whose name they did not know. Sent ashore to inquire of the natives, they came back and said, "It is a kangaroo." Many years passed before it was known that when the natives were asked to name the animal and said, "Kangaroo," they meant, "What did you say?"

1142   Robert Falson Scott, the explorer, applied to Lloyd George for assistance in the financing of his last, fatal Polar expedition. The then Chancellor referred him to a certain wealthy man, also of some prominence in the political scene. "How did you succeed,' asked Lloyd George, when the explorer again called on him.

"He gave me a thousand pounds," was the reply, "but he has undertaken to raise 20 thousand pounds if I can persuade you to come with me, and a million if I manage to leave you there."

RELATED SUBJECTS: *Scientists* 1116-1122; *Travel* 1791-1796

SEE ALSO: *Cynicism* 169; *Pagan Gods* 1661

MATHEMATICIANS

1146 When the Greek philosophers found that the square root of 2 is not a rational number, they celebrated the discovery by sacrificing 100 oxen.

1147 Pascal's genius for geometry began to appear before he was even twelve years old, in the room where he passed his hours of play; he procured a piece of charcoal, and drew diagrams on the floor, trying to make a circle, perfectly round, a triangle with equal sides and angles, a perfect parallelogram and like things. He discovered all this unaided, and then turned his attention to the properties of these figures and their mutual relations and proportions. But as his father had with such great care concealed from him all mathematical works, the poor boy did not even know the names of the figures he drew. Compelled to make his own definitions, he called a circle "a round," and a line "a bar," etc., and with these very primitive definitions proceeded to construct his axioms, till at last he wrought out complete demonstrations!

Step by step he advanced in his studies, one discovery opening the door to another; and so far did he push his researches, that without ever seeing a mathematical work, he got to the thirty-second proposition of the book of Euclid.

1148 The sculptor Jacob Epstein tells this story: "When I was doing Professor Albert Einstein's bust he had many a jibe at the Nazi professors, one hundred of whom had condemned his theory of relativity in a book. 'Were I wrong,' he said, 'one professor would have been enough!'"

1149 Edison approached the mathematical aspects of his science with that same practical instinct and native ability that characterized every other phase of his work. He often succeeded in beating the mathematicians on his staff to the draw in the search for correct formulae, seeming to arrive at his conclusions through infallible instinct and native genius.

"These mathematicians make me tired," he often said, "You ask them to work out a sum and they take a piece of paper, cover it with rows of a's and b's and x's and y's; decorate them with a lot of little numbers, scatter a mess of fly specks around them and then give you an answer that's all wrong."

1150   This story is told of, and possibly by, Albert Einstein, who was asked by his hostess at a social gathering to explain his theory of relativity. Said the great mathematician, "Madam, I was once walking in the country on a hot day with a blind friend, and said that I would like a drink of milk.

"'Milk?' said my friend, 'Drink I know; but what is milk?'

"'A white liquid,' I replied.

"'Liquid I know; but what is white?'

"'The color of a swan's feathers.'

"'Feathers I know; what is a swan?'

"'A bird with a crooked neck.'

"'Neck I know; but what is this crooked?'

"Thereupon I lost patience. I seized his arm and straightened it. 'That's straight,' I said; and then I bent it at the elbow. 'That's crooked.'

"'Ah!' said the blind man, 'now I know what you mean by milk!'"

1151   At a gathering of mathematicians, someone undertook to discourse upon the meaning of Einstein's theories. After he had run on tediously for nearly an hour, someone interrupted to say, "I think you are greater than Einstein himself. Twelve men understand Einstein—but nobody understands you."

1152   Sir William Rothenstein was in Berlin doing a portrait of Einstein. The mathematician was always accompanied to the studio by a solemn, academic looking individual who sat in a corner throughout the sittings. Einstein, not wishing to waste any time, was putting forth certain tentative theories, to which the silent companion replied only by an occasional nod or shake of the head.

When the work was concluded, Rothenstein, who was curious, asked Einstein who his companion was.

"That's my mathematician," said Einstein, "who examines problems which I put before him and checks their validity. You see, I am not myself a good mathematician."

1153   Asked one day for a mathematical formula for success in his life, Albert Einstein gave the following:

"If a is success in life, the formula is, a equals x plus y plus z, x being work and y being play."

"And what is z?" he was asked.

"Z," he said, "is keeping your mouth shut."

1154   Once the Gershwin family happened to be discussing the Einstein theory. "Imagine," began George, "working for twenty years on an idea and then being able to write it down in three pages!"

"It was probably very small print," was Pop Gershwin's comment.

> RELATED SUBJECTS: *Learned Men* 1081-1095; *Scientists* 1116-1122; *Statistics* 2221-2222

> SEE ALSO: *Professors* 1028; *Wealth* 2184

COMMON SENSE

1156   Lincoln once said to Chauncey Depew, "They say I tell a great many stories; I reckon I do, but I have found in the course of a long experience that common people, take them as they run, are more easily informed through the medium of a broad illustration than in any other way, and as to what the hypercritical few may think, I don't care."

1157   This is one of the favorite stories of Dr. Karl Compton, the noted physicist of M. I. T. His sister lives in India. She was having a simple electrical installation done by a native electrician. He troubled her so much for instructions that she at last said irritably, "You know what I want; just use your common sense and do it."

The electrician salaamed politely and said, "Madam, common sense is a rare gift of God. I have only a technical education."

> RELATED SUBJECTS: *Stupidity* 576-583; *Erudition* 1071-1076; *Learned Men* 1081-1095

> SEE ALSO: *Machinery* 2272

LITERATURE

1161   Two passengers were overheard in a literary discussion on the Brooklyn express.

"Whatcher favorite readin'?"

"Popeye, Superman, and Flash Gordon."

"Howcha like O. Henry?"

"Naw, the nuts get in my teeth."

1162 The magazine which published "The Old Curiosity Shop" came to America by sailing vessel. As interest in Dickens' story mounted from week to week, the crowds became larger on the New York wharf waiting to buy copies as soon as the boat docked. By the time the story reached its last chapter these crowds had grown to such numbers and to such a pitch of suspense that they swarmed, five or six thousand strong, upon the wharf and could not wait until the ship docked. When they spied the captain on the deck they called out across the narrowing water the question that burned in everyone's heart: "Did little Nell die?"

RELATED SUBJECTS: *Authors* 1166-1219; *Books* 1221-1224; *Libraries* 1226; *Language* 1231-1233; *Newspapers* 1236-1248; *Magazines* 1251-1252; *Art* 1256; *Music* 1303-1306; *Plays* 1386-1388

SEE ALSO: *Eating* 20; *Critics* 1096; *Authors* 1216

AUTHORS

1166 Meeting one's literary idol face to face is sometimes a sad experience, according to George Dolby, who was Dickens' lecture manager.

"During the progress of a reading," he tells, "my attention was drawn to a gentleman who was in a most excited state. Imagining him to be ill and wanting assistance, I said, 'What's the matter with you?'

" 'Say, who's that man on the platform reading?'

" 'Mr. Charles Dickens,' I replied.

" 'But that ain't the real Charles Dickens, the man as wrote all them books I've been reading all these years?'

" 'The same.'

" 'Well, all I've got to say about it then is that he knows no more about Sam Weller'n a cow does of pleating a shirt, at all events that ain't my idea of Sam Weller, anyhow.' And he clapped his hat on his head and left in a state of high dudgeon."

1167 The Emily Dickinson house in Amherst has been converted into a shrine, preserving the memory and relics of the distinguished American poetess. During his administration, President Coolidge, chancing to pass through Amherst, stopped off at the Dickinson shrine to do it honor.

In deference to the President, he was shown throughout the house and permitted to see and handle many relics carefully shut away from the general public. At last, in the small upper room in which Emily Dickinson had done much of her writing, the greatest special privilege was conferred upon him. Stooping down, his guide opened a locked chest and removed from it a packet of the holograph manuscripts of some of her most famous poems. These were put into Coolidge's hand. He examined them with interest and handed them back making, at the same time, his only comment on the entire tour, "Wrote with a pen, eh? I dictate."

1168 Nicholas Murray Butler and Professor Brander Matthews of Columbia University were having a conversation, and Prof. Matthews was giving his ideas as to plagiarism, from an article of his own on that subject.

"In the case of the first man to use an anecdote," he said, "there is originality; in the case of the second there is plagiarism; with the third, it is lack of originality; and with the fourth it is drawing from a common stock."

"Yes," broke in President Butler, "and in the case of the fifth, it is research."

1169 Henry James could never rest content with the phrases that came to his tongue. He simply couldn't leave the English language alone; he would extract a word from his verbal storehouse, drop it, substitute another, then a third, and so on until he had constructed a veritable pyramid of synonyms. This terrible word-malady broke out once at Prince's Restaurant as he gave the waiter his order:

"Bring me . . . fetch me . . . carry me . . . supply me . . . in other words (I hope you are following me) serve—when it is cooked . . . scorched . . . grilled I should say—a large . . . considerable . . . meaty (as opposed to fatty) . . . chop."

1170 While Voltaire was living in retirement in Geneva, he was visited by the Italian Casanova. Voltaire had been reading some recent works by Haller, the Bernese savant, and praised him to his guest. "That is commendation which is indeed ill requited," said Casanova. "I have heard that Haller, far from returning your compliment says that your writing is more than half nonsense." "Ah well, then," returned the famous wit with a wry smile, "it may be that we were both mistaken in our judgment."

1171 One day Dr. Johnson received a message from Oliver Goldsmith that his landlady had called in an officer to arrest him for non-payment of his bill. Johnson immediately sent him a guinea and himself proceeded to the scene of battle at his own best speed. When he arrived Goldsmith had already broken the guinea to procure a bottle of Madeira, and being well stimulated by the contents, was berating his landlady soundly when Johnson entered. The heavy angel interrupted his eloquence to inquire if he had any means of raising money, whereat Goldsmith produced the manuscript of a novel. This Johnson pocketed, hurried away to Newberry the bookseller, and returned shortly with £60. This was the "Vicar of Wakefield."

1172 On the last three days of July the genius of English narrative stood in the pillory—in Cheapside first and then in the Temple. He had a triumph there. The notable "Hymn to the Pillory," which he had composed in prison, was chanted by the crowd. The flower-girls of the district wreathed the pillory with chaplets of their own weaving. Money, said to have been subscribed by the High Church faction "for his torment," circulated mysteriously among the audience, who spent it in liquor with which they drank his health. Still we are not to forget that the creator of "Crusoe" stood three times in the pillory, victim of clerical hatred.

1173 Lord Craven during the reign of King James I was anxious to meet Ben Johnson, the poet. When the latter learned of it he proceeded to call on his lordship. He was in a very shabby condition and the porter insulted him and asked him to go about his business. The poet, enraged, returned the compliments. Lord Craven, hearing the disturbance came out to inquire about it.

"I understand your lordship wishes to see me," said the poet.
"You, friend!" exclaimed Lord Craven. "Who are you?"
"Ben Johnson."

"No, no—you can't be Ben Johnson who wrote 'The Silent Woman'; you look as if you could not say Boo to a goose."

"Boo, then!" cried Ben.

His lordship laughed and profusely apologized: "You are Ben Johnson after all."

1174 Sir Walter Scott told this story: "One morning last Spring I opened a huge lump of a despatch . . . the contents proved to be a MS play, by a young lady of New York who kindly requested me to read and correct it, equip it with prologue and epilogue, procure for it a favorable reception from the manager of Drury Lane, and make Murray or Constable bleed handsomely for the copyright; and inspecting the cover I found that I had been charged five pounds odd for the postage. This was bad enough,—but there was no help, so I groaned and submitted. A fortnight or so after, another packet, of not less formidable bulk arrived, and I was absent enough to break its seal too without examination.

Conceive my horror when out jumped the same identical tragedy of 'The Cherokee Lovers,' with a second epistle from the authoress, stating that, as the winds had been boisterous, she feared the vessel entrusted with her former communication might have foundered, and therefore judged it prudent to forward a duplicate."

1175 At an unguarded moment Piron was buttonholed by a poetaster who, standing his victim in a corner, announced that he was going to read him the five entire acts of a tragedy he had just dashed off. After hearing the first scene, Piron perceived that the play was nothing but a potpourri of verses pillaged from other poets. So as he stood wearily listening he took off his hat and made a low bow to each quotation he recognized. The author at length lifted his eyes, observed Piron's repeated salutation, and asked him why he bowed so often. "Why," said Piron as he edged away, "that is the way I am accustomed to recognize old friends when I find them."

1176 Albert Smith once wrote an article in "Blackwood's," signed "A.S."

"Tut," said Douglas Jerrold, on reading the initials, "what a pity Smith will tell only two-thirds of the truth."

1177 Self-criticism is an admirable human trait. It is demonstrated in this story about Samuel Goldwyn. A ghost writer, who had been doing a series of articles purporting to be by Goldwyn, became sick and one of the pieces was done by a substitute ghost. Goldwyn, upon reading this article, expressed some dismay, saying, "This is not up to my usual standard."

1178 Bernard Shaw's name first became familiar to the general public as a result of scurrilous attacks, disguised as interviews, made upon him by a section of the London evening press. The interviewer would force his way into Shaw's modest apartment, apparently for no other purpose than to bully and insult him.

Many people maintained that Shaw must be an imaginary personage. Why did he stand it? Why didn't he kick the interviewer downstairs? Failing that why didn't he call the police? It seemed difficult to believe in the existence of a being so Christian as this poor persecuted Shaw appeared to be. Everyone talked about him.

As a matter of fact, the interviews were written by Shaw himself.

1179 When Jean Baptiste Rousseau wrote his ode "To Posterity," Voltaire, doubtful of its quality, remarked, "This poem will not reach its destination."

1180 Nathaniel Hawthorne, having lost his government position, went home, dejected and almost desperate. His wife, after a time, learning the reason for his gloom, instead of giving way to reproaches, set pen and ink on the table, and, lighting a fire in the grate, put her arms about his shoulders and said, "Now you will be able to write your book."

He took heart of grace and the world was enriched with "The Scarlet Letter."

1181 When Spenser had finished the "Faërie Queen," he carried it to the Earl of Southampton, the great patron of the poets of those days. The manuscript being sent up to the Earl, he read a few pages, and then ordered the servant to give the writer twenty pounds. Reading further, he cried in rapture, "Carry that man another twenty pounds!"

Proceeding still, he said, "Give him twenty pounds more." But at length he lost all patience, and said, "Go, turn the fellow out of the house, for if I read on I shall be ruined."

1182 Dr. Johnson was asked by Miss Brooke, a would-be authoress, to read a play she had just written, called "The Siege of Sinope." In an offhand manner she informed the Doctor that she wanted his criticism because she had too many irons in the fire to give her play the correction that she felt it might need. Without expressing any curiosity about the manuscript, the Doctor replied: "In that case, Madam, I would say: Put your tragedy where your irons are."

1183 Dryden and Otway lived opposite each other in Queen Street. Otway coming one night from the tavern chalked upon Dryden's door, "Here lives John Dryden; he is a wit."

Dryden knew his handwriting, and, next day, chalked on Otway's door: "Here lives Tom Otway; he is oppo-site."

1184 The record of Shakespeare's wit is hardly hilarious. There was the pun àpropos of his god-paternity to one of Ben Johnson's children. Ben found him in an attitude of thought and asked him the reason. Will replied that he was pondering what to give his godchild and had just decided:

"I' faith, Ben, I'll e'en give him a dozen of good latten spoons, and thou shalt translate them."

1185 On one occasion a group was assembled, including Oscar Wilde and Frank Harris. Harris, it seems, was addicted to plagiarism in his conversation and on this occasion told as his own an anecdote which every one recognized as a paraphrase of a story of Anatole France. A silence followed the story, which Wilde at last broke. "Frank," he said gravely, "Anatole France would have spoiled that story."

1186 When Wordsworth said to Lamb, "I believe I could write like Shakespeare, if I had a mind to try it." "Yes, n-nothing is w-wanting but the m-mind," came Lamb's answer as swiftly as the stutter would allow.

1187 An Englishman being left alone with Richardson, observed to him "he was happy to pay his respects to the author of 'Sir Charles Grandison,' for at Paris and at the Hague and in fact, at every place I have visited it is much admired." Richardson appeared not to notice the compliment, but when all the company were assembled addressed the gentleman with,

"Sir, I think you were saying something about 'Sir Charles Grandison.'"

"No sir," he replied, "I do not remember ever to have heard it mentioned."

1188   Queen Elizabeth, being much enraged against Dr. Heyward, author of the "Life of Henry the Fourth," had ordered her law officers to proceed against him, and, amongst others, inquired of Lord Bacon "if there was not treason in the book."

Bacon readily answered, "No, madam, I cannot answer for there being treason in it, but I am certain it contains much felony."

"How?" eagerly exclaimed her Majesty, "how, and wherein?"

"In many passages," replied Bacon, "which he has stolen from Tacitus."

1189   Lillah McCarthy asked George Bernard Shaw why he had come to live in England instead of seeking his inspiration among the Dublin poets — George Moore, A. E., Yeats and the others. He answered: "Lord bless you, I'm old enough to be A. E.'s father; and George Moore had not discovered Ireland then. He was in Paris studying painting. He hadn't even discovered himself. The Ireland that you know did not exist. I could not stay there, dreaming my life away on the Irish hills. England had conquered Ireland; so there was nothing for it but to come over here and conquer England. Which, you will notice, I have done pretty thoroughly."

1190   William Dean Howells once read a poem which had been brought to him by an aspiring young writer. "This is a magnificent poem," said Howells. "Did you write it unaided?"

"Yes, sir," said the young man. "Every word of it."

Mr. Howells rose and said, "I'm very glad to meet you, Lord Byron. I was under the impression that you had died at Missolonghi a good many years ago."

1191   Boswell, dining one day with Dr. Johnson, asked him if he did not think that a good cook was more essential to the community than a good poet.

"I don't suppose," said Dr. Johnson, "that there's a dog in the town but what thinks so."

1192   An American had been crying aloud for an opportunity to meet H. G. Wells, the author, for whose works he had an ardent admiration. At one of these luncheons, it was arranged that he should sit next to Mr. Wells, and all through the luncheon he had a wonderful time talking to the source of his admiration. After the luncheon a friend said to him: "Well, you had your opportunity at last to meet your patron saint, didn't you?"

"Who is that?" he blandly asked.

"H. G. Wells," was the answer.

"H. G. Wells?" he echoed in surprise. "I haven't met Wells. I wish I could."

"Well," was the reply, "you certainly talked enough to him during the luncheon."

"What?" he gasped in sheer amazement. "You don't mean to say that was H. G. Wells, the author? . . . Good Heavens, man, I told that man the whole plot in detail of 'Mr. Britling Sees It Through,' and when I asked him if he had ever read the book, he said he had not."

1193   Sir Lewis Morris was complaining to Oscar Wilde about the neglect of his poems by the press. "It is a complete conspiracy of silence. What ought I to do, Oscar?"

"Join, it," replied Wilde.

1194   The main pattern of Shelley's life was an alternation of sleeping and reading. He was, in fact, always fatigued from night reading, and had a habit of falling asleep by day, anywhere, suddenly, like a child. At Oxford he read about sixteen out of every twenty-four hours, his eyes always in a book when eating or when walking, whether in country lanes or on the streets. . . . It was his habit at this time to read standing, where possible. Trelawney reported that he left Shelley at ten one morning, standing at the mantel in his study, reading and returning at six, found him in the same position still reading, looking pale and exhausted.

1195   Some of the admirers of the 18th Century German poet Klopstock made a journey from Gottingen to Hamburg to ask him to explain a difficult passage in his works. Klopstock received them graciously, read the passage, and said: "I cannot recollect what I meant when I wrote it, but I remember it was the finest thing I ever wrote, and you cannot do better than devote your lives to the discovery of its meaning."

1196   John Erskine one time went to lecture at the University of Pennsylvania. The President of the University had never met

Dr. Erskine, and did not immediately succeed in finding him when he went to meet him on the station platform. When the two men had at last identified one another, the President of the University said, "I asked one gentleman if he were Dr. Erskine, and he said emphatically, 'I should say not!' I asked another one and he said, 'I wish I were.' That proves that at least one of them had read your books."

"Yes," said Erskine. "But which one!"

1197 When D'Angeau, a Parisian writer, heard that all rank and merit were threatened with destruction on the breaking out of the Revolution, he exclaimed: "Well, come what will, I have two hundred verbs well conjugated in my escritoir!"

1198 When George Bernard Shaw, as a young man, emerged from his native Ireland and moved to England he began writing a column for a London weekly publication. At that time Oscar Wilde was enjoying his vogue as a wit and epigram-maker. One evening an acquaintance, calling upon Wilde, happened upon a copy of the paper to which Shaw was a contributor and reading therein one of Shaw's characteristic articles which was signed with the author's initials, said to his host:

"I say, Wilde, who is this chap G. B. S. who's doing a department for this sheet?"

"He's a young Irishman named Shaw," said Wilde. "Rather forceful, isn't he?"

"Forceful," echoed the other, "well, rather! My word, how he does cut and slash! He doesn't seem to spare anyone he knows. I should say he is in a fair way to make himself a lot of enemies."

"Well," said Wilde, "as yet he hasn't become prominent enough to have any enemies. But none of his friends like him."

1199 Soon after Goldsmith's death, some people dining with Dr. Johnson were commenting freely on some parts of Goldsmith's works which in their opinion, showed neither talent nor originality. To this Dr. Johnson listened for some time, when at length his patience being exhausted he arose with great dignity, looked them full in the face, and exclaimed, "If nobody were allowed to abuse poor Goldsmith but those who could write as well, he would have few censors."

1200 Goldsmith and Johnson one time had an argument on the merits of Warburton, the writer. Goldsmith asserted that

Warburton was a weak writer. Dr. Johnson refuted this, saying, "Warburton may be absurd, but he will never be weak; he flounders well."

1201 Sophocles wrote tragedies to the very end of his long life. On account of this zeal for writing he seemed to be neglecting his business affairs so his sons summoned him to court that a jury might pronounce him incompetent to manage his estate on the ground of senility. Then the old man is said to have recited to his judges a play which he had just finished and had in his hands, the "Oedipus at Colonnus," and to have asked whether the poem seemed the work of a man in his dotage. After his recitation he was freed by a vote of the jurors.

1202 Somebody told Jerrold that a friend of his, a prolific writer, was about to dedicate a book to him.

"Ah!" replied Jerrold gravely, "that's an awful weapon he has in his hands!"

1203 Barry Cornwall tells how he once said something in Lamb's presence which he thought possessed some smartness.

Lamb commended him with a stammer.

"Very well, my dear boy, very well; Ben" (taking a pinch of snuff) "Ben Jonson has said worse than that—and b-b-better."

1204 At the Garrick Club in London the witty librettist, W. S. Gilbert, was once making light of Shakespeare, to the horror of most of those surrounding him. "All right then," said Gilbert in answering to their protests. "Let us take this passage for example:

'I would as lief be thrust through a quickset hedge,
    As cry, "Plosh," to a callow throstle.' "

"Why, that's perfectly clear," insisted one of his hearers, rising to the defense of the Bard. "It just means that this birdlover would rather get himself all scratched up in the thorny bush than disturb the bird's song. What play is the passage from?"

"No play," said Gilbert, "I made it up—and jolly good Shakespeare too."

1205 Frank Harris, Whistler and Oscar Wilde were playing billiards one day. Whistler uttered a bon mot. Whereupon Wilde enviously said, "I wish I had said that."

"Don't worry, Oscar," retorted Harris, "you will."

1206 Dryden, when about to compose, had himself "blooded and purged."

1207 William Blake, English mystic, poet, and artist said, "I write when commanded by the spirits, and the moment I have written I see the words fly about the room in all directions. It is then published and the spirits can read. My manuscripts are of no further use. I have been tempted to burn my manuscripts, but my wife won't let me."

1208 Stevenson's prose tales often came to him as dreams. "In the small hours one morning," writes his wife, "I was awakened by cries of horror from Louis. Thinking he had a nightmare I awakened him. He said angrily: 'Why did you awaken me? I was dreaming a fine bogey tale.' "
    This was "Dr. Jekyll and Mr. Hyde."

1209 The power of the pen is excellently illustrated by an incident in the war between the ancient Greeks and Romans. A group of Athenians were seized and held captive at Syracuse. To help pass the time they enacted many scenes from the plays of Euripides. Their captors were so favorably impressed by the beauty of the verses that instead of treating their prisoners cruelly as was their custom, they persuaded them to continue their play-acting and held them as honored guests.
    Upon their return to Athens, the former captives went to the home of Euripides and informed him of the effect of his plays upon the supposedly heartless men of Syracuse. So great was their gratitude towards the great dramatist that they treated him as though he had actually rescued them in combat on the field of battle.

1210 Boileau, in presenting a poet to M. d'Hemery, addressed him, "Sir, I present to you a person who will give you immortality; but you must give him something to live upon in the meantime."

1211 DuBose Heyward was once lecturing in Detroit. After his talk, a group of local women insisted upon questioning him as to his opinion of their local laureate, Edgar A. Guest. After vainly seeking to side-step the issue, Heyward was at last driven to acknowledge that he did not consider Mr. Guest's work poetry. Great indignation resulted.

"Mr. Heyward," snapped one fearsome lady, "what kind of car do you drive?"

The poet and novelist was compelled to admit that he drove none.

"Eddie Guest," said the lady cuttingly, "drives a Packard."

1212   "Doctor," said Frederick Reynolds, the dramatist, to Dr. Baillie, the celebrated physician, "don't you think that I write too much for my nervous system?"

"No, I don't," said Dr. Baillie, "but I think you write too much for your reputation."

1213   In his later years a lady called upon Mark Twain to express her enthusiasm for his work. She wanted to kiss his hand. He accepted it with perfect dignity and seriousness. "How God must love you!" said the lady. "I hope so," said Mark Twain gently. After she had gone, he observed as gently and without a smile, "I guess she hasn't heard of our strained relations."

1214   An author was reading some bad verses in his poem to a friend in a very cold apartment. The critic cried out in a shaking fit:

"My dear friend, either put fire into your verses or your verses into the fire or I shall not be able to stand here any longer."

1215   After coming out of jail Frank Harris decided that he would rather commit suicide than go in again; and as he always had a contempt for Court orders and ignored everything, he felt liable to arrest at any moment. So that he might not again suffer indignity, he carried with him a small packet of cyanide of potassium, which he proposed to swallow before the hand of the Law could touch him.

On his last trip to New York he was packing up at quarantine when a steward came along and told him he was wanted by the captain. Harris' heart fell. Here it was. He concealed the packet of poison in his right hand and followed the steward, and when he saw the captain talking to a tall, smooth, well-fed man he knew it could only be the worst.

"You wanted me?" gulped Frank.

The captain inclined his head toward the third man, who

was eyeing Frank keenly.

"Mr. Frank Harris?" asked the American.

Frank wished he wasn't, but admitted the stigma.

"Pleased to meet you, Mr. Harris," said the large man, extending his hand. "I'm the mayor, and I've come right off the tug-boat to tell you . . . that we are honored to offer you the freedom of our great city."

Hastily Frank changed the poison packet into his left hand and greeted the mayor.

1216   Shortly after the sensational reception accorded the publication of his marvelous translation of "The Arabian Nights," Sir Richard Burton made the following statement:

"For thirty years I served Her Majesty at home and abroad without acknowledgment or reward. I publish a pornographic book, and at once earn 10,000 pounds and fame. I begin at last to understand the public and what it wants."

1217   At one time, before they had achieved the fame that later came to them, Dorothy Parker and Robert Benchley shared a tiny office in the Metropolitan Opera House building. When Benchley was out in the search for Eldorado, Miss Parker frequently found herself oppressively lonely in the gloomy cubby-hole. No one ever came to see them.

She solved this problem adroitly and procured for herself no end of company by inducing the sign painter to put on the office door, instead of their names, the word "Gentlemen."

1218   On the subject of proof reading some authors are a menace to their publishers, while others suffer from legitimate grievances. In one such instance an author, Ward Dorrance, wrote to his publishers on the subject of the proofs of his book: "In all the proof that has reached me windrow has been spelled window. If, in the bound book, windrow still appears as window, then neither rain nor hail nor gloom of night nor fleets of riot squads will prevent me from assassinating the man who is responsible. If the coward hides beyond my finding, I shall step into Scribner's and merely shoot up the place, Southern style."

1219   The import of Thomas Hardy's birth was so little appreciated that he was thrown aside for dead. Presently he must have been so in fact, had not the nurse glancing up from

attending the mother, cried out suddenly, "Dead! Stop a
minute. He's alive enough, sure!"

RELATED SUBJECTS: *Literature* 1161-1162; *Books* 1221-
1224; *Playwrights* 1376-1385

SEE ALSO: *Dullness* 193; *Eccentricity* 202, 208; *Gentlemanliness* 256; *Long-Windedness* 357; *Modesty* 386,
388; *Patience* 391; *Practical Joking* 433, 434; *Quarrelsomeness* 466; *Rough and Ready* 505; *Vanity* 626;
Women 841; *Infidelity* 904; *Births, Birthdays* 1011,
1013; *Critics* 1099; *Newspapers* 1244; *Magazines* 1251;
Painting 1288; *Miracles* 1616; *Deathbed Scenes* 1764,
1775; *Swimming* 1892; *Taxes* 2193; *Poverty* 2202,
2206, 2211; *Stealing* 2590

BOOKS

1221 It was an Englishman, met in a train somewhere in
Europe, who startled Mark Twain by saying abruptly, "Mr.
Clemens, I would give ten pounds not to have read your
'Huckleberry Finn'!" And when Mark looked up, awaiting an
explanation of this extraordinary remark, the Englishman
smiled and added: "So that I could have again the great
pleasure of reading it for the first time."

1222 Sir John Malcolm once asked Warren Hastings, who
was a contemporary and a companion of Dr. Johnson and
Boswell, what was his real estimation of Boswell's "Life of
Johnson?"

"Sir," replied Hastings, "it's the dirtiest book in my library."
Then proceeding, he added: "I knew Boswell intimately; and
I well remember when his book first made its appearance,
Boswell was so full of it that he could neither think nor talk
of anything else: so much so, that meeting Lord Thurlow
hurrying through Parliament Street to get to the House of
Lords, where an important debate was expected, for which he
was already too late, Boswell had the temerity to stop and
accost him with: "Have you read my book?"

"Yes, damn you!" replied Lord Thurlow, "every word of it;
I could not help myself."

1223   Coleridge was always a tremendous reader. While he was a student at Christ's Hospital, he used to spend his free time wandering aimlessly about London, shivering in front of the windows of book-shops and print-shops. Once, while so standing, he got, in his own words "absent-mindedly involved" with "the coat-tail pocket" of a stranger, who "at first took him for a thief, then was so charmed by his conversation that he made him free of a library in Cheapside." Thenceforth "he would run all risks in skulking out to get the two volumes to which he was entitled daily."

1224   When Dr. Johnson was told that Rousseau's "Confessions" would contain every motive that had induced him to act in every situation—"Then," replied he, "if he was an honest man, his book will not be worth a farthing."

RELATED SUBJECTS: *Literature* 1161-1162; *Authors* 1166-1219; *Libraries* 1226

SEE ALSO: *Borrowing* 125; *Practical Joking* 432; *Censors* 2354

LIBRARIES

1226   The famous American orator, Robert Ingersoll, was the owner of a remarkable and celebrated library of atheistical books. An interviewer once asked Ingersoll what the library had cost him. Thinking it over a moment, Ingersoll replied, "It certainly cost me the Governorship of Illinois, and possibly even the Presidency of the United States."

RELATED SUBJECTS: *Literature* 1161-1162; *Books* 1221-1224

SEE ALSO: *Borrowing* 126; *Modesty* 380; *Books* 1223; *Bigotry* 1629

LANGUAGE

1231   On New Year's Eve, a Negro in Harlem added a new word to the language. He stood on a street corner and shouted: "Hallalouyear!"

Before morning revelers all over the city were shouting "Hallalouyear!"

1232 "Why don't you buy a dictionary?" asked the man whose friend repeatedly consulted him as to the spelling of certain words.

"What would I do with a dictionary?" was the reply. "If I can't spell the words, I couldn't find 'em, and if I can spell 'em, I don't need a dictionary."

1233 "What's status quo, Daddy?"

"Son," said his father gravely, "that's just the name of the mess we're in."

RELATED SUBJECTS: *Speeches* 756-782; *Talking* 806-818; *Literature* 1161-1162

SEE ALSO: *Bishops* 1495

NEWSPAPERS

1236 Booth Tarkington, while stopping at a little Indiana town, lost one of his dogs.

"Have you a newspaper in town?" he asked of the landlord.

"Right across the way, there, back of the shoemaker's," the landlord told him. "The 'Daily News'——best little paper of its size in town."

The editor, the printer, and the printer's devil were all busy doing justice to Mr. Tarkington with an "in-our-midst" paragraph when the novelist arrived.

"I've just lost a dog," Tarkington explained after he had introduced himself, "and I'd like to have you insert this ad for me: 'Fifty dollars reward for the return of a pointer dog answering to the name of Rex. Disappeared from the yard of the Mansion House Monday night.'"

"Why, we were just going to press, Sir," the editor said, "but we'll be only too glad to hold the edition for your ad."

Mr. Tarkington returned to the hotel. After a few minutes he decided, however, that it might be well to add, "No questions asked" to his advertisement, and returned to the "Daily News" office.

The place was deserted, save for the skinny little freckle-faced devil, who sat perched on a high stool, gazing wistfully out of the window.

"Where is everybody?" Tarkington asked.

"Gawn to hunt th' dawg," replied the boy, without removing his gaze from the distant fields.

1237 They called Eleanor Roosevelt "God's gift to newspaper women" because she made it easier for women to get news of the White House, and because she made jobs for them by making much news which only women could get. No previous First Lady held press conferences or gave news directly. Nevertheless, there was painful truth as well as humorous fiction in the Women's National Press Club skit in which a frazzled inmate of the "Eleanor Roosevelt Home for Exhausted Newspaper Women" clasped her hands, and petitioned Heaven: "Dear God, let me pray the prayer they say that Franklin (Roosevelt) prays. Just for one day, God, please make her tired! Dear God, just for one day!"

1238 A Metropolitan paper once chartered a locomotive to rush a green reporter to a near-by town to scoop all rivals with first news of a fire that was burning the place down. A couple of hours later the managing editor got a telegram from the bright young man reading: "Have arrived at the fire. What shall I do?"

The editor replied: "Find the place where the fire is hottest and jump in!"

1239 One of the first big assignments that fell to Maury H. B. Paul as a young society editor was the covering of the seasonal opening of the Metropolitan Opera House. He had not been long in New York and was not familiar enough with the personalities to identify the occupants of the lavish boxes.

He resorted to the device of slipping around the corridor during the act and copying the names from the brass plates on the doors. The following day he was summoned to the office of his employer, Frank Munsey.

"I have just had a telephone call from Mrs. Stuyvesant Fish," said Munsey. "She has read your account of the Metropolitan première. She thought you might be interested to know that you have succeeded in opening half the graves in Woodlawn Cemetery."

Thus Mr. Paul learned, the hard way, that the name of the original box-owner is usually left on the door no matter who subsequently may occupy it.

1240 When Heywood Broun, as a cub reporter, once went to interview Senator Smoot for the "N.Y. World," the legislator from the Mormon State pompously said, "No, I have nothing to say."

"I know," coldly replied young Broun, "now let's get down to the interview."

1241 In an upstate New York town, certain busybodies began to carp about the carelessness of the grammar and general diction of the editor of the local weekly newspaper. Having heard echoes of this, that dignitary rose at the next town meeting and said, "I hear I been criticised somewhat by some of you folks for usin' poor grammar. I have three good reasons for it. To begin with, I don't know any better. If I did, none of you would know the difference; and more than that, if I spoke and wrote any better than I do, I'd be managing editor of a big New York paper at a decent salary and you farmers would lose the best darned editor in Herkimer county."

1242 Wendell Phillips once addressed an abolitionist meeting in Boston where the audience was hostile to him. They yelled and sang and completely drowned his voice. The reporters were seated in a row just under the platform. Phillips made no attempt to address the howling audience, but bent over and seemed to be speaking in a low tone to the reporters. By and by the curiosity of the audience was excited; they ceased to clamor and tried to hear what he was saying to the reporters. Phillips looked at them coldly and said:

"Go on, gentlemen, go on. I do not need your ears. Through these pencils I speak to thirty millions of people."

1243 A man who considered himself a humorist sent a selection of his original jokes to the editor of a newspaper, and confidently awaited a check. He was much elated when, a few days later, he received a letter bearing the imprint of the newspaper. Upon opening it, however, instead of a check, he found a brief note: "Dear Sir: Your jokes received. Some we have seen before, some we have not seen yet."

1244 When Robert Bridges came back from America, he told how when he evaded the interviewers who met him on the boat, they got back at him by printing in their papers in their largest caption: "The King's Canary Refuses to Sing."

1245 While in Denver on the "Tribune," Eugene Field hung on the wall: "God bless our proofreader. He can't call for him too soon."

1246 The editor of a tiny small-town newspaper had cherished for many years a set of old-fashioned wooden scarehead type of some 60 point size. On more than one occasion his assistants had tried to induce him to use it, but he always firmly vetoed the idea.

One summer the old man went away for a short fishing trip. In his absence a cyclone struck the town; tore the steeple off the church, unroofed several houses, sucked a couple of wells dry, and scattered a few barns around. No bigger calamity had hit the town in years. So, figuring "Now's our chance," his assistants got down the 60 point type from the shelf and set up a sensational front page headline with it.

Two days later the editor came storming into the office in a high dudgeon. "Balls of fire!" he shouted. "What d'ye mean by taking down that type for a cyclone? All these years I've been savin' that type for the Second Coming of Christ!"

1247 It was at the Yale-Princeton game on Thanksgiving Day, 1890, that Richard Harding Davis risked his job. His managing editor, Arthur Brisbane, had a sidelines ticket but he was accompanied by a friend who was behind the fence without one. Let Reporter Davis turn over his pass to the friend and retire to the stands. Davis refused pointblank and with undiplomatic emphasis. He was reporting this game, it was best done from the sidelines, there was his post, and there he was staying, he informed his chief. Otherwise, he remarked, McClay would take his head off. Rather than the fury of his city editor, he would chance the wrath, once removed, of his managing editor. Brisbane and guest relegated themselves to the stands.

When Brisbane told the story at the office that night, a subordinate asked him if Davis was to be fired.

"No," said the editor, "raise his salary!"

1248 Out of newspaper offices come some very extravagant yarns. There is the one told about Chapin, famous New York editor, who made it a strict rule that his employees were not to hang around the office on "days off."

A certain reporter on his staff fell in with a friend on his day off, Thursday, and they went on a "bat" that lasted for six days. On the seventh day, a trifle weak but cold sober, the reporter, realizing that he was in for trouble, decided that the best thing to do would be to go to the office and get it over with.

When the boss came in the reporter was waiting in his office. Without waiting for an explanation, Chapin shouted, "What the hell are you doing here on your day off? Get out of here and don't come back until tomorrow at nine."

RELATED SUBJECTS: *Literature* 1161-1162; *Magazines* 1251-1252

SEE ALSO: *Boners* 107, 109, 113, 114, 117, 119; *Brevity* 131, 133; *Exaggeration* 224; *Extravagance* 232; *Patriotism* 403; *Vanity* 614, 618; *Gossip* 825, 826; *Sickness* 1701; *Death* 1747; *Cabinet Members* 1953; *Advertising* 2101

MAGAZINES

1251 "Dear Jack London," wrote the editor of a well-known magazine. "If I don't receive your story within twenty-four hours, I'll come up to your room and kick you downstairs. And I always keep my promises."

London sent this reply:

"Dear Dick: If I did all my work with my feet, I'd keep my promises too."

1252 The distinguished editor, the late George Horace Lorimer, was obliged, as are all editors, to reject by far the greater number of stories sent to him.

In the early days of his career when a great burden of editorial reading fell to him he once received a letter from an indignant woman, who said, "Last week you rejected my story. I know that you did not read it for, as a test, I pasted together pages 15, 16 and 17, and the manuscript came back with the pages still pasted. You are a fraud and you turn down stories without even reading them."

Mr. Lorimer replied: "Madam, at breakfast when I open an

egg, I don't have to eat the whole egg to discover it is bad."

RELATED SUBJECTS: *Literature* 1161-1162; *Authors* 1166-1219; *Newspapers* 1236-1248

SEE ALSO: *Women* 842; *Literature* 1162

ART

1256 Someone called, "Monsieur Degas!" It was Vibert, the well-known painter of "The Cardinals."

"You must come to see our exhibition of watercolors," he said. Then he gave a sidelong glance at the old mackintosh Degas was wearing, and added: "You may find our frames and rugs a little too fancy for you, but art is always a luxury, isn't it?"

"Yours, perhaps," retorted Degas; "but mine is an absolute necessity."

RELATED SUBJECTS: *Literature* 1161-1162; *Painting and Drawing* 1261-1293; *Sculpture* 1296-1297; *Architecture* 1301-1302; *Music* 1303-1306; *Plays* 1386-1388

PAINTING AND DRAWING

1261 Of Correggio the painter it is told that upon seeing one of the works of Raphael, he could only express his feelings by exclaiming with a noble pride in their common art: "And I too am a painter!"

1262 Tolstoy tells the following story about Brulov, the Russian artist.

"One day, in correcting a sketch made by one of his pupils, he added a stroke or two with his own brush, and immediately put the breath of life into what had been a very mediocre piece of work. 'But my sketch is entirely changed,' said the pupil, 'and all you've done is to add a few strokes to it.'

"'The reason for that,' answered Brulov, 'is that Art entered the thing just where those strokes began.'"

1263 Degas rarely ever indulged in anything more than mildly biting repartee except when art or "the established order" was attacked. Bonnet, for instance, was showing him a picture by one of his pupils, representing a warrior drawing his bow.

"Just see how well he aims!" said Bonnet.

"Aiming at a prize—isn't he?" replied Degas.

1264 Although the French public at first said only that cubism was crazy, a leading art merchant added, "I am now buying Picasso not because I have any taste for him but because he will be worth a lot of money someday."

1265 Honoré de Balzac lived many years in a cold and all but empty attic. There was no flame in his fireplace, no picture on his wall. But on one wall he inscribed with charcoal: "Rosewood paneling with commode;" on another, "Gobelin tapestry with Venetian mirror," and in the place of honor over the fireless grate, "Picture by Raphael."

1266 When someone asked the famous painter Orpen: "How do you mix your colors?" he answered: "With brains, sir."

1267 When Tintoretto was a little boy he entered Titian's studio, but that master could not foresee the artistic in the boy and sent him home after three days, with the message, "He will never be anything but a dauber."

1268 The artist Turner invited Charles Kingsley, the author, to his studio to view his picture of a storm at sea. Kingsley was wrapt in admiration.

"How did you do it?" he exclaimed.

"I wished to paint a storm at sea," answered Turner, "so I went to the coast of Holland and engaged a fisherman to take me out in his boat in the next storm. The storm was brewing, and I went down to his boat and bade him bind me to its mast. Then he drove the boat out into the teeth of the storm. The storm was so furious that I longed to be down in the bottom of the boat and allow it to blow over me. But I could not; I was bound to the mast. Not only did I see that storm and feel it, but it blew itself into me till I became part of the storm. And then I came back and painted that picture."

1269 Cézanne observed that Ambroise Vollard was looking with some curiosity at a row of big druggist's pots set out on the floor, and bearing abbreviated Latin inscriptions: Jusqui., Aqu., Still., Ferug., Rib., Sulf., Cup., and volunteered:

"That, Monsieur, is my paint box. I am going to show 'em that with drugs I can paint beautiful things, while they, with their fine colors, make nothing but drugs!"

1270   Orozco is a deeply embittered soul; a veritable glare comes from behind the very thick lenses of his glasses. He is one-armed; his body has a tortured twist. But in personal relations Orozco is never bitter. He is the kindliest man I know, solicitous toward other folk, warmly compassionate . . . His early work, not sufficiently academic, was derided in Mexico. Disheartened, he decided to go to the United States where artistic experimentation seemed to have more of a chance. But at the American border a comprehensive set of drawings was seized in the customs and declared indecent. They were torn up and ground under the feet of our outraged officials, who in those days of contempt for Mexico saw no reason for being considerate of any Mexican, least of all an artist with dubious drawings. Only half a dozen of those early drawings—the House of Tears series—survived, and they are among the finest things Orozco has ever produced.

1271   At a period of Donatello's life he went to Pisa to execute some works there which were found so wonderful that the Pisans broke out into transports of delight, praising the artist to the skies. Oddly enough, however, this excessive praise proved distasteful to the sculptor. He declared that he must go back to Florence for the whimsical reason, that where he was praised by everybody he would soon forget all he knew, grow lazy and self-satisfied, where as at home in Florence he was notoriously abused and found fault with and thus forced always to produce his best, "the constant blame forcing him," as he put it, "to study and consequently to greater achievements."

1272   Samuel F. B. Morse, who was a painter before he invented the telegraph, once asked a physician friend to look at his painting of a man in death agony. "Well," Morse inquired after the doctor had scrutinized it carefully, "what is your opinion?"

"Malaria," said the doctor.

1273 Alfred Steiglitz, the husband of Georgia O'Keeffe, has also always been the exclusive handler of her paintings. In most cases he has been reluctant to part with them at all. Occasionally he would name, in a sort of irritation, a sum which he regarded as safely beyond the pale. He once demanded $25,000 for a series of five flower paintings. To his astonishment the price was accepted without question. Miss O'Keeffe was so dumbfounded that for three months she was unable to paint.

1274 In 1906, Gertrude Stein, posed eighty times for Picasso's portrait of her, after which he wiped the face off, saying he couldn't "see" her any more, and then finished the likeness in Spain, where he couldn't see her at all. He also gave her this portrait because, as he later said, at that time in his career the difference between a gift and a sale was, after all, negligible. He also said, when friends complained that the portrait didn't look like her, that someday she'd look like the portrait.

1275 A philosopher called upon a young art student who had just set to work in his first studio after a brilliant course in the art schools of Europe. They talked of the problems relating to beauty, ideals and ambitions. Upon his departure the philosopher paused upon the threshold of the studio and said to the young painter:

"Your art will cease to be great art unless you keep in touch with humanity."

1276 A rich merchant of Genoa commissioned Donatello to carve for him a colossal head. When the model was finished the Genoese objected to the price, saying that he had been engaged only a month on it, and that the sum asked was equal to half a florin a day.

Donatello, turning round, exclaimed that it was possible in a moment to destroy the work of a year, and with a sudden push he threw the head to the ground, where it broke into a hundred pieces.

"It was clear," he said, "that the purchaser ought to confine himself to vegetables and leave art alone."

1277 The works of Millais, the painter, had been collected in a gallery in London, and a friend, Lady Constance Leslie, went early in the day to the exhibition. Going up the stairs, she encountered the painter going out with head bowed down. As she greeted him and he looked up she saw tears in his eyes. "Ah, dear Lady Constance," he said, "you see me unmanned. Well, I'm not ashamed of averring that in looking at my earliest pictures I have been overcome with chagrin that I so far failed in my maturity to fulfill the full forecast of my youth."

1278 When Sir Humphry Davy returned from a visit to Paris he was asked how the picture galleries had impressed him. "The finest collection of frames that I ever saw," he said.

1279 Mark Twain once visited the artist Whistler in his studio and was looking over his pictures. He started to touch one canvas. "Oh," cried Whistler, "don't touch that! Don't you see it isn't dry yet?"

"I don't mind," said Mark Twain, "I have gloves on."

1280 The fine American painter, Georgia O'Keeffe, was slow in appreciating the monetary value of her work, and has never ceased to be somewhat indifferent to it. Characteristic of her reactions was the day when the first sale of one of her pictures occurred. The canvas brought $400. Miss O'Keeffe, who was standing nearby while the transaction was completed, became pale; not because of the sum of money but at the thought that she would never see her painting again.

1281 Whistler once undertook to get a fellow painter's work into the autumn salon. He succeeded and the picture was hung. But the painter, going to see his masterpiece with Whistler on varnishing day, uttered a terrible oath when he beheld it! "Good gracious," he groaned. "You're exhibiting my picture upside down."

"Hush," said Whistler, "the committee refused it the other way."

1282 Correggio was yet in the prime of life when he completed his great work, "The Assumption of the Virgin," which he painted on the ceiling of the dome of the cathedral at Parma. So ignorantly unappreciated was his masterly performance by the canons, his employers, that they not only refused the unfortunate artist the price they had agreed upon, but paid him five hundred crowns, which was all they would allow, in copper. Correggio was carrying home this money to his family who were living in great poverty in a neighboring village, when overcome by the heat of the weather, and the weight of his coppers, he was tempted to slake his thirst at a spring by the wayside, and the consequence was an inflammatory attack, which soon proved fatal.

1283 The great moral satirist, Hogarth, was once drawing in a room where many of his friends were assembled, and among them a young lady. As she stood by Hogarth, she expressed a wish to learn to draw caricature. "Alas! young lady," said Hogarth, "it is not a faculty to be envied. Take my advice, and never draw caricature—by the long practice of it I have lost the enjoyment of beauty. I never see a face but distorted. I have never the satisfaction to behold the human face divine."

1284 Abe Lincoln was shown a picture done by a very indifferent hand, and asked to give an opinion of it.

"Why," said Lincoln, "the painter is a very good painter and observes the Lord's commandments."

"What do you mean by that, Mr. Lincoln?"

"Why, I think," answered Lincoln, "that he hath not made to himself the likeness of anything that is in the heaven above, or that is in the earth beneath or that is in the waters under the earth."

1285 On one occasion a woman said to Whistler: "I just came up from the country this morning along the Thames, and there was an exquisite haze in the atmosphere which reminded me so much of your little things. It was really a perfect series of Whistlers."

"Yes, madam," responded Whistler gravely, "Nature is creeping up."

1286 Degas stopped to look at each canvas, and presently gave a little exclamation of disgust.

"To think," he remarked, "that not one of these fellows has ever gone so far as to ask himself what art is all about!"

"Well, what is it all about?" countered the critic.

"I have spent my whole life trying to find out. If I knew I should have done something about it long ago."

1287 Whistler completed a portrait for a wealthy and highly placed client, who was dissatisfied with the finished work. "I really think, Mr. Whistler," he explained, "that it's a bad work of art."

Whistler shrugged and looked coolly at the man. He said, "But then you must admit that you're not a good work of nature."

1288 Whistler once admired a picture Rossetti was painting, and some time afterward asked him how it was going. "All right," said Rossetti. "I have ordered a stunning frame for it."

Later Whistler saw it framed, but not at all advanced in execution. "You've done nothing to it since I saw it, have you?"

"No-o," said Rossetti, "but I've written a stunning sonnet on the subject."

"Then," replied Whistler, "take out the picture and frame the sonnet."

1289 A painter was advised to turn physician: for now all his faults were seen; then they would be buried.

1290 Whistler detested Turner. Unwittingly, a lady approached him one day requesting, "Mr. Whistler, my husband has discovered in an auction shop what he thinks are two genuine Turners. Would you be kind enough to come and tell us whether they're genuine Turners or imitation Turners."

"Madam," said Whistler, "that's a fine distinction."

1291 Helen Westley, the actress, while playing in a Theatre Guild show in Chicago, decided to see the sights of the city. Some days later, a culture-bitten colleague enthusiastically raised the subject of her visit to the galleries of the Art Institute. "The room of contemporary American painters is superb!" she chanted.

"I prefer the Rembrandt Room," commented Frank Reicher. Then everyone turned questioningly to the noted character actress.

"And which room in the Museum do you prefer, Helen?"

"I?" remarked the incorrigible Miss Westley, without blinking an eyelash, "why I prefer the Ladies Room."

1292 At a showing of the work of Rockwell Kent, a woman, who had been gazing at one of his celebrated angels, approached him and said, "No angel ever looked like that!"

"Have you ever seen an angel, Madam?" asked Kent.

1293 Ambroise Vollard once told Degas of a painter who had come to him, exclaiming, "At last I have found my true style!"

"Well," said Degas, "I'm glad I haven't found my style yet. I'd be bored to death."

RELATED SUBJECTS: *Art* 1256; *Sculpture* 1296-1297; *Architecture* 1301-1302

SEE ALSO: *Eccentricity* 205; *Generosity* 248; *Modesty* 390; *Practical Joking* 435, 436; *Rough and Ready* 499, 506; *Snobbishness* 551; *Beauty* 668; *Age* 676; *Flirtation* 861; *Churchmen* 1451; *Popes* 1501; *Doctors* 1669; *Deathbed Scenes* 1765; *Advertising* 2107; *Real Estate* 2142; *Poverty* 2205, 2206; *Civilians in War* 2340, 2344

SCULPTURE

1296 A cobbler detected a fault in the shoe-latchet of one of Apelles' sculptures and the artist, recognizing his superior information, rectified the fault. The cobbler, blown up by his success, next ventured to criticize the legs, for which he was indignantly kicked out. "Keep to your trade," said the sculptor. "Let not a cobbler overstep his last."

1297 This is a story told by Anatole France. Rodin had just finished an imposing statue of the poet, Victor Hugo, standing upright on the crest of a rock, with Muses and Ocean deities circling about him. One morning the sculptor brought a troupe of journalists to his studio to contemplate the new work. Unfortunately, the evening before, he had left the window open and, as a terrible storm had broken out during the night, a stream of water had reduced the huge group to a formless pulp. Victor Hugo had flopped down into a sea of mud.

Rodin opened the door and allowed his guests to go in first. Suddenly he beheld the disaster. He all but tore his beard with despair. But the chorus of praise had already begun:

"Wonderful! Marvelous! Victor Hugo rising from this bed of slime, what a symbol! Master, it is a stroke of genius! You have tried to represent the ignominy of an epoch in which the inspiration of the bard alone survived, noble and pure. How beautiful!"

"Do you think so?" Rodin asked timidly.

"Of course! It is the masterpiece of masterpieces."

ARCHITECTURE

1301   That celebrated landmark of Paris, the Eiffel Tower, has been the butt of much abuse in its time. Balzac is said to have fled screaming from the sight of it, saying that he could not endure its colossal vulgarity.

William Morris, the English poet, appears to have shared a somewhat similar view. During a long stay in Paris he very nearly cloistered himself in the restaurants of the Eiffel Tower, not only taking all his meals but even doing much of his writing there.

"You're certainly impressed by the Tower," someone once remarked to him.

"Impressed," said Morris, "I stay here because it's the only place in Paris where I can avoid seeing the damn thing!"

1302   An Egyptian architect was commissioned by one of the Pharaohs to build a lighthouse at the mouth of the Nile. On a piece of rock, duly selected, Cnidus, the architect, erected the house of light. Engraved upon the cement which covered the outside of the lighthouse was the name of Pharaoh.

In a few years the effect of wind and rain had worn the cement away and Pharaoh's name had vanished. Then it was discovered that the wily Cnidus had engraved his own name in the masonry beneath.

MUSIC

1303   "No, Madam," replied Dr. Johnson to the lady who had asked him if he liked music, "but of all noises, I think music is the least disagreeable."

1304 President Ulysses S. Grant had a violent dislike of music. One time during a concert at Peabody Institute in Baltimore he turned to Robert Winthrop sitting next to him and said, "Why, Mr. Winthrop, I know only two tunes. One is, 'Yankee Doodle' and the other isn't."

1305 At the first performance of the celebrated "Miserere" of Lully before the Court of Louis XIV in the chapel of Versailles, the monarch being on his knees during the whole time, necessarily kept his Court in the same position. At its conclusion the King asked the Count de Grammont his opinion of it. "Sire," he replied, "the music is very soft to the ears, but very hard to the knees."

1306 The musical world is full of smart alecs, tricksters and faddists; such as the so-called tune detectives, who delight in singling out musical phrases which may appear identically in the work of a number of different composers.

Such men ignore the fact that music is a form of language in which the words and phrases are common stock, to some degree, much as with the spoken word. Moreover it is by no means uncommon for a composer to pay some colleague the compliment of quotation, again as practiced in the literary world. This is sometimes carried to the length seen in some of the notable variations upon themes.

Brahms waited until the rich maturity of his talents before composing his first symphony. When this great work was in its final rehearsal, before the première playing, there was in the auditorium a certain officious musical upstart fond of seizing opportunities to display his great musical learning. This person hastened to the podium at the end of the rehearsal and, pulling at Brahms' coat-tail, said "Meister, in the fourth movement there is a theme which is very similar to that used by Beethoven in the fourth movement of the Ninth Symphony."

Brahms wheeled majestically upon the upstart. "Any ass knows that!" he roared.

RELATED SUBJECTS: *Literature* 1161-1297; *Art* 1256; *Composers* 1311-1326; *Conductors* 1331-1339; *Operas and Concerts* 1341-1348; *Instrumentalists* 1351-1363; *Singers* 1366-1368; *Dancers* 1371; *Plays* 1386-1388

SEE ALSO: *Boners* 114

COMPOSERS

1311 "I feel," said Max Dreyfus to George Gershwin, "that you have some good stuff in you. It'll come out. It may take months, it may take a year, it may take five years, but I'm convinced that the stuff is there. I'll tell you what I'm willing to do: I'll gamble on you. I'll give you thirty-five dollars a week, without any set duties. Just step in every morning, so to speak, and say, 'Hello.' The rest will follow."

1312 Something of this unwinking poker-faced, toneless comicality is in the routine George—the George Gershwin away from his ruled paper, his old Steinway grand. He will inform the reporters that he has just received the $50,000 he demanded of the movie people for the rights to use his "Rhapsody in Blue" in Whiteman's film, "The King of Jazz." "That's more than Beethoven or Schubert ever got for a composition, eh? I guess that wouldn't make them turn over in their graves!"

1313 The Master's (Brahms') intolerance, however, was of longer standing than his last illness. A generation before, in the middle seventies, this quality lost him his warm friend and zealous propagandist, the conductor Hermann Levi. Brahms was visiting Levi in Munich when, in the course of a musical conversation, Levi mentioned the names of Gluck and Wagner in the same connection. Whereupon the Master shouted angrily: "One doesn't pronounce these two names like that, one after the other!" He rushed from the room, and left town the following day.

1314 Toward the end of his life Brahms confided to a friend: "Recently I started various things, symphonies and so on, but nothing would work out well. Then I thought: I'm already too old, and resolved energetically to write no more. I considered that I had all my life been sufficiently industrious and had achieved enough; here I had before me a care-free old age and could enjoy it in peace. And that made me so happy, so contented, so delighted—that all at once the writing began to go."

1315 Mascagni, the composer of Cavalleria Rusticana, once heard an organ-grinder playing excerpts from his opera underneath his window. The composer, annoyed by the slow tempo of the playing, rushed into the street.

"Here, here," he cried to the street-musician, "I am Mascagni —I will show you how to play this music correctly." Thereupon, he gave the crank-handle of the barrel-organ a few rapid turns.

The next day Mascagni, hearing the barrel-organist again, put his head out of the window and read the following sign over the hurdy-gurdy: "Pupil of Mascagni."

1316 Mendelssohn's friend Madame Frege sang to him a song with the words:

"Time marches on by night as well as day,
And many march by night who fain would stay."

"Oh, that has a dreary sound!" the composer cried with a shudder—"but it is just what I feel."

He then suddenly rose, as pale as death, and paced the room hurriedly, complaining that his hands were as cold as ice.

He died within a month.

1317 A lad once asked Mozart how to write a symphony. Mozart said, "You're a very young man. Why not begin with ballads?"

The aspirant urged, "You composed symphonies when you were 10 years old."

"Yes," replied Mozart, "but I didn't ask 'how?'"

1318 Robert Fuchs, a reminiscent composer, was present one day when a highly Brahmsian composition of his was played to Brahms, and nearly fainted with embarrassment when the Master, assuming innocent bewilderment, asked him: "But what piece of mine is that?"

1319 Brahms attended a rehearsal of his clarinet quintet, and was so touched that tears came to his eyes. To cover his emotion he marched across the room, closed the first violin part and growled: "Stop the terrible music!"

1320 When Nietzsche one day observed to Wagner that in "Figaro" Mozart had invented the music of intrigue, Wagner replied: "On the contrary! In 'Figaro' Mozart dissolved the intrigue in music."

1321 While George Gershwin was at work on the "Rhapsody in Blue," his father thrust his head into the room. "Make it good, George," he counselled, "it might be important." So, indeed, it proved as Pa Gershwin was able to demonstrate irrefutably to a doubting Thomas. "Of course it's a great piece! Doesn't it take fifteen minutes to play?"

1322   Brahms hated to be called Meister (Master) or Tonkunstler (musical artist), for, he contended, "You might as well call me 'Cobblemaster' or 'Maker of Clay Stoves,' and have done with it!"

1323   The composer, Gounod, had a fabulous memory. When he was about 19 he had attended a rehearsal of "Roméo et Juliette," which was still in manuscript and was being directed by the composer, Berlioz. The next day he called upon Berlioz, sat at the piano and proceeded to play the entire finale of the opera from memory. The composer stared at him in terror and astonishment. Had his work been pirated? Was it some incredible coincidence?

"Where the devil did you get that music?" he demanded.
"At your rehearsal yesterday," replied Gounod.

1324   Irving Thalberg once sought to persuade the composer, Arnold Schoenberg, to write the score for the film, "The Good Earth." The producer's representative found the composer unenthused over the idea, and tried to work him up about its possibilities.

"Think of it," he said, "you've got a scene with a terrific buildup; a storm, wheat fields swaying in the wind. The earth trembles. In the midst of the earthquake and storm O-Lan gives birth to a baby. What an opportunity for music."

"With so much going on," said Schoenberg, "what do you want with music?"

1325   When the American composer, George Gershwin, died, a man of sentiment combined with musical aspirations wrote an elegy in his honor. He sought out Oscar Levant. Reluctantly Levant granted him a hearing. Eagerly the man rendered the piece with his own hands and then turned expectantly toward Levant, seeking approbation.

"I think it would have been better," Levant said, "if you had died and Gershwin had written the elegy."

1326   At the premiere performance of César Franck's symphony the gentle, benign old composer, who had seldom ventured out of his organ loft, was seated in the audience. The stupid and blasé assemblage were hostile to this fine work which did not until later find its proper appreciation. One pompous and arrogant woman, who chanced to be seated directly behind the composer, remarked loudly in the interim between two of the movements, "Who is the creature who writes this abominable music?"

The gentle Franck turned around in his seat and said courteously, "Madam, it is I."

RELATED SUBJECTS: *Music* 1303-1306; *Operas and Concerts* 1341-1348

SEE ALSO: *Drinking* 41; *Boners* 115; *Eccentricity* 206; *Generosity* 247; *Kindness* 316; *Pompousness* 426; *Practical Joking* 437; *Deathbed Scenes* 1766

CONDUCTORS

1331 One of the great traditions of contemporary music is the astounding and infallible memory of Arturo Toscanini. One time early in his career, when Toscanini was a cellist, he formed an acquaintance with the voilinists, Romanini and Enrico Polo, and with Bolzoni, the composer. Bolzoni once composed an Adagio which the group performed on a special occasion. More than a year later the two violinists and Toscanini again met. But Bolzoni was absent. "What a pity," exclaimed someone, "That Bolzoni has the score. If he had left us a copy we might have had that quartet we liked so much."

Toscanini said, "Give me a pencil and paper."

Whereupon he proceeded to write down all four parts of the Adagio from memory.

1332 The fine conductor, Bruno Walter, is a man of a gentle and sensitive temperament. The first time that he conducted the New York Philharmonic the noted cellist, Alfred Wallenstein, occupied the first cellist's chair. Walter was annoyed and embarrassed by the fact that Wallenstein ignored him throughout rehearsal and concerts alike, gazing everywhere in the auditorium, except at the conductor, while playing. Where another man might have flown into a rage, Walter merely asked that Wallenstein come to speak privately with him.

"Tell me, Mr. Wallenstein," said Walter mildly, "what is

your ambition?"

"I should like some day to be a conductor."

"Well," said Walter gently, "I only hope you never have Wallenstein in front of you."

1333 The eminent conductor, Malcolm Sargent, was conducting a Royal Choral Society rehearsal of "The Messiah." He was displeased with the women's section's rendering of "For Unto Us a Child is Born." Calling for attention, he begged, "Just a little more reverence, please, and not so much astonishment."

1334 When Basil Cameron, the conductor, was starting on his musical career he looked round for a good name and decided on Von Hindenburg. And a good name it was, up to the beginning of August 1914, when Von Hindenburg quietly disappeared like so many "Germans" of the period. In his case, however, the public was astounded to hear that the brilliant young conductor they had admired was commanding the German Army.

1335 A certain young violinist came to Leopold Stokowski with a very forceful and impressive letter of introduction from an old and respected friend of the notable conductor. "I'm very sorry that there's no opening for you now in the orchestra," Stokowski explained, "but if you can stay in Philadelphia for a while, I'll be glad to place you at the first opportunity."

The chance came little more than a week later, when the second violinist was rushed to the hospital for an appendectomy only a few hours before a concert. Stokowski called the young aspirant and said, "We're playing a Beethoven cycle. Can you manage the second violin in the Seventh and Eighth Symphonies?"

Eagerly the young man assured him he could. In the opening passages of the Seventh Symphony that night the conductor listened sharply for the strains of the second violin and noted that the new-comer seemed to be doing well. Glancing at him, he was shocked to see an expression of great agony and anguish on the violinist's face. "Heavens," he thought, "there must be a curse on the second violin. Will he be able to last out the program!"

As the symphony progressed from movement to movement, the second violinist appeared to writhe and grimace in increasing torture. Stokowski's concern began to change to anger and irritation. At the intermission, seeking to control himself, he went to the musician's dressing room and demanded, "Are you sick?"

"Why, no," said the young man.

"Is there anything paining you?"

"Not at all."

"Then," shouted Stokowski angrily, "you must not approve of my conducting."

"Oh, sir," said the musician, "it's a privilege to play under you."

"Then why on earth were you making such outlandish faces?"

"Oh, that—" said the young man. "Well, you see, sir, I just don't like the music."

1336 The first time the musical instrument called "the Serpent" was used at a London concert over which the German composer Handel presided, he was so much surprised at the coarseness of its tones that he called out sharply: "Vat de devil is dat?" On being informed it was the Serpent, he replied: "It never can be de serpent vat seduced Eve."

1337 The noted conductor, Eugene Goosens, is fond of a story about a titled Englishman of no real musical education or ability, who desired to be a conductor. He hired a symphony orchestra and a costly concert hall and, willy-nilly, began conducting a rehearsal in preparation for the launching of a great concert. He had no ability whatsoever to control the orchestra and the musicians found themselves struggling to keep time against the erratic and vague gestures of their conductor. The rehearsal got nowhere and, after a couple of hours, everyone was hot, tired and irritable. At this time, in the midst of a slow, stately passage, the kettle drummer, who was rattled, anticipated an attack by some 12 bars and came crashing in. Flying into a fury, the conductor hurled down his baton, glared at the players, and shouted, "Who did that?"

1338 During a rehearsal a second violinist grazed the string next to the one he had intended to play. The sound of this slip was almost inaudible. Few people would have noticed it. But Toscanini stopped the orchestra, pointed his baton at the culprit without hesitation, and cried out sharply, "One string will be quite enough, if you please."

1339 Once, when the Philharmonic was rehearsing César Franck's Symphony under the direction of Toscanini, he interrupted the rehearsal and protested that the clarinetist was playing a wrong note. The clarinetist denied the charge, and repeated the passage from his score before him.

"The note is A," Toscanini said, "Not A Flat."

"No, no," said the clarinetist, and came forward with his score to prove it. Toscanini peered nearsightedly at the page.

"This is an error," he said, and, sending for the full conductor's score, which he never used, he opened it and demonstrated the error of which the clarinetist himself was innocent, an error in the part-copyist's work.

> RELATED SUBJECTS: *Music* 1303-1306; *Operas and Concerts* 1341-1348

OPERAS AND CONCERTS

1341 Walking with a friend one day, Fritz Kreisler passed a large fish shop where a fine catch of codfish, with mouths open and eyes staring, were arranged in a row. Kreisler suddenly stopped, looked at them, and clutching his friend by the arm, exclaimed:

"Heavens! That reminds me—I should be playing at a concert!"

1342 So dependent on the adulation of his audience was Franz Liszt that he is said to have paid women 25 francs to faint at his concerts. The swoon was always timed to occur just before the climax of his most popular run. Liszt would leap from his piano-stool, pick up the swooner and leave the rest of the audience impressed by his brilliance and dismayed by their own stolidity. Once, however, the hired fainter forgot to faint. Liszt's fingers flew up the keys—but he could not finish the run. So he fainted himself.

1343 Joseph Choate, the lawyer, had no taste for music. Once he was persuaded by his daughter to accompany her to the opera. He looked at the libretto helplessly and said, "Helen, expound to me this record lest I dilate with the wrong emotion."

1344 After his concert in a Midwestern town, Paderewski was found backstage in a silent, preoccupied mood. One of his aides asked if he were ill.

"No, no," the great musician replied, "but some friends were missing. The gray-haired couple. They were not in their usual seats in the fourth row."

The aide was surprised. "I didn't know you had friends in this town. Did you know them well?"

"I knew them very well," Paderewski explained, "but I never met them. I liked the way they listened. Every time I have played here for 20 years I have always played for them." He shook his head gravely. "I hope there is nothing seriously wrong."

1345 According to C. R. W. Nevinson, "It was a privilege to paint Mark Hambourg, a dear friend. Never have I met a man with such a gift for penetrating to the heart of things and by the use of a few vivid phrases he will lift any conversation out of the ordinary. I remember sitting beside him at an after-dinner concert, when Moiseivitch was playing. The audience, all men and women of 'culture,' were anything but attentive, smoking, drinking, coughing, picking, wriggling, but the waiters and waitresses stood entranced, their eyes on the master. 'Look,' said Mark. 'Look at the effect of education. It kills all concentration. The lower classes are the only people left who can listen, and can respond to the highest emotions.'"

1346 In Boston the famous tenor, Beniamino Gigli was singing "Faust." The stage of the Boston Opera House was not as adequately equipped as that of the Metropolitan. There was a trap door which sank down in order that Mephistopheles might conduct Faust to Hell. As Gigli stepped on this and began to sink, something went wrong and he became stuck midway and could not get any further, though he made every effort to squeeze through. In the midst of the predicament which was now clearly evident to all the audience, the voice of a slightly inebriated Irishman roared from the top gallery, "Thank God. I'm safe at last! Hell is full!"

1347 Brahms' kindness often revealed a finely imaginative quality. During his concert tour in Hungary with Joachim, the audience one evening consisted of a solitary man. The violinist was all for giving him back his money and closing before the start. "No," said Brahms, "our unique partisan does not deserve such disrespect. Let us go on with the program." So they began, and soon were enthusiastically playing whatever their fortunate solo audience suggested.

1348 A story is told by Deems Taylor about the first performance in Carnegie Hall of the extremely modernistic "Ballet Méchanique" by George Antheil. The composition might be classed as an extreme of extremes; and among the unorthodox instruments augmenting the orchestra were 10 grand pianos, 6 xylophones, a player piano, a fire-alarm siren, an airplane propeller and several automobile klaxons.

The audience, which had been attentive and quiet previously, began to fidget after the start of the music. The general excitement and consternation mounted, until finally, after eight minutes of the composition, a man in one of the front rows raised a white handkerchief tied to his cane. Whereupon the entire audience burst into laughter.

RELATED SUBJECTS: *Music* 1303-1306; *Composers* 1311-1326; *Conductors* 1331-1339; *Instrumentalists* 1351-1363; *Singers* 1366-1368; *Dancers* 1371

SEE ALSO: *Newspapers* 1239

INSTRUMENTALISTS

1351 Once when Paderewski played before Queen Victoria, the sovereign exclaimed with enthusiasm, "Mr. Paderewski, you are a genius!"

"Ah, Your Majesty," he replied, "perhaps, but before I was a genius, I was a drudge."

1352 Sam Ward told this story of Paganini. "The master held a guitar across his lap. 'Your young friend is musical?' enquired he. 'Fanatico!' replied Gear. 'Then, he shall hear me practice for tomorrow night's concert.' Taking the guitar he converted that little-understood instrument into an orchestra of bewildering and harmonic sonority. Now it seemed a battle, with the clash of swords, shouts of combatants, the roll of the drum. Then wails of pain and grief appeared to emerge from the sounding board over which his fingers flew like what the Westerners call 'greased lightning.' The performance lasted perhaps half an hour, and the dampness of his dishevelled locks indicated the intensity of the emotion and the exertions that expressed it.

"When the maestro received, with a sad smile, our frantic applause, I inquired whether he was going to rehearse on the violin his programme for the morrow. He shook his head: 'I never rehearse the violin. My practice is the gymnastics of the guitar, to be sure of my suppleness of finger and delicacy of touch. My violin never fails me.'"

1353   A musical lady was playing once on the harpsichord for Dr. Johnson who appeared very much bored with the proceedings. As she finished she turned apologetically to him:

"Do you know, doctor, that selection is very difficult?"

"Difficult, madam," answered Dr. Johnson. "Would to heaven it had been impossible."

1354   Paderewski was once traveling incognito through Germany. He stopped for the night at a small Inn in the Black Forest. In the main room of the Inn was an old battered piano. Paderewski asked the landlord if he might try it. Upon doing so, he found that the instrument was not only badly out of tune but that a number of the keys were stuck and would strike no sound at all. He remarked upon this to the landlord. The latter, offended at the criticism of his piano, replied, "If you were a good pianist you could skip over those keys so it wouldn't matter."

1355   A young lady called one day on Rubinstein, the great pianist, who had consented to listen to her playing.

"What do you think I should do now?" she asked when she had finished.

"Get married," was Rubinstein's answer.

1356   Dr. Axel Munthe, seated in the lounge of the Victoria Louise, was enthusiastically hailed by a brother physician.

"What a genius you are!" Thus the brother physician ended a long eulogy.

But Dr. Munthe smiled and said: "A genius, eh? Well, at his villa in Biarritz Sarasate was once called a genius by a famous critic. But Sarasate frowned and shook his head.

" 'A genius!' he said. 'For thirty-seven years I've practiced fourteen hours a day, and now they call me a genius!' "

1357 Paderewski once explained that he practiced faithfully every day. "If I miss one day's practice," said he, "I notice it. If I miss two days, the critics notice it. If I miss three days, the audience notices it."

1358 Fritz Kreisler, the violinist, found himself in Hamburg one evening with an hour to spare before taking his boat to London where he was to play the following evening. So he wandered into a music shop. The proprietor asked to see his violin which he carried under his arm. In a moment he disappeared, to reappear with two policemen. One laid his hand on Kreisler's shoulder and said, "You are under arrest."

"For what?" asked Kreisler.

"You have Fritz Kreisler's violin."

"Well, I am Fritz Kreisler."

"Come, come," said the policeman, "you cannot pull that one on us. Come to the station."

Kreisler's boat sailed in an hour. He had to do some quick thinking.

"I looked around," he says, "and in the corner I saw a victrola. I asked the proprietor if he had any of Fritz Kreisler's records; he produced 'The Old Refrain,' put it on for me, and played it through. 'Now,' I said, 'let me have my violin.' Then, with whatever skill I may command I played 'The Old Refrain.' When I was through I said, 'Are you satisfied now?' "

With profuse apologies they bowed him out to freedom.

1359 It is said that Jascha Heifetz and Mischa Elman were dining together in a restaurant much frequented by artists. The waiter approached the table with an envelope which bore simply the inscription, "To the World's Greatest Violinist."

Heifetz, who had picked it from the tray, bowed and handed it across the table and said, "For you, Mischa."

Elman read it and said, "No, no," and handed it back. "Something for you, Jascha."

Thus they shilly-shallied back and forth until finally Heifetz was persuaded to open it. He drew out the letter and unfolded it. It began, "Dear Fritz."

1360 There is a legend which would have it that, when Jascha Heifetz made his triumphant New York debut, among the audience were the other violinist, Mischa Elman, and the distinguished pianist, Josef Hofmann. The hall was crowded and it was an evening in Spring. The concert progressed and the audience was spellbound by the genius of Heifetz. As the music went on Elman became increasingly nervous and fidgety, running his finger frequently around the inside of his collar and mopping at his forehead with a handkerchief. In the pause between two selections, he leaned over and whispered to Hofmann, "Awfully hot in here, isn't it?"

Hofmann smiled and whispered back, "Not for pianists."

1361 Mischa Elman, the violinist, takes delight in telling the following story.

"While visiting a friend of the family I was asked to play something to the assembled group of people. For an urchin of seven, as I was at that time, I flatter myself I rattled off Beethoven's 'Kreutzer Sonata' finely. The Sonata has in it several long and impressive rests. In one of these rests a motherly old lady leaned forward, patted my shoulder and said, 'Play something you know, dear.'"

1362 Jascha Heifetz arrived in great haste at Radio City, perilously near to being late for a radio concert with the NBC Symphony Orchestra. He hastened into the elevator carrying his violin in its case.

"You'll have to go in the freight elevator with that," said the operator.

"I have no time," said Heifetz, "I'm in a hurry."

"I don't care," said the operator. "All musicians with instruments have got to ride in the freight elevator."

"Look," said the exasperated musician, "I'm Jascha Heifetz."

"I don't care if you're Rubinoff," said the operator, "you've got to ride in the freight elevator."

1363 "Ole Bull (celebrated 18th Century Norwegian violinist) was a man of singular and beautiful simplicity of character. He spoke English with much expression and had quaint turns of dialect as original as they were unstudied. He was describing the grandeur of the hills and fiords of his native land and its deep forests resounding with musical cataracts when someone exclaimed: 'Did you play to them, Ole?'

"'No,' he replied, 'I listened.'"

RELATED SUBJECTS: *Music* 1303-1306; *Operas and Concerts* 1341-1348

SEE ALSO: *Conductors* 1335

SINGERS

1366   Catherine II was treating her court to concerts by Catterina Gabrielli the celebrated Italian soprano. The Empress had asked the artist to come to St. Petersburg without stating any definite price. Gabrielli determined, however, that a royal patron should be royally charged; and when at the end of the season Catherine inquired of her entertainer what she was to be paid for her singing, she replied, "Five thousand ducats."

"Five thousand ducats!" the Empress exclaimed. "Why not one of my field marshals is paid as much as that."

"Well, then," retorted Gabrielli like a flash, "Your Majesty had better get one of your field mashals to sing for you."

1367   Samuel Foote once asked a man why he forever sang one tune.

"Because it haunts me," replied the other.

"No wonder," said Foote. "You continually murder it."

1368   During rehearsals of Verdi's great opera, "Otello," by an American opera company, the tenor, who was preparing for the chief role, was perplexed by certain instructions given him by the stage director. This dignitary insisted that at a certain moment, nearing a climax in the action, while the chorus was singing and while there was a rest of a matter of only a few bars in the tenor role, that he should go to the back of the stage and return again toward the footlights to resume singing. It required swift timing and was seemingly utterly senseless from the point of view of dramatic action. The tenor protested. The stage director would not yield. "It is the tradition of the part," he insisted.

"Why?"

"I don't know. It is the tradition. You must do it."

"Who created this role?"

"Tamagno."

Unable to do anything but accede, the tenor carried the incident in his memory. A year or so later, being in Italy, he sought out the great, aged tenor, Tamagno. And, being granted an interview, said:

"Maestro, I wish to ask you about a certain piece of business in the role of Otello."

The old man heard him out and was obviously puzzled. In an effort to recollect his motive, he peered for a time at the pages of the score.

"Yes, yes," he said at last, "it is very simple. Note that in the final passage Otello must sing a high B flat. So while the chorus was singing I went upstage to spit."

> RELATED SUBJECTS: *Music* 1303-1306; *Operas and Concerts* 1341-1348

> SEE ALSO: *Eating* 21; *Reputation* 77; *Melancholy* 368; *Vanity* 620; *Fatness* 689; *Courtships* 852; *Operas* 1346; *Actors* 1423

DANCERS

1371 Finley Peter Dunne, the "Mr. Dooley" of humorous fame, once went to see Isadora Duncan perform. The famous dancer wore very few clothes, and as a result of their lack, looked even plumper than usual. A floodlight threw calcium beams on her. As Dunne was leaving, one of the patronesses hailed him.

"Oh, Mr. Dunne," she twittered, "how did you enjoy the madame's dancing?"

"Immensely," said Dunne. "Made me think of Grant's Tomb in love."

> RELATED SUBJECTS: *Music* 1303-1306; *Operas and Concerts* 1341

THEATRE AND FILM

PLAYWRIGHTS

1376 It is reported that Sam Goldwyn telephoned to George Bernard Shaw and attempted to drive a bargain for the film rights to some of his plays. Shaw's terms were stiff and Goldwyn endeavored to whittle them down by an appeal to the artist.

"Think of the millions of people who would get a chance to see your plays who would otherwise never see them. Think of the contribution it would be to art."

"The trouble is, Mr. Goldwyn," Shaw replied, "that you think of nothing but Art and I think of nothing but money."

1377   Sir Herbert Beerbohm Tree, to a would-be dramatist:
      "My dear Sir: I have read your play. Oh, my dear Sir!
                          "Yours faithfully."

1378   "Not all your plays are successes, I suppose, Sir James," someone remarked to J. M. Barrie at a dinner party.
      In the manner of one imparting a confidence, Barrie leaned toward him and said, "No, some Peter out and some Pan out."

1379   Clare Boothe's first produced play, "Abide with Me," was a failure. The playwright, however, was evidently possessed of some ebulliency on the occasion of its opening. Richard Watts, drama critic, reported, "One almost forgave 'Abide with Me' its faults when its lovely playwright, who must have been crouched in the wings for a sprinter's start as the final curtain mercifully descended, heard a cry of 'Author,' which was not audible in my vicinity, and arrived to accept the audience's applause just as the actors, who had a head start on her, were properly lined up and smoothed out to receive their customary adulation."

1380   Richard Brinsley Sheridan, threatening to cut his son Thomas off with a shilling, he immediately replied, "Ah father, but where will you borrow the shilling?"

1381   Boyer, a French dramatic author, had been fifty years writing without success. That he might prove whether his condemnation was not on account of the prejudice of the critics, he gave it to be understood that the new tragedy of "Agamemnon" was the production of a young man lately arrived at Paris. The piece was received with great applause, even by Racine himself, who was the great scourge of Boyer. The next night the tragedy was hissed, Boyer having made it known that he was the author.

1382 Oscar Wilde arrived at his club one evening, after witnessing a first production of a play that was a complete failure.

"Oscar, how did your play go tonight?" said a friend.

"Oh," was the lofty response, "the play was a great success but the audience was a failure."

1383 Cumberland, a third rate dramatist, was jealous of Sheridan's reputation and lost no occasion to talk him down. An acquaintance of Sheridan's, meeting him on the street one day, informed him that Cumberland was telling everyone how he had gone to see "The School for Scandal" and had thought it a very bad thing—couldn't see how people saw anything funny in it at all.

"Why, did he not laugh at my comedy?" asked Sheridan, pretending the deepest concern.

"No."

"Well then, I must say that is very ungrateful in Mr. Cumberland, for I laughed at his last tragedy until I almost split my sides."

1384 "When I wrote 'Major Barbara,' the characters were modelled on people I knew. The likenesses were unmistakable, and therefore I was anxious to make sure that no words used in the play could hurt the originals. I read the play to an old dear friend of the family. All went well till I came to the lines: 'Never call me Mother again.' 'Oh,' said she, 'you must not say that for those are the very words used by . . . (the character copied in the play), and used in tragic circumstances.'"

Shaw paused. Bridges opened his eyes, "remarkable coincidence," he said and closed his eyes again.

1385 A librettist accosted De Wolf Hopper at the stage entrance to Weber & Fields.

"I wish to explain the story of my new opera," he began. "The hero is stranded on a desert island, and the natives make him King. You see now the splendid beginning for complications."

"I do," said the comedian, "and I know them well; they are chiefly of a financial character, if memory serves me." And he fled.

RELATED SUBJECTS: *Plays* 1386-1388

SEE ALSO: *Producers* 1395; *Audiences* 1441; *Hollywood* 1449

PLAYS

1386 The play "Merrily We Roll Along," famous for its reverse sequence of events, was a succes d'estime but was otherwise disappointing to its authors, George S. Kaufman and Moss Hart. Attempts were made to analyze the reason for the play's failure. According to Kaufman, the best diagnosis of the trouble was made by Herman Mankiewicz, who said, "Here we have this young man: a successful playwright, wealthy, honored, loved by beautiful women, the owner of yachts, sought out by everyone, and the problem is, how the Hell did the poor son-of-a-gun ever get himself into such a jam!"

1387 On the first night of the performance of one of Douglas Jerrold's pieces, a successful playwright rallied him on his nervousness.

"I," said this colleague, "never feel nervous on the first night of my pieces."

"Ah, my boy," Jerrold replied, "you are always certain of success. Your pieces have all been tried before."

1388 The influence of antiquity is perpetual. The art and literature of the ancient Greeks and Romans is evident in most of the things about us in modern everyday life. Many artists owe their great success to emulating the ancient classics, the masterpieces of many writers are based on the great dramas of Euripides, Sophocles and Aeschylus. Corneille notably patterned his plays on the Greek idea. His "Andromaque" is a well-known example. The classic basis of this play earned for him probably the highest praise ever accorded a dramatist. Napoleon, a great lover of the classics, exclaimed after seeing "Andromaque," "If Corneille were alive I would make him King!"

RELATED SUBJECTS: *Playwrights* 1376-1385; *Producers* 1391-1397; *Directors* 1401-1403; *Actors* 1406-1431; *Audiences* 1436-1441

SEE ALSO: *Critics* 1102, 1103; *Playwrights* 1378, 1382; *Sin and Sinners* 1647

PRODUCERS

1391 When Gary Cooper had finished making a certain picture for Samuel Goldwyn, another producer, Hunt Stromberg, exercised the option which he held on Cooper's services. Goldwyn called the other producer on the 'phone, and in an aggrieved tone, said, "It isn't that I mind your taking Cooper. But you could have been nicer about it. You could at least have called me up and said, 'Sam, I need Cooper right away, if it doesn't interfere with your plans.' Then, I'd have said, no."

1392   How Producer Gabriel Pascal acquired the film rights to Bernard Shaw's plays—a mine of entertainment material practically every producer in Hollywood has tried to buy at one time or another—is an utterly implausible story. In 1935, after spending six months in Hollywood doing nothing, Pascal, who had made one successful picture in England and a succession of shorts, left in disgust. He arrived in London, and out of a clear sky called on Shaw, whom he had never met, saying he wanted to produce his plays. When Shaw asked how much capital he had to do it with, Pascal replied: "Fifteen shillings and sixpence—but I owe a pound."

Delighted as much with this effrontery as with Pascal's obvious admiration for his work, Shaw gave him a pound to pay his debts, and agreed to the experiment. The successful "Pygmalion" was the result.

1393   Sam Goldwyn, impressed by the wide sale of Radcliffe Hall's "The Well of Loneliness," expressed a desire to purchase the film rights. "You can't film that," he was advised. "It deals with Lesbians." "So all right," replied Goldwyn, "where they got Lesbians, we'll use Austrians."

1394   To Billy Rose came a seedy looking individual with a startling proposition.

"I'll do an act in your show that will be the greatest sensation ever presented. You can advertise it in advance, and get $100 a ticket. If you'll put $25,000 in escrow for my wife, I'll then commit suicide in the full view of your audience."

"It's a natural!" said Rose, simulating enthusiasm, "but just a minute. What will you do for an encore?"

1395   They say that Samuel Goldwyn read the first script submitted by a new writer attached to the studio and summoned the hopeful to his desk. "This is a perfect scenario," said Goldwyn. "It is the first time in my life that I've seen a perfect scenario. There's absolutely nothing wrong with it. I want you to have a hundred copies made so I can distribute them to all the other writers so that everybody should see a really perfect script. And hurry," he called as the thrilled and excited writer hastened out of the office, "before I start rewriting it."

1396   The film producer, Darryl Zanuck, of whom Eddie Cantor has said, "Zanuck is Goldwyn without the accent," once epitomized the Hollywood approach in speaking of "Les Misérables," which he was about to film, referring to it as Lee's Miserables," depicting it as " 'I'm a Fugitive from a Chain Gang' in costume."

1397   The following incident occurred at the Flea Show in Paris. One of the dear creatures which acted as coachman to the great flea-coach, managed to hop off his box, and elected a rather stout lady standing near, as his resting-place. The proprietor of the show, who had spent much time and patience upon the education of his insect, was in despair, and the lady was asked if she would mind making a search for the missing flea.

She accordingly retired to a private room, and in a few minutes returned triumphant, carefully holding the captive in the most approved flea-style. She handed him to the showman who started and changed color, and returning the flea to the lady remarked:

"Madame, this is not my flea!"

> RELATED SUBJECTS: *Plays* 1386-1388; *Hollywood* 1446-1449

> SEE ALSO: *Parties* 519; *Authors* 1177; *Composers* 1324; *Playwrights* 1376; *Funerals* 1776

DIRECTORS

1401   John Barrymore once asked the great Russian director, Constantin Stanislavski, how he selected his artists. "I choose them by means of this," said Stanislavski, picking up a pin. "Now, you go into the next room."

Barrymore went out and in a moment Stanislavski said, "You may come in now. Please look for the pin."

The Russian watched as Barrymore picked up the glasses from the table, looked under them and lifted each plate. He felt along the surface of the tablecloth, lifted the corner, and there was the pin.

Stanislavski clapped his hands: "Very good—you are engaged! I can tell a real actor," he explained, "by the way he looks for a pin. If he prances around the room, striking attitudes, pretending to think very hard, looking in ridiculous places—exaggerating—then he is not good."

1402 One day at rehearsal Sir Herbert Tree asked a youthful actor to "step back a little." The player did so. Tree eyed him critically—and went on rehearsing. After a time he repeated his request: "A little further back." The youth obeyed. Surveying him, Tree went on with his work. Shortly afterwards he again asked him to step still further back.

"If I do," expostulated the youth, "I shall be right off the stage."

"Yes," said Tree, "that's right."

1403 This story concerns the Hollywood director, Joseph von Sternberg, who came to sword's points with Sam Jaffe when the actor was appearing in "The Scarlet Empress" under Von Sternberg's direction.

Mr. Jaffe deemed certain arbitrary instructions to be improper, and disputed the point.

"Mr. Jaffe," screamed Von Sternberg, "I am Von Sternberg, I have 10,000 followers."

"You're very fortunate," said Jaffe coldly, "Jesus Christ had only 12."

RELATED SUBJECTS: *Plays* 1386-1388; *Actors* 1406-1431

SEE ALSO: *Actors* 1425, 1426

ACTORS

1406 Someone remarked to Adolph Menjou that the depredations of the draft were working havoc in the ranks of Hollywood's romantic leading men. "That is true," said Menjou, "and it will be the first time that some of our leading ladies will be playing opposite men their own age."

1407 No actress could ever have enjoyed a more touching tribute than that once received by Helen Hayes when she was portraying the role of Mary of Scotland. As darkness was falling after the matinee one winter's afternoon, she encountered outside the stagedoor a small boy gazing at her adoringly. After several successive matinees he still appeared faithfully; then, one time he impulsively stepped forward thrusting something into her hand and fled down the street. Miss Hayes found herself holding a small box. Opening it she found a little gilded medal bearing the inscription, "Scholarship Medal, Public School 42, 1933."

1408   When Alfred Lunt and Lynn Fontanne, a notably devoted husband and wife, started rehearsing "At Mrs. Bean's," a play in which it was necessary for Miss Fontanne to strike Mr. Lunt in the face, she found she couldn't hit him. She pulled her hand back and let go—and then stopped dead before she struck. Her husband begged her to do it, but after 30 minutes she still couldn't. Finally Mr. Lunt shouted: "For God's sake, Lynn, you're the lousiest actress I've ever played opposite!"

The Fontanne hand made a direct hit. Mr. Lunt yelped with pain, then grinned. But when they put on the show he had to whisper, "Don't be lousy, dear," each time before she would hit him.

1409   A film salesman was trying to sell the latest Clark Gable picture to a cinema proprietor in the wilds of Venezuela. "Clark Gable is dead," he was told. "You recall the film 'Parnell'?"

"Yes. A box-office winner."

"Si, señor, but, the Gable he died in that."

"Look here, I don't . . ."

"I tried to show another Gable film after that," went on the Venezuelan. "And what happen? Hell broke loose. Señor, my clients see the Gable die in one picture. Cannot one believe one's own eyes? So far as this village is concerned, Gable is dead."

1410   Robert Palmer, the 18th Century actor, was in the early part of his life a bill-sticker, which circumstance was pretty generally known to the performers. One evening, being dressed for Sir Brilliant Fashion, he strutted into the green-room, with sparkling buckles on his shoes and at his knees, and a brilliant ring on his finger. One of the company inquired if they were real. "I wear nothing but diamonds," replied Palmer. "I congratulate you," said John Bannister, "for I remember when you wore nothing but paste." This occasioned a war, which was heightened by Mrs. Jordon crying out—"Stick him against the wall, Bob—stick him against the wall."

1411   Miss Clara Morris told the following story of her own experience:

"Somewhere in the wide world there is an actor—and a good one—who never eats celery without thinking of me. It was years ago, when I was playing Camille. In the first scene, you will remember, the unfortunate Armand takes a rose from Camille as a token of love. We had almost reached that point, when, as I glanced down, I saw that the flower was missing from its accustomed place on my breast.

"What could I do? On the flower hung the strength of the scene. However, I continued my lines in an abstracted fashion, and began a still hunt for that rose or a substitute. My gaze wandered around the stage. On the dinner table was some celery. Moving slowly toward it, I grasped the celery and twisted the tops into a rose form. Then I began the fateful lines:

" 'Take this flower. The life of a camelia is short. If held and caressed it will fade in a morning or an evening.'

"Hardly able to control his laughter, Armand spoke his lines which ran: 'It is a cold, scentless flower. It is a strange flower.' I agreed with him."

1412   John Kemble was performing one of his favorite parts at some country theatre and was interrupted from time to time by the squalling of a child in the gallery, until at length, angered by this rival performance, Kemble walked with solemn steps to the front of the stage, and addressing the audience in his most tragic tones, said, "Ladies and gentlemen, unless the play is stopped, the child cannot possibly go on."

1413   A pushing young actor who was understudy in one of Mr. Barrie's plays found his opportunity one night through the illness of his principal. He accordingly flooded his managerial and influential acquaintances with telegrams announcing: "I play So-and-So's part tonight." Except that the theatre was comparatively empty this breathless disclosure produced no result, other than a telegram in reply from Mr. Barrie to this effect: "Thanks for the warning."

1414   When John Barrymore was playing Hamlet on Broadway, Jane Cowl attended one of the matinees. She was not inaudible while watching it, and the audience soon knew she was there. Barrymore became aware of her presence, also, but didn't acknowledge it until the end of the performance. In making his curtain speech he bowed in the direction of the famed lady's box. "And in conclusion," he said, "may I take this opportunity to thank Miss Cowl for the privilege of co-starring with her this afternoon."

1415 During a theatrical engagement at Manchester, Kemble and Lewis were walking one day along the street, when a chimney-sweeper and his boy came up. The boy stared at them with open mouth and exclaimed:

"They be play-actors."

"Hold your tongue, you dog," said the old sweep, "you don't know what you may come to yourself."

1416 Lillah McCarthy tells of Lord Lucas that, "He wanted me to play a season of Shakespeare and knew how much I wished it; and one day he came to the theatre with a cheque. 'Here's the money for Shakespeare. I've sold my pig-farm. I like his pearls better than my pigs!'"

1417 Beerbohm Tree was once trying to get a well-known actor back into his company. He invited the man to call and received him in his dressing room as he was making up.

"How much would you want to come back?" inquired Mr. Tree, busy with his paint pots. The actor named an exorbitant salary to which Tree replied as he went on making up:

"Don't slam the door when you go out, will you?"

1418 Sam Ward told this story. "I remember awaiting in Rachel's box at the Théâtre Français, in the summer of 1855, the arrival of the great tragedienne, after the curtain had dropped upon her performance of Phèdre, the memory of which is still fresh with many now living. She hardly used a gesture or made a motion to depart from the statuesque repose of her inspired declamation. It was Jules Janin who took me to her dressing room, who placed my hand upon her costume, the white chlamys, and called my attention to the fact that it was wringing-wet!"

1419 An extra came up to Helen Westley, elderly character actress, on a movie set. "Why, Miss Westley," she gushed, "what are you doing in this picture?"

"My dear," the reply sped back, "hadn't you heard? I furnish the sexagenarian appeal."

1420   Alfred Lunt and Lynn Fontanne made one movie while I was in Hollywood. When they were asked to see the rushes (uncut scenes in the picture) Lynn saw them alone and was horrified. She rushed home to her husband.

"Well?" said Alfred.

"I was awful," said Lynn wildly, "terrible, unbelievable. I can't go on with it."

"How was I?" asked her husband.

"Oh, charming, dear, perfectly wonderful, as you always are. You'll have to do a little something about your makeup, because you look as though you didn't have any lips. But Alfred, I can't go on with this. My voice sounds impossible and I haven't any eyes, and my face is entirely expressionless and I don't seem to know what to do with my hands and feet."

There was a long pause.

"Alfred," said Lynn, "I tell you I can't go on. What'll I do?"

"No lips, eh?" said Alfred.

1421   It was Dorothy Parker who commented acidly about the performance of a certain prominent American actress, saying, "She certainly ran the gamut of emotions from A to B."

1422   Someone remarked to Mrs. Siddons that applause was necessary to actors, as it gave them confidence. "More," replied the actress, "it gives us breath."

1423   At a dinner in Hollywood, Charlie Chaplin entertained the guests throughout the evening by imitating people they knew: men, women and children, his chauffeur, his Jap servants, his secretaries. Finally he sang at the top of his voice an aria from an Italian Opera—sang it superbly. "Why Charlie, I never knew you could sing so beautifully," someone exclaimed.

"I can't sing at all," Chaplin rejoined. "I was only imitating Caruso."

1424   Jacob Adler, the great actor of the Yiddish theatre, was reputed to have many progeny scattered along his trail, aside from the numerous family of distinguished actors who have descended from him. Not infrequently some claimant to his paternity would present himself. Once, while the great actor was in his dressing room, such a young man gained entrance to him and introduced himself, saying, "I'm your son." Adler peered intently at the youth for a moment. "So you are—so you are," he said, and turning to his valet he said, "Give the boy a pass."

1425 The late John Barrymore used to tell of the confusion that prevailed in an old stock company with which he had once played repertory. The vast number of plays, the frequency and inconsistency with which they were performed, rendered confusion more or less inevitable. One evening Barrymore found himself unable to remember his lines. Faking a piece of business, he sidled over into the wings and hastily called to the director, "What's the line, what's the line?"

The director sighed wearily and asked, "What's the play?"

1426 "Many are called, but few are chosen" might well be the motto emblazoned above the doors of the Hollywood casting directors.

One hopeful young actor was turned down time and again by the same company. Despairing, yet determined, he made a final effort. Approaching one film director, he said, "It's now or never, if you want me in one of your pictures. I now have many companies after me."

"You have?" asked the director, his interest aroused by this statement. "What companies?"

"Well," said the actor seriously, "there's the telephone company, the electric and gas companies, the milk company . . ."

The director laughed—the actor got a job.

1427 Roger Kemble, father of the famous Mrs. Siddons, had once expressly forbidden the young lady to marry an actor.

She defied this parental instruction, wherewith Kemble upbraided her not only for her disobedience but for the aggravating circumstance that she had married undoubtedly the most incompetent member of his company.

"Exactly," replied the defiant bride. "Nobody can call him an actor."

1428 William Randolph Hearst, according to a legend, once invited Will Rogers to come to San Simeon for a weekend. Hearst had assembled a considerable company, and Rogers was the star guest whom Hearst did not fail to show off to his best advantage. A few days later Hearst received from Rogers a bill for several thousand dollars for services as a professional entertainer. He called Rogers on the phone and protested, saying, "I didn't engage you to come as an entertainer. I invited you as a guest."

Rogers snapped, "When people invite me as a guest, they invite Mrs. Rogers too. When they ask me to come alone, I go as a professional entertainer."

1429   Once in the dressing room of Katherine Cornell those old stagers, Mrs. Leslie Carter and Mrs. Patrick Campbell, chanced to meet. They were introduced as "surely being acquainted with one another."

"Honored. Honored," said Mrs. Campbell grandly, shaking Mrs. Carter's hand. Then turning to a by-stander she confided in a loud stage-whisper, "I thought she was dead."

1430   When someone was lamenting Samuel Foote's unlucky fate of being kicked in Dublin, Dr. Johnson said he was glad of it. "He is rising in the world," said he. "When he was in England, no one thought it worth while to kick him."

1431   At the finish of the filming of "Bill of Divorcement," Katherine Hepburn turned to John Barrymore and said, "Thank God, I don't have to act anymore with you!"

"Oh," he replied, "I didn't know you ever had, darling."

RELATED SUBJECTS: *Plays* 1386-1388; *Producers* 1391-1397; *Directors* 1401-1403; *Audiences* 1436-1441

SEE ALSO: *Reputation* 76; *Devotion* 172; *Eccentricity* 207; *Long-Windedness* 360; *Memory* 373; *Rudeness* 519; *Shrewdness* 527, 529; *Fatness* 685; *Handicaps* 702, 704; *Introductions* 791; *Names* 831; *Women* 843; *Divorce* 911; *Babies* 958; *Directors* 1401; *Sermons* 1549; *Kings* 1987; *Parliament* 1999

AUDIENCES

1436   When John Barrymore was playing "Redemption" in New York . . . he struggled against a particularly croupy audience. When it came to the scene where he, as a derelict, is being questioned by the prefect of police, and was asked if he couldn't say anything for himself, he waved his hand out toward the audience, and cried:

"Say anything! How can I say anything with that bunch of trained seals out there?"

1437   An old farmer went to the movies for the first time. He watched the proceedings with interest, especially one scene in which a group of girls started to undress to go swimming. During this process a train passed by and in the next scene they were shown in the water.

The old man had gone into the show early in the afternoon. Late that evening, an usher, seeing him still in his seat, came up to him and asked why he stayed through so many performances.

"Waal," drawled the old codger, "I figger that one of these times that train is goin' to be late."

1438   True or not, it is a good story. Orson Welles once lectured in a small Middle-Western town before an audience sparse almost to invisibility. He opened his remarks with a brief sketch of his career; "I'm a director of plays, a producer of plays. I'm an actor of the stage and motion pictures. I'm a writer and producer of motion pictures. I write, direct and act on the radio. I'm a magician and painter. I've published books. I play the violin and the piano." At this point he paused and surveyed his audience, saying, "Isn't it a pity there's so many of me and so few of you!"

1439   Rachel, the celebrated French actress, once remarked after an opening night at the theatre:

"Mon dieu! When I came out on the stage the audience simply sat there open mouthed."

"Oh, nonsense!" rudely interrupted a younger rival of hers: "They never all yawn at once."

1440   A person threw the head of a goose on the stage of the theatre. The manager, advancing to the front, said: "Gentlemen, if any one among you has lost his head, do not be uneasy, for I will restore it at the conclusion of the performance."

1441   After the première performance of "Arms and the Man," Bernard Shaw was called upon to take a bow. As he stepped forward upon the stage amidst the applause, a loud voice called from the balcony, "Come, come, Shaw, you know all this stuff is balderdash."

Shaw good-naturedly looked up toward the balcony and

called back, "I quite agree with you, my friend, but who are you and I against so many?"

RELATED SUBJECTS: *Plays* 1386-1388; *Actors* 1406-1431

SEE ALSO: *Patriotism* 396; *Babies* 960

HOLLYWOOD

1446 W. C. Fields has crowned perhaps all other estimates of Hollywood with one observation. Someone asked him whether he had ever had the D.T.'s since coming to Hollywood. "I don't know," said Fields, "I don't know. There's no way of telling where the D.T.'s leave off and Hollywood begins."

1447 James Thurber, the "New Yorker" cartoonist, attended one of Hollywood's super-colossal premieres. When they were leaving the theatre Thurber asked a writer friend what he thought of the picture.

"I thought it stank," replied the friend in no uncertain terms. "What did you think of it?"

"I can't say I liked it that well," replied Thurber.

1448 Typical of Hollywood is the authentic story of the first effort made by the now prominent star, Roland Young, to get into the movies; or more accurately the movies' first effort to get him. Young became an unquestioned star of the legitimate stage over night with his success in the play, "The Last of Mrs. Cheney." The films purchased the story and desired to bring its celebrated leading man to Hollywood to appear in the screen version; but when Young arrived on the coast, he was sent back to New York. They decided he wasn't the type.

1449 The popular writer Edgar Wallace was once portraying to a friend the fabulous glories of the film industry. "I write a scenario in a couple of days and get a fortune for it. You ought to try it."

"It's too baffling for me," his friend said ruefully. "I was once asked to submit something to a film company. I sent them four scenarios—and got back nine."

RELATED SUBJECTS: *Producers* 1391-1397; *Directors* 1401-1403; *Actors* 1406-1431

SEE ALSO: *Rough and Ready* 507; *Divorce* 911; *Producers* 1396; *Actors* 1406

RELIGION AND MORALS

CHURCHMEN

1451   While Raphael was engaged in painting his celebrated frescoes, he was visited by two cardinals who began to criticize his work, and found fault without understanding it.

"The Apostle Paul has too red a face," said one.

"He blushes to see into whose hands the Church has fallen," answered the angry artist.

1452   Julian Huxley tells this: "I recall the story of the philosopher and the theologian. The two were engaged in disputation and the theologian used the old quip about a philosopher resembling a blind man, in a dark room, looking for a black cat —which wasn't there.

" 'That may be,' said the philosopher, 'but a theologian would have found it.' "

1453   When the learned John Selden was a member of the Assembly of Divines at Westminster he delighted to puzzle them by curious quibbles. Once they were gravely engaged in determining the exact distance between Jerusalem and Jericho; and one of them, to prove it could not be great, observed, "that fish were carried from one place to the other." At which the resourceful Dr. Selden observed: "Perhaps it was salt fish?" This again threw the Assembly into confusion.

1454   The theologian, Leonard Bacon, was present at a religious conference. He had made a certain statement on the floor whereupon a member, opposed to his views, burst forth with the exclamation, "Why, I never heard of such a thing in all my life."

"Mr. Moderator," appealed Bacon, "I cannot allow my opponent's ignorance, however vast, to prejudice my knowledge, however small."

1455   Shortly before his death Chief Justice Melville Fuller presided at a church conference. During the progress of a heated debate a member arose and began a tirade against universities and education, thanking God that he had never been corrupted by contact with a college.

"Do I understand the speaker thanks God for his ignorance?" interrupted the Chief Justice.

"Well, yes," was the answer. "You can put it that way if you wish."

"All I can say then," said the Chief Justice, "is that the member has a great deal to thank God for."

1456 At a gathering in London, where a furious theological controversy occurred, Dean Swift lost his temper and boisterously asked a stranger who sat next to him: "On which side, sir, are you? Are you an atheist or a Deist?"

"Oh, neither, Sir," was the immediate reply; "I am a dentist."

> RELATED SUBJECTS: *Ministers* 1461-1477; *Priests* 1481-1483; *Rabbis* 1486-1488; *Bishops* 1491-1498; *Popes* 1501-1504; *Evangelists* 1511-1516; *Missionaries* 1521; *Churches* 1526-1528; *Church Services* 1531-1538

> SEE ALSO: *Eating* 7; *Authors* 1172

MINISTERS

1461 Henry Ward Beecher asked Park Benjamin, the poet and humorist, why he never came to hear him preach. Benjamin replied, "Why, Beecher, the fact is, I have conscientious scruples against going to places of amusement on Sunday."

1462 John Wesley, in a considerable party, had been maintaining with great earnestness the doctrine of Vox populi vox Dei against his sister. At last the preacher, to put an end to the controversy, said, "I tell you, sister, the voice of the people is the voice of God."

"Yes," replied his sister mildly, "it cried: 'Crucify him! Crucify him!'"

1463 A young minister who was temporarily filling a city pulpit made the following request in his prayers: "May the brother who ministers to this flock be filled full of fresh veal and new zigor."

1464 "Can I lead a good Christian life in New York City on $15 a week?" a young man once asked Dr. S. Parkes Cadman.

"My boy," was the reply, "that's all you can do."

1465   "I am thankful that the Lord has opened my mouth to preach without any larning," said an illiterate preacher.

"A similar event took place in Balaam's time," replied a gentleman present.

1466   John Wilkes was once asked by a Roman Catholic gentleman in a warm dispute upon religion: "Where was your religion before Luther?" "Did you wash your face this morning?" inquired the facetious alderman. "I did, sir." "Then pray where was your face before it was washed?"

1467   A Presbyterian minister of the early days settled near the headwaters of the Susquehanna. A good man, he was, but full of humor and ready with his repartee on all occasions.

Jack Rickitt, a quasi-parishioner, but who was more punctual at the river than at Church, presented the minister one Monday morning with a fine string of pickerel. The minister thanked him gravely for the gift.

"But parson," suggested Jack, still retaining the fish, "those fish were caught yesterday. Perhaps yer conscience won't let you eat 'em."

"Jack," replied the minister, holding out his hands toward the string, "there's one thing I know—the pickerel were not to blame!"

1468   Sydney Smith, the clergyman, had a combat of wit with a friend. His defeated antagonist intending to cast a slur on Smith's vocation, fired back: "If I had a son who was an idiot, I would make him a parson."

"Your father was of a different opinion," was Sydney Smith's answering thrust.

1469   The Reverend Doctor Edgar DeWitt Jones propounded the specifications of a good minister. "He should get religion like a Methodist; experience it like a Baptist; be sure of it like a Disciple; stick to it like a Lutheran; pray for it like a Presbyterian; conciliate it like a Congregationalist; glorify it like a Jew; be proud of it like an Episcopalian; practice it like a Christian Scientist; propagate it like a Roman Catholic; work for it like a Salvation Army lassie; enjoy it like a colored man."

1470   Jerome D. Engel, the famous Baptist preacher, was once vacationing at a well-known shore resort. One of the local churches had expected to have its pulpit filled on Sunday morning by a "supply" or visiting minister. At the last minute, the visitor was unable to appear, and the church found itself with no one to conduct services. The leaders of the church scurried around distractedly in search of a preacher, and were unable to to find anyone. At last, chancing to hear of the presence in town of the eminent divine, one of the church members sought out Engel and begged for his services. Graciously, the minister consented. Delighted and relieved, the committeeman said, "You know, Dr. Engel, we'd have been willing to accept a poorer preacher, but it was impossible to find one."

1471   In the Southern states the church of the élite is generally the Episcopal. There is a legend concerning an eminent Episcopal divine who was once asked, after a dissertation, "Pastor, is it possible for a man to achieve salvation outside of the Episcopal church?"

The minister replied, "It is conceivable that such a possibility might exist. However, no gentleman would avail himself of it."

1472   Jerome D. Engel, the famous Southern Baptist divine, was strolling along the seawalk during a Church Convention at Charleston. He came upon an old colored man who was fishing from the pier. For some time Engel watched the Negro patiently waiting for a bite. At last he pulled in a fish of repulsive appearance, seeming to be something between a toad and a bullhead. Knowing little about so worldly a matter as fishing, Engel asked, "What kind of fish is that, George?"

"Dey calls it a Baptist fish," croaked the old man.

"A Baptist fish?" inquired Engel sceptically.

"Sho'," answered the fisherman, throwing his catch back into the sea. "Dey calls dem dat 'cause dey spoils so fast after dey is taken out of de water."

1473   George Ade, automobiling in Indiana, dined at a country hotel among a roomful of ministers. The ministers, who were holding a convention in the town, were much amused when Mr. Ade's identity was disclosed to them. One of them said during dinner: "How does a humorist of your stamp feel, sir, in such reverend company as this?"

"I feel," said Mr. Ade promptly, "like a lion in a den of Daniels."

1474   Reverend Henry Ward Beecher entered Plymouth Church one Sunday and found several letters awaiting him. He opened one and found it contained the single word "Fool." Quietly and with becoming seriousness he announced to the congregation the fact in these words:

"I have known many an instance of a man writing a letter and forgetting to sign his name, but this is the only instance I have ever known of a man signing his name and forgetting to write the letter."

1475   A new clergyman in town sought the services of the best local physician, a man irregular in his church attendance. The medical treatment was prolonged, and the young pastor, worried over the accumulating expense, spoke to the doctor about the matter of his bill.

"I'll tell you what I'll do, Pastor," said the doctor, "I hear you're a pretty good preacher and you seem to think I'm a fair doctor. We'll make a bargain. I'll do all I can to keep you out of Heaven, and you do all you can to keep me out of Hell, and it won't cost either of us a cent."

1476   Bursting with her news, Mrs. Meadows hurried to her neighbor's house.

"Have you heard, Mrs. Smith? The minister's son has decided to become a jockey. Of course you know that he was supposed to go to the Theological Seminary this year."

Mrs. Smith, more of the woman of the world than her friend, replied drily, "Well, I must say that he'll bring a lot more people to repentance that way than he would as a minister."

1477   Some years ago a theological tempest in a teapot raged over the issue of Fundamentalism versus Modernism. Dr. Harry Emerson Fosdick, of the Riverside Church in New York, was in the forefront of this fray.

There is a legend that, at this time, Dr. Fosdick was awakened in the small hours of the morning by the persistent ringing of his telephone. He climbed out of bed and hastened to answer it, and sleepily said, "Hello."

A voice came over the wire, saying, "Ish thish Mr. Foshdick?"

Dismayed the minister said, "Yes, this is Dr. Fosdick speaking."

"Dr. Harry Emerson Foshdick?"

"Yes, yes," was the impatient answer, "what is it you want?"

"Dr. Foshdick, I want to know the difference between Fundamentalism and Modernism."

Exasperated, Dr. Fosdick said, "Good Heavens, man, that's not something I can explain to you over the telephone, and obviously you're in no condition to hear. Come around to my study tomorrow and I'll be glad to answer your questions."

"But, Dr. Foshdick," insisted the voice, "I can't wait until tomorrow. I must know now."

Angrily Dr. Fosdick said, "Why can't you wait until tomorrow? Why do you have to know now?"

"Becaush," said the voice patiently, "tomorrow I won't give a damn."

RELATED SUBJECTS: *Churchmen* 1451-1456; *Church Services* 1531-1538; *Sermons* 1541-1559

SEE ALSO: *Smoking* 64; *Boners* 116; *Hypocrisy* 302; *Laziness* 327; *Prejudice* 449; *Love* 849; *Marriage* 878; *Home Life* 999; *Sermons* 1543, 1549; *Miracles* 1619; *Sin and Sinners* 1647; *Doctors* 1671; *Deathbed Scenes* 1772; *Golf* 1862; *Political Parties* 1907; *Poverty* 2209; *Salaries* 2254; *Horse* 2287; *Parrot* 2292; *Witnesses* 2504, 2505; *Wills* 2607

PRIESTS

1481 The Rev. Alexander Doyle of the Paulist Fathers is a clever speaker and a warm advocate of abstinence and tight-closed saloons for Sunday. Among his auditors was a country girl who was deeply impressed by the preaching of Father Doyle. She wrote home to her mother this bit of criticism.

"I never get tired of going to hear the sermons in the Paulist Church, Mother. Father Doyle is such a lovely preacher that you would think every word he said was true!"

1482 Curran said to Father O'Leary:

"Reverend Father, I wish you were St. Peter."

"Why," said the priest.

"Because, then you would have the keys of heaven, and could let me in."

"I had better have the keys," said Father O'Leary, "of another place, and then I could let you out."

1483 A new Protestant pastor had come to town and his clerical dress was not unlike that of a priest. He chanced to pass several little Catholic boys on the street, and a number of them tipped their hats and chorused, "Good evening, Father." No sooner had the minister passed than one of the boys turned on his companions in disgust, "Father! He's no father—he's got three kids!"

> RELATED SUBJECTS: *Churchmen* 1451-1456; *Church Services* 1531-1538; *Sermons* 1541-1559

> SEE ALSO: *Vanity* 628

RABBIS

1486 A place-hunter in Prussia, having asked Frederick the Great for the grant of some rich Protestant bishopric, the king expressed his regret that it was already given away, but broadly hinted that there was a Catholic abbacy at his disposal. The applicant managed to be converted in a week, and to be received into the bosom of the true church; after which he hastened to his friend, the king, and told him how his conscience had been enlightened. "Ah!" exclaimed Frederick, "how terribly unfortunate! I have given away the abbacy. But the chief rabbi is just dead, and the synagogue is at my disposal; suppose you were to turn Jew?"

1487 Applying for a post as keeper at the Bronx Zoo, a burly Irishman came to the question, "What is rabies and what can you do about it?"

The applicant wrote: "Rabies is Jewish priests, and you can't do anything about it."

1488 A certain Jewish man had left Pinsk to go to work in Minsk. For six months he had been away. He had a short vacation and was very anxious to get back home to see his wife and children. It was late on a Friday afternoon, however, and his friend said, "Look, you shouldn't travel on the Sabbath. It's against religion. Stay over with me until the Sabbath is over. Be my guest."

"No," said the other, "I'm anxious to get back to Pinsk. Six months I've been away."

"Six months," said his friend. "So what's another day? You shouldn't travel on the Sabbath. Stay with me. I've got a nice house. I'll give you nice Jewish meals."

After much argument, the man yielded, against his better judgment, and remained over the Sabbath. Even then his friend would not let him go and insisted on detaining him yet another day, entertaining him practically to exhaustion. At last he announced his departure.

"I can't stay another minute. I'm going right away."

"All right," said his host at last, and as his friend was about to leave the house he presented him with a bill for food and lodging. Outraged, the man cried, "What kind of a business is this! You make me stay against my will; you won't let me go. You insist that I be your guest. You keep me overtime—then you give me a bill! I won't pay it."

Equally firmly, his host insisted that he must pay. Finally he said, "All right. We'll consult the rabbi."

They sought out the rabbi. He heard the whole story, stroked his beard, and pored at length over the books of the Law. At last, after recapitulating the whole case, he delivered his verdict: "You must pay."

The victim flew into a rage. They thrashed the case back and forth many times. But the rabbi was adamant: "You must pay."

At last, weary and desirous only of getting to Pinsk, the man drew out his wallet and paid the money, demanding a receipted bill. His friend took the money, receipted the bill, and then handed the money back again, saying, "Forget it!"

"What!" screamed the other in despair. "You force me to be your guest; you won't take no for an answer; you keep me there; you give me a bill; you drag me to the rabbi; he tells me I must pay; I pay. And now you give me back the money. What is this?"

"Ah," said his friend, "I just wanted you to see what kind of a dope we have got for a rabbi in Minsk."

RELATED SUBJECTS: *Churchmen* 1451-1456

SEE ALSO: *Wealth* 2181

BISHOPS

1491   "Pat," casually asked the contractor of his workman, "didn't you once tell me that you had a brother who was a bishop?"

"Yes."

"And you are a bricklayer. It surely is a funny world. Things in life aren't divided equally, are they, Pat?"

"No, that they ain't, sor," said Pat as he proudly slapped the plaster along the line of bricks, "my poor brother couldn't do this to save his loife, sor."

1492   Somebody jested with a noted British jurist, Lord Salisbury, noting that a bishop was a man of greater authority than he. "A judge can do no more than say, 'You be hanged.' A bishop has the power to say, 'You be damned.' "

"That may be true," said Salisbury, "but when a judge says, 'You be hanged,' you are hanged!"

1493   Some years ago a person requested permission of the Bishop of Salisbury to fly from the top of the spire of that Cathedral. The good Bishop, with an anxious concern for the man's spiritual as well as temporal safety, told him he was very welcome to fly to the Church, but he would encourage no man to fly from it.

1494   When Archbishop Patrick J. Ryan of Philadelphia was a very young priest he was stationed at a Parish in St. Louis, where Archbishop Kendrick presided over the diocese. The latter lived in a very small, unpretentious house, scarcely in keeping with his position in the Church.

One day when Father Ryan was passing the house of the Archbishop, accompanied by a Chicago priest who was visiting St. Louis, he pointed out the house as the residence of the head of the local church. The Chicago priest said with surprise:

"Why, you should see the splendid residence we have in Chicago for our Archbishop."

"Yes," said Father Ryan, "but you should see the splendid Archbishop we have in St. Louis for our residence."

1495   An eminent English Bishop, who had sojourned in America for some time, was speaking of his adoption of American slang. "I now say to my chauffeur, 'Step on the gas,

George,' but I have not yet had the courage to say to the Archbishop of Canterbury, 'O.K., Chief.' "

1496 When the Reverend Whitefield became so popular a character it was agitated in the Privy Council that some method should be used to stop his preaching. Lord Chesterfield being present, turned on his heel and said: "Make him a bishop and you will silence him at once."

1497 One time Phillips Brooks was about to embark for Europe. A friend suggested jokingly that possibly he would bring a new religion back with him. He cautioned that if this was so, he should be careful, it might be difficult to get a new religion through the Customs House.

"I doubt it," said Bishop Brooks. "In all likelihood any new religion popular enough to import would have no duties attached to it."

1498 Bishop Manning of New York is fond of recalling the occasion upon which he was introduced in great dignity to a Negro congregation by its Negro pastor as, "a sounding brass and a tinkling cymbal."

RELATED SUBJECTS: *Churchmen 1451-1456*

SEE ALSO: *Smoking 65; Profanity 67, 68; Memory 374; Pompousness 423; Marriage 877; Sermons 1553; Believers 1593; Hypochondriacs 1720; Stealing 2582*

POPES

1501 Michelangelo, when painting in the Pope's chapel the picture of Hell and the souls of the damned, made one of the latter so exact a resemblance of a cardinal who was his enemy, that everyone immediately applied to Pope Clement, desiring it might be effaced; to which the latter replied, "You know that I have power to deliver a soul out of purgatory, but not out of Hell!"

1502 New made Popes were formerly seated on a chair with a hole in it, from whence they threw money to the people. The design of this delicate throne was to intimate to the newly elected Pope, that he was subject to the calls of nature like other men.

1503   When Sixtus the Fifth aspired to the Popedom he counterfeited old age for fifteen years. During the conclave assembled to elect a new Pope, he leaned upon a crutch and appeared remarkably infirm. His plan took so well that the Cardinals elected him, expecting that he would die soon. But shortly after his election he performed the "miracle" of his own cure.

1504   Goethe, walking through Rome with a friend, said to him, "There is not a relic of primitive Christianity here; and if Jesus Christ was to return to see what his deputy was about, he would run a fair chance of being crucified again."

RELATED SUBJECTS: *Churchmen* 1451-1456

SEE ALSO: *Quick Thinking* 483

EVANGELISTS

1511   One of the Lincoln stories has it that, during his 1846 campaign for Congress, he attended a preaching service of Peter Cartwright. The Evangelist called on all who wished to go to Heaven to stand up. All rose but Lincoln. The Evangelist called for all to rise who did not want to go to Hell. "I am grieved," said Cartwright, "to see Abe Lincoln sitting back there unmoved by these appeals. If he doesn't want to go to Heaven and doesn't want to escape Hell, will he tell us where he does want to go?"
    Lincoln got up slowly and said, "I'm going to Congress."

1512   An evangelist was exhorting his hearers to flee from the wrath to come. "I warn you," he thundered, "that there will be weeping, and wailing and gnashing of teeth!"
    At this moment an old woman in the gallery stood up. "Sir," she shouted, "I have no teeth."
    "Madam," returned the evangelist, "teeth will be provided."

1513   An eloquent evangelist who was holding a meeting had been interrupted on several occasions by the departure of some one of the audience. He determined to stop it by making an example of the next person. Therefore, when a young man arose to depart in the middle of his sermon he said: "Young man, would you rather go to hell than listen to this sermon?"

The young man stopped midway up the aisle and turning slowly answered: "Well, to tell the truth, I don't know but I would."

1514   A traveling Negro evangelist was fond of making spectacular finales for his revival meetings. Coming to a church, he arranged for his usual climax by secreting in the rafters of the ceiling a small Negro boy with a caged dove. At the height of his sermon the parson would shout for the Holy Ghost to come down, whereupon the dove was to be released to fly about. The moment came, and fervent in his cry, the preacher called out, "Holy Ghost come down!" Nothing happened. Again he raised his arms heavenward and said, "Holy Ghost come down!" Nothing happened, and in the expectant hush the little Negro boy poked his head over the rafters and called down, "A yaller cat is dun et the Holy Ghost, shall I thrown down de yaller cat?"

1515   That aggressive American revivalist, Dwight Moody, once passed through a large crowd in a Chicago railway station distributing tracts on temperance.

One of those to receive this material was a benign elderly gentleman who glanced at the paper in his hand and peered quizzically at Moody.

"Are you a reformed drunkard?" he asked.

"No, sir, I'm not!" cried Moody in indignation.

"Then," answered the old gentleman, "why don't you reform?"

1516   Billy Sunday, the rootin', tootin', sawdust-trail evangelist, was once interrupted in his harangue by a heckler, who shouted the question, then famous in all agnostic or atheistic circles, "Who was Cain's wife?"

Billy Sunday shot back the reply, "I respect any seeker of knowledge, but I want to warn you, young man, don't risk being lost to salvation by too much inquiring after other men's wives."

RELATED SUBJECTS: *Revivals* 1576-1578; *Conversions* 1621-1625

SEE ALSO: *Conversions* 1621

MISSIONARIES

1521   A missionary told how she was once describing the loving character of the Christians' God to a company of her Chinese sisters. As she went on in her holy enthusiasm, picturing God's real character as full of mercy to the sinful and the suffering, one of the Chinese women turned to her neighbor and said, "Haven't I often told you that there ought to be a God like that."

RELATED SUBJECTS: *Conversions* 1621-1625

SEE ALSO: *Long-Windedness* 344

CHURCHES

1526   Many years before the popularity of Florida as a winter resort, John D. Rockefeller, Sr., was in the habit of spending his winters at Augusta, Georgia.

While there he always attended the colored Baptist church on the first Sunday of his stay, and the white Episcopal and Methodist churches the following two Sundays.

The Methodist minister, intrigued by this invariable schedule, once asked the Baptist preacher if he knew why Mr. Rockefeller always visited his church first.

"Why, that's easy," replied the preacher. "You Methodists burn electricity, the Episcopalians use gas, but we'uns burn kerosene oil."

1527   There had been a series of severe electrical storms in Orange, New Jersey, and the vestrymen of a certain church in that town had discussed the advisability of placing lightning rods on the edifice. So they went to call on Thomas Edison, the inventor, to get his opinion.

"I think, sir," said their spokesman, "that lightning rods are a mighty good thing on a building. What do you think?"

"What sort of building is it?" asked Edison impatiently.

"A church."

"By all means put them on," said the great inventor. "You know Providence is absent-minded at times."

1528   Harpo Marx is not a religious man. He has never entered a synagogue but once since his Bar Mitzvah. On this occasion he entered a synagogue in search of his bootlegger. He got his pocket picked.

RELATED SUBJECTS: *Churchmen* 1451-1456; *Church Services* 1531-1538

SEE ALSO: *Prejudice* 451; *Poverty* 2210; *Salaries* 2253

CHURCH SERVICES

1531 One day the telephone in the office of the Rector of President Roosevelt's Washington church rang, and an eager voice said, "Tell me, do you expect the President to be in church this Sunday?"

"That," the Rector explained patiently, "I cannot promise. However, God will be there and that will be incentive enough for a reasonably large attendance."

1532 Rebuking her small son for not going to church willingly, his mother said, "You go to the movies for entertainment and you go down to Freddie's house, and over to Tommie's house, and you have a nice time. Now don't you think it is only right that once a week you should go to God's House, just for one hour?"

The boy thought it over and said, "But, Mom, what would you think if you were invited to somebody's house and every time you went, the fellow was never there!"

1533 An extreme instance of tongue-twistedness is found in the case of the nervous and confused usher on Easter morning when the church was crowded to overflowing. Finding a lady somewhat disconcerted at being unable to occupy her usual place, he hastened up and said, "Mardon me, padam, but this pie is occupewd. May I sew you to another sheet?"

1534 In a small and impoverished Negro community, the church had no other hall to hold its services than a large room below a second-story dance hall with a wild reputation. Often, when evening service was being held, it was difficult for the preacher to make himself heard above the stomping and clatter from above. The building was ramshackle, and one night in the midst of a sermon a particularly vigorous jive was in progress above. There was the splintering of a plank, and looking upward in alarm, the parson saw, protruding through a hole that had given way in the ceiling, the solid and buxom leg of a Negress. In consternation, he at once called out, "Any man what raises his eyes to the ceiling De Lawd will strike blind."

A hushed silence fell over the congregation, when the quavering voice of an aged Negro at the rear of the church was heard to remark, "Waal, I'll risk one eye on it anyhow."

1535　The noted Baptist preacher, Jerome D. Engel, was once annoyed by an old gentleman who fell asleep during his sermon on several consecutive Sundays. A small boy habitually accompanied the old gentleman and, after service one morning, Engel spoke to the boy in the vestry and said, "My lad, who's the elderly gentleman with whom you attend church?"

"Grandpa," was the reply.

"Well," promised Engel, "if you will only keep him awake during the sermon, I will give you a nickel each week."

This seemed advantageous to the lad, and for the following two weeks the old gentleman listened attentively. But the third week, he once again dropped off soundly to sleep and Engel was vexed. Sending for the boy, he said, "Didn't you agree to keep him awake every week for a nickel?"

"Yes, sir," said the boy, "but now Grandpa gives me a dime not to disturb him."

1536　In a small Scottish church, a sexton was painstakingly pursuing his duties, seeing that everyone had his place and was properly quiet during the sermon.

Suddenly he spied an old Scotswoman with an ear trumpet. Being unfamiliar with this device, he hurried over to her and in a low voice said, "One toot and you're oot."

1537　In the later years of his ministry, the Southern preacher, Jerome D. Engel, became slightly hard of hearing. A legend has it that at one service during the announcement period, Engel informed the congregation about new hymnals which were being ordered and which were to be purchased individually by the congregation. When he had finished the announcement, the Deacon of the church arose to remind the audience that the following Sunday was the regular day for the baptism of infants. Engel, not hearing clearly and thinking the deacon had made reference to the books, hastily added, "All you who haven't any, can get as many as you want, by calling on me, at 75¢ a piece."

1538 A woman engaged an Irish maid from the city to serve at her country estate. The girl was a devout Catholic and suffered from the fact that the only church of any description within reach of her new place of employment was a Christian Science temple. Feeling the necessity to worship in somewise she at last attended services there. Upon her return her employer asked, "Well, Mary, how did you like the Christian Science services?"

"Faith," said Mary, "it was mighty quare. I went in and sat down and after a time a man on one side of the church got up and told what Mary Baker Eddy had done for him; then another man got up and told what Mary Baker Eddy had done for him. And next a woman in front of me got up and told what Mary Baker Eddy had done for her, and it went on until I couldn't stand it any longer, and I got right up and told what Lydia E. Pinkham had done for me."

> RELATED SUBJECTS: *Sermons* 1541-1559; *Collections* 1561-1569; *Sunday School* 1571; *Revivals* 1576-1578; *Prayer* 1606-1612
>
> SEE ALSO: *Hypocrisy* 301

SERMONS

1541 The well-known and popular preacher, Charles Spurgeon, was admonishing a class of Divinity students on the importance of making the facial expressions harmonize with the speech in delivering sermons. "When you speak of Heaven," he said, "let your face light up and be irradiated with a Heavenly gleam. Let your eyes shine with reflected glory. And when you speak of Hell—well, then your every-day face will do."

1542 Mark Twain occasionally attended the services of Dr. Doane, later Bishop of Albany, but then Rector of an Episcopal church in Hartford. One Sunday morning Twain said to him at the end of the service, "Dr. Doane, I enjoyed your service this morning. I welcomed it like an old friend. I have, you know, a book at home containing every word of it."

"You have not," said Dr. Doane indignantly.

"I have so."

"Well, you send that book to me. I'd like to see it."

"I'll send it," promised Twain. The following day he sent Dr. Doane an unabridged dictionary.

1543   A visiting minister was eating breakfast with his host, before the morning service at which he was to speak. He ate very little, explaining that it is not good for a preacher to eat heavily before a sermon. The housewife had prepared the meal with great care and felt somewhat peeved at the apparent lack of appreciation of her cooking. She could not attend the service, as she had the dinner to prepare.

When her husband got home she inquired:

"Well, how was he?"

The husband, drawing a sigh, replied:

"He might just as well of et."

1544   When a Scotch minister told his neighbor that he had preached two hours and a half the day before, the neighbor said to him, "Why, minister, were you not tired to death?"

"Aw, na," said he, "I was as fresh as a rose, but it would have done your heart good to see how tired the congregation was."

1545   A minister named Craig purchased a whistle and when his hearers went to sleep, he emitted from it a very shrill sound. All were awake and sat up to hear him. "You are certainly smart specimens of humanity," said he, as he slowly gazed at his wondering people; "when I preach the gospel you go to sleep, when I play the fool you are wide awake."

1546   "I ought not to be surprised by anything at my time of life," said a well-known minister, "but one of my flock did manage to take my breath away. I was preaching about the Father's tender wisdom in caring for us all; illustrated by saying that the Father knows which of us grows best in sunlight and which of us must have shade. 'You know you plant roses in the sunshine,' I said, 'and heliotrope and geraniums; but if you want your fuchsias to grow they must be kept in a shady nook.' After the sermon, which I hoped would be a comforting one, a woman came up to me, her face glowing with pleasure that was evidently deep and true. 'Oh, Dr. ——, I am so grateful for that sermon,' she said, clasping my hand and shaking it warmly. 'My heart glowed for a moment, while I wondered what tender place in her heart and life I had touched. Only for a moment, though. 'Yes,' she went on fervently, 'I never knew before what was the matter with my fuchsias.' "

1547   George Whitefield, the celebrated preacher, was on one occasion describing a blind man's approach unknowingly to the edge of a precipice.

"Tap, tap, went his stick, feeling the way. Shuffle, shuffle, came his feet. Rods of distance dwindled to yards, yards dwindled to inches. The last full step took him to the edge; his stick reached into vacancy and slipped from his hand: he moved forward to retrieve it; he lifted one foot over vacancy"— and the skeptical, licentious Lord Chesterfield, who was in the audience, leaped to his feet, crying out: "My God! He's gone!"

1548   The celebrated preacher, Rowland Hill, was greatly annoyed whenever any noise diverted the attention of his hearers from what he was saying. On one occasion, a few days before his death, he was preaching to a crowded congregation, and in the middle of his discourse observed a commotion in the gallery.

"What's the matter there," he exclaimed. "The devil seems to have got among you!"

A plain, country-looking man started to his feet, and addressing Mr. Hill in reply, said:

"No sir—it aren't the devil as is doing it! It's a fat lady what's faint; and she is a very fat 'un, sir, as don't seem likely to come to again in a hurry."

"Oh, that's it—is it?" observed Mr. Hill, drawing his hand across his chin. "Then I beg the lady's pardon—and the devil's too."

1549   Garrick said he would give a hundred guineas if he could say "Oh!" as well as the Rev. Whitefield.

1550   Dr. South, when preaching before Charles II observed that the monarch and his attendants began to nod; and some of them soon after snored. On this he broke off his sermon, and said, "Lord Lauderdale, let me entreat you to rouse yourself; you snore so loud, that you will awake the king."

1551   "My brethren," said the satirical Dean Swift in a sermon, "there are three kinds of pride—of birth, of riches, and of talent. I shall not speak of the latter, none of you being liable to that abominable vice."

1552 A somewhat self-satisfied and greatly inexperienced young preacher one Sunday supplied the pulpit of a country church. After services he asked one of the church fathers what he thought of his sermon. "Now, I'll tell you," said the old man, "I'll put it in a sort of parable. I recollect Archie Tucker's first deer hunt. He was kind of green. He followed the deer all right, but he followed it all day in the wrong direction."

1553 A prominent bishop tells of the Sunday morning when he was approached after the service by an old lady, who said in a tone of appreciation, "Bishop, you'll never know what your service meant to me. It was just like water to a drowning man!"

1554 A certain minister recounted a harrowing experience which befell him during one of his sermons. Just as he was beginning his address, an elderly lady of stern mien marched down and seated herself directly beneath him in front of the pulpit. She opened up a little kit, assembled the various parts of a rather elaborate hearing mechanism and affixed it to her ears. After not more than 10 minutes of his discourse, she suddenly took off the ear-pieces, unscrewed the mechanism and packed it neatly away in its little box, and sat with her hands in her lap throughout the rest of the sermon.

1555 "I believe you have never heard me preach, Charles?" said Coleridge, referring to the days of his Unitarian ministry.
   "Yes," retorted Lamb. "I-I never heard you do anything else."

1556 When the celebrated Reverend Whitefield preached before seamen in New York some two hundred years ago he used the following graphic description to describe the plight of sinners:
   "Well, my boys, we have a clear sky, and are making fine headway over a smooth sea before a light breeze, and we shall soon lose sight of land. But what means this sudden lowering of the heavens, and that dark cloud arising from beneath the western horizon? Don't you hear distant thunder? Don't you see those flashes of lightning? There is a storm gathering! Every man to his duty! How the waves rise and dash against the ship!

The air is dark! The tempest rages! Our masts are gone! The ship is on her beam ends! What next?"

At this point the congregation of tars arose as one man and shouted: "Take to the long boats!"

1557 It is told of John Wesley that when he saw some of his hearers asleep he stopped in his discourse and shouted: "Fire! Fire!"

The sleepers were alarmed, and waking up, cried out: "Where, sir, where?"

"In hell!" replied Wesley solemnly—"In hell for those who sleep under the preaching of the word."

1558 A clergyman in a Lawrence church on a recent occasion discovered, after beginning the service, that he had forgotten his notes. As it was too late to send for them, he said to his audience, by way of apology, that this morning he should have to depend upon the Lord for what he might say but in the afternoon he would come better prepared.

1559 An admirer of a distinguished clergyman remarked in his praise: "President Holley was an excellent preacher—he never put any religion or politics in his sermon."

RELATED SUBJECTS: *Speeches* 756-782; *Ministers* 1461-1477; *Church Services* 1531-1538

SEE ALSO: *Liars* 335; *Long-Windedness* 342; *Handicaps* 701; *Wife* 932; *Collections* 1568

COLLECTIONS

1561 Andrew Carnegie told this story: One day he found himself in a sleepy little town in Georgia on a Sunday, and he determined to visit the colored church. When the plate was passed he dropped a fifty dollar banknote on it. The old man who passed the plate put it down at once, examined the note carefully on both sides, then counted the change in the plate. Then he marched solemnly to the front with the plate and whispered to the pastor, nodding first at the fifty dollar note and then at Mr. Carnegie. The minister put the plate on the pulpit, fingered the note, blinked once or twice and said: "Bre'ren, de Lawd hab be'n mighty good to us dis day. De collec'shun mounts to one dollar en twenty-fo cents, 'en ef de fifty dollar bill wha' dat man wid de grey ha'r 'en beard put in de plate, am good, we have fifty-one dollahs 'en twenty-fo' cents. Let us t'ank de Lawd, en pray dat it may be a good bill."

1562   Wishing to develop his son's character, a father once gave him a penny and a quarter as he was departing for church, and said, "Now, son, you put whichever one you want in the collection plate."

When the boy got back, his father asked which coin he had given. The young fellow said, "Well, just before they sent around the plate the preacher said, 'The Lord loveth a cheerful giver,' and I knew I could be a lot more cheerful if I gave the penny, so I gave it."

1563   A young hopeful, setting out for Sunday School one morning, was given two nickels, one for the collection plate and one for himself. As he was rambling down the street he played with the coins. One of them slipped out of his hand, rolled away from him and disappeared irretrievably into the sewer. The youngster gazed ruefully down through the grate for a moment and then said, "Well, there goes the Lord's nickel."

1564   A very old lady and a very small boy were seated side by side in the pew of the church. As the collection plate was being passed the little boy noticed that the lady seemed to be fumbling fruitlessly in her purse.

Leaning toward her he whispered, "Here, you take my dime. I can hide under the seat."

1565   The Rev. Sydney Smith, preaching a charity sermon frequently repeated the assertion that, of all nations, Englishmen were most distinguished for generosity and the love of their species. The collection happened to be inferior to his expectations and he said that he had evidently made a great mistake, for that his expression should have been, that they were distinguished for the love of their specie.

1566   The Vicar of St. John's Church in Waterloo, England, contrived an original way of dispensing with annual Church bazaars. To all the members of his congregation he sent the following bill: "Bus fare . . . admission . . . wear and tear on clothes and tempers . . . tea . . . useless articles . . . total . . . Please remit."

The sums received were in excess of any previously raised.

1567   In the church meeting the suggestion had been made and well received that a drive be undertaken to raise money to buy a chandelier for the church. A crusty old elder, however, arose and said, "It's tomfoolery and extravagant frippery. It will not only cost money to buy the durn thing and install it, but next we'll have to hire somebody to play it."

1568   "Brudren," said a darky minister down South, "brudren, I'se got a five-dollar sermon, and a two-dollar sermon, an' a one-dollar sermon, an' I want dis here indelicate audience to take up a collection as to which one ob dem dey can afford to hear."

1569   The official board of the church had called a meeting in order to seek a means of raising funds for much-needed repairs. The little church was literally falling apart and the pastor, stirred by a very real emotion, having been connected with this parish for nearly twenty years, made a moving speech.

Great was his and the other members' surprise when the most miserly member of the board rose and offered to start the fund with a contribution of five dollars. As he spoke a bit of plaster fell and hit him on the head. A trifle dazed, he rose again and said, "Reckon I'd better make that fifty dollars."

From the back of the hall came a pleading voice. "Hit him again, Lord!"

> RELATED SUBJECTS: *Generosity* 241-248; *Stinginess* 556-566; *Church Services* 1531-1538

> SEE ALSO: *Long-Windedness* 344; *Shrewdness* 541; *Stinginess* 557; *Collection* 2179

SUNDAY SCHOOL

1571   "Which is the first and most important sacrament?" asked a Sunday-school teacher of a girl preparing for confirmation.

"Marriage," was the prompt response.

"No, baptism is the first and most important sacrament," the teacher corrected.

"Not in our family," said the pupil haughtily, "we are re-spectable."

RELATED SUBJECTS: *Church Services* 1531-1538

SEE ALSO: *Patriotism* 401; *Collections* 1563; *Fishing* 1852

REVIVALS

1576 At one time, Henry Ward Beecher used to amaze earnest inquirers at revival meetings by asking them, instead of the expected questions about their souls, how much exercise they took and whether their bowels moved regularly. He called this "clinical theology": it enabled him, as he said, to distinguish in his penitents between "dyspepsia and piety."

1577 Jerome D. Engel, when conducting one of his celebrated revivals in Philadelphia, stopped a small newsboy and asked him the way to the post-office.

"Down this street three squares and turn to the left."

"You seem a bright little fellow," said Engel, a man of considerable self-esteem. "Do you know who I am?"

"Naw."

"I am the famous preacher who is holding the revival over in the big tabernacle. If you will come to my meeting tonight I will show you the way to Heaven."

"Aw, go on," said the youngster, "you don't even know the way to the post-office."

1578 The Negro Baptist minister was exhorting his flock, "Come, my children. Get your sins washed away."

One of the congregation spoke up, "I already have. Over at the Methodist church."

"Brother Jones," sternly replied the minister, "you ain't been washed, you just been dry cleaned."

RELATED SUBJECTS: *Evangelists* 1511-1516; *Devout Persons* 1601-1602; *Conversions* 1621-1625

SEE ALSO: *Hypocrisy* 302; *Evangelists* 1514

BIBLE

1581 A bigoted old churchgoer, firmly set in his notions, rebuffed his neighbor who was speaking of a new American version of the Bible. Said he, "If the King James version was good enough for St. Paul, it's good enough for me."

1582 The Rev. Dr. W. S. Rainsford once told of the futility of trying to comfort people with Bible texts.

"Whenever I tried to persuade an Irish member of my flock to pay more attention to his church duties, he would make the excuse that it took him all his time to earn a living, and he would touch my heart by his expatiation upon the difficulty of making money.

"But Patrick," I protested, "man does not live by bread alone."

"No, y'r Riverance," replied Patrick, "Sure, an' he needs a bit o' mate an' some vegetables as well!"

1583 Someone remarked in President Grant's presence that Sumner did not believe in the Bible. "Why should he?" asked the President, "he did not write it."

1584 On one occasion, when Mrs. William Gladstone was entertaining visitors, conversation turned on the Bible, and there was a lively argument on the meaning of a certain passage.

Presently one of the callers, hoping to end the discussion, remarked devoutly:

"There is One alone who knows all."

The cloud vanished from Mrs. Gladstone's face and she smiled sunnily as she said:

"Yes, and William will be down in a few minutes."

1585 Mark Twain was fond of telling the story of the small boy's account of Elijah in his less ingratiating mood.

"There was a prophet named Elijah. One day he was going up a mountainside. Some boys threw stones at him. He said, 'If you keep on throwing stones at me I'll set the bears on you and they'll eat you up.' And they did, and he did, and the bears did."

1586 Greatly distressed by the prevailing ignorance of the villagers in the small village in which she was vacationing, an old lady persuaded the schoolteacher to give some lessons to some of the more illiterate adults.

Meeting one of these pupils on the street one day she asked kindly, "Well, John, I guess you can read your Bible by this time."

"Bless your heart, ma'am," was the grateful reply, "I was out of the Bible and into the baseball news over a week ago."

RELATED SUBJECTS: *Churchmen* 1451-1456; *Church Services* 1531-1538; *Sermons* 1541-1559

SEE ALSO: *Liars* 335; *Society* 796; *School Classrooms* 1053; *Rationing* 2357

BELIEVERS

1591   Chateauneuf, keeper of the seals of Louis XIII, when a boy of only nine years old, was asked many questions by a bishop, and gave very prompt answers to them all. At length the prelate said, "I will give you an orange if you will tell me where God is."

"My lord," replied the boy, "I will give you two oranges if you will tell me where he is not."

1592   When John Jay was asked how it was possible for him to occupy his mind after his retirement from public life, he replied with a smile, "I have a long life to look back upon and an eternity to look forward to."

1593   Parson Paten was so much averse to the Athanasian Creed that he would never read it. Archbishop Secker having been informed of his recalcitrance, sent the archdeacon to ask him his reason. "I do not believe it," said the priest.

"But your metropolitan does," replied the archdeacon.

"It may be so," rejoined Mr. Paten, "and he can well afford it; he believes at the rate of seven thousand pounds a year, and I only at fifty."

1594   Four gentlemen—a Baptist, Presbyterian, Methodist and Roman Catholic—met by agreement to dine on fish. Soon as grace was said, the Catholic rose, armed with a knife and fork, and taking about one-third of the fish, including the head, removed it to his plate, saying with great satisfaction: "The Pope is the head of the church." Immediately the Methodist minister arose, and helping himself to about one third, embracing the tail, said: "The end crowns the work." The Presbyterian now thought it was time for him to move, and taking the remainder of the fish to his plate, exclaimed: "Truth lies between the two extremes."

Our Baptist brother had nothing before him but an empty plate, and the prospect of a slim dinner, so seizing a bowl of melted butter, he dashed it over them, exclaiming: "I baptize you all."

1595 Shortly before the death of Thoreau, a pious aunt visited him and asked, "Have you made your peace with God, Henry?"

"I don't know that we ever quarrelled," he replied.

1596 Abraham Lincoln once remarked to a friend that his religion was like that of an old man named Glenn in Indiana, whom he heard speak at a church meeting and who said: "When I do good I feel good; when I do bad, I feel bad; and that's my religion."

> RELATED SUBJECTS: *Devout Persons* 1601-1602; *Prayer* 1606-1612; *Miracles* 1616-1619; *Conversions* 1621-1625; *Bigotry* 1626-1629; *Superstition* 1631-1636; *Atheists and Agnostics* 1651-1659
>
> SEE ALSO: *Football* 1858; *Stool Pigeons* 2591

DEVOUT PERSONS

1601 Henry M. Stanley, the famous deliverer of Dr. Livingstone from darkest Africa, one time came to Edison's laboratory to see the great inventor demonstrate his new invention, the phonograph.

Having heard the machine and been tremendously impressed by it, he asked, "Mr. Edison, if it were possible for you to hear the voice of any man whose fame is known in the history of the world, whose voice would you prefer to hear?"

"Napoleon," Edison answered without hesitation.

"No, no," said Stanley with an overtone of disapproval, "I should like to hear the voice of Our Savior."

"Oh, well," replied Edison slightly embarrassed by his

guest's religious feeling, "You know I like a hustler."

1602 An ignorant coal miner, a devout man, was chided because he had not succeeded in converting his three sons. He defended himself with these words: "I tells 'em to pray and they won't pray, and I tells 'em again to pray and they won't pray, and I knocks 'em down and they won't pray."

> RELATED SUBJECTS: *Devotion* 171-173; *Believers* 1591-1596; *Prayer* 1606-1612; *Miracles* 1616-1619; *Conversions* 1621-1625; *Bigotry* 1626-1629
>
> SEE ALSO: *Church Services* 1538

PRAYER

1606 To a clergyman during the early war period Lincoln made a significant remark. "Let us have faith, Mr. President," the minister said with great solemnity, "that the Lord is on our side in this great struggle."

To which Lincoln quietly retorted, "I am not at all concerned about that, for I know that the Lord is always on the side of the right; but it is my constant anxiety and prayer, that I and this nation may be on the Lord's side."

1607 A pious lady had prayed St. Raboni for the conversion of her husband—a few days after, he died—whereupon the widow exclaimed, "What a gracious saint is Raboni, he even gives us more than we pray for."

1608 Bion was sailing in a vessel, when a great storm came on. The mariners, who were wicked and dissolute fellows, called upon the gods; but Bion said, "Peace; let them not know you are here."

1609 After the capture of Ticonderoga, Ethan Allen, the American patriot, hurried home to his family in Bennington, Vermont, and while there attended a Thanksgiving service at the Old First Church. Town history says that during the long prayer in which the Rev. Mr. Dewey was giving all the credit for the victory to the Lord, Allen interrupted: "Parson Dewey, Parson Dewey!" At the third call, the minister paused and opened his eyes.

"Please," said Allen, "mention to the Lord about my being there."

1610 Dr. Franklin, when a child, found the long graces used by his father before and after meals very tedious. One day, after the winter's provisions had been salted: "I think, father," said Benjamin, "if you were to say grace over the whole cask, once for all, it would be a vast saving of time."

1611 It was said that Oliver Cromwell, the English statesman and soldier, usually said the following grace before meals: "Some people have food but no appetite; others have appetite, but no food. I have both. The Lord be praised."

1612 The new preacher had finished his sermon in which he had listed all the human wants that he thought the Lord should gratify.

The deacon asked the old Negro janitor who had listened patiently throughout this sermon, if he did not think the minister had offered up a good prayer.

"Ah most suttinly does, boss. Why that man asked de Lawd fo' things de othah preacher didn't even know He had."

RELATED SUBJECTS: *Believers* 1591-1596; *Devout Persons* 1601-1602; *Miracles* 1616-1619

SEE ALSO: *Shortness* 694; *Congress* 1941; *Bosses* 2234; *Civil War* 2329

MIRACLES

1616 Caedmon was so unlettered that he had to retire for shame from the Refectory at Whitley Abbey when the harp, passing from hand to hand during dinner, approached him with its implication that he must recite. "On one of these occasions," as narrated by Bede, "it happened to be Caedmon's turn to keep guard at the stable during the night and overcome with vexation, he quitted the table and retired to his post of duty, where, laying himself down, he fell into a sound slumber. In the midst of his sleep, a stranger appeared to him, and, saluting him by his name, said: 'Caedmon, sing me something.' Caedmon answered: 'I know nothing to sing; for my incapacity in this respect was the cause of my leaving the hall to come hither.' 'Nay,' said the stranger, 'but thou hast something to sing.' 'What must I sing?' said Caedmon. 'Sing the Creation,' was the reply; and thereupon Caedmon began to sing verses which he had never heard before.

"Caedmon then awoke, and he was not only able to repeat the lines which he had made in his sleep, but he continued them in a strain of admirable versification. In the morning he hastened to the town reeve, or bailiff of Whitley, who carried him before the Abbess Hilda; and there, in the presence of some of the learned men of the place, he told his story, and they were all of the opinion that he had received the gift of song from Heaven."

1617 On February 10, 1872 Mr. Wallace Wright publicly challenged Mrs. Mary Baker Eddy—

"1st. To restore the dead to life again as she claims she can.

"2nd. To walk upon the water without the aid of artificial means as she claims she can.

"3rd. To live 24 hours without air, or 24 days without nourishment of any kind without its having any effect upon her.

"4th. To restore sight when the optic nerve has been destroyed.

"5th. To set and heal a broken bone without artificial means."

Mr. Wright ended the controversy by the exultant announcement on Feb. 17 that his opponent and her Science were practically dead and buried.

1618 A Negro preacher addressed his flock with great earnestness on the subject of Miracles, as follows:

"My beloved, friends, de greatest ob all miracles was 'bout the loaves and fishes. Dey was 5000 loaves and 2000 fishes, and de twelve apostles had to eat 'em all. De miracle is dey didn't bust."

1619 John Wesley, the hymnist, was nominated a special person by divine fiat. When a baby, he was miraculously saved from his father's burning office. Just after his escape the roof fell in. This incident contributed so strongly to his later evangelism, giving him the conviction that he had been saved by God for a special mission, that he adopted a device found on some of the contemporary prints, of him, namely, a house in flames, with this motto from the prophet, "Is he not a brand plucked from the burning?"

RELATED SUBJECTS: *Believers* 1591-1596; *Prayer* 1606-1612; *Superstition* 1631-1636

SEE ALSO: *Popes* 1503; *Boats* 1816

CONVERSIONS

1621 During the Civil War the late Colonel Gabe Bouch organized a regiment which he controlled as a dictator.

"I am an humble servant of the Lord," said an itinerant evangelist who had wandered into camp one day, "endeavoring to save the souls of the unfortunate. I have just left the camp of the Massachusetts, where I was instrumental in leading eight men into the paths of righteousness."

"Adjutant," thundered Colonel Bouch, after a moment's pause, "detail ten men for baptism. No d—d Massachusetts regiment shall beat mine for piety."

1622 George Cruikshank having become a teetotaller, showed all the vehement zeal of a convert. Douglas Jerrold, meeting him shortly after his conversion, exclaimed, "Now, George, remember that water is very good anywhere—except upon the brain."

1623 A woman was testifying of her conversion at a revival meeting. She said: "I was very foolish and vain. Worldly pleasures, and especially the fashions, were my only thought. I was fond of silks, satins, ribbons and laces. But, my friends, when I saw they were dragging me down to perdition I gave them all to my sister."

1624 A young man, who had formerly attended Dr. Bethune's meetings, after an absence of a few years called upon him and said: "Dr. Bethune, I have become a Christian since I saw you, and have joined the army of the Lord."

"I am very glad to hear it," said the doctor, and added, "With what denomination have you become connected?"

"The Baptists."

"Oh the Baptists," said Dr. Bethune. "Why they are not the army, but the navy of the Lord."

1625 A Methodist in America, bragging how well he had instructed some Indians in religion, asked one of them "if he had not found great comfort last Sunday, after receiving the sacrament."

"Aye, master," replied the savage, "but I wished it had been brandy."

RELATED SUBJECTS: *Evangelists* 1511-1516; *Revivals* 1576-1578; *Miracles* 1616-1619

SEE ALSO: *Rabbis* 1486; *Devout Persons* 1602; *Jail* 2563

BIGOTRY

1626　"What did the Puritans come to this country for?" asked a teacher in a class of American history.

"To worship in their own way, and make other people do the same," was the reply.

1627　The Young Men's Christian Association appointed a committee to go to President Lincoln to protest his appointment of the Rev. Mr. Shrigley as hospital chaplain in the army. When they first approached the President, mentioning Mr. Shrigley's name, he misunderstood them and thought that they had come to praise his choice, and said:

"Oh yes, I have sent it to the senate. His testimonials are highly satisfactory, and the appointment will no doubt be confirmed at an early date."

Hastily the committee spokesman protested:

"But, sir, we have come not to ask for the appointment, but to solicit you to withdraw the nomination, on the ground that Mr. Shrigley is not evangelical in his sentiments."

"Ah!" said the President, "that alters the case. On what point of doctrine is the gentleman unsound?"

"He does not believe in endless punishment," was the reply.

"Yes," added another member of the committee, "he believes that even the rebels themselves will finally be saved; and it will never do to have a man with such views hospital chaplain."

The President was silent for a moment. Then, regarding the expectant faces about him, he said with emphasis: "If that be so, gentlemen, and there be any way under heaven whereby the rebels can be saved, then let the man be appointed!"

1628　There are few more tragic records of the struggle of the human mind and spirit against bigotry than this text of Galileo's recantation before the "Holy Inquisition."

"But because I have been enjoined by this Holy Office altogether to abandon the false opinion which maintains that the sun is the center and immovable, and forbidden to hold, defend, or teach the said false doctrine in any manner, and after it had been signified to me that the said doctrine is repugnant to the Holy Scripture . . . I abjure, curse, and detest the said heresies and errors . . . and I swear that I will never more in future say or assert anything verbally, or in writing, which may give rise to a similar suspicion of me."

1629 In connection with the destruction of the 700,000 manuscript volumes of the Alexandrian Library, the Caliph Omar said:

"Either these books conform to the Koran or they do not. If they do, they are not needed; if they do not, they are positively harmful. Therefore, let them be destroyed."

> RELATED SUBJECTS: *Hypocrisy* 301-303; *Prejudice* 441-452; *Tolerance* 601-603; *Devout Persons* 1601-1602; *Superstition* 1631-1636; *Censors* 2351-2355

> SEE ALSO: *Courage* 153; *Bible* 1581

SUPERSTITION

1631 Coleridge, when asked by a lady if he believed in ghosts, replied, "No, madam, I have seen too many to believe in them."

1632 Carefully explaining the correct procedure in serving meals, the wealthy society lady ended her little lecture to the new maid by saying, "Now, Mary, don't forget. You always serve from the left and take the plates from the right."

"I won't forget, Ma'am," answered the girl in a conciliating tone of voice, "but what's the matter? Superstitious or something?"

1633 Lincoln told this story: a balloon ascension occurred in New Orleans before the war, and after sailing in the air for several hours the aeronaut, who was arrayed in silks and spangles like a circus performer, descended in a cotton field where a gang of slaves were at work. The frightened Negroes took to the woods—all but one venerable darky, who was rheumatic and could not run, and who, as the resplendent aeronaut approached, having apparently just dropped from heaven, said "Good-mornin', Massa Jesus; how's yo' pa?"

1634 When the first telephone line was put in for King Ibn Saud in Arabia, Moslem religious leaders protested against such innovations and works of the Devil from the land of the Infidel. Ibn Saud listened to their complaint, and gave judgment: "If the telephone is really a work of the Devil, the holy words of the Koran will not pass over it; if the holy words do pass over it, it assuredly cannot be the work of the Devil. So we will appoint two mullahs, one to sit in the Palace and one in the telephone exchange, and they are to take turns reading a passage from the Holy Book, and we will see." By this test the religious leaders were convinced.

1635 A snake having twined itself round a key, which was declared by the seers to be a portent, Leotychidas remarked: "It would have been more of a portent if the key had twined itself round a snake."

1636 General Emilio Mola, second in command with the Spanish fascists, was killed in an airplane crash. When peasants picked him up, they found he was in his stocking-feet. A brother officer explained that a Gypsy had once told the General he would die with his boots on, and he therefore always took his shoes off when in an airplane.

RELATED SUBJECTS: *Prejudice* 441-452; *Stupidity* 576-583; *Devout Persons* 1601-1602; *Bigotry* 1626-1629

SEE ALSO: *Dictators* 2001; *Judges* 2492

PROHIBITIONS AND RESTRICTIONS

1641 Here we have just another proof that most conceptions of personal morality depend largely upon whose ox is being gored. As the Negro parson was preaching fervently against all the common sins, ranging from murder to simple crapshooting, a devout old Negress swayed and rocked in her pew, murmuring, "Amen—Amen. Praise God!" at each prohibition. Then the parson started on the subject of snuff dipping, at which the pious old Negress sat bolt upright and muttered to herself, "Now he done stop preachin' and took to meddlin'."

1642   A little lesson in morality was imparted to the youngster who asked his father, "What is a 'necessary evil?'"

"One that we like so much we don't want to abolish it," replied his parent.

> RELATED SUBJECTS: *Drinking* 36-55; *Smoking* 61-65; *Profanity* 66-68; *Gambling* 71-74; *Ministers* 1461-1477; *Sermons* 1541-1559; *Bigotry* 1626-1629; *Sin and Sinners* 1646-1647; *Censors* 2351-2355; *Laws* 2596-2599

> SEE ALSO: *Behavior* 1; *Drinking* 45; *Tolerance* 602; *Censors* 2355

SIN AND SINNERS

1646   An old Negro preacher, wearied of the many complaints he heard about the temptations placed in the paths of members of his congregation by Satan: "Folks is all de time making out dat Satan is runnin' after them fo' to tempt them. De truth is, dere is so many people pulling at the Debil's coattails, he ain't got de time to chase nobody."

1647   In the days of the great Edwin Booth most ministers considered it a sin to attend theatrical performances. However, one clergyman, anxious to see the great actor perform, sent Mr. Booth a letter asking if he might be permitted to enter the theatre by a private door as he did not wish anyone to see him going into such a place.

"Sir," was Booth's reply, "there is no door in my theatre through which God cannot see."

> RELATED SUBJECTS: *Drinking,* 36-55; *Smoking* 61-65; *Profanity* 66-68; *Gambling* 71-74; *Conscience* 146-147; *Hypocrisy* 301-303; *Conversions* 1621-1625; *Prohibitions and Restrictions* 1641-1642

> SEE ALSO: *Drinking* 36; *Conscience* 146; *Hypocrisy* 302; *Vanity* 628; *Ministers* 1464; *Chiseling* 2128

ATHEISTS AND AGNOSTICS

1651   The noted agnostic, Colonel Robert Ingersoll, during a visit with Henry Ward Beecher, noted a beautiful globe portraying the constellations and stars of the heavens. "This is just what I've been looking for," he said after examining it. "Who made it?"

"Who made it?" repeated Beecher in simulated astonishment. "Why Colonel, nobody made it; it just happened."

1652   Someone once charged David Hume, the agnostic, with being inconsistent because he went to hear the orthodox, Scotch minister, John Brown. Hume replied, "I don't believe all that he says, but he does. And once a week I like to hear a man who believes what he says."

1653   A Portuguese sculptor, upon his death bed, had a crucifix placed before his eyes by a confessor, who said, "Behold that God whom you have so much offended. Do you recollect him now?"

"Alas! Yes, Father," replied the dying man, "it was I who made him."

1654   When Phillips Brooks was recovering from an illness, and was denying himself to all visitors, Robert G. Ingersoll, the agnostic, called. The bishop received him at once.

"I appreciate this very much," said Mr. Ingersoll, "but why do you see me when you deny yourself to your friends?"

"It is this way," said the bishop, "I feel confident of seeing my friends in the next world, but this may be my last chance of seeing you."

1655   Once, while addressing an open-air meeting, an atheist asked Bishop Carpenter if he believed that Jonah was swallowed by the whale.

"When I get to heaven I will ask Jonah," said his lordship.

"But supposing," the other persisted, "he is not there?"

"Then you will have to ask him," was the quick retort.

1656   The late Dr. Jowett, the famous master of Balliol College, Oxford, was met one day in the "quad" by an undergraduate who informed him that he, for his part, could find no positive evidence of the existence of God.

"Well, Mr. B.," said Dr. Jowett tartly, "if you do not find a God by five o'clock this afternoon, you will leave this college!"

1657   One day, when D'Alembert and Condorcet were dining with Voltaire, they proposed to converse of atheism, but Voltaire stopped them at once. "Wait," said he, "till my servants have withdrawn. I do not wish to have my throat cut tonight."

1658   During the riots of 1780 most persons in London, in order to save their houses from being burnt or pulled down, wrote on their doors, "No Popery!" Old Grimaldi, to avoid all mistakes, wrote on his, "No Religion!"

1659   The little Louis Napoleon did not respond with particular susceptibility to his religious education. In the course of it, he stumbled upon one of the puzzling problems which is remarked upon by many young theological students.

His instructor had portrayed with great melodrama the anguish and suffering of Christ. Louis manifested little reaction.

"Aren't you grieved," demanded his teacher, "to think how these wicked men behaved to our Lord?"

"Well," objected Louis, "if He was all powerful, why did He let them?"

RELATED SUBJECTS: *Cynicism* 166-170; *Believers* 1591-1596

SEE ALSO: *Shrewdness* 538; *Libraries* 1226; *Churchmen* 1456; *Evangelists* 1516

PAGAN GODS

1661   According to a story told by Roy Chapman Andrews, the famous explorer, the Living Buddha of Mongolia, a personage only a stage less exalted than the Great Lama of Tibet, was a man of original ideas. One of the regular ceremonies of his office was the laying on of hands to many worshippers and lesser priests who came daily for his blessing. The Buddha conceived a mass blessing. He had a small American Delco generator in his palace. This he rigged up with a wire stretching down a long areaway. The many pilgrims would line up clutching the wire and each received a memorable blessing as the Living Buddha threw the switch by his throne.

Dr. Andrews was invited to partake of the blessing, which courtesy he could not refuse. He reports that the shock nearly knocked him over.

RELATED SUBJECTS: *Believers* 1591-1596; *Superstition* 1631-1636

SEE ALSO: *Buying and Selling* 2066

DOCTORS

1666 Dr. Samuel Garth, the celebrated physician of Pope's time, loved wine to excess. At a favorite club of which he was a member, he once remained to drink to a late hour. A companion said to him, "Really, Garth, you ought to quit drinking and hurry off to your patients."

"It is no great matter," replied Garth, "whether I see them tonight or not; for nine of them have such bad constitutions that all the physicians in the world can't save them; and the other six have such good constitutions that all the physicians in the world can't kill them."

1667 A certain person coming to a doctor said, "Sir, when I awake from sleep I have a dizziness for half an hour, and then I feel all right."

"Get up after the half-hour," the physician replied.

1668 Senator Beveridge told this story: "I once saw two famous physicians introduced at a reception. They were deservedly famous, but they were of opposing schools; and the regular, as he shook the other by the hand, said loudly:

"I am glad to meet you as a gentleman, sir, though I can't admit that you are a physician."

"And I," said the homeopathist smiling faintly, "am glad to meet you as a physician, although I can't admit you are a gentleman."

1669 Whistler had a French poodle of which he was extravagantly fond. The poodle was seized with an infection of the throat, and Whistler had the audacity to send for the great throat specialist Sir Morell Mackenzie. Sir Morell, when he saw that he had been called in to treat a dog, didn't like it much, it was plain. But he said nothing. He prescribed, pocketed a big fee, and drove away. The next day he sent post-haste for Whistler, and Whistler, thinking he was summoned on some matter connected with his beloved dog, dropped his work and rushed like the wind to Mackenzie's. On his arrival Sir Morell said gravely: "How do you do, Mr. Whistler? I wanted to see you about having my front door painted."

1670 Professor Charles A. Beard relates this story:

A young doctor returned to the village of his birth and called upon the old family physician.

"I suppose that you intend to specialize," remarked the elder.

"Oh, yes," replied the youth, "in the diseases of the nose; for the ears and throat are too complicated to be combined with the nose for purposes of study and treatment."

Thereupon the family physician inquired: "Which nostril are you concentrating on?"

1671 Stephen Leacock tells this story: "Years ago when I first got my Ph.D. degree, I was inordinately proud of it and used to sign myself 'Dr. Leacock' in season and out. On a trip to the Orient I put my name down that way on the passenger list of the liner. I was just getting my things straight in my cabin when a steward knocked and said: 'Are you Dr. Leacock?' 'Yes,' I answered. 'Well, the captain's compliments, doctor, and will you please come and have a look at the second stewardess's leg?'

"I was off like a shot, realizing the obligations of a medical shot. But I had no luck. Another fellow got there ahead of me. He was a Doctor of Divinity."

1672 Before Oliver Wendell Holmes was a writer, he practiced medicine, and taught anatomy at Harvard and Dartmouth. As a practitioner he was not successful, for people were a bit doubtful about the flippant youth, who posted the following sign above his office door: "Small fevers gratefully received."

1673 A doctor was aroused in the middle of the night by a phone call from a man to whose family he had not had occasion to render medical services for some time. "Doctor," said the excited man, "please come over right away. My wife is in great pain and I'm sure it's appendicitis." The doctor had been sleepily mulling over the medical history of the family and said, "Well now, it probably isn't anything like that. I'll come around first thing in the morning. Don't worry. Probably just indigestion."

"But, doctor, you've got to come. I'm positive it's appendicitis," protested the alarmed husband.

"Oh come, Mr. Johnson," the doctor said, somewhat irritably, "I took out your wife's appendix almost two years ago. You know as well as I do that she hasn't got another one."

"That's all right," said the husband, "but I've got another wife."

1674 The patient was lying on the stretcher waiting to be pushed into the operating room. "I'm so nervous," he remarked to a sympathetic young woman standing by. "This is my first operation."

"So am I," said the young lady, "my husband is the doctor and it is his first too."

1675 "I don't understand it," the doctor said to the patient who was still complaining. "Have you carried out all my instructions."

"All but one, doctor. I am not able to take that two mile walk every morning that you suggested. I get too dizzy."

"Dizzy?" asked the doctor. "What do you mean?"

"You see," said his patient, "I forgot to tell you. I'm a lighthouse keeper."

1676 Robert Smith, brother of Sydney Smith, and an ex-Advocate-General, on one occasion engaged in an argument with a physician over the relative merits of their respective professions.

"I don't say that all lawyers are crooks," said the doctor, "but you'll have to admit that your profession doesn't make angels of men."

"No," retorted Smith, "you doctors certainly have the best of us there."

1677 Alexandre Dumas, the French novelist, being the guest one day of Dr. Gistal, an eminent doctor of Marseilles, was asked by his host after dinner to enrich his album with one of his witty improvisations.

"Certainly," replied Dumas with a smile, and drawing out his pencil he wrote under the eyes of the doctor, the following lines:

> "Since Dr. Gistal came to our town,
>> To cure diseases casual and hereditary,
>> The hospital has been pulled down"—

"You flatterer!" exclaimed the doctor, mightily pleased. But the poet went on—

>> "And we have made a larger cemetery."

1678 A physician was talking over some of his cases with a layman friend. A bit maliciously the friend remarked, "Say, doctor, I hear that that man you treated for a liver ailment died of a heart attack."

Outraged at this slur against his professional skill, the doctor shouted, "See here, my good man, when I treat someone for liver trouble, he dies of liver trouble."

1679   A patient going to a doctor for his first visit was asked, "And whom did you consult before coming to me?"

"Only the village druggist," was the answer.

"And what sort of foolish advice did that numbskull give you?" said the doctor, his tone and manner denoting his contempt for the advice of the layman.

"Oh," replied his patient, with no malice aforethought, "he told me to come and see you."

> RELATED SUBJECTS: *Scientists* 1116-1122; *Doctors' Fees* 1681; *Psychiatrists* 1686-1687; *Hospitals* 1691; *Dentists* 1696-1697

> SEE ALSO: *Eating* 22; *Gambling* 72; *Gratitude* 264; *Long-Windedness* 362; *Melancholy* 366, 367; *Handicaps* 706; *Births* 1015; *Scientists* 1122; *Authors* 1212; *Painting* 1272, 1289; *Instrumentalists* 1356; *Ministers* 1475; *Sickness* 1704; *Hypochondriacs* 1718, 1719; *Medicines* 1728; *Prisoners* 2366; *Lawyers* 2531

DOCTORS' FEES

1681   "I reckon you get paid right handsome for looking after the rich Johnson boy," observed the cleaning woman to the doctor.

"Why, yes. I get pretty good fees," he replied, somewhat amused. "Why do you ask?"

"I just hope you won't forget that it was my boy what threw the brick that hit him."

> RELATED SUBJECTS: *Doctors* 1666-1679

PSYCHIATRISTS

1686   A Jewish mother was much distressed over the problem of her young son who was afraid to eat the popular dish known as kreplach. She took the boy to a psychiatrist for consultation. After hearing the case, the doctor said, "Now, madam, this is very simple. Take the boy home, take him out in the kitchen, and show him the ingredients that go into the dish. And then, show him how kreplach is made. That should probably eliminate the condition."

Hopefully the mother followed his advice. On the kitchen table she put out a small square of dough beside which was a small mound of prepared chopped meat. "Now," she said, "there's nothing here you should mind." The lad beamed and nodded encouragingly. The mother then put the meat in the center of the dough and folded over one corner. The boy smiled and all seemed to be going well. She folded over the second corner and the third. The boy was nodding and the experiment seemed to be progressing most favorably. Then she folded over the fourth and final corner; whereupon the boy groaned and muttered, "Oi, kreplach!"

1687 A man came to a psychiatrist and proceeded to unfold before the doctor his life story, covering his childhood experiences, his emotional life, his eating habits, his vocational problems, and everything else he could think of. "Well," said the doctor, "it doesn't seem to me as though there were anything wrong with you. You seem as sane as I am."

"But, doctor," protested the patient, a note of horror creeping into his voice, "it's these butterflies. I can't stand them. They're all over me."

"For Heaven's sake," cried the doctor, recoiling, "don't brush them off on me!"

RELATED SUBJECTS: *Eccentricity* 196-209; *Doctors* 1666-1679

SEE ALSO: *Students* 1036

HOSPITALS

1691 In West Virginia a contest was once held for a name for a new county hospital. The first prize was a free appendectomy.

RELATED SUBJECTS: *Doctors* 1666-1679; *Sickness* 1701-1707; *Diseases* 1721

SEE ALSO: *Doctors* 1674

DENTISTS

1696 After the war, General Pershing found himself in need of dental care. Following the advice of his dentist, he had a number of teeth removed. Great was his indignation when he learned that these teeth were being sold as souvenirs under the name, "Famous General's Teeth."

He hurriedly sent out his aides to round up the molars. There is no record of what he said when they returned with a total of 175 teeth, all purported to be his.

1697 A patient called his dentist for an appointment. "So sorry," said the dentist, "not today. I have eighteen cavities to fill." Whereupon he hung up the phone, picked up his golf bag and departed from his office.

RELATED SUBJECTS: *Doctors* 1666-1679

SEE ALSO: *Churchmen* 1456

SICKNESS

1701 C. R. W. Nevinson, English painter, tells one of the finest of all sick-bed stories: "Then came pleurisy, culminating in pneumonia that nearly ended my life. The telephone was at my bedside, and in order that I should not be disturbed we were supposed to be cut off from all incoming calls. One night, however, when the night nurse had gone out of the room the bell rang. Instinctively I reached out my hand.

"'Yes,' I quavered.

"'"Daily Blank" speakin',' announced a very Cockney voice. 'Is 'e gone yet?'

"It hurt me to laugh and I maintained my gravity by thinking they should not have left it to the office boy.

"'No,' I said. 'He's still with us.'

"I then said that the patient had expressed a desire that certain matters should be remembered in his obituary notice, and I dictated a paragraph which the voice assured me it had taken down. I wished him good-bye.

"'Good-bye,' said the voice. 'An' if 'e goes within the next hour give's a scoop will yer?'

"I promised to do my best in difficult circumstances, and rang off."

1702 The steward attempted to encourage the suffering passenger. "Don't be downhearted, nobody's ever died of seasickness."

"Oh," moaned the sufferer, "how can you be so cruel! Only the hope of death has kept me alive so far."

1703 "Could there be anything worse," an ailing friend once wrote complainingly to Mark Twain, "than having a toothache and an earache at the same time?"

Mark Twain wrote back: "Rheumatism and St. Vitus' Dance."

1704 Looking down at the sick man, the doctor decided to tell him the truth.

"I feel that I should tell you. You are a very sick man. I'm sure that you would want to know the facts. Now—is there anyone you would like to see?"

Bending down toward his patient, the doctor heard him feebly answer, "Yes."

"Who is it?"

In a slightly stronger tone the sufferer said, "Another doctor."

1705 Demetrius would at times tarry from business to attend to pleasure. On such occasions he usually feigned indisposition. His father, coming to visit him, saw a beautiful young lady retire from his chamber. On his entering, Demetrius said, "Sir, the fever has left me."

"I met it at the door," replied the father.

1706 The old-timer had been sick in bed for weeks. The local doctors had been unable to help or to diagnose. The old codger insisted that he didn't need anybody's help, but specialists were called in over his protests. When they had gone, his friends and relatives asked the old man what they had said.

"Told you I was all right," he said triumphantly. "Them gentlemen used a lot of big words I couldn't understand but they finally said, 'Well, no use worrying about it or arguing over it. The autopsy will soon give us the answer.'"

1707 Abraham Lincoln was once confined to the White House with a bad cold. A Congressman, who had called to express his sympathy, was interrupted in the middle of his solemn words by the President, who said laughingly, "Well—I expect colds."

And looking down at his large feet he continued, "There's so much of me on the ground, you know."

RELATED SUBJECTS: *Doctors* 1666-1679; *Hospitals* 1691; *Poor Health* 1711-1712; *Hypochondriacs* 1716-1720; *Diseases* 1721; *Medicines* 1726-1731; *Death* 1746-1749

SEE ALSO: *Doctors* 1674; *Office Seekers* 1967; *Stocks* 2147

POOR HEALTH

1711 Daniel Webster described in this way his last interview with John Adams: "While I was with him and conversing on the common topics of the day, someone, a friend of his, came in and made particular inquiry of his health. John Adams answered, 'I inhabit a weak, frail, decayed tenement; battered by the winds and broken in upon by the storms, and, from all I can learn, the landlord does not intend to repair.'"

1712 It is related that during the Civil War Senator Douglas was approached by a constituent, at a time when the most momentous battles were being fought, when the very fate of the Union was hanging in the balance.

"Oh, Mr. Douglas!" exclaimed this constituent, "I am so glad to see you! Tell me—is there—have you any news?"

"Thank you!" answered Senator Douglas gravely. "Thank you—I am feeling much better!"

RELATED SUBJECTS: *Sickness* 1701-1707; *Hypochondriacs* 1716-1720; *Diseases* 1721

SEE ALSO: *Drinking* 42; *Congress* 1947

HYPOCHONDRIACS

1716 Hypochondriacs should never go to medical lectures. Invariably they become afflicted with symptoms of any disease they hear about. One such man, having returned from a lecture on diseases of the kidney, immediately called upon his doctor.

The doctor attempted to explain that in that particular disease there were no pains or discomfort of any kind.

"I knew it," gasped the hypochondriac. "My symptoms exactly."

1717 "When I meet a man whose name I cannot remember," Disraeli said, "I give myself two minutes, then if it is a hopeless case, I always say, 'And how is the old complaint?' "

1718 A lady much afflicted with nervous complaints went to consult the celebrated surgeon Dr. Abernethy (18th Century). The rough and caustic manner in which he catechised her, so discomposed the fair one's weak spirits, that she was thrown into a fit of hysterics. On parting, she put the usual fee into his hands in the form of a sovereign and a shilling. Dr. Abernethy pocketed the sovereign with one hand, and with the other presented the shilling to her, saying gravely, "Here, madam, take this shilling, go to the next toy-shop, buy a skipping-rope, and use it every day; it will do you more good than all my prescriptions."

1719 A lady who went to consult the blunt Dr. Abernethy, began a description of her complaint thus: "Whenever I lift my arm, it pains me exceedingly."

"Why, then, madam," said the doctor impatiently, "you are a great fool for lifting it."

1720 A certain Archbishop, getting along in years, had been worried for some time that he would fall a victim to a paralytic stroke. One evening, while playing chess with a very charming young lady, he suddenly became very agitated, and feeling that his presentiment had been fulfilled, he fell back in his chair, murmuring, "Your move."

Alarmed, his partner hurried to his side. "Are you ill?" she asked.

"It has come," the Archbishop replied, "at last it has come, my right side is paralyzed."

"How can you be so sure?"

"I have been pinching my leg," weakly said the Archbishop, "and there is absolutely no feeling."

"Oh," said the charming young lady, blushing profusely, "Your Grace, I do beg your pardon, but it was my leg you were pinching."

RELATED SUBJECTS: *Imagination* 306; *Pessimism* 411; *Sickness* 1701-1707; *Poor Health* 1711-1712

DISEASES

1721 The founder of Washington's famous Smithsonian Institution, James Smithson, was long troubled by an obscure illness which none of the many doctors consulted were able to diagnose.

"I earnestly desire," he remarked one time, "that you perform an autopsy to discover what is the matter with me, for I am dying to know what my ailment is."

> RELATED SUBJECTS: *Doctors* 1666-1679; *Hospitals* 1691; *Sickness* 1701-1707; *Medicines* 1726-1731
>
> SEE ALSO: *Painting* 1272

MEDICINES

1726 An old lady, on her way to a summer resort, kept pestering the conductor to tell her when they would reach Ellenville.

Finally, harried by her constant questioning, he pleaded with her to bother him no more, that he would tell her as soon as they reached the town. Becoming busy with all his duties, the train reached and passed Ellenville with the conductor forgetting all about the old lady. Suddenly recollecting her anxiety about the place, he backed up the train and as it pulled into the little station, he hurried out and told the woman, "Here you are now—in Ellenville. I'll help you with your baggage."

"Oh, thank you," replied the dear old lady. "Never mind. I'm not getting off here. My daughter just told me that when I got to Ellenville, it would be just about time to take another of my pills."

1727 Many years ago an English sailor who had broken his leg was advised to send to the Royal Society an account of the remarkable manner in which he had healed the fracture. He did so. His story was that, having fractured the limb by falling from the top of a mast, he had dressed it with nothing but tar and oakum, which had proved so wonderfully efficacious that in three days he was able to walk just as well as before the accident. This remarkable story naturally caused some excitement among the members of the society. No one had previously suspected tar and oakum of possessing such miraculous healing powers. Several letters accordingly passed between the Royal Society and the humble sailor, who continued to assert most solemnly that his broken leg had been treated with tar and oakum, and with these two applications only. The Society might have remained puzzled for an indefinite period had not the man remarked in a postscript to his last letter:

"I forgot to inform your honors, by the way, that the leg was a wooden one."

1728   "Pray Dr. Abernethy, what is the cure for gout?" asked an indolent, luxurious citizen of the famous doctor.

"Live on sixpence a day, and earn it!" was the pithy answer.

1729   When one of Dr. Chapman's patients revolted at a monstrous dose of medicine, and said: "Why, doctor, you don't mean such a dose as this for gentlemen?"

The doctor replied: "Oh no, but for 'working' men."

1730   "Now be sure," the farmer's wife cautioned the druggist, "to label them bottles plain; which one is for the horse, and which one is for my husband. I don't want nothing to happen to that horse before Spring plowing!"

1731   A man, having hurt his forehead, was advised to rub it with brandy. Some days after, being asked if he had done so, he answered, "I have tried several times, but can never get the glass higher than my mouth."

RELATED SUBJECTS: *Doctors* 1666-1679; *Hospitals* 1721; *Sickness* 1701-1707; *Diseases* 1721

SEE ALSO: *Drinking* 43; *Melancholy* 367; *Handwriting* 733; *Hypochondriacs* 1718; *Deathbed Scenes* 1770

ACCIDENTS

1736   "Rastus," said his friend who had been reading in the paper of a number of fatal accidents, "if you had to take your choice 'twixt one or 'tother, which would you ruther be in, a collision or an explosion?"

"Man—a collision," said Rastus.

"How come?"

"Why man, if you's in a collision thar you is, but if you's in an explosion whar is you?"

RELATED SUBJECTS: *Injury* 1741; *Accidental Death* 1751

INJURY

1741   An enthusiastic lady told a group of friends in delight of the opportunity she had had to apply the knowledge she had acquired in her First Aid class. "It was wonderful," she said, "it was so fortunate that I had had the training. I was crossing Fifth Avenue at 57th Street and heard a crash behind me. I turned around and saw a poor man who had been struck by a taxicab. He had a compound fracture of the leg, was bleeding terribly, was unconscious and seemed to have a fractured skull. Then all my First Aid came back to me; and I stooped right down and put my head between my legs to keep myself from fainting!"

RELATED SUBJECTS: *Accidents* 1736; *Accidental Death* 1751

DEATH

1746   One day when the Sultan was in his palace at Damascus a beautiful youth who was his favorite rushed into his presence, crying out in great agitation that he must fly at once to Baghdad, and imploring leave to borrow His Majesty's swiftest horse.

The Sultan asked why he was in such haste to go to Baghdad. "Because," the youth answered, "as I passed through the garden of the Palace just now, Death was standing there, and when he saw me he stretched out his arms as if to threaten me, and I must lose no time in escaping from him."

The young man was given leave to take the Sultan's horse and fly; and when he was gone the Sultan went down indignantly into the garden, and found Death still there. "How dare you make threatening gestures at my favorite?" he cried; but Death, astonished, answered: "I assure Your Majesty I did not threaten him. I only threw up my arms in surprise at seeing him here, because I have a tryst with him tonight in Baghdad."

1747 Mark Twain, being a celebrity, turned the famous erroneous announcement of his death into a well-known quip. More difficult was the situation of the obscure man whose death was mistakenly noted in his local paper. The "corpse" hastened to the editor to protest. "I'm awfully sorry," the editor replied. "And it's too late to do much about it. The best thing I can do for you is to put you in the 'Birth Column' tomorrow morning, and give you a fresh start."

1748 It is recorded that Xerxes, the King of Persia, who had gathered vast forces at the Hellespont for the invasion of Greece, caused a lofty seat to be set up on a hill from which he could survey them. "But when he saw," says Herodotus, "the whole Hellespont hidden by his ships, and all the shores and plains of Abydos thronged with men, Xerxes first declared himself happy, and presently he fell a-weeping. . . .'For,' he said, 'I was moved to compassion when I considered the shortness of all human life, seeing that of all this multitude of men not one will be alive a hundred years hence.' "

1749 A philosopher who went to call on a sick friend, was told at the door:
"He is already departed."
"Well, tell him I called," replied the philosopher.

> RELATED SUBJECTS: *Hospitals* 1691; *Sickness* 1701-1707; *Diseases* 1721; *Accidental Death* 1751; *Natural Death* 1756-1757; *Deathbed Scenes* 1761-1775; *Funerals* 1776-1778

> SEE ALSO: *Absent-Mindedness* 86; *Brevity* 131; *Cheerfulness* 143; *Cowardice* 157; *Extravagance* 232; *Quick Thinking* 482; *Stinginess* 564; *Husband* 916; *School Classrooms* 1052; *Literature* 1162; *Composers* 1316; *Producers* 1394; *Prayer* 1607; *Superstition* 1636; *Diseases* 1721; *Funerals* 1778; *Kings* 1976; *Collection* 2178; *Bankruptcy* 2198; *Begging* 2217; *Horse* 2288

ACCIDENTAL DEATH

1751 The new foreman was puzzling over the formal papers which had to be filled out explaining the details of the casualty in which Murphy, one of his workmen, had lost his life by falling from a high scaffold. At last he managed to complete all of

the task except for one more unfilled line which seemed to
stump him. Finally, licking his pencil, he applied himself
firmly to the section headed, "Remarks," and wrote, "He didn't
make none."

> RELATED SUBJECTS: *Accidents* 1736; *Injury* 1741; *Death*
> 1746-1749

NATURAL DEATH

1756   "Scrope Davies," said Lord Byron, "is a wit and a man
of the world and feels as much as such a character can do."

Davies was a great gambler and was always backing horses,
and when at Cambridge, as a student, he had a peculiar habit
of attempting to cut his throat after every Newmarket meeting when he lost. Indeed, so frequently did he amuse himself
in this way that on one occasion the doctor who was sent for
declined to hasten himself when he heard it was Scrope's throat
that he was required to attend to, saying: "There is no danger
of him, I have sewn him up six times already."

Scrope Davies was enabled to survive this little peculiarity
for over forty years and died a natural death in Paris.

1757   Sir Samuel Garth, the London doctor, lay dying. The
presence of officious friends troubled him; and, when he saw his
doctors consulting together, he raised his head from his pillow,
and said with a smile, "Dear gentlemen, let me die a natural
death." After he had received extreme unction, a friend approached him, and asked how he was feeling. "I am going on
my journey," was the answer. "They (pointing to the doctors)
have greased my boots already."

> RELATED SUBJECTS: *Sickness* 1701-1707; *Diseases* 1721;
> *Death* 1746-1749; *Accidental Death* 1751; *Deathbed
> Scenes* 1761-1775

> SEE ALSO: *Insurance* 2136

DEATHBED SCENES

1761   During his last illness a number of Pennsylvania politicians called upon Thaddeus Stevens to pay their respects and

in the course of conversation one of them remarked on his appearance.

"Ah, gentlemen," he said, "it is not my appearance that I am concerned about just now, but my disappearance."

1762 Shortly before his death, Judge John Marshall Harlan of the U. S. Supreme Court became partly conscious and spoke his farewell words to those who were at his bedside: "Goodbye, I am sorry to have kept you all waiting so long."

1763 An old French countess, of the most exquisite politeness, was about to breathe her last, when she received a call from an acquaintance ignorant of her mortal illness. The answer sent down from the chamber of the departing sufferer was eminently unique.

"The Countess de Rouen sends her compliments to Madame de Calais, but begs to be excused, as she is engaged in dying."

1764 A few hours before his death, Marcel Proust asked his servant to bring to his bed a certain page from his manuscript wherein the death agony of one of his characters was described —because "I have several retouchings to make here, now that I find myself in the same predicament."

He wrote like a maniac to the end.

1765 Three days before Blake's death he was working on the "Ancient of Days." He sat bolstered up in bed, and tinted it with his choicest colors, and in his happiest style. He touched and retouched it—held it at arm's length, and then threw it from him, exclaiming: "There! That will do! I cannot mend it." He saw his wife in tears . . . "Stay, Kate!" cried Blake. "Keep just as you are—I will draw your portrait—for you have ever been an angel to me." And so he did—and it was his last work.

1766 Dr. Arne, the Eighteenth Century English composer, died as he had lived. His intimate friend, Vernon, the favorite singing actor of Drury Lane Theatre described his end:

"I was talking on the subject of music with the doctor, who suffered much from exhaustion, when in attempting to illustrate what he had advanced, he in a very feeble and tremulous voice sang part of an air, during which he became progressively more faint until he breathed his last! Making, as our immortal Shakespeare expresses it, 'a swan-like end, fading in music.'"

1767 When Curran, the witty English lawyer of the 18th Century, lay on his deathbed, he was told by his physician that he coughed rather easier than before. "In faith, so I think I ought, for I have been practicing all night."

1768 When Lord Holland was on his deathbed, his friend George Selwyn called to inquire how his Lordship was, and left his card. This was taken to Lord Holland, who said: "If Mr. Selwyn calls again, show him into my room. If I am alive, I shall be glad to see him. If I am dead I am sure he will be delighted to see me."

1769 Louis XIV lingered in a prolonged deathbed agony, during the whole of which, the courtiers of his chamber were required to be in attendance. After some days of his slow decease, the King opened his eyes and remarked faintly, "Gentlemen, I must apologize for being such an unconscionable time dying."

1770 When John Donne, the English poet, was dying the great physician Doctor Simon Faxe told him he might be restored "by cordials and drinking milk twenty days together"; but the Dean loathed milk and "passionately refused to drink it." Upon the doctor's insisting, he did try it for ten days, then said he would rather die than continue since he didn't fear death.

1771 Scrope Davies, the witty gambler and friend of Byron, was lying on his deathbed. He had seriously taken leave of his physician who told him that he could not live beyond eight o'clock next morning. Exerting the small strength left to him he called the doctor back. "Doctor," he whispered, "I'll bet you five guineas I live till nine."

1772 A clergyman came to a man near to death and said: "Dear friend, do you know who died to save you?"

"Oh, meenister, meenister," said the dying man, "is this the time for conundrums?"

1773 Alonzo Cano, a Spanish artist, when a priest presented to him a crucifix badly executed, turned his eyes away and refused to look at it, but when one of good workmanship was brought to him, he devoutly embraced it and expired.

1774 When the chieftain Rob Roy Macgregor was on his deathbed, a gentleman whom he had reason to consider as an enemy came to see him. On being requested to admit the visitor to his bedside he said, "No enemy shall see Rob Roy in the posture of defeat. Raise me up, put on my clothes, buckle on my arms, then admit him." He was obeyed: the guest was received with cold civility by the dying man, and in a short time departed. "Now," said Rob Roy—"now help me to bed, and call in the piper." The piper appeared; Rob Roy shook hands with him, and desired him to play "Cha tuile mi tuile-adgh" and not to cease while he continued to breathe. He soon expired, with the "voice of war" pealing around him.

1775 A moving example of deserted genius was the poet, Heinrich Heine. When the great German lyricist lay on his mattress deathbed in a poverty-ridden Parisian garret, all had forsaken him except his friend, Hector Berlioz, the composer. Moved by this sole demonstration of loyalty the dying poet commented bitterly, "I always thought you were an original, Berlioz."

RELATED SUBJECTS: *Sickness* 1701-1707; *Diseases* 1721; *Death* 1746-1749; *Natural Death* 1756-1757

SEE ALSO: *Vanity* 614; *Generosity* 244; *Atheists* 1653; *Natural Death* 1757

FUNERALS

1776 Charles Dillingham and Florenz Ziegfeld, both eminent producers and both now deceased, were pall-bearers at the funeral of the great escape artist, Houdini. As they lifted the beautiful and heavy casket to their shoulders, Dillingham whispered to Ziegfeld, "Suppose he isn't here."

1777 A Chinese servant asked permission of his master to attend the funeral of a friend, also Chinese. The man gave his permission and jokingly added, "I suppose you will follow the old Chinese custom of putting food on the grave."

"Yes, sir," was the answer.

"And," still laughing, the man said, "when do you suppose the food will be eaten?"

The man was somewhat shaken out of his Occidental complacency when his servant replied, "As soon, sir, as the friend you buried last week will smell the flowers you put on his grave."

1778 Lord Chesterfield, a little before his death, was so infirm, whenever he went out in his coach the horses were generally led step by step. In this situation he was one morning met by an acquaintance, who congratulated his lordship on being able to take the air. "I thank you kindly sir," says his lordship; "but I do not come out so much for the air, as for the benefit of rehearsing my funeral."

> RELATED SUBJECTS: *Death* 1746-1749; *Accidental Death* 1751; *Natural Death* 1756-1757

> SEE ALSO: *Boners* 117; *Devotion* 172; *Stinginess* 562; *Vanity* 621, 623; *Wife* 929; *Civilians in War* 2339; *Lawyers* 2528

LONGEVITY

1781 Fontenelle was continually being told by his doctors that what he liked to eat was bad for him. Toward the end of his life, one warned him that he must give up coffee, explaining at great length in the most appalling medical terms, that it was a slow poison and would eventually ruin his system. In a tone of deep conviction the nonagenarian replied, "Doctor, I am inclined to agree with you that it is a slow poison—very slow, for I have been drinking it for the past 80 years." Coffee-lovers may derive some comfort from the fact that Fontenelle came within a month of living to be a hundred years old.

1782 Until Joseph Chamberlain, British Prime Minister, was seventy, he seemed to hold the secret of perpetual youth. Someone asked him what the secret of his good health was. He smiled and said, "Never walk if you can drive; and of two cigars always choose the longest and the strongest."

> RELATED SUBJECTS: *Age* 671-678; *Insurance* 2136-2140

RECREATION AND SPORTS

RELAXATION

1786 When Maxim Gorky visited America he was taken to Coney Island by friends who wanted him to behold this huge playground swarming with holiday throngs. They took him through the crowded concessions, where he saw one dizzy contraption after another, swinging people through the air, swirling them in eccentric curves, shooting them down breathtaking inclines. They took him underground and overground, into bewildering mazes, museums of freaks, palaces of jugglers, theatres of dancing ladies and living statuary. They were giving Maxim Gorky the time of his life! Finally, at the end of what may have seemed to them a perfect day, they asked him how he had liked it. He was silent for a moment. Then he said, very simply, "What a sad people you must be!"

> RELATED SUBJECTS: *Diligence* 176-177; *Laziness* 326-327

TRAVEL

1791 One day in the Yosemite Valley, a traveller was told that there was an old man in the office of the hotel who in 1851 had been one of the company that had discovered the Yosemite. Eagerly he seized the opportunity of finding out what it was like to be the first of civilized men to behold one of nature's most marvellous works. "It must have been wonderful," he said, "to have the Valley burst suddenly upon you."

The old man spat over the edge of the veranda and looked reflective for a moment. "Well," he said, "I'll tell ye. If I'd ha' knowed it was going to be so famous I'd ha' looked at it."

1792 A tourist journeyed by camel to see the great Pyramids. He was swept away by the beauty of the desert night and the work-a-day world seemed to fade away from his remembrance. After absorbing all the glamour of the experience and desiring to preserve every detail of the dream-like world in which he found himslf, he remounted his steed, at the same time asking his Arab guide, "What is the name of my camel?"

"Greta Garbo," replied the guide.

1793 There is the story of a Harvard man who spent some days in Egypt, and enjoyed during that time the services of a French-speaking native guide and courier. As they parted, the guide requested, "Sire, teach me words of English with which I may attract your countrymen." The Harvard man did so.

Some time later, he returned to Egypt, looked up his guide, and said, "How did you make out with the English I taught you?"

"Sire," said the guide, "some there were who smiled and came with me, others there were who were angered and turned away."

The phrase he had been taught was, "To Hell with Yale!"

1794 In the days of the Underground Railway many Southern Negroes conceived of Canada, the ultimate objective of most runaway slaves, as a kind of free Paradise. Old Uncle Jake had the notion that he would like to get there. He asked a friend how one might get to Canada, and was told that if he were to travel far enough all the way up the length of the Mississippi he could get there. The old Negro had no geographic sense, but he had a considerable desire for liberty. Sneaking off early one morning, he took his battered rowboat and headed upstream, rowing as vigorously and intently as he could. The current was swift and the old man, working feverishly without looking to the right or the left, barely held his own and, by the end of the day, actually lost some six or twelve feet of distance. At this time, he was aroused from his intense concentration by an acquaintance who hailed him from the shore, "What you doin' out there in that boat, Jake?"

"Fo' de Lord's sake," exclaimed Jake. "Who on earth knows me way up here in Canada!"

1795 The poet, John Godfrey Saxe, had his bag packed for a trip when a friend encountered him and asked, "Where are you going?"

"To Boston, Deo volente."

"What route is that?" his acquaintance asked.

"By way of Providence, of course," replied Saxe.

1796 Texas is a big state. Easterners so far into the Middle West as Chicago have a lot to learn about it. An instance is the Chicago firm that sent a wire to its traveling representative in El Paso, saying that as long as he was in Texas anyway, he might as well clear up a little affair in Texarkana. The salesman wired back: "Be cheaper send man from Chicago. Closer than I am."

Astonished, his home office checked with the map and sent out a man from Chicago.

> RELATED SUBJECTS: *Explorers* 1141-1142; *Trains* 1801-1802; *Porters* 1806; *Autos* 1811; *Boats* 1816

> SEE ALSO: *Eating* 9; *Reputation* 77; *Curiosity* 161; *Exaggeration* 223; *Stupidity* 576, 577, 582; *Universities* 1021; *Porter* 1806; *Presidents* 1939

TRAINS

1801 One time Winston Churchill almost missed a train and Mrs. Churchill was alarmed. Sir Edward Marsh, Churchill's private secretary, tried to calm her by saying, "Winston is such a sportsman, he always gives the train a chance to get away."

1802 Mrs. Theodore Roosevelt, the younger, after having been absent from home for several days, wired her husband to meet her at a certain station. Hurrying to be on time, Colonel Ted arrived at the station just in time to see the train whizz through at a great speed. Somewhat bewildered, he stared at the speeding cars and was more astonished to see his wife standing on the very back platform frantically waving an important looking envelope in her hand. Spying him, she threw it at him, and, the train rounding a corner, she disappeared from sight.

Scrambling about in the bushes into which the envelope had fallen, the Colonel finally found it and quickly opened it. He was amused and somewhat relieved to read:

"Dear Ted: This train doesn't stop here."

> RELATED SUBJECTS: *Travel* 1791-1796; *Porters* 1806

> SEE ALSO: *Absent-Mindedness* 81; *Exaggeration* 221; *Practical Joking* 431; *Medicines* 1726; *Public Relations* 2111; *Debt* 2172

PORTERS

1806 A gentleman, considerably inexperienced in travel, had made a transcontinental touring trip. As he was about to disembark he was in some doubt as to what sum he should give the Pullman porter who had catered to him throughout most of the journey. "Sam," he asked, "what's the average tip you get?" "Five dollars," replied Sam. Whereupon he was presented with that sum. Overcome and embarrassed, Sam shuffled his feet for a moment, and then said, "Well, Boss, Ah reckon Ah ought to tell you that so far you is de fust one what's come up to the average."

> RELATED SUBJECTS: *Travel* 1791-1796; *Trains* 1801-1802; *Servants* 2276-2283

AUTOS

1811 An old mountaineer was on his way to the town. He decided to use the new highway that had just been completed. Just as he was about to steer his horse onto the road, an automobile whizzed by. The old man had never before seen one of these new-fangled machines. Open-mouthed he stared after it. Scarcely a minute passed and, following in close pursuit, came a motorcycle cop. The old man was astounded. Muttering to himself he said, "Well, by gol! Who'da thunk that thing could have a colt?"

> RELATED SUBJECTS: *Travel* 1791-1796
>
> SEE ALSO: *Chiseling* 2126; *Machinery* 2272; *Rationing* 2356

BOATS

1816 An old lady on a sinking ship was told that they had no other hope but to trust in Providence.
"Has it come to that?" said she.

> SEE ALSO: *Accuracy* 92; *Prayer* 1608; *Sickness* 1702; *Parrot* 2293

SPORTS
BASEBALL

1821 The New York Yankees were playing an exhibition game with a Texas University. The college team was doing very well in holding the New York team to a close score. Then Lou Gehrig came to bat. There were two runners on base. It was three and two for Gehrig, when suddenly, the pitcher threw one right down the slot.

Gehrig swatted and the ball sailed clean over the park and disappeared from sight. The college catcher raged up to the pitcher.

"Why don't you watch your signals," he stormed. "You might have known that guy would slap it a mile."

"Yes," the pitcher said with a sigh of contentment, "I know. But I got to thinking. I knew I'd never pitch a Big League game and I knew I'd probably never get to see a game at the Yankee Stadium. And I sure did want to see Gehrig bust just one!"

1822   Woodrow Wilson was a lifelong baseball fan. During the harassing and anguished days of the War the only chance he had to attend the sport was the occasion of a Red Cross benefit game played in Washington.

Returning from this, he found one of his advisers, Mr. Garfield, waiting with troubling news about a coal shortage.

"Oh hang it all, Garfield," said the President, "I've just been to a ball-game and I wish I could say, three strikes and out to this job."

1823   A baseball game was being held for a charity affair. The committee could only find eight men who were available to play. Seeking to make up the team, they persuaded an old fellow who had never played before to fill in. His first time up at bat he smacked the ball and hit it over the fence of the ball park. His teammates cheered, and they and the spectators together kept yelling at the man to run. "Why, shucks," said he, "what's the use of running. I'll buy another ball for you."

1824   Now a member of a minor league team, a former big time baseball player, was regaling his teammates with stories of his former prowess.

"Was I fast! Lissen, you guys, when I played for the Giants, every time I hit one of my many home runs I reached first base before the spectators could hear the crack of the bat. Then when I rounded second, the second baseman usually said something that made me sore, so I slapped the third baseman in the catcher's mouth. Not bad, eh?"

RELATED SUBJECTS: *Football* 1856-1858; *Golf* 1861-1869

SEE ALSO: *Zanies* 643; *Bible* 1586

BILLIARDS

1826 Finding no other means of recreation in the small town in which he was stranded, the travelling salesman wandered into the local poolroom.

Indicating his desire to play a game, he was shown to the only table in the place and was given a set of balls of the same uniform, dirty-gray color.

"Hey," he said to the proprietor, "how do you expect me to play with these. I can't tell the red from the white."

"Oh, that's all right. You'll get to know them by their shape."

1827 A farmer, from way back in the country, came into town one day with his pockets fairly well lined from the sale of his crops. Seeking to appear worldly, he walked into a saloon and gaming house over the entrance to which was a great sign proclaiming, BILLIARDS.

Strolling up to the bar with a simulated air of assurance the farmer slapped a coin on the counter and said, "Gimme a glass of them there billiards."

The barkeeper took a long look at him and, sizing up the situation, made no comment. Going into the none too immaculate kitchen behind the bar he came forth with a large, foamy glass of dark and dangerous dishwater which he shoved across the counter to his customer. The farmer, with his eyes slightly popping, drank it down in one long draught. Banging the glass back down on the counter he wiped his mouth and said, "Waal, efen I warn't an old and hardened billiard drinker, I'd 'a said that there was dishwater!"

BULL FIGHTING

1831 At a party in Paris, the American bullfighter, Sidney Franklin, was cornered by a dowager who took him severely to task for the alleged cruelty of his art. She would have none of his careful explanations, but pattered on endlessly about the "poor, helpless bulls." After ten minutes of this, Franklin came to the limit of his patience.

"Madam," he said, "I can't agree with you. I have killed many bulls, but I have always spared them the ultimate cruelty— not one did I ever bore to death!"

SEE ALSO: *Prize Fighting* 1886

CARD PLAYING

1836 You can't beat Texas! A supercilious and wealthy New Yorker asked a clerk in his hotel if there were not a card game which he could get into.

"There is a poker game now going on in Room 600," said the clerk, "but you'd better look out. They play for mighty high stakes."

The New Yorker sniffed at the implication and went to seek the game. Entering the room he found a table surrounded by grim-faced, flinty-eyed Texans, methodically sorting and handling their cards. Stepping up brashly, the New Yorker drew out a hundred-dollar bill from his pocket and threw it on the table, saying, "I hear you boys play for big money. Well, give me chips for that." No one said a word. The dealer motioned him to a chair, looked him coldly in the eye and deliberately pushed across the table at him—one white chip.

1837 Horne Took, the sly wit, being asked by George III whether he played at cards, replied, "I cannot, Your Majesty, tell a king from a knave."

1838 A bridge expert was being harassed by many questions from the hopeful bridge player. "And do tell me, Mr. Jacoby, how would you have played the hand, under the same circumstances."

"Under an assumed name, Madam," said Mr. Jacoby tersely, and made a quick exit.

1839 Dr. Parr was a constant and conscientious whist player. Nothing annoyed him more than to have as his partner one who could not match his skill at the game. One evening he was coupled with just such a player. As the evening wore on, he became increasingly disgusted. When his hostess came to the table and asked how the game was going, Dr. Parr exploded, "As well as could be expected, Madam, considering that I have three adversaries."

1840 The following is without a doubt a nice description of a "friendly" game of bridge:

The old quarrel between North and South has spread out to include East and West, and is now called contract bridge.

DANCING

1841 There is a legend of doubtful authenticity about Tommy Hitchcock, who, at a certain dance, was paired off for one number with a young woman to whom he had not been formally introduced. Slightly apologetic he said, "I'm afraid I am not dancing very well this evening; I'm a little stiff from polo." His partner answered coldly, "It doesn't make any difference to me where you come from."

FISHING

1846 "Uncle" Joe Cannon, the late Speaker of the House, was once telling Chauncey Depew, in somewhat lurid terms, about a fish he had nearly caught.

"About the size of a whale, wasn't it?" asked Depew.

"I was baitin' with whales," said "Uncle" Joe.

1847 Daniel Webster liked to commune with plain people whom he encountered. On one of his fishing excursions he wanted to try a certain brook and he drove to the house of a certain Mr. Baker whom he knew nearby, and asked permission to leave his horse a few hours. Mr. Baker volunteered to go with Webster and show him just where the people usually fished at that brook. The old man pointed out the spot. The ground was very muddy—Mr. Webster sank in half-way up his leg. Said he, "Rather miry here, Mr. Baker."

Mr. Baker answered, "Yes, I know it, and that's the worst on't."

The mosquitoes began to bite annoyingly. With the hand that was not holding his fishing rod Webster was busy all the time slapping and scratching. Said Webster, "These mosquitoes are pretty thick and hungry."

Baker answered, "Yes, I know it. That's the worst on't."

Now the heat in the damp, low ground became intense. Mr.

Webster wiped his forehead and rested. Then he said, "It's very hot down in these bushes, Mr. Baker."

And Baker answered, "Yes, I know it. That's the worst on't."

Webster resumed his fishing and after an hour's struggle with the heat, the bushes, the mire and the mosquitoes Webster said, "There seem to be no fish here, Mr. Baker."

Came the answer, "Yes, I know it. That's the worst on't."

1848   Mark Twain, according to one story, was returning from a trip to the Maine woods. Chumming up in the smoking car with a homespun New Englander occupying the same seat, Mark said, "Stranger, it's the closed season for fishing up here, but, just between you and me, I've got two hundred pounds of the finest rock bass, out there in the baggage car, that you ever laid eyes on."

"Waal," drawled Mark's new acquaintance, "that's interestin', but d'ye know who I am?"

"Not guilty," replied Mark. "Who are you?"

"Waal," came the reply, "I'm the State Game Warden."

Quoth Mark: "Now doesn't that beat the Dutch? Say, d'ye know who I am, Warden? I'm the damnedest liar in the United States!"

1849   Anyone who is discouraged at the lack of results being yielded by his efforts should take heart with the point of view of the country lad who hailed the city fisherman by the creek and asked, "How many fish yer got, Mister?"

"None yet," he was told.

"That ain't bad," replied the boy, "there was a feller fished here for two weeks and he didn't get any more than you got in half an hour."

1850   A seasoned old fisherman found his neighbor on the bank of the stream one day to be a rank greenhorn at the art of angling. This personage fished for some hours doing practically everything wrong. Notwithstanding this, from the sheer operation of the law of averages, the beginner finally got a bite. Feverishly he reeled and reeled and reeled until at last, some miracle having saved his line, he had wound his small catch all the way up to the tip of his pole. Overcome with the excitement of it all, he turned to the experienced fisherman and said, "Now what shall I do? Now what shall I do?"

"Looks to me," said the old-timer laconically, "as though

there was nothing left for you to do except climb up the pole and git him."

1851 For the first time in their long married life, Mrs. Smith had persuaded her husband to take her fishing with him.

Seated by the side of the stream, Mr. Smith was silently doing his best to make a catch. The guide with them was also engrossed only in the business at hand. But Mrs. Smith kept chattering away, asking all the questions she could think of.

Suddenly she spied a strip of oily water, seeming to cross the lake like a broad smooth street.

"Oh, guide, guide, what's that streak over there?"

"Where, ma'am?" asked the guide, endeavoring to bait a hook.

"Right over there. What is it?"

"Why that, ma'am," drawled the guide, "that's just where the road went across the ice last winter."

1852 During the course of the Sunday School session, the teacher called upon one of the pupils to recite some parables. "Do you know the parables, Johnnie?" she asked.

"Yes, ma'am."

"Well, I want you to tell us about the one that you like the best."

"That's easy, ma'am, I like the one where somebody loafs and fishes."

1853 An old colored man was sitting by the side of a stream patiently waiting for a bite. A youngster, ambling along the banks, stopped to watch him.

"Say, uncle, how many you caught?"

"Well, sonny, ef I ketch dis heah one I'm after, and two mo', I'll have three."

1854 Mr. Jones and Mr. Glover were lunching together. As their various friends passed the table, Mr. Jones would stop them and, in glowing terms, describe his success on his recent fishing trip.

Glover, amused by the enthusiastic Mr. Jones, finally said, "Say, I notice that in telling about that fish you changed the size of it for each different listener."

"Yes, sure, I never tell a man more than I think he will believe."

FOOTBALL

1856 Coach Dana X. Bible of Texas A. and M. College delivered perhaps the quietest, shortest, most effective pep talk in recent football history. His team had been badly trounced in the first half of one of their big games. The interval between halves was one of silence and gloom in which the coach said nothing. At last, as the team prepared to go out again on the field, he looked them over slowly and deliberately and said, "Well, girls, shall we go?"

They won the game.

1857 The football game between Notre Dame and Yale was in full swing. The score was tied. The spectators were yelling wildly; the players were grimly determined that their side would win.

About the middle of the third quarter time was called at the request of the Yale center. Walking up to the referee he said, "Look here, Mr. Referee, I don't like to complain but every time we get tangled up in a scrimmage play that big Irish center bites me. What do you think I should do about it?"

"Well," snapped the referee, "the only thing I advise is that you play him only on Fridays."

1858 In Belfast they still tell you about the football game that took place between the 100 percent Catholics and the 100 percent Protestants. A Limey attended that game, and when the Catholics made a skillful play he applauded and when the Protestants in their turn scored he again joined in the shouting. At this point an Irishman jabbed the Limey in the back and said:

"My God, man, haven't you got any religion at all?"

GOLF

1861 Don Marquis, author and playwright, once had a bet on with an expert golfer. The stakes were five dollars a hole and in the bargain, Don Marquis gave the expert two strokes.

Before starting the game, the expert turned to Marquis, just before teeing off for his first drive, and said, "Now where do I get my two strokes?"

"I don't care where you take the second," said Don Marquis, "but the first has to be a stroke of apoplexy."

1862 A certain preacher was chagrined by the fact that one of his friends and golfing companions invariably beat him. His companion, an older man, said, "Don't take it too hard. You win in the end. You'll probably be burying me one of these days."

"I know," said the preacher, "but even then it will be your hole."

1863 Real devotees of the game of golf are fanatics of a peculiar breed. There was the case of such a man, who returned home after a long day on the links. His wife greeted him, and observed that their young son, William, had come in only a moment before. "He says he's been caddying for you all day."

"Is that so?" replied the sportsman. "Somehow I thought that boy seemed mighty familiar."

1864 The late Justice McKenna, of the United States Supreme Court, was an earnest but poor golfer. Deciding that his game might be improved, he hired an instructor to teach him the finer points.

One day, while practicing on a golf course near Washington, he missed, teeing off. He tried three or four times, but each time his club hit several inches behind the ball. His instructor watched silently. Finally the Justice, becoming disgusted, glared at the still stationary ball and muttered, "Tut—tut!"

Gravely the instructor walked toward him—"Sir," he said, "you'll never learn to play golf with them words."

1865 Searching frantically for almost an hour, two novices at the game of golf attempted to find their balls which they had driven into the rough.

About to give up they were approached by a sweet old lady who had been watching them sympathetically. "I don't wish to interfere, gentlemen, but would it be cheating if I were to tell you where the balls are?"

1866 A foursome at golf were going around on a course which had as its hazard a deep ravine. Three of them were caught and two of them decided to forfeit the hole rather than take a chance on having too many strokes chalked up against them. The other decided to take his chances.

He disappeared into the ravine and the others gathered around to watch his progress. Finally the ball appeared and bounced up onto the green.

"How many strokes?" asked one.

"Three."

"But we heard six."

"Three of them were echoes."

1867 The golfer, annoyed at the loss of his ball, started to scold his caddie for not having been more careful in watching its flight.

Replying thoughtlessly, attempting to excuse himself, the caddie said, "Well, sir, it don't usually go anywhere, so it sort of took me unprepared like."

1868 A couple of day laborers, on their way home from work, stopped to watch a game of golf. They saw a golfer drive his ball into the rough; watched as he toiled to extricate himself. Then he got into a sand trap and labored, throwing up huge clouds of sand, to get himself out of his difficulty.

Finally, after getting on the green, he managed to putt the ball into the cup. One of the laborers, a burly Irishman, had been watching all this with a most sympathetic eye. Unable to repress his verbal sympathy, he said, "Now, mister, yez arre in a helluva fix!"

1869 A new member of a golf club was led to the first tee. Surrounded by grinning spectators he teed off and, with an almost miraculous drive, landed the ball in the first hole. Noticing no sign of anything from his watchers, who were in fact struck speechless by this feat, he marched off to the second tee. Taking his stance he again drove at the ball, and again it went into the cup.

Waving his club as though in near disappointment he said, "Gosh, I sure thought I'd missed it that time."

RELATED SUBJECTS: *Baseball* 1821-1824; *Football* 1856-1858

SEE ALSO: *Stinginess* 565; *Dentists* 1697

HORSE RACING

1871   "I thought you were sick yesterday," the employer said to the clerk.

"Yes, sir, I was," replied Jones.

"Well," retorted his employer, "you certainly didn't look very sick when I saw you at the races yesterday afternoon."

"I didn't? You should have seen me after the end of the fourth race."

1872   Leaning from her window one fine Spring morning, a woman noticed a poorly dressed man standing in front of a vacant store located just under the window. She noticed that, in passing, many people stopped to give the man money. Impressed and sympatheic, the woman put a two-dollar bill in an envelope, scribbled on a piece of paper, "Godspeed," and tossed it down to him.

A few days later, she saw the man again. This time he was walking back and forth in front of the building where she lived and looking perplexedly up at her window. As she walked out of her house, he came up to her and said, "Say, lady, I've been looking for you. Here's your $52. 'Godspeed' won at twenty-six to one."

RELATED SUBJECTS: *Gambling* 71-74; *Horses* 2286-2288

SEE ALSO: *Gambling* 72; *Liars* 333; *Ministers* 1476; *Natural Death* 1756

HUNTING

1876   A Californian went out to follow up a grizzly bear and was gone three days. Then he turned up without his game. "Lost the trail, Bill, I suppose," said one of his cronies.

"Naw, I kept on the trail all right."

"Then what's the matter?"

"Waal, the footprints was getting too fresh, so I quit."

1877 An old hunter was holding his usual court before a group of summer visitors in the small town. "How many bears did you kill?" asked one of them.

"Oh, 'bout a hundred."

"Say, you must have had plenty narrow escapes."

"Young man," replied the old-timer, "if thar was any narrer escapes, 'twas the bears had 'em."

1878 An eager sportsman accosted one of the natives in the small Maine town where he was spending his vacation.

"Is there much good hunting around here?" he asked eagerly.

The native glanced around him for a minute then said, "Well, sure, there's plenty huntin', but damned little findin'."

1879 A cowboy from one of the many dude ranches in the Rockies was spending his day off doing a little hunting. Sighting an eagle, he took aim and brought the bird down. He scrambled down the crag and retrieved his game. As he slung the bird over his shoulder he saw one of the customers from the dude ranch approaching him.

"I say," said the Easterner in a patronizing sort of tone, "I was watching you. You should have saved that shot. Why the fall alone would have killed the eagle."

RELATED SUBJECTS: *Fishing* 1846-1854

SEE ALSO: *Exaggeration* 225; *Gratitude* 262; *Sermons* 1552

MISCELLANEOUS CONTESTS

1881 There is a legend of an Indian chief who was wont to try the strength of his youths by making them run in a single effort as far up the side of a mountain as each could reach by his main strength. On an appointed day, four left at daybreak. The first returned with a branch of spruce, indicating the height to which he had attained. The second bore a twig of pine. The third brought an Alpine shrub. But it was by the light of the moon that the fourth made his way back. Then he came, worn and exhausted, and his feet were torn by the rocks.

"What did you bring, and how high did you ascend?" asked the chief.

"Sire," he replied, "where I went there was neither spruce nor pine to shelter me from the sun, nor flower to cheer my path, but only rocks and snow and barren land. My feet are torn, and I am exhausted, and I have come late, but—"

And as a wonderful light came into his eyes, the young brave added:

"I saw the sea."

1882   A dinner in honor of the winning members of the track meet was being held at the local hotel. Various honors were given them in the form of medals and blue ribbons. Each presentation was accompanied by a toast. Toward the end of the evening the prize honor of all, a beautiful silver cup, was awarded the young man who had won the gruelling mile run, the major event of the meet.

The boy accepted the cup and a toast was proposed amid shouts of "Speech! Speech!"

He won more than the ordinary cheers and shouts of the crowd when he said:

"Gentlemen, I have won this cup by the use of my legs. I trust I may never lose the use of my legs by the use of this cup."

1883   Mr. Block was always annoying the members of his local club with stories of his great physical prowess. One day a new member, already tired of the boasting and blustering, determined to quash him once and for all.

"Block," said the new member, "I'll bet you that I can wheel something in a wheelbarrow from this clubhouse to the gate, and you can't wheel it back."

Mr. Block looked the newcomer over carefully. Not an impressive looking man, small and puny. He could think of nothing that this man could do that he couldn't top.

"O.K.," he said, "I'll take you up on that."

The newcomer smiled blandly. A wheelbarrow was brought to the clubhouse steps.

Rubbing his hands in great glee, the new member grasped the handles of the barrow, motioned to Block and said, "All right, get in."

PRIZE FIGHTING

1886   Jack Johnson, the Negro heavyweight champion, who became a prominent figure in Mexico, was scheduled to face barehanded a bull in the ring. Some days later he was asked how it had gone.

He wrinkled up his brow, rolled his eyes and boomed: "Ah sure wuz scared. Ah'd rather fight a hundred men than one bull any day."

1887 John L. Sullivan was once interviewed by a reporter who asked him why he had never become a boxing instructor.

"Well, son, I tried it once," said the famous fighter. "A husky young man took one lesson from me and went home a little the worse for wear. When he came around the second time he said, 'Mr. Sullivan, it was my idea to learn enough about boxing from you to be able to lick a certain young fellow I've got it in for. But I've changed my mind. If it's all the same to you, Mr. Sullivan, I'll just send this fellow down here to take the rest of my lessons for me.'"

SWIMMING

1891 Bernard Shaw was enjoying a swim in a pool during a stay in South Africa; so were some boys who knew nothing of the august author. One small boy was "dared" by his playmates to "duck the old man" for a shilling. He accepted, but when he was close to his victim, panic seized him. Shaw turned, saw the youngster, and asked him what he wanted. In halting accents, the boy revealed the plot and the shilling bet.

"Well," said Shaw, looking sternly at the youngster, "if you wait a moment while I get my breath, I'll let you push my head under water."

He did, and the small boy swam back triumphantly to collect his shilling.

1892 The greatest and most mysterious of all Shelley's preoccupations was with water, boats and swimming. He was apparently fascinated by water as a great element, and time and again prophesied his death by drowning. But it was typical of Shelley's humorless absolutism where his fancy was involved that he was without fear in the business, and never troubled to learn either to navigate or to swim.

In 1816 the friendship that sprang up with Byron at Geneva was based partly on mutual literary admiration, and partly on their common love of boating. Byron knew something of sailing and navigation, and they took a trip together around the lake in an open boat. They nearly foundered in a sudden storm one night. After Byron had got the sail down and while the water poured in and the wind roared in the darkness, they sat in furious argument, Byron, proud of his power as a swimmer, declaring that he would save Shelley when they sank, Shelley equally determined that he would not be saved.

1893   Although unable to swim, Shelley was forever invading pools and streams . . . One day when Trelawney, a powerful swimmer, jumped into a deep pool in the Arno, Shelley immediately jumped in after him and lay "like a conger eel" on the bottom till Trelawney fished him up with some difficulty, Shelley protesting as soon as he could breathe that truth lay always "at the bottom of the well" and that "in another minute I should have found it."

1894   Impressing upon his class an admiration for notable feats of physical prowess the teacher related the exploit of a vigorous man who swam three times across a broad river, in the morning, before breakfast.

There was a giggle from one of the youngsters in the class.

"Well," said the teacher with some irritation, "what is it that seems to be so amusing? I see nothing amusing."

"It's only this, sir," replied the pupil. "I was wondering why he didn't make it four times and get back on the side where he left his clothes."

1895   A certain American soldier, attached to one of the American Tank Units fighting with the British in the Libyan campaign, had been carried by the exigencies of the service many miles deep into the heart of the desert with his comrades. This outpost of the Front had been quiet for days. The soldier found himself one afternoon with a few hours' leave.

It was with some surprise that his commanding officer spotted the man striding purposefully across the sands clad in his bathing trunks.

"Murphy!" shouted the officer in some astonishment. "Where in blazes do you think you're going?"

"Why, sir," said the soldier, "I just thought while I had a couple of hours off I'd take a dip in the surf."

"Are you crazy?" demanded the officer. "The ocean is 500 miles from here!"

"Beautiful big beach, isn't it?" said the soldier.

SEE ALSO: *Fatness* 688

GOVERNMENT AND RULERS

POLITICS

1896 There is a story how Eyre, the surveyor, called upon his friend and neighbor, Lord Lyndhurst, the Chancellor of England. "I find," said he, "your lordship has changed your politics."

"Yes," said Lord Lyndhurst, "and is ready to change them again if you will make it worth his while."

1897 President Wilson had been asked to receive a group of Irish-American leaders who wished to present a paper. He had consented to do so, with the proviso that Daniel F. Cohalan should not accompany them. During the War Cohalan had been a great disturber. Nevertheless the committee had shown up, headed by Cohalan. Tumulty was urging the President to relent. "Oh, Governor," he pleaded, "this will make a terrible impression on his followers." Cohalan was an influential political leader.

The President took out his watch. "That's just what I wanted it to do, Tumulty; but I think it will make a good impression on decent people."

1898 The following is a statement attributed to the late G. K. Chesterton:

"The mere proposal to set the politician to watch the capitalist has been disturbed by the rather disconcerting discovery that they are both the same man. We are past the point where being a capitalist is the only way of becoming a politician, and we are dangerously near the point where being a politician is much the quickest way of becoming a capitalist."

1899 In Washington, during the career of the notorious Huey Long, a political follower of the Louisiana senator was pleading with him to procure him the nomination, which would be equivalent to election, for representative from a certain Louisiana district.

"I can't do that," Long said. "It's all your own fault. Even I couldn't get you elected. Not after that story about the hotel episode in New Orleans."

"That story is a damned lie!" cried the aspiring politician. "Why there isn't even any Hotel Episode in New Orleans."

1900 When Oliver Cromwell first coined his money, an old cavalier looking on one of the new pieces, read this inscription on one side: "God is with us,"—on the other—"the Commonwealth of England." "I see," said he, "that God and the Commonwealth are on different sides."

1901 A New Jersey Congressman once brought two citizens of that state to visit the President. Seeking to impress Lincoln, he introduced them as being "among the weightiest men in southern New Jersey."

Upon their departure, Lincoln said to one of his aides who was standing by, "I wonder that end of the state didn't tip up when they got off it."

> RELATED SUBJECTS: *Political Parties* 1906-1907; *Campaigning* 1911-1920; *Elections* 1921; *Public Officers* 1926

> SEE ALSO: *Cynicism* 170; *Discretion* 181; *Quick Thinking* 485; *Rough and Ready,* 503, 504; *Stupidity* 581; *Births* 1012; *Explorers* 1142; *Cabinet Members* 1951

POLITICAL PARTIES

1906 Thaddeus Stevens, once going into the room of the Committee on Elections of which he was a member, found a hearing going on. He asked one of his Republican colleagues what was the point in the case. "There isn't much point to it," was the answer. "They are both damned scoundrels."

"Well," said Stevens, "which is the Republican damned scoundrel? I want to go for the Republican damned scoundrel."

1907 Senator George W. Norris had made a speech in Norfolk, Nebraska, the night before and was taking a walk after breakfast when he noticed some men hitching a horse in a livery stable across the street. One of them recognized him and crossed over hurriedly introducing himself as a preacher in a place twelve miles away, in haste to get home to deliver his sermon.

The preacher wanted to shake his hand. "I have followed

your record in Congress," he said, "and I came down to your meeting last night to hear you talk. Mr. Norris, I am so anxious to have you succeed that every night on bended knees I ask God to guard and protect you and see that you are elected to the Senate in order that your activities may have a wider scope. Why, I get so enthusiastic that I almost feel as though I ought to vote for you myself!"

"Well, my good friend, if that's the way you feel about it, why don't you vote for me?"

"Oh, Mr. Norris, I never could do that. I am a Democrat."

RELATED SUBJECTS: *Politics* 1896-1901; *Campaigning* 1911-1920; *Elections* 1921; *Office Seekers* 1966-1970

SEE ALSO: *Campaigning* 1911

CAMPAIGNING

1911 Once Theodore Roosevelt was making a political speech during one of his campaigns, when a heckler interrupted him from the large crowd with a repeated and slightly inebriated cry, "I am a Democrat."

Roosevelt was generally a dangerous man to heckle. Pausing in his speech and smiling with oriental unction, he leaned forward and said, "May I ask the gentleman why he is a Democrat?"

The voice replied, "My grandfather was a Democrat, my father was a Democrat, and I am a Democrat."

Roosevelt said, "My friend, suppose your grandfather had been a jackass, and your father had been a jackass, what would you be?"

Instantly the reply came back, "A Republican!"

1912 Sam Houston, when running for Governor of Texas, overlooked no prospective voters. He went around to most of the farmhouses and personally harangued the inmates, getting their promises to vote for him.

At one such farmhouse he had gotten the farmer's promise of a vote, and seeing the lanky son of the house pass by, sized him up as another prospective supporter.

"Son," he said to the boy, "you look old enough to vote; how old are you?"

"Waal, I was 21 last April, but I didn't bow my head when

dad ast the blessin', so he sot me back two years . . . so now I can't vote."

1913   A candidate for a minor county office had depicted himself as a true man of the people. A delegation once called on him at his country home. The candidate recieved them in his shirt sleeves and with a pitchfork in his hand. Saying that he was busy, he consented to talk with them if they would conduct the little meeting in the barn, where he had some hay to pitch into the loft. They all trotted down to the barn but found no hay there.

"Hiram," asked the candidate of his hired man, "where's the hay?"

"Sorry, sir," was the man's reply, "I ain't had time to throw it back since you threw it up for yesterday's delegation."

1914   "Fellow-citizens," said the candidate, "I have fought against the Indians. I have often had no bed but the battlefield, and no canopy but the sky. I have marched over the frozen ground till every step has been marked with blood."

His story told well, till a dried-up looking voter came to the front.

"Did you say yer'd fought for the Union?"

"Yes!" replied the candidate.

"And agin the Indians?"

"Yes, many a time."

"And that you had slept on the ground with only the sky for a kiver?"

"Certainly."

"And that your feet bled in marching over the frozen ground?"

"That they did," cried the exultant candidate.

"Then I'll be darned if you hain't done enough for your country. Go home and rest. I'll vote for the other fellow."

1915   The political speaker found himself repeatedly interrupted by a heckler who shouted, "Liar!" again and again during his discourse. His patience exhausted, the speaker at last said, "If the gentleman will be good enough to tell us his name as well as his calling, we shall be pleased to hear from him."

1916   To the revilings of a local Conservative, a Liberal candidate for a parliamentary vacancy in Surrey replied, "The gentleman taunts me with not having been born in this district as he was. Let me tell the gentleman that my only excuse is that I am a Lancashire man from choice, while he is one by necessity. If there is any difference between us, it is that I came into this country with my pants on, while the gentleman came into it with his off."

1917 When Mr. Thomas Sheridan, son of the celebrated Richard Brinsley Sheridan, was a candidate for the representation of a Cornish borough, he told his father, that if he succeeded, he should place a label on his forehead with the words "to let," and side with the party that made the best offer.

"Right, Tom," said the father, "but don't forget to add the word 'unfurnished.'"

1918 On one occasion Lord Macaulay had an unpleasant experience at Edinburgh. He was re-contesting a seat in that constituency, and was standing side by side with his opponent on the balcony one evening, when he was suddenly struck by a dead cat. The member of the audience who threw the animal at once apologized and said that he had intended it for his opponent.

"Well," said Macaulay, "I wish you had meant it for me and struck him."

1919 Political orators are not known for their gentle remarks when attacking an opponent. A particularly vicious example of this is the remark made by John Randolph about Edward Livingston.

"He is a man of splendid abilities, but utterly corrupt. Like a rotten mackerel by moonlight, he shines and stinks."

1920 Shortly after his entrance into political life Disraeli stood for a certain Middlesex borough in the Conservative interest. It was a "personally conducted" canvass, and, among others, the future Prime Minister solicited the vote and interest of a well-to-do but somewhat irascible farmer, who was supposed to be rather doubtful in his political convictions.

"Vote for you!" he shouted when Mr. Disraeli made known the object of his call. "Why, I'd vote for the devil sooner."

"Oh, quite so!" said Mr. Disraeli, suavely, "but in event of your friend not standing, may I hope for your interest?"

ELECTIONS

1921 There is the story of a Yankee farmer who promised his vote to the Democratic candidate for Selectman and ten minutes later promised it to the Republican nominee. To his wife's rebuke he replied cannily:

"Did you notice how pleased each of the candidates were?"

"Yes."

"Well, I pleased them both, and on election day I'll please myself, and then we shall all be pleased together."

PUBLIC OFFICES

1926 The typically parliamentary mind suffers considerably from the necessity of departing from orderly procedure. This was clearly demonstrated in the meeting of the Town Council of a small city on the West Coast. The session was interrupted by a mild earthquake shock, and all present hastened out of the building to safety. The clerk found himself severely perplexed by the problem of concluding his formal minutes of the meeting in the proper manner. After mulling over the problem for a considerable length of time, he was inspired to the following conclusion, "On motion of the City Hall, the Council adjourned."

PRESIDENTS

1931 Lincoln was once asked if he did not find the office of the Presidency with all its attendant ceremonies rather tiresome at times.

Lincoln replied, "Yes, sometimes. In fact, I feel sometimes like a man who was ridden out of town on a rail, and said: 'If it wasn't for the honor of the thing, I'd rather walk!'"

1932 On the reception of the news of the death of Washington, Napoleon addressed the following letter to the consular guard and the army:

"Washington is dead! That great man who fought against tyranny, and consolidated his country's freedom. His memory will be always dear to Frenchmen, and to all free men in both worlds—but especially to the French soldiers, who, like him and the American soldiers, have struggled for liberty and equality. The First Consul, therefore, orders that for ten days black crêpe shall be suspended from all the flags and standards of the Republic."

1933 John Bach McMaster, the historian, told this story of Abraham Lincoln.

When he was a very small boy he was taken to a reception at the White House. The guests were lined up and led past the President under the watchful eyes of the ushers. No one was allowed to come very close or to shake his hand. One old man, who had come a long distance just for this occasion, was very disappointed at not having shaken hands with the President. Just before leaving the line the old-timer waved his hat at the President and shouted, "Mr. President, I'm from up in York state where we believe that God Almighty and Abraham Lincoln are going to save this country."

Jovially the President waved back at him. "My friend, you're half right," was his reply.

1934 During the first year of the war Peter Harvey, the pompous friend and biographer of Daniel Webster, went to Washington, and on his return was asked how he liked President Lincoln.

"Well," he said, "Mr. Lincoln is a very singular man. I went in to see him, and told him that I'd been an intimate personal friend of Daniel Webster; that I had talked with him so much on the affairs of the country that I felt perfectly competent to tell him what Mr. Webster would advise in the present crisis; and thereupon I talked to Mr. Lincoln for two solid hours, telling him just what he should do and what he should not do; and would you believe it, sir, when I got through, all Mr. Lincoln said was, as he clapped his hand on my leg, "Mr. Harvey, what tremendous great calves you have got!"

1935 Jefferson Davis insisted on being recognized by his official title as commander or President in the regular negotiation with the U. S. Government. This Mr. Lincoln would not consent to.

Mr. Hunte thereupon referred to the correspondence between King Charles the First and his Parliament as a precedent for a negotiation between a constitutional ruler and rebels. Mr. Lincoln's face then wore that indescribable expression which generally preceded his hardest hits, and he remarked: "Upon questions of history, I must refer you to Mr. Seward for he is posted in such things, and I don't profess to be; but my only distinct recollection of the matter is that Charles lost his head."

1936 The last story of Calvin Coolidge's occupancy of the White House concerns the Hoover inauguration. It had poured rain. As he and Mrs. Coolidge were leaving Washington by train he watched the rain spattering on the window for a little while and remarked, "A lot of people got wet today, all right."

1937 When Lincoln was criticized by a deputation sent to call on him he said, "Gentlemen, suppose all the property you were worth was in gold, and you had put it in the hands of Blondin to carry across the Niagara River on a rope. Would you shake the cable and keep shouting—'Blondin, stoop a little more—go a little faster—lean a little more to the north—lean a little more to the south?' No, you would hold your breath as well as your tongue, and keep your hands off until he was safe over. The Government is carrying an immense weight. Untold treasures are in our hands. We are **doing** the very best we can. Don't badger us. Keep quiet, and we will get you safe across."

1938 A newspaper correspondent visited Coolidge at Plymouth, watched the automobiles rolling by, and said:

"It must make you proud to see all these people coming by here, merely to look at you sitting on the porch. It shows that although you are an ex-President you are not forgotten. Just look at the number of those cars."

"Not as many as yesterday," replied Mr. Coolidge. "There were 163 then."

1939 When Mrs. Calvin Coolidge went abroad after her husband's death she feared there would be an unnecessary fuss made over the wife of an ex-President. But the friend with whom she was travelling said, "Don't worry. In the little places where we'll be stopping they don't know one President of the United States from another. People won't bother you." And no one did—until in a small Italian town they received word that reservations had been made for them in the next town. This sounded ominous. When they reached the hotel in question they were received pompously by the manager. Bowing profoundly, he said, "We are proud to welcome the wife of the great President of the United States. Will you register, Mrs. Lincoln?"

1940 "I think the White House should set an example of a standard of decent living for those who have to work in somebody else's house," Mrs. Roosevelt explained, as she planned to make the servants' quarters "humanly livable." The kitchens had not previously been improved in a quarter of a century. Even the upper servants who do no basement or kitchen work, felt the impact of Mrs. Roosevelt's improvements of the working conditions of White House servants. One of the oldest Negro doormen, who had served the White House for administration after administration, suddenly spoke one day for himself and his fellows. An old friend of the Roosevelts was departing after a few days' visit. She commented on the courtesy and graciousness of the colored servants in the White House. He thanked her with the proper dignity. She said she had always loved to visit the White House, but she was not sure she would like it so much again, after the Roosevelts left.

The liveried man dropped his dignity and her bags, turned,

and exclaimed, "Oh, Ma'am, I don't know what we'll do without Mrs. Roosevelt here!"

RELATED SUBJECTS: *Politics* 1896-1901; *Campaigning* 1911-1920; *Elections* 1921; *Office Seekers* 1966-1970; *United States* 2031-2032

SEE ALSO: *Ambition* 96; *Boners* 107, 109; *Brevity* 133; *Economy* 211, 212; *Honesty* 292; *Kindness* 314; *Modesty* 381, 383, 384; *Prejudice* 441; *Homeliness* 652; *Tallness* 696; *Talking* 813; *Friendship* 867; *Church Services* 1531; *Prayer* 1606; *Baseball* 1822; *Congress* 1943, 1948; *Freedom* 2037; *Taxes* 2191; *Civil War* 2326; *Detectives* 2557; *Stealing* 2589

CONGRESS

1941　When Edward Everett Hale was Chaplain of the Senate, someone asked him, "Do you pray for the senators, Dr. Hale?" "No, I look at the senators and pray for the country," he replied.

1942　Laboulaye said, in one of his lectures, that Jefferson, who had become so completely imbued with French ideas as even to admire the unicameral system of legislation, one day visited Washington at Mount Vernon, and, in the course of the conversation that ensued, the comparative excellence of the two systems came up for consideration. After much had been said on both sides, finally, at the tea-table, Washington turning sharply to Jefferson, said, "You, sir, have just demonstrated the superior excellence of the bicameral system, by your own hand."

"If How is that?" said Jefferson.

"You have poured your tea from your cup out into the saucer to cool. We want the bicameral system to cool things. A measure originates in one house, and in heat is passed. The other house will serve as a wonderful cooler; and, by the time it is debated and modified by various amendments there, it is much more likely to become an equitable law! No, we can't get along without the saucer in our system."

1943　Fiume was said by Colonel House to have been one of the causes of the United States Senate's rejection of the Treaty of Versailles. One day at his apartment in New York, several years after the Peace Conference, while I was discussing with the Texan the sabotage of the pact at Washington, the Colonel spun this amusing yarn:

"When Mr. Wilson told me of his decision to oppose the cession of the Adriatic port to the Italians, I said: 'Mr. President, aren't you afraid the Senate is going to be highly displeased when it hears about Fiume?'

"The President replied: 'I suppose it will, as soon as it learns where Fiume is!'

"Somehow or other, that aspersion of the Senate's geographical knowledge," House continued, "got back to Washington. Lodge & Co. never forgave it!"

1944 The late Senator Henry Cabot Lodge was talking about the ineffectiveness of most Congressional investigating committees.

"Some of them," he observed, "remind me of Si Hoskins. Si got a job at shooting muskrats, for muskrats overran a mill-owner's dam. There, in the lovely Spring weather, Si sat on the grassy bank, his gun on his knee. Finding him one morning, I said: 'What are you doing, Sir?'

"'I'm paid to shoot the muskrats, sir. They're underminin' the dam.'

"'There goes one now!' said I. 'Shoot, man! Why don't you shoot?'

"Si puffed a tranquil cloud from his pipe and said: 'Do you think I want to lose my job?'"

1945 Once the House was making an effort to secure a quorum, and, as is usually done in such cases, telegrams were sent to members who were absent. One man, who was delayed by a flood on the railroad, telegraphed Thomas B. Reed, Speaker of the House, saying:

"Wash-out on line; can't come."

Reed telegraphed back: "Buy another shirt and come on next train."

1946 "Congress is so strange," commented Boris Marshalov, a Russian actor and dramatic coach, after a visit to the spectators' gallery of the House of Representatives. "A man gets up to speak and says nothing. Nobody listens—and then everybody disagrees."

1947 The nervous condition resulting from high tension in our national capital in war time is indicated by the case of the weary Congressman who paused in the drugstore of his hotel and asked for a box of aspirin tablets. "Sorry, sir," said the clerk. "We're all out of everything for headaches."

1948 Ward Lamon told this story of President Lincoln, whom he found one day in a particularly gloomy frame of mind. Lamon said, "The President remarked, as I came in, 'I fear I have made Senator Wade of Ohio my enemy for life.'

" 'How?' I asked.

" 'Well,' continued the President, 'Wade was here just now urging me to dismiss Grant and in response to something he said, I remarked: "Senator, that reminds me of a story." '

" 'What did Wade say?' inquired Lamon of the President.

" 'He said in a petulant way,' the President responded: ' "It is with you, sir, all story, story! You are the father of every military blunder that has been made during the war. You are on your road to hell, sir, with this government, by your obstinacy, and you are not a mile off this minute." '

" 'What did you say then?'

" 'I good naturedly said to him,' the President responded, ' "Senator, that is just about from here to the Capitol, is it not?" ' He was very angry, grabbed up his hat and cane, and went away.' "

> RELATED SUBJECTS: *Politics* 1896-1901; *Political Parties* 1906-1907; *Campaigning* 1911-1920; *Elections* 1921; *Parliament* 1996-2000

> SEE ALSO: *Boners* 108; *Gentlemanliness* 255; *Liars* 333; *Long-Windedness* 346, 347, 351; *Politeness* 420; *Prejudice* 441; *Quick Thinking* 471; *Rough and Ready* 496, 497; *Shortness* 692; *Evangelists* 1511; *Poor Health* 1712; *Political Parties* 1906; *Army* 2402

CABINET MEMBERS

1951 When Attorney-General Bates resigned in 1864, the Cabinet was left without a Southern member. A few days before the meeting of the Supreme Court, which then met in December, Mr. Lincoln sent for Titian G. Coffey, and said: "My Cabinet has shrunk up North, and I must find a Southern man.

I suppose if the twelve apostles were to be chosen nowadays, the interest of locality would have to be heeded."

1952 Lincoln received many complaints because of the stern dictatorial methods employed by the Secretary of War, Stanton. He finally silenced them by saying:

"We may have to treat Stanton as they are sometimes obliged to treat a Methodist minister I know out West. He gets wrought up to so high a pitch of excitement in his prayers and exhortations that they put bricks in his pockets to keep him down. But I guess we'll let him jump awhile first."

1953 When former Prime Minister Menzies of Australia was sworn into office, various representatives of the press were on hand to interview him. The reporter from the radical press said, somewhat bluntly, "I suppose, Mr. Prime Minister, that you will consult the powerful interests that control you in choosing your Cabinet?"

"Young man," snapped the Prime Minister, "keep my wife's name out of this."

> RELATED SUBJECTS: *Politics* 1896-1901; *Public Offices* 1926; *Presidents* 1931-1940

> SEE ALSO: *Drinking* 37; *Ambition* 96; *Modesty* 384; *Diplomats* 2022

GOVERNORS

1956 A certain Colonel on the staff of the Governor died suddenly. Many applicants for his position were clamoring to be heard. Before even the funeral had taken place, one of these managed to detain the Governor for a moment, asking, "Would you object to my taking the place of the Colonel?"

"Not at all," snapped the Governor. "Speak to the undertaker."

> RELATED SUBJECTS: *Politics* 1896-1901; *Political Parties* 1906-1907; *Campaigning* 1911-1920; *Elections* 1921

> SEE ALSO: *Drinking* 54; *Generosity* 243; *Politeness* 417; *Quick Thinking* 484; *Rough and Ready* 502; *Civil War* 2326; *Jail* 2561

MAYORS

1961 A mayor of a city in southern Italy, in an address of welcome to the King of Italy, said: "We welcome you in the name of our five thousand inhabitants, three thousand of whom are in America."

> RELATED SUBJECTS: *Politics* 1896-1901; *Political Parties* 1906-1907; *Campaigning* 1911-1920; *Elections* 1921
>
> SEE ALSO: *Boners* 112; *Laws* 2597

OFFICE SEEKERS

1966 One time, Abraham Lincoln drawled, he read a story of a certain King who wanted to go hunting, and asked the Court Minister if it would rain. The Minister told him the weather would be fair. Setting out, the royal party met a farmer riding a jackass. He warned the King it was going to rain. The King laughed, went on, and no sooner got started hunting than a heavy downpour drenched him and his party. He went back, threw out the Minister, and called for the farmer.

"Tell me how you knew it would rain."

"I did not know, Your Majesty. It's not me, it's my jackass. He puts his ear forward when it's going to be wet."

The King sent the farmer away, had the jackass brought and put in place of the Minister.

"It was here," said Lincoln, "that the King made a great mistake."

"How so?" asked some of the audience.

"Why, ever since that time, every jackass wants an office. Gentlemen, leave your credentials with me and when the war is over you'll hear from me."

1967 A Commissioner to the Hawaiian Islands was to be appointed, and eight applicants had filed their papers, when a delegation from the South appeared at the White House on behalf of a ninth. Not only was their man fit—so the delegation urged—but was also in bad health, and a residence in that balmy climate would be of great benefit to him.

President Lincoln was rather impatient that day, and before the members of the delegation had fairly started in, suddenly closed the interview with this remark:

"Gentlemen, I am sorry to say that there are eight other applicants for that place, and they are all 'sicker'n' your man."

1968 An old acquaintance of President Lincoln visited him in Washington. Lincoln desired to give him a place. Thus encouraged, the visitor, who was an honest man but wholly inexperienced in public affairs or business, asked for a high office, Superintendent of the Mint.

The President was aghast, and said:

"Good gracious! Why didn't he ask to be Secretary of the Treasury, and have done with it?"

Afterward, he said: "Well, now, I never thought Mr. ——— had anything more than average ability, when we were young men together. But, then, I suppose he thought the same thing about me, and—here I am!"

1969 To someone who wanted an appointment which was already filled, Lincoln sent the following telegram:

"What nation do you desire General Allen to be made quarter-master-general of? This nation already has a quarter-master-general.—A. Lincoln."

1970 Master (Geoffrey) Chaucer was a man of law, for he had studied at the Temple, probably about the time when he is said to have cudgelled a friar in Fleet Street; he was a soldier, and had been taken captive in the wars; he was a courtier and an ambassador, and had negotiated a royal marriage. There was probably ground, therefore, for supposing that were he given an office of profit under the Crown he would take his pleasure and leave the duties to be performed by others, as was not uncommon in those days. Wherefore he was bound down to this close bargain: "That the said Geoffrey write with his own hand the rolls touching the same office, and continually reside there, and do and execute all things pertaining to the said office in his own proper person, and not by his substitute."

> RELATED SUBJECTS: *Politics* 1896-1901; *Public Offices* 1926; *Presidents* 1931-1940
>
> SEE ALSO: *Rabbis* 1486

KINGS AND EMPERORS

1971 The late King George the Fifth, in his domestic setting, was quite an average husband and family head. When, on social occasions, he would talk too long to someone or express himself too rashly, Queen Mary would prod him gently with her umbrella and murmur, "Now, George." Also when palace guests would admire the Cloisonné, the Wedgwood, the Chippendales, etc., the King would always refer to his wife, saying, Now, May, you know about this."

1972 It is reported that King Victor Emanuel, when asked what he thought of the African campaign, replied very enthusiastically: "If Italy wins, I shall be King of Ethiopa; if the Ethiopians win, why then I shall be King of Italy again."

1973 It is said that the late King George the Fifth and the Princess Victoria, his sister, were accustomed to have a brief chat on the telephone at the same hour every morning. Their conversations were of a personal, highly informal, and often joking sort. One morning when her phone rang at the accustomed time, the Princess picked up the instrument and said, "Hello, you old fool."

The voice of the operator broke in, saying, "I beg your pardon, Your Royal Highness, His Majesty is not yet on the line."

1974 In the work of James I entitled "True Law of Free Monarchies," is laid down, "That a free Monarchy is one in which the Monarch is perfectly free to do as he pleases."

1975 James Brevoort, the correspondent of Washington Irving, wrote from Paris of the unceremonious manner in which the Chamber of Deputies legislated General Lafayette out of his great office. Louis Philippe attempted to smooth matters by offering him the title of Honorary Commander-in-Chief of the National Guard for life, to which the veteran hero of two hemispheres replied: "How would Your Majesty be pleased with the title of Honorary King of the French?"

1976 Peter the Great was so much affected by the death of Peter, his son by Catherine I, that he shut himself up at Peterhof, intending to starve himself to death; and forbade every person, of whatever description, under pain of death, to disturb his retirement. The senate assembled on this desperate resolution of the prince, and Dolgorouki undertook to drive him from it. He went and knocked at the door of the room where Peter was shut up. "Whoever you be," cried the Czar with a terrible voice, "fly off, or I will open the door and knock out your brains."

"Open, I say," replied Dolgorouki in a firm tone, "it is a deputy from the senate come to ask you whom you wish to have named as emperor in your room, since you have resigned."

Peter, struck with the courageous zeal of Dolgorouki, opened, embraced his faithful courtier, yielded to his councils, and resumed the reins of government.

1977   Alexander III (of Russia), the grandson of Nicholas I, begged his son Nicholas II to continue the good work his great-grandfather had initiated in setting the principle of primogeniture firmly on its feet. At long last they had managed to maintain it unbroken for a second generation, twice in succession handing on the throne from father to son. "Now remember," Alexander III enjoined his son, "that when I pass the scepter to you on my death, you are not to let it pass out of your hands except to your eldest son on your death. Remember! No brothers! No women! No uncles! Always the eldest son. Is that clear?"

"Yes, Papa."

"Promise me."

"Yes, Papa."

1978   Louis Napoleon was present at the opening of the Chambers, and remarked afterwards, very seriously: "There's no doubt, Papa, you made a very fine speech."

"Well, Louis," returned Napoleon the Third, "when you grow up, it will be your job to make the speeches."

"But then what will you do?" asked Louis innocently.

1979   At a dinner during the First World War the German Kaiser was being discussed. Opinions differed about him. Some of the diners attacked him savagely. Others insisted he was a fine man despite his shortcomings. J. M. Barrie, the playwright, listened in silence, then without looking up from his plate, remarked dryly, "He is an infernal scoundrel but that is his only fault."

1980   The first Napoleon, dining at a table full of monarchs, when he heard one of them deferentially alluding to the Bonaparte family as being very old and noble, exclaimed, "Pish! My nobility dates from the day of Marengo!"

1981 The Duke of York meeting King Charles the Second, attended only by two persons, expressed his surprise that the King should so expose himself. "No man," replied the Monarch, "will take away my life to make you King."

1982 Nicholas II at the moment was playing tennis at Peterhof. When the Emperor was handed a telegram he had two tennis balls in his left hand, the racket raised, ready to serve, in his right. He took the telegram with the right hand raising racket and telegram to his eyes, reading:

"Russian Fleet annihilated at Shushima Stop Nearly all our ships sunk."

The Czar shoved the telegram into his trouser pocket. "Thirty-fifteen," he said, and served.

1983 James I would say to the lords of his council, when they sat upon any great matter, and came to him from council, "Well, you have sat, but what have you hatched?"

1984 One day in a gathering of family and friends, Napoleon the Third observed, "We are a mixed lot here. We represent all parties. Conneau there is a republican, and always was. Madam Lebreton is an orleanist. The Empress is a legitimist, and I am a socialist, as we all know."

"But, in that case," spoke up little Louis Napoleon, "who are the Bonapartists?"

The Emperor put an arm around him, "You are the Bonapartist, dear child."

1985 Seeing his young grandson deeply engrossed in his studies, the late King George V of England stopped to see what was interesting the child.

"And who are you studying about now?" he asked, giving the youngster a friendly pat on the head.

"About Peter Warbeck," was the reply.

"And who was he?"

"Oh," answered the boy, "he's just someone who pretended he was the son of a king. But he wasn't really; he was the son of respectable parents."

1986 Suetonius relates how at a royal feast the Roman emperor Caligula suddenly burst out in uproarious laughter. He laughed and laughed, and the rest of the company, in order to be polite and save their lives, laughed with him. The fun-smitten host at length fell back in his chair exhausted, and a guest near his chair respectfully inquired the reason for his merriment. The jovial monarch with a wave of his fat hand over the crowded banquet-hall, replied: "Nothing, but that upon a single nod of my head, you would all have your throats cut."

1987 Benjamin Constant had such a command of the language, that when he chanced to displease his audience by an expression, he would go on substituting synonyms till he suited them. For example: "I am anxious to spare the Crown"—a murmur; "the Monarch"—the murmurs continued; "the Constitutional King"—the murmurs are hushed.

1988 Disraeli, in conversation with a friend, disclosed the secret of his ascendancy in royal favor. "When talking with the Queen," he said, "I observe a simple rule of conduct; I never deny; I never contradict; I sometimes forget."

1989 When Charles V retired in weariness from the greatest throne in the world to the solitude of the monastery at Yuste, he occupied his leisure for some weeks in trying to regulate two clocks. It proved very difficult. One day, it is recorded, he turned to his assistant and said: "To think that I attempted to force the reason and conscience of thousands of men into one mould, and I cannot make two clocks agree!"

1990 Disraeli, explaining his popularity with the queen said, "Gladstone speaks to the queen as if she were a public department. I treat her with the knowledge that she is a woman."

1991 A gentleman begging the Duke of Buckingham to employ his interest for him at Court, added, that he had nobody to depend upon but God and his Grace. Then said the Duke: "Your condition is desperate; you could not have named two beings who have less interest at Court."

1992 A German prince in a dream saw three rats, one fat, another lean, and a third blind. He sent for a learned Bohemian gipsy to interpret the dream.

"The fat rat," she answered, "is your prime minister, the lean rat is your people, and the blind rat is yourself."

1993 When Napoleon, after a series of victories, came to visit annexed Belgium, he found, on entering Ghent, a triumphal arch erected by the Guild of Butchers. It was inscribed:

"The little butchers of Ghent to Napoleon the great (butcher)."

PARLIAMENT

1996 One night Burke severely attacked some acts of the Government. George Onslow arose and haughtily said that he must call the honorable member to a sense of his duty, and that no man should be suffered in his presence to insult the sovereign.

Burke, in reply, gravely addressed the Speaker: "Sir, the honorable member has exhibited much ardor but little discrimination. He should know that, however, I may reverence the king, I am not at all bound, nor at all inclined to extend that reverence to his ministers. I may honor his majesty, but, sir, I can see no possible reason for honoring," and he glanced round the treasury bench at Mr. Onslow and the other ministers, "his majesty's man-servant, and maid-servant, his ox, and his ass!"

1997 During one of his much admired debates in Parliament, Sheridan was annoyed by the persistence of a well-meaning fellow, who kept punctuating, by the exclamation, "Hear, Hear!", almost all of his most telling remarks.

In the course of discussion, Sheridan took occasion to describe a political enemy as, "wishing to play the rogue but having only sense enough to act the fool. Where," he cried forcefully, "where shall we find a more foolish knave or a more knavish fool than he?"

"Hear! Hear!" was the annoying response.

Sheridan swung about and thanked him forthwith, sitting down amid a general roar of laughter.

1998 A young peer once asked Disraeli what course of study he had best take to qualify himself for speaking so as to gain the ear of the House of Lords.

"Have you a graveyard near your house?" asked Disraeli.

"Yes," was the reply.

"Then," said Disraeli, "I should recommend you to visit it early of a morning and practice upon the tombstones."

1999 A nobleman wished Garrick to be a candidate for the representation of a borough in Parliament. "No, my lord," said the actor, "I would rather play the part of a great man on the stage than the part of a fool in Parliament."

2000 At one time the House of Commons had sat in a long and ineffectual session. Mr. Papham, speaker of the House of Commons, was summoned by Queen Elizabeth, who said to him, "Now, Mr. Speaker, what has passed in the Commons' House?"

He replied, "If it please Your Majesty—seven weeks."

RELATED SUBJECTS: *Politics* 1896-1901; *Congress* 1941-1948; *Kings and Emperors* 1971-1993

SEE ALSO: *Liars* 334; *Long-Windedness* 345, 349; *Patriotism* 402; *Age* 675; *Speeches* 766, 767; *Campaigning* 1916; *Freedom* 2039; *War* 2318; *Stealing* 2581

DICTATORS

2001 Adolf Hitler is known to frequent astrologers, soothsayers and others of that ilk. A certain astrologer was asked by him, "On what day will I die?"

After peering over his charts, the astrologer announced, "You will die on a Jewish Holiday."

Much perturbed, Hitler demanded, "Which one?"

"I do not know," replied the astrologer.

Hitler became very angry, "You must know," he shouted, "I insist upon the truth."

"I do not know," persisted the astrologer, "because any day you die will be a Jewish Holiday."

2002 When that late and noble statesman, Neville Chamberlain, was about to depart from the fatal Munich Conference, Herr Hitler said to him, "Mr. Chamberlain, vud you be so kind as to gif me your umbrella for a keepsake?"

"No, no," said Chamberlain, "I can't do that."

"But, Mr. Chamberlain, it vud mean so much to me. I request it of you. Please!"

"I'm sorry I can't oblige you," said Chamberlain.

Hitler flew into a rage. "I insist!" he screamed, stamping on the Prime Minister's foot.

"No," said Chamberlain firmly, "It's impossible. You see—the umbrella is mine."

2003 According to a story circulating in Rome, Mussolini dies and goes to Paradise, where he is greeted warmly by Napoleon. "God will be here in a few minutes," says Napoleon. "Since you are new here, you should probably be warned that we rise when he enters."

"What! I get up? Don't forget that I am the Duce."

"I am Caesar," states a voice. "Yet I have the manners to rise."

"Not I!" says Mussolini. The argument is becoming warm when Machiavelli approaches.

"Peace, friends," he exclaims. "I will arrange everything."

Three solemn knocks announce the coming of God.

"Attention!" thunders Machiavelli. "Here comes the photographer!"

Whereupon Mussolini hops to his feet, folds his arms, sticks out his chin and chest.

Peace reigns.

2004 Sir Oswald Moseley, one time leader of the British Fascist movement, had once staged a most effective setting for his rabble-rousing. In a concentration of spotlights he marched stiffly up to the platform accompanied by an escort of Black Shirts and faced the audience. Solemnly, in a hush of silence, he raised his right arm high in the Fascist salute. From the balcony issued a shrill voice, "Yes, Oswald, you may leave the room!"

2005 In the days of Mussolini's higher prestige, it is said that he was once stranded in a small town due to the breaking down of his automobile. He went into a local cinema. When his picture appeared on the screen everyone rose but he remained seated. The manager of the theatre came forward, tapped him on the shoulder, whispering in his ear, "I feel the same way but you'd better stand up. It's safer."

2006 Calamy, the celebrated Presbyterian minister, on one occasion objected to Cromwell assuming the supreme power as Protector, as being in his opinion, both unlawful and impracticable. Cromwell observed: he "cared little about the lawfulness; but why may I ask you is it impracticable?"

"Oh!" observed the divine, "it is impracticable inasmuch as it is against the voice of the people; you will have nine in ten against you."

"Very well, sir," replied Cromwell, "but what if I should disarm the nine and put the sword into the tenth man's hand: would that not do the business, think you?"

The events which succeeded proved that Cromwell not only entertained the opinion he thus expressed, but that he also acted upon it.

2007 Frank Gannett, American newspaper publisher, spent three hours one afternoon in No. 10 Downing Street, where Prime Minister Stanley Baldwin cocked his feet on an old-fashioned roll-top desk, smoked pipe after pipe, and opened his mind to Gannett. Baldwin had already announced in the House of Commons that the frontier of Britain was on the Rhine.

"What do you intend to do about that man across the Rhine?" Gannet asked.

"If a python gets out of a cage," replied Baldwin, "one man would be a fool to try alone to get him back. But several men can get him back without much trouble. No; we are not going to tackle him alone."

2008 King Victor Emmanuel of Italy has long been known as the very silent partner in the management of his country. One day the King and Mussolini were walking about the palace gardens discussing affairs of state. The King dropped his handkerchief. Mussolini, still mindful of the fact that the code of behavior called for him to pick it up, was just about to stoop for it when the King stopped him.

"Permit me," he said. "This is about the only thing you have been letting me put my nose into these days."

2009 In Italy the underground wiseacres are asking, "What's the difference between Christianity and Fascism?"

The answer is, "In Christianity one man sacrifices himself for all. Under Fascism all men sacrifice themselves for one."

2010 Mussolini died and went to Heaven. He received a tremendous ovation. Millions of angels sang and praised him. He was given a crown and put on a great throne. Looking around he was surprised to notice that his crown and his throne were both bigger than those of God the Father. Even he was unprepared for this. "How is it?" he asked of God.

"You are greater than I," said God respectfully. "I gave your people one day of fasting a week. You have given them seven. I gave them faith. You have taken it away."

2011 In the year when the 20th anniversary of Fascism was "celebrated," a stranger was riding through the streets of Naples in a carriage. They passed a bakery and he saw a great mob of people storming the place. He asked the driver about it and the cabby, afraid to speak, said that it was a film being made. Not much farther along another mob of people was seen outside a grocery. "What's that?" asked the stranger.

"The second scene," said the driver.

Further along a similar mob was besieging a butcher. Without waiting to be asked, the cab driver said, "This is the third scene."

"What's the name of this picture, anyway?" asked the passenger.

"Twenty years after," said the driver.

INTERNATIONAL RELATIONS

2016 According to F. W. Wile, "It was the President himself (Wilson) who told us of one of his conversations with Signor Orlando about Fiume. The Italian premier argued that, as the population, language and institutions of the city were overwhelmingly Italian, Italy's claim to the city was indisputable.

" 'Well, Mr. Prime Minister,' rejoined Mr. Wilson, 'I hope you won't press that point with respect to New York City, or you might feel like claiming a sizable piece of Manhattan Island.' "

> RELATED SUBJECTS: *Diplomats* 2021-2027; *War* 2316-2323
>
> SEE ALSO: *Honor* 297; *Dictators* 2002, 2007

DIPLOMATS

2021 According to diplomatic procedure, the representative of a foreign country, before being actually presented to the President, always exchanges with him the text of the speeches.

On one such occasion this formality never reached its ordinary climax. Instead of stiltedly repeating the already familiar words, President Roosevelt greeted the foreign diplomat with, "Now, Mr. Minister, I've read your remarks and you've read mine, so suppose we dispense with the speeches and have a friendly chat."

2022 After the Russo-Japanese War, Admiral Togo, Commander of the victorious Japanese fleet, visited the United States and was cordially received. A state dinner was tendered him at which it fell to the lot of William Jennings Bryan, then Secretary of State, to propose a toast to Togo. Bryan, a staunch Prohibitionist, would not touch champagne, and it was feared that some diplomatic impasse might arise from the difficulty. Bryan, however, rose at the proper time, picked up his glass of water and said, "Admiral Togo has won a great victory on water, therefore I will toast him in water. When Admiral Togo wins a victory on champagne, I will toast him in champagne."

2023 When Lady Baldwin of Bewdley visited Manhattan with her husband (Stanley Baldwin), she wanted to see the

General Motors Futurama at the New York World's Fair, but did not want to stand in line. So Earl Baldwin telephoned the British Consulate; the Consulate called the British Embassy in Washington; the Embassy cabled the Foreign Office in London; the Foreign Office appealed to Ambassador Joe Kennedy. Resourceful Joe sent a cable direct to General Motors' Building at the Fair. A press agent there called Lady Baldwin at the Waldorf (cost, 5 cents), told her to come right out, he'd see that she was well taken care of.

2024   Henry VIII, in a spell of temper against his rival Francis I, King of France, commissioned a clergyman named Bonner to deliver an insolent and threatening message to the French court. The clergyman realized it would be a risky job and protested that he could never hope to get back to England alive if he dared to talk to the French king in the manner Henry VIII wished.

"Don't worry about that," said the monarch soothingly. "If the King of France puts you to death, I will cut off the heads of all the Frenchmen I can get my hands on."

"That may be, your majesty," replied Bonner, tapping his head: "but of all the heads in England, there is none that fits my shoulders as well as this one does."

2025   Among the guests at a luncheon, was the wife of the Finance Minister of one of the neutral countries. Her gown was very décolleté but nature had not endowed her with the necessary charms to wear such a garment. German Foreign Minister Rantzau gazed at her and then murmured, "She is just like her husband, an uncovered deficit."

2026   When James B. Reynolds was Assistant Secretary of the Treasury, Senator Root sent for Mr. Reynolds one day to discuss with him some matter concerning a trade conference in Paris which Mr. Reynolds had been selected to attend.

"I suppose," said Mr. Root, "you speak French?"

"Well, yes," responded Mr. Reynolds. "I know a little French. I have no trouble to make the waiters and the cab drivers understand me."

"I see," said Mr. Root. "But, Mr. Reynolds, suppose there should be no waiters and cab drivers at the conference?"

2027   The famous Marshal Villars, having given some offense to the mistress and ministers of Louis XIV, occasion was soon found to send him on very dangerous service in Germany. When coming to take his farewell of the king, the marshal thus expressed himself:

"Sire, I leave your Majesty surrounded by my enemies, while I go to be surrounded by yours."

RELATED SUBJECTS: *Tact* 586-591; *International Relations* 2016

SEE ALSO: *Long-Windedness* 350; *Quick Thinking* 474; *Congress* 1943

UNITED STATES

2031 Judge T. Lyle Dickey of Illinois related that when the excitement over the Kansas-Nebraska bill first broke out, he was with Lincoln and several friends attending court. One evening several persons, including himself and Lincoln, were discussing the slavery question. Judge Dickey contended that slavery was an institution which the Constitution recognized, and which could not be disturbed. Lincoln argued that ultimately slavery must become extinct. "After a while," said Judge Dickey, "we went upstairs to bed. There were two beds in our room, and I remember that Lincoln sat up in his nightshirt on the edge of the bed arguing the point with me. At last we went to sleep. Early in the morning I woke up and there was Lincoln half sitting up in bed. "Dickey," said he, "I tell you this nation cannot exist half slave and half free."

"Oh, Lincoln," said I, "go to sleep."

2032 Cobden used to tell the following anecdote: "When in America I asked an enthusiastic young lady why her country could not rest satisfied with the immense unoccupied territories it already possessed, but must ever be hankering after the lands of its neighbors; when her somewhat remarkable reply was:

"Oh, the propensity is a very bad one, I admit, but we came honestly by it, for we inherited it from England."

RELATED SUBJECTS: *Presidents* 1931-1940; *Freedom* 2036-2042; *Equality* 2046

FREEDOM

2036 "You do not know what you are advising us to do," replied the Spartans to a Persian envoy who urged them to submit to Xerxes, "for you know what it is to be a slave, but the sweetness of freedom you have never tasted. If you felt it, you would tell us to fight for it, not with spears only, but with axes."

2037 When the Emancipation Proclamation was taken to Lincoln by Secretary Seward, for the President's signature, Lincoln took a pen, dipped it in ink, moved his hand to the place for the signature, held it a moment, then removed his hand and dropped the pen. After a little hesitation, he again took up the pen and went through the same movement as before. Lincoln then turned to Seward and said:

"I have been shaking hands since nine o'clock this morning, and my right arm is almost paralyzed. If my name ever goes into history, it will be for this act, and my whole soul is in it. If my hand trembles when I sign the Proclamation, all who examine the document hereafter will say: 'He hesitated.' "

2038 At a little stream on the Swiss frontier, a Swiss and a Nazi were fishing from the opposite sides of the water. Great success had attended the Swiss, and he had a handsome string to show for his efforts; whereas the Nazi had not had so much as a nibble.

"Why is it," called the German across the water, "that you have so much better luck? Are we not using the same bait?"

"Well," said the Swiss, "on this side the fish aren't afraid to open their mouths."

2039 On August 1, 1836, the British Parliament abolished slavery in the West Indies, but the decree was not to go into effect for a year. On July 31, 1837, a year later, twenty thousand slaves came together in Jamaica. They put on white robes, and at eleven o'clock at night they all knelt down, and with faces turned upward they waited for an hour. As the clock struck twelve the twenty thousand former slaves rose up and shouted joyously:

"We are free! We are free!"

2040 Years ago there was an insurrection in Massachusetts. There were thousands of men in arms against the State authorities. One of the leaders, Luke Shay, spoke thus at Springfield:

"My boys," said he, "they talk to you about liberty; they tell you that liberty means the right to do what you have a mind to.

That is not liberty. Liberty is the right to make other folks do what you want to have them do."

2041   Harold Laski has this story to tell: I discussed recently with a Hindu I knew—a man of great culture—the question of Indian Independence. "If England were to withdraw from India," I said, "wouldn't the country relapse into a state of anarchy—much like what it was in the 18th Century when Clive and Hastings laid the foundations of the British Raj?"

My friend assented sadly, "Yes, I suppose you are right."

"And that would be followed by a tyranny, or several tyrannies, would it not?"

"Yes, probably."

"And then the pendulum would swing back to anarchy again?"

"Yes," he said, "yes, I am afraid it would!" Then, after a long pause, he added, "but it will be our tyranny and our anarchy!"

2042   Having been subordinated and suppressed for eighteen years, Catherine the Great revelled in doing what she pleased. "O Freedom," she wrote, "The soul of all things; without thee there is no life." But when the miners and other serfs of the land rebelled, she decided that freedom was too precious to be scattered around, and she wrote to Vyazemsky, who had quelled the revolt with cannon: "The Russian Empire is so vast that any other form of government than that of an autocratic emperor would be detrimental, for every other form fulfills itself more slowly and embodies passions which dissipate its strength."

RELATED SUBJECTS: *Equality* 2046; *Woman's Suffrage* 2051-2052; *Revolutions* 2061-2064

SEE ALSO: *Courage* 152; *Shrewdness* 535; *Engagement* 857; *Presidents* 1932; *Kings* 1974

EQUALITY

2046   The liberal historian Mrs. Catherine Macaulay used to debate with Doctor Johnson the question of social equality. One day at dinner in her house the Doctor put on a grave face and said, "Madam, your arguments have converted me to your way of thinking. I am convinced that all mankind should stand upon an equal footing; and, to give you proof, Madam, that I am in earnest, here is a very sensible, civil, well-behaved fellow-citizen—your footman; I desire that he may be allowed to sit down and dine with us." This proposition the hostess of course indignantly rejected, much to the Doctor's amusement. Later, he said, reporting his victory from his armchair, "I thus showed her the absurdity of her levelling doctrine. She has never liked me since. Your levellers wish to level down as far as themselves; but they cannot bear levelling up to themselves."

RELATED SUBJECTS: *Freedom* 2036-2042; *Woman's Suffrage* 2051-2052; *Socialism* 2056-2057; *Revolutions* 2061-2064

WOMAN'S SUFFRAGE

2051   Among the ardent feminists arrested during the suffragette movement in England was an elderly crusader, often in jail for the Cause, and a young thing sentenced for the first time and taking it very hard. They were assigned to adjoining cells. Anon the older woman heard the younger sobbing. She rapped energetically on the dividing wall, and called:

"There, there, dear, don't cry! Put your trust in God—She will protect you!"

2052   One evening when Lloyd George was addressing a meeting of hostile suffragettes, one woman, in an ugly mood, rose and said, "If you were my husband I would give you poison."

Lloyd George, noted for his ready wit, snapped back, "My dear lady, if I were your husband I would take the poison."

RELATED SUBJECTS: *Women* 841-843; *Equality* 2046

SOCIALISM

2056   One rainy day, standing at a window with Sidney Webb (Lord Passfield), I asked him how the Socialists were going to bring about all these great changes. He pointed to the rain, gentle, steady, incessant, and said in a voice no less gentle: "I want the Socialists to work like that: without noise, without fuss." And then (using another simile): "Under the earth are the burrows of the moles; we must work as they work, unobtrusively, slowly and gradually undermining the existing system until, one day, it subsides."

2057 Andrew Carnegie was once visited by a socialist who preached to him eloquently the injustice of one man possessing so much money. He preached a more equitable distribution of wealth. Carnegie cut the matter short by asking his secretary for a generalized statement of his many possessions and holdings, at the same time looking up the figures on world population in his almanac. He figured for a moment on his desk pad and then instructed his secretary, "Give this gentleman 16¢. That's his share of my wealth."

RELATED SUBJECTS: *Freedom* 2036-2042; *Equality* 2046; *Revolutions* 2061-2064; *Wealth* 2181-2187

REVOLUTIONS

2061 On the afternoon of July 14, 1789, the Duc de La Rochefoucauld-Liancourt brought to King Louis XVI at Versailles the news of the capture of the Bastille. The King exclaimed, "Why, this is a revolt!"
"No, sire," replied the Duke, "it is a revolution."

2062 The character of the natural revolutionary is typified by the Irishman who was cast ashore upon a beach after a shipwreck. Weak and exhausted from his struggle with the waves, the castaway staggered along the sands until he encountered a man. "What place is this?"
He was answered. "Is there a government here?" he asked next.
"Of course," was the reply.
"Then—I'm agin it!"

2063 During the time of the French Revolution, when the months in France were named Thermidor, Floreal, Nivose, etc. —Sheridan proposed to extend the innovation to the English language, beginning with January, as—"Freezy, Sneezy, Breezy, Wheezy, Showery, Lowery, Flowery, Bowery, Snowy, Flowy, Blowy, Glowy."

2064 A man living in a village outside Paris during the Revolution met a friend fresh from the city and asked what was happening. "It's awful," was the reply, "they're cutting off heads by the thousand."

"Good Heavens! Surely not heads," he cried. "Why, I'm a hatter!"

RELATED SUBJECTS: *Kings and Emperors* 1971-1993; *Dictators* 2001-2011; *Freedom* 2036-2042; *Equality* 2046; *Socialism* 2056-2057; *War* 2316-2323; *Civil War* 2326-2329

SEE ALSO: *Shrewdness* 538; *Authors* 1197

BUSINESS, INDUSTRY AND POSSESSIONS

BUYING AND SELLING

2066 Among the Romans, the deity who presided over commerce and banking was Mercury, who, by a strange association, was also the god of thieves and of orators. The Romans, who looked upon merchants with contempt, fancied there was a resemblance between theft and merchandising and they easily found a figurative connection between theft and eloquence; hence, thieves, merchants, and orators, were placed under the superintendence of the same deity. On the seventeenth of May, in each year, the merchants held a public festival, and walked in procession to the temple of Mercury, for the purpose, as the satirist said, of begging pardon of that deity for all the lying and cheating they had found it convenient to practice, in the way of business, during the preceding year.

2067 One time in Mexico, Carleton Beals had fallen into the habit of buying two oranges from an orange woman near his house. One day, when he was planning to give a party, he undertook to buy her entire stock of four dozen oranges.

Severely she said, "Here are your two," and handed him his usual purchase.

"But this time I want to buy all the rest of them."

"Why," she said, outraged, "you can't. What do you think I would do all the rest of the day with no oranges to sell!"

> RELATED SUBJECTS: *Stores* 2071-2072; *Bargaining* 2076-2082; *Price* 2086; *Salesmen* 2091-2097; *Advertising* 2101-2108; *Competition* 2116; *Credit* 2166-2167; *Businessmen* 2236-2237

> SEE ALSO: *Shrewdness* 526, 536; *Practical Joking* 434; *Clothing* 718

STORES

2071 A certain flower store in New York has a sign on its walls, saying, "Kindly desist from telling us to make up your order 'nice, nice, nice.' You worry yourself and the sales help needlessly. You must realize it is a great strain on the salesmen to be told to 'make it nice' by one customer after another. Your order will be carefully executed without unnecessary reminders."

2072 The story is told of an ingenious young man who desired to present his sweetheart with a gift. He decided that perfume would be appropriate, but he did not know the name of the brand she used, and was too shy to ask her. He solved the problem by taking her little pet dog for a walk. Snatching the animal into a store, he proceeded to instruct the astonished clerk to wave the stoppers of a large number of perfumes under the nose of the rather indifferent dog. At last came a perfume which caused the animal to jump up excitedly and wag its tail. On this evidence he bought his gift which turned out to be right.

RELATED SUBJECTS: *Buying and Selling* 2066-2067; *Price* 2086; *Advertising* 2101-2108

SEE ALSO: *Honesty* 290; *Quick Thinking* 492; *Names* 831, 834; *Congress* 1947; *Advertising* 2105; *Collection* 2178; *Bosses* 2231

BARGAINING

2076 Georges Clemenceau, "The Tiger" of France, told this story:

"One day in a little village in the East Indies, I noticed a little statuette, and said to the dealer, 'I like your statuette. How much is it?'

" 'Because it's you,' he answered, '75 rupees.'

" 'Because it's you,' I answered, 'I offer you 45 rupees.'

"He raised his hands to heaven.

" 'Forty-five rupees! You're making fun of me! What if anyone happened to hear of it?'

" 'Forty-five rupees,' I said.

"Then he made a fine gesture of indignation. 'Impossible! I'd rather give it to you.'

" 'Agreed!' I took the statuette, stuffed it into my pocket, and said, 'You are extraordinarily kind, and I thank you. But it is quite evident that this gift can only come from a friend to a friend. Consequently you won't take it amiss if I in turn make you a gift.'

" 'Naturally not.'

" 'Well, here are 45 rupees to use in good works.'

"He took them and we parted, enchanted with each other."

2077 Shrewd bargaining is typified by the woman who entered one of the large department stores of New York and ordered a yard of silk which had been priced at 35¢ a yard. After her purchase, there was left a remnant of one and a half yards, and the clerk suggested that she take it also. "What do you want for it?" she asked. "Oh, 20¢," replied the clerk. "All right," said his customer, "I'll take it and you can keep the yard you just cut off."

2078 William F. Hallstead of Scranton was General Manager of the Delaware, Lackawanna Railway. One day a Lackawanna County farmer walked into his office and bluntly asked for a pass to New York and return. Mr. Hallstead, who knew the old fellow very well, said: "Look here, Silas, suppose I should drop in on you some day and ask you to hitch up and drive me to Honesdale and return, what would you think of me?"

The old farmer thought for a moment, and in a slow drawl, replied, "Waal, I think it would be gol darn cheeky; but Mr. Hallstead, suppose I was driving to Honesdale anyway, and you asked me for a ride, what would you think of me if I refused?"

Mr. Hallstead saw the point and Silas got the pass.

2079 An English firm cabled Edison and offered him "Thirty thousand" for one of his patents.

"Too cheap, Edison," said a friend.

"Too cheap?" repeated Edison. "The thing isn't worth half of that."

His friends induced him to cable back: "It is yours."

Within a fortnight he received a draft for one hundred and fifty thousand dollars. It had turned out, of course, that the English firm had meant the amount in pounds.

Edison wanted to cable that some mistake had occurred, but his friends intervened.

"Well," he said, "it beats me."

2080 It happened on one of those downtown Manhattan streets where the cloak-and-suiters rush out and seize the passers-by by the arm. "Look," said one of them eagerly to the man he had seized, "a fine suit; the best; nice cut; fine quality materials. To you, $15." "No," said the customer, trying to break from him. "Look," said the clothier, dragging his victim a little closer to the shop, "a very special cut, with cuffs even; the last suit. To you, special, $12." "No," said the man, trying to pull free. "An opportunity that shouldn't be passed up," continued the salesman, "Look, because it's early, to start the day right, the first sale—$8."

"Nothing doing," snarled the customer. "My God," wailed the proprietor, throwing his hands up into the air, "such a person. To make the thing right, to start the day; I start something, I should finish it. I'm giving it to you for nothing." "Not without two pair of pants!" said the customer.

2081 At one time the great copper magnate, Fritz Augustus Heinze, struggled bitterly with John D. Ryan, head of Standard Oil's copper holdings, for control of rich copper deposits at Butte, Montana.

The transaction had nearly stalled when the two men at last met face to face in secrecy, and conferred privately for many hours far into the night. Negotiations broke down again at a point when they were a half million dollars apart in their ideas and it seemed as though a real impasse had been reached. No other channels of negotiation were left open. Abruptly one of them said, "All right, let's toss a coin to see which one gives up the half million."

Probably never before or since has this much money fallen with the fall of a coin.

2082 Soon after Sir William Johnson had been appointed superintendent of Indian affairs in America he wrote to England for some suits of clothes richly laced. When they arrived Hendrick, king of the Mohawk nation, was present and particularly admired them. In a few succeeding days Hendrick called on Sir William and acquainted him that he had had a dream. On Sir William's enquiring what it was, he told him that he had dreamed that he had given him one of those fine suits he had lately received. Sir William took the hint and immediately presented him with one of the richest suits. The Indian chief, highly pleased with the generosity of Sir William, retired. Some time after this, Sir William happening to be in company with Hendrick, told him that he had also had a dream. Hendrick being very solicitous to know what it was, Sir William informed him, that he had dreamed that he (Hendrick) had made him a present of a particular tract of land (the most valuable on the Mohawk River) of about 5,000 acres. Hendrick presented him with the land immediately, remarking shrewdly: "Now, Sir William, I will never dream with you again. You dream too hard for me."

RELATED SUBJECTS: *Honesty* 286-294; *Shrewdness* 526-541; *Buying and Selling* 2066-2067; *Competition* 2116; *Chiseling and Swindling* 2121-2132

SEE ALSO: *Playwrights* 1376; *Church Services* 1535; *Horses* 2286

PRICE

2086 Walking in the country, Douglas Jerrold, plucking a buttercup, was wont to say, "If it cost a shilling a root, how beautiful it would be!"

RELATED SUBJECTS: *Economy* 211-213; *Buying and Selling* 2066-2067; *Stores* 2071-2072; *Bargaining* 2076-2082

SEE ALSO: *Inventors* 1126; *Painting* 1273, 1276, 1282; *Bargaining* 2080; *Public Relations* 2112; *Machinery* 2272

SALESMEN

2091 James H. Rand, of Remington, Rand, Inc. was, at the outset of his career, a salesman for a bank-equipment firm. Frank A. Munsey, the eccentric publisher and financier, was about to open banks in Baltimore and Washington. Rand called upon Munsey to sell him equipment, and the publisher cross-questioned him minutely as to the merits and demerits, desirability and undesirability of all types of equipment. Finally he said, "All right, I'll give you a letter to my Washington manager. You can go to him for the order."

Delighted, Rand took the letter and hastened to Washington. He talked to Munsey's manager and got an order for $25,000 worth of equipment. In his zeal he forgot all about the letter and did not even present it. Back in New York several days later, Rand suddenly found the letter in his pocket. Curious, he opened it. Munsey's instructions to his manager had been, "Learn all you can from this man, but don't buy anything from him if you can help it."

2092 The traveling salesman was anxious to gain admission to the office of a prominent industrialist, the establishing of business relations with whom would be the highlight of his whole trip. But the man in question was difficult to see. Entering his outer office, he gave his card to the secretary. It was taken within and, through the partly opened door, the salesman saw the executive tear it in half and throw it into the waste basket. The secretary returned meanwhile and stated that her employer would not see him. "May I have my card back?" asked the salesman. Slightly embarrassed, the secretary reported to her superior who sent her back out again with a nickel and a message that he was sorry, but the card had been destroyed. More than equal to the occasion, the salesman drew another card from his wallet and gave it to the girl. "Take this back to him," he said, "and tell him I sell two cards for a nickel."

He got his interview and he got his order.

2093 The executive was taken down a peg.

"You may well feel proud of yourself, young fellow," he said to the life insurance agent, "I've refused to see seven insurance men today."

"I know," said the agent, "I'm them."

2094 "We need to have the whole place re-equipped all over electrically," said the office manager to his boss.

"Send for Markman of our sales force," snapped the boss. "He hasn't done anything but wire the house since he's been on the road."

2095 The sales manager was delivering a terrific dressing down to one of his salesmen. He became so abusive in his anger that the culprit protested, saying, "Don't talk to me that way. I take orders from no one."

"That's what I'm raising Hell about," snapped the manager.

2096 An advertising salesman arrived at a large Chicago hotel and took a room. He carried with him only a small grip and the hotel porter asked for the tags for his trunks.

"I have none," said the salesman.

"Why, I understood you was a salesman," said the porter.

"That's right, I am. But I don't need any trunks. I sell brains."

The porter scratched his head and said, "Well, sir, Boss, you is the first traveling salesman what's ever come here without no samples."

2097 "I owe my success as a salesman," said the speaker, addressing the gathering of young men being trained for this profession, "to the first five words which I invariably utter when a woman opens the door, 'Miss, may I speak to your mother?'"

> RELATED SUBJECTS: *Buying and Selling* 2066-2067; *Bargaining* 2076-2082; *Competition* 2116; *Insurance* 2136-2140; *Real Estate* 2141-2142

> SEE ALSO: *Travel* 1796; *Real Estate* 2141

ADVERTISING

2101 During Mark Twain's days as a newspaperman, he was editor of a small Missouri newspaper. One day he got a letter from a subscriber, stating that he had found a spider in his paper, and asking if this was an omen of good or bad luck.

Twain wrote: "Finding a spider in your paper is neither good luck nor bad. The spider was merely looking over our paper to see which merchant was not advertising so that he could go to that store, spin his web across the door and lead a life of undisturbed peace ever afterward."

2102 The famous tenor, Giovanni Martinelli, was once asked if he smoked. "Tobacco! I would not think of it!" said the singer. "But," said one of the reporters, "didn't you once endorse a cigarette and say that it did not irritate your throat." "Of course I endorsed it, and it is true that the cigarettes did not hurt my throat. I never smoked them."

2103 "This," said the manager of the store, "is an inferior grade of shoe. I'm an honorable business man and I refuse to pass it off as anything better. Put it in the window and mark it—'A Shoe Fit for a Queen.' A Queen does not have to do much walking."

2104 One of the great press agents was the late Dexter Fellows who functioned in that capacity for Ringling Brothers and Barnum and Bailey. He knew he had the greatest show on earth. He once entered a newspaper office in the Mid-West and announced without preliminaries, "I am Dexter Fellows of the circus."

"What circus?" someone asked.

"Good Lord, man," he said, with all the horror of sacrilege on his face, "if you were in London and heard a man say 'God Save the King,' would you interrupt him and ask what king?"

2105 Unique in the entire field of advertising is S. Klein, celebrated New York dress merchant. Klein advertises only occasionally to announce, in connection with holidays or other special days, that his store will be closed, in order to keep immense crowds from being disappointed and needlessly cluttering up Union Square. He dares not advertise in any other way for, on the one or two times in the past when he attempted to do so, the result was an actual riot in Union Square, with cordons of police and fleets of squad cars required to restore peace.

2106 From the Lost and Found Column of a Nashville paper: Bird or Hat:—Flew in or blew in out of car passing Dannaker's Service Station, Franklin Road. It's sorta round with green and red polka dot quills or feathers in it. If you've lost a hat or a bird, drive by and see it—it's funny.

2107 When the famous Pre-Raphaelite painter Burne-Jones visited the U. S. he one day received a circular letter from a firm engaged in the sale of dried fruit, inviting him to compete for a prize to be given for the best design to be used in advertising their wares. Only one prize, the circular stated, was to be given, and all unsuccessful drawings were to become the property of the firm.

After reading the circular, and not to be outdone by the

audacious request, Sir Philip sat down and wrote the following letter in reply:

"Manager, Dried Fruit Company:

"Dear Sir: I am offering a prize of fifty cents for the best specimen of dried fruit, and should be glad to have you take part in the competition. Twelve dozen boxes of each kind of fruit should be sent for examination, and all fruit that is not adjudged worthy of the prize will remain the property of the undersigned."

2108   A certain small boy had been steeped in radio advertising, comic strip promotions, and general conversations on the subject of vitamins. His mother one day offered him some little candies. "These are good," the child said. "What vitamins do they have?"

"Oh, none in particular," replied his mother.

The child was astonished. "Do you mean to say they're just for fun?" he asked.

> RELATED SUBJECTS: *Buying and Selling* 2066-2067; *Stores* 2071-2072; *Public Relations* 2111-2112; *Competition* 2116
>
> SEE ALSO: *Talking* 810; *Newspapers* 1236; *Salesmen* 2096; *Chiseling* 2122; *Evidence* 2521

PUBLIC RELATIONS

2111   In one of his political speeches in the early days of the N.R.A., Hugh "Ironpants" Johnson revived a story which probably dates from the days of Chauncey Depew and Rufus Choate, demonstrating the usual futility of letters of complaint.

It concerns the case of the man who was tormented by bedbugs in his sleeping car and who wrote an indignant letter about the matter to the general passenger agent of the railroad.

He was cautioned by his friends that he would probably not receive so much as a reply, and his satisfaction was great when, in due course, he received an apologetic letter assuring him that such a thing could never happen again. His elation was quashed a moment later, however, by the discovery of the inter-office memo which had inadvertently been inserted with the letter and which said tersely, "Send this s.o.b. the bug letter."

2112   Seeking to establish closer ties with its consumers, a gas and light company in a small town held a party at which its customers were addressed by a member of the firm, who made a gallant effort to extol the virtues of the company, and, telling of its use to the community, he said, "Think of all the good this company has done. If I may be permitted a pun, it may well be said, 'Honor the Light Brigade.'"

From the audience a raucous voice called out, "Oh what a charge they made."

> RELATED SUBJECTS: *Speeches* 756-782; *Advertising* 2101-2108
>
> SEE ALSO: *Police* 2551

COMPETITION

2116   A young and conscientious fellow ran a newsstand in front of a bank. One day a friend of his stopped by and asked him for a loan of five dollars.

"Sorry," said the young man, "I'm afraid I couldn't do that. You see I have an agreement with the bank."

"You—an agreement with the bank. What do you mean?"

"Well, you see, it's this way. I don't give loans. The bank doesn't sell newspapers. It's a perfect agreement. I'm sorry, but I'm bound."

> RELATED SUBJECTS: *Ambition* 96-97; *Diligence* 176-177; *Quick Thinking* 471-492; *Bargaining* 2076-2082; *Salesmen* 2091-2097; *Advertising* 2101-2108; *Chiseling and Swindling* 2121-2132
>
> SEE ALSO: *Chiseling* 2131, 2132

CHISELING AND SWINDLING

2121   Colonel Putnam told the story of an Indian upon the Connecticut River who called at a tavern in the fall of the year for a dram of rum. The landlord charged him two coppers for it. The next spring, at the same house, he called for another, and had to pay three coppers.

"How is this, landlord—last fall you asked but two coppers for a glass of rum; now you ask three?"

"Oh," says the landlord, "it costs me a great deal to keep a head of rum over the winter—as much as to keep a horse over the winter."

"I can't see that," says the Indian. "He won't eat so much hay —maybe he drink as much water."

2122 A farmer advertised a "frog farm" for sale, claiming that he had a pond that was thoroughly stocked with fine bull-frogs. A prospective buyer appeared and was taken late one warm evening to the pond that he might hear the frogs. The "music" made so favorable an impression on the buyer that the sale was made. Soon afterward the purchaser proceeded to drain the pond in order to catch and market the frogs. To his surprise, when the water was drained out of the pond, he found that all the noise had been made by one old bull-frog.

2123 A poor Irishman applied to one of the overseers of the poor for relief.

"Och, yer honor," said he, "sure I'd be starved long since, but for me cat."

"But for what?" asked the astonished interrogator.

"My cat," rejoined the Irishman.

"Your cat—how so?"

"Sure, yer honor, I sold her eleven times for sixpence a time, and she was always home before I could get there meself."

2124 In the days before gold coins were withdrawn from circulation, they were invariably an object of interest to small boys, not to mention adults. A paternal gentleman making a purchase in the store of little Abie's father permitted the child to hold in his hand and examine a shiny five-dollar gold piece. To his consternation, as very young children will do, the child popped the small coin into his mouth and swallowed it. "Do not worry. Do not worry," said the proprietor, "I'll take him into the back and hold him up by the heels and shake him." The store owner was gone for some little time. At last he appeared apologetically with some change, and said, "Too bad we couldn't have worked quicker. Here's two dollars and fifty cents. Abie has digested the rest."

2125 The folly which is ineradicable from human nature is neatly summed up by the case of the middle aged school teacher who invested her life savings in a business enterprise which had been elaborately explained to her by a swindler. When her investment had disappeared and the wonderful dream was shattered, she went to the office of the Better Business Bureau, which was able at once to confirm her darkest fears. "Why on earth," asked the man, "didn't you come to us first? Didn't you know about the Better Business Bureau?"

"Oh, yes," said she sadly, "I've always known about you. But I didn't come because I was afraid you'd tell me not to do it."

2126 Not all inhabitants of the Tobacco Road region of Georgia are as indigent as the Lester family. Witness the case of the motorist who had become bogged down in the sticky clay of an unpaved Georgia road, and had paid $10 to be pulled out by a Georgia cracker with a team of mules. "I should think," said the motorist, just about to get into his car to continue, "that you would be pulling people out of this stuff day and night."

"Nope," drawled the mule driver, "at night's when we tote the water for the roads."

2127 A lesson well learned is demonstrated by the remarks made by a man who had, at one time in the past, lost a great deal of money in a gold mine speculation. When asked by a friend to define the term, "bonanza," he said, "A bonanza is a hole in the ground owned by a champion liar."

2128 Farmer Jones had a very beautiful horse of which he was very proud. One day he drove him into town and carefully tied the animal to the hitching post in front of the local tavern. Two thieves, hurrying through the town, happened to spy the horse and decided to steal it. Realizing that the horse was much too fine and valuable an animal to be stolen in the ordinary manner, they decided on a stratagem to carry out their plan.

One of them hurriedly untied the horse and rode swiftly away. The other remained by the post.

The farmer finally emerged from the tavern. Seeing that his horse was not where he had left him he was just about to shout when the thief walked up to him. In a sad, low tone he said, "Sir, I am your horse. Years ago I sinned and for my sins I was punished. I was changed into a horse. Today my sentence is over, and I can be released if you will be so kind."

The farmer, amazed yet touched by this story, sent the man away wishing him luck in his new life.

Several weeks later Farmer Jones went to a fair in a neighboring town. Great was his surprise to see his own horse for sale there. Gazing long at the animal to make sure that his eyes did not deceive him, he walked over and whispering in the horse's ear said, "So—you've sinned again."

2129 A man whom Dr. Johnson reproved for following a useless and demoralizing business, said: "You know, doctor, that I must live."

Dr. Johnson replied: that "he did not see the least necessity for that."

2130 Whether Laurie Marks, the New York gambler, implicated in the swindle once practiced on the Bank of Liverpool, really did commit suicide by jumping overboard from a steamer, was under discussion by a group of police officials. Ex-Inspector Byrnes, who had known Marks well, had the following to say:

"Marks is not dead. He is too much of a gambler for anything like suicide, and if a search were made for him he would be found in some of the great cities. Marks would as soon think of suicide as of going into hiding in a village or backwoods community. Once when he was seriously ill Marks refused to go to a quiet resort, saying he preferred to go to some place where things were moving and sandwiches were $2 apiece, for then he would know he had a chance to get somebody else's money."

2131 A certain merchant prince was raising his small son with an eye to equipping him for the harsh realities and cutthroat competition of the world. As one object lesson he put the youngster on a high mantelpiece and coaxed him to jump into his arms. The boy did this repeatedly until he had built up a certain confidence. On the last jump the father stepped aside and the child crashed to the floor. Lifting up the whimpering youngster the father said, "Now then, let that be a lesson to you. Never trust anyone—not even your own father."

2132 Cornelius Vanderbilt wrote the following letter to certain business rivals:

Gentlemen:

You have undertaken to cheat me. I will not sue you, for law takes too long. I will ruin you.

Sincerely yours,
Cornelius Vanderbilt

INSURANCE

2136 The life insurance office was taken aback by the old man of 97 years, who wished to take out a policy. His application was turned down. Whereupon the old gentleman said with annoyance, "You folks are making a big mistake. If you look over your statistics you'll find that mighty few men die after they're 97."

2137 Insurance agents are sometimes faced with difficult problems when the answer to the required questions put to applicants for insurance touch upon sensitivities or family scandals.

In one such instance the consummation of a deal was held up for a long time by the refusal of the prospective insured to give the cause of his father's death. After much wheedling the agent extracted from his client the information that the father had been hanged, but could not induce him to state this on the insurance blank.

"All right," said the agent, "we'll put it this way."

And in the troublesome blank he wrote: "Fell from scaffold; death instantaneous."

The problem was solved.

2138 Fire insurance is a more delicate legal problem than life insurance, as it is somewhat easier to set fire to your barn than to cut your own throat to collect for it.

A certain merchant heavily insured his warehouse. As he signed the papers concluding the deal, he said in a tone of jocularity, "Now if this warehouse were to burn down tonight, how much would I get?"

"No less than 10 years," said the agent grimly.

2139 When an insurance adjuster returned from investigating a blaze, his boss asked what had caused the fire.

"Friction," the investigator replied tersely.

"Something rubbing together, eh?"

"Yeah," the adjuster added, "the fire was caused by rubbing a $3,000 insurance policy against a $2,000 house."

2140 A hearing was being held to determine whether or not it was, as some seemed to think, an incendiary fire. The adjuster was questioning some of the villagers attempting to find out if the fire had been started for the purpose of collecting insurance. One of those under questioning was an old man, deaf as a post. Unable to hear the questions being fired at him, he turned to his wife, a puzzled look on his face.

At the top of her voice she shouted, "What the man wants to know is was the Jobson's fire kotched er was it sot?"

RELATED SUBJECTS: *Longevity* 1781-1782; *Salesmen* 2091-2097

SEE ALSO: *Salesmen* 2093

REAL ESTATE

2141 Groucho Marx, after much evasion, finally succumbed to the blandishments of a realtor who wanted to show him a palatial ocean-front estate which was for sale. The salesman drove the comedian up the mile-long, beautifully landscaped approach, escorted him through the house, the stables, the gardens, the kennels, babbling of the wonders of this dream palace by the sea. Groucho patiently plodded after him, nodding gravely, apparently much impressed. Finally he was ushered out on the flagged terrace and the salesman waved proudly toward the broad expanse of the Pacific.

"Now what do you think?" he challenged.

"I don't care for it," replied Groucho thoughtfully and he waved in turn at the view. "Take away the ocean and what have you got?"

2142 An artist who wanted a home among the Taconic Hills of Vermont was talking the matter over with a farmer who allowed that he had a house for sale. "I must have a good view," said the artist. "Is there a good view?"

"Well," drawled the farmer, "from the front porch yuh kin see Ed Snow's barn, but beyond that there ain't nuthin' but a bunch of mountains."

RELATED SUBJECTS: *Buying and Selling* 2141-2142; *Salesmen* 2091-2097

FINANCE AND WEALTH

SEE ALSO: *Universities* 1018; *Painting* 1264; *Politics* 1898; *Lawyers' Fees* 2543

STOCKS AND BONDS

2146 During the hectic days following the crash of 1929, many discussions of the whys and wherefores were overheard along Wall Street. One of the more honest and direct explanations of his plight was the following:

"I hear that you lost quite a lot of money in the crash. Were you a bull or a bear?"

"Neither, just a plain, simple jackass."

2147 A stock broker, suffering a slight nervous breakdown from the constant pressure of fluctuating business, was taken to a hospital to rest.

While more or less in a daze, he overheard his nurse say, as she handed the patient's chart to the doctor, "Temperature today, 102."

Weakly the broker raised his head and said, "When it reaches 102½, sell," then wearily fell back against his pillow.

RELATED SUBJECTS: *Buying and Selling* 2066-2067; *Wealth* 2181-2187; *Bankruptcy* 2196-2198; *Businessmen* 2236-2237

SEE ALSO: *Gossip* 822

BANKS

2151 The Hon. Hugh McCulloch, Secretary of the Treasury during Lincoln's second term, was once announced with a delegation of New York bankers. As the party filed into the room he preceded them and said to the President, in a low voice:

"These gentlemen from New York have come on to see the

Secretary of the Treasury about our new loan. As bankers they are obliged to hold our national securities. I can vouch for their patriotism and loyalty, for, as the good Book says, 'Where the treasure is, there will the heart be also.' "

To which Lincoln quickly replied: "There is another text, Mr. McCulloch I remember, that might equally apply, 'Where the carcass is there will the eagles be gathered together.' "

2152 Judge Giles Baker of a Pennsylvania county was likewise cashier of his home bank. A man presented a check one day for payment. He was a stranger. His evidence of identification was not satisfactory to the cashier.

"Why, Judge," said the man, "I've known you to sentence men to be hanged on no better evidence than this!"

"Very likely," replied the judge. "But when it comes to letting go of cold cash we have to be mighty careful."

2153 Upon being questioned as to the occupation of his father, the young man replied, "He cleans out the bank."

"Janitor or president?" was the final question.

2154 Pausing for a moment before completing the transaction before him, the teller in the bank peered at the young lady and asked, "I'm sure that this check is all right, but could you show me some positive identification?"

The young lady seemed about to turn away; then, in a faltering tone, she said, "I have a mole on my thigh just above the knee."

2155 A young bride walked into a bank to cash a check. She was somewhat taken aback when the clerk informed her that the check would have to be indorsed by her before it could be cashed.

"Why, it's a good check. My husband sent it to me. He's away on business."

"Yes, madam, it's perfectly all right. But, please sign it on the back so that your husband will know that you got the money."

The bride walked to the writing desk, seemed to be lost in deep contemplation for a moment, and then returned to the teller's window and handed the check to him.

Great was his surprise when he saw scrawled across the back of the check: "Your loving wife, Ethel."

2156 Returning home one evening a father was accosted by his daughter in the hallway of their home.

Indignantly the daughter said, "Father, why in the world did you tell me to put my money in such a bank? Why it's absolutely on the rocks."

"What," said her father, "why that's one of the strongest banks in the country. What do you mean by such a statement?"

Waving a check in the air, his daughter replied, "Look at this. It's my check for $25.00 and it was returned today by the bank and marked 'No Funds.'"

2157 A stranger in Chicago, a New Yorker, stopped a little boy and asked him the way to the Fifth National Bank, adding, "Direct me there, son, and I'll give you a dollar."

Suppressing a grin, the boy replied: "O.K., boss, just follow me."

About half a block farther, the boy stopped and pointed to the building nearest them. "Here you are, sir."

The man, chagrined by his gullibility, handed the boy the dollar but couldn't help saying, "That certainly was an easily earned dollar."

"That's right," said the boy, "but don't forget that bank directors in Chicago are highly paid."

2158 A man working as a teller in a bank bumped into an old friend of his one day.

Seeing that the bank teller seemed very preoccupied, the friend said, "What is the matter with you?"

"Well, there is a lot of trouble down at the bank. We are going through a complete reorganization."

"Why?"

"It seems that we had more vice-presidents than depositors," replied the bank teller as he walked away.

RELATED SUBJECTS: *Loans* 2161-2164; *Credit* 2166-2167; *Debt* 2171-2174; *Wealth* 2181-2187

SEE ALSO: *Exaggeration* 222; *Extravagance* 231; *Hypocrisy* 302; *Buying and Selling* 2066; *Salesmen* 2091; *Competition* 2116; *Loans* 2162; *Collection* 2176; *Bankruptcy* 2196; *Bosses* 2233; *Stealing* 2583

LOANS

2161   According to Cicero, "When Cato was asked what was the most profitable feature of an estate, he replied: 'Raising cattle successfully.' What next to that? 'Raising cattle with fair success.' And next? 'Raising cattle with but slight success.' And fourth? 'Raising crops.' And when his questioner said, 'How about money-lending?' Cato replied: 'How about murder?' "

2162   It is said that Henry Clay once asked the Riggs Bank for a $250 loan on his personal note. There was no reflection upon his credit, the bank replied, but it was a necessary formality in connection with this particular institution to have an indorser.

Clay happened upon Daniel Webster and asked him if he would be kind enough to indorse for him.

"Certainly," said Webster, "but look here, I need some money myself. Why not make the note for $500 and you and I will split it."

This was done, and to this day the note is in the Riggs bank, unpaid.

2163   Having persuaded Benjamin Franklin to lend him $50, his "poor relation" asked for a sheet of paper in order to give him a note for the sum.

"What," said Franklin, "do you want to waste my stationery as well as my money?"

2164   The famous French satirical writer, Voltaire, was worth $500,000 at the age of 40. But he did not earn his money from books. He made most of it by lending money to needy noblemen. He would lend an heir to an estate a large sum on condition that he would pay him 10% interest on the amount as long as both of them lived. The heir would be neither required nor allowed to pay off the principal; and the agreement ended only when Voltaire died. Voltaire picked only younger men and, because of his tubercular appearance, had no difficulty in getting clients. It is said that when a prospective buyer hesitated, the satirist would cough in a way that always closed the deal.

RELATED SUBJECTS: *Borrowing* 121-126; *Banks* 2151-2158; *Credit* 2166-2167; *Debt* 2171-2174; *Collection* 2176-2179

CREDIT

2166 The Vicar of Sheffield, the Rev. Dr. Sutton, once said to the late Dr. Peech, a veterinary surgeon:

"Mr. Peech, how is it that you have not called upon me for your account?"

"Oh," said Dr. Peech, "I never ask a gentleman for money."

"Indeed," said the Vicar, "then how do you get it if he doesn't pay?"

"Why," replied Dr. Peech, "after a certain time I conclude he is not a gentleman, and then I ask him."

2167 Those who believe in a strictly cash business have as their shining example the small son of a mountaineer, who was accosted by a revenuer.

"Where's your pappy?" asked the officer.

"Pappy's up at the still."

"Where's your mother?"

"She's up at the still too."

"I'll give you a dollar," said the officer, "if you'll take me up there."

"All right," said the boy, "give me the dollar."

"I'll give it to you when we get back," said the officer.

"No sir, mister, give it to me now," insisted the boy. "You ain't a-comin' back."

> RELATED SUBJECTS: *Buying and Selling* 2066-2067; *Banks* 2151-2158; *Loans* 2161-2164; *Debt* 2171-2174; *Wealth* 2181-2187; *Salaries* 2251-2254

> SEE ALSO: *Salaries* 2252

DEBT

2171 A friend once observed to Sheridan, "Being of an illustrious Irish family, it is strange that your name has not an O prefixed to it."

"True," replied Sheriden, "no family has a better right to it. We owe everybody."

2172 The train came to a sudden stop. People started to look out of the window and then, hurriedly dropped back into their seats as they saw that the cause of the stop was a hold-up.

The robbers came through the train ruthlessly stripping the money, jewels and valuables from the passengers. One man seemed to become more and more nervous as the bandits approached the seat where he sat with his friend. Finally, drawing a ten-dollar bill from his pocket he leaned toward his friend and said, "Here, Jerry. Here's the ten dollars I owe you."

2173 Charles Fox, the English Statesman, once received a severe reprehension from his father who asked him how it was possible for him to sleep, or enjoy any of the comforts of life, when he thought about the immense sums he owed. "Your lordship need not be in the least surprised," answered Charles; "your astonishment ought to be how my creditors can sleep."

2174 Richard Brinsley Sheridan, the playwright, wit and spendthrift, being dunned by a tailor to pay at least the interest on his bill, answered: "It is not my interest to pay the principal, nor my principle to pay the interest."

RELATED SUBJECTS: *Borrowing* 121-126; *Banks* 2151-2158; *Loans* 2161-2164; *Credit* 2166-2167; *Collection* 2176-2179; *Taxes* 2191-2194; *Bankruptcy* 2196-2198

SEE ALSO: *Borrowing* 122

COLLECTION

2176 A meeting of bank directors included J. Edward Simmons and Russell Sage. In the course of a general conversation Mr. Simmons remarked:

"Money isn't everything—is it, Mr. Sage?"

"No," replied Mr. Sage thoughtfully, "the work of collecting it is very important."

2177 A new technique of collection was practiced by the man who called up his debtor and demanded payment of a long outstanding account.

"I can't give it to you now," was the answer, as usual.

"Give it to me now," replied his ingenious creditor, "or I'll tell all your other creditors you've paid me."

2178 A Canadian butcher, many of whose customers' accounts were in bad standing, put a sign in his window: "This business will soon close because of bad debts. Names and amounts will be posted here."

The business is now thriving.

2179 Benjamin Franklin, noted for so many different things, was also known as one of the best money raisers of his generation. He set forth his principles on this subject thus:

"First, call upon all those whom you know will give something; next apply to those you are uncertain whether they will give or not, and finally to those you are sure will give nothing, for in some of these you may be mistaken."

> RELATED SUBJECTS: *Banks* 2151-2158; *Loans* 2161-2164; *Debt* 2171-2174; *Taxes* 2191-2194; *Bankruptcy* 2196-2198

> SEE ALSO: *Debt* 2174

WEALTH

2181 One day a rich but miserly Chassid came to a Rabbi. The Rabbi led him to the window. "Look out there," he said, "and tell me what you see."

"People," answered the rich man.

Then the Rabbi led him to a mirror, "What do you see now?" he asked.

"I see myself," answered the Chassid.

Then the Rabbi said, "Behold—in the window there is glass and the mirror there is glass. But the glass of the mirror is covered with a little silver, and no sooner is a little silver added than you cease to see others and see only yourself."

2182 Some years ago while Baron Rothschild and a nobleman friend were taking a pleasure trip along the Rhine a young lad on the boat noticed the end of a silk handkerchief sticking out of Rothschild's pocket. With visions of the fabulous value of a Rothschild handkerchief he took the end of the handkerchief and gently tugged at it. At this point the nobleman turned to the Baron and whispered: "Baron, that boy beside you is taking your handkerchief."

"Let him alone," said the Baron. "We all had to start small."

2183 For a certain invention the Western Union Company offered Thomas Edison one hundred thousand dollars. He could not grasp the idea of such a sum, and wouldn't take the money. "Safer with you," he said. "Give me six thousand dollars a year for seventeen years."

2184 Julius Rosenwald, the Chicago multi-millionaire, who once said, "I never could understand the popular belief that because a man makes a lot of money he has a lot of brains"— was fond of telling the following story: "A certain man won a million dollars on number 14. When asked how he had figured it out, he said: 'I had a dream. One night I saw in my dream a great big 9, and next I saw a 6, so I used my brains and figured that 9 and 6 is 14.'"

2185 The usual group of respected citizens were assembled to address the graduating class of the local high school. One of them, a self-styled, self-made millionaire, began and ended his speech by saying, "And all my success in life I owe to one thing; pluck, pluck, pluck."

A voice from the back of the auditorium, emanating from a bored but eager graduate said, to the somewhat disconcerted speaker, "We know, sir, but how about telling us something about how and whom to pluck?"

2186 Dr. Johnson, being asked by a young nobleman what had become of the gallantry and military spirit of the old English nobility, replied, "Why, my lord, I'll tell you what has become of it: it has gone into the city to look after a fortune."

2187 Certain government officials approached President Lincoln with the request that they be given control over funds now in the hands of other branches of the governmental set-up.

Lincoln answered them with this story:

"You are very much like a man in Illinois whose cabin was burned down, and, according to the kindly custom of early days in the West, his neighbors all contributed something to start him again. In his case they had been so liberal that he soon found himself better off than before the fire, and got proud. One day a neighbor brought him a bag of oats, but the fellow refused it with scorn, and said, 'I am not taking oats now; I take nothing but money.'"

TAXES

2191 President Roosevelt has frequently been a guest, in years past, on the Nourmahal, luxurious yacht belonging to Vincent Astor. He was once invited to take a winter cruise.

"Oh, don't put that big thing in commission just for me," he protested.

"Mr. President, the Nourmahal is in commission all year round," said its owner.

"Well," rejoined the President, "I guess we'll have to raise taxes on the rich again."

2192 A New York man received from the Bureau of Internal Revenue a "Second Notice" that his tax payment was overdue, and carrying with it dire threats as to what would be done if it was not immediately forthcoming. Hastening to the Collector's office, the man paid up and said, "I would have paid this before but I didn't get your first notice."

"Oh," replied the clerk, "we've run out of first notices, and besides, we find that the second notices are a lot more effective."

2193 A commentary on the artist and society is found in the incident of Joseph Conrad and the offer of knighthood that was sent him in a long blue official envelope, bearing the legend "On His Majesty's Service."

For weeks this lay untouched on Conrad's desk. At last the Prime Minister sent a messenger to see what had happened. Conrad, it transpired, had been afraid to open it. He thought it was the income tax.

2194 Theodore Hook, the English poet, was entertaining a party at his cottage at Fulham with comic song improvisations, when in the middle of it his servant entered with, "Please, sir, here's Mr. Winter, the tax-collector; he says he has called for taxes." Hook would not be interrupted, but went on at the pianoforte, as if nothing had happened, with the following stanza: —

"Here comes Mr. Winter, collector of taxes.
I advise you to pay him whatever he axes:
Excuses won't do; he stands no sort of flummery.
Though Winter his name is, his presence is summary."

RELATED SUBJECTS: *Wealth* 2181-2187; *Laws* 2596-2599

SEE ALSO: *Babies* 962; *Critics* 1105; *Bishops* 1497

BANKRUPTCY

2196 The following note was found among the effects of a businessman after his death. He had long been known for his frequent lapses into bankruptcy.

"I hereby name the following six bankers to be my pall-bearers. Since they have carried me for so long during my lifetime, they might as well finish the job now."

2197 Forced into bankruptcy for the fifth time, the merchant was going over his accounts with his lawyer and accountant.

"It looks pretty bad this time," said the accountant, "can't see how you will be able to pay more than 4 cents on a dollar."

"What," retorted the merchant, "I've always paid ten cents on the dollar. And I'm going to do it this time too. Yes, sir, even if I have to take it out of my own pocket."

2198 Abraham Ibn Ezra was an old Hebrew scholar who lived centuries ago. He was known far and wide as a most unlucky man. Everything he did seemed doomed to failure. In fact, so perverse was his fortune, he once remarked jestingly that should he go into the shroud business, mankind would suddenly cease to die.

RELATED SUBJECTS: *Economy* 211-213; *Extravagance* 231-232; *Credit* 2166-2167; *Debt* 2171-2174; *Poverty* 2201-2211

SEE ALSO: *Farmers* 2312

POVERTY

2201 When Abraham Lincoln once was asked to tell the story of his life, he replied: "It is contained in one line of Gray's 'Elegy in a Country Churchyard': 'The short and simple annals of the poor.'"

2202 In December 1846, Edgar Allan Poe, being in the direst need, inserted a notice in "The Express":

"We regret to learn that Edgar A. Poe and his wife are both dangerously ill with the consumption, and that the hand of misfortune lies heavy upon their temporal affairs. We are sorry to mention the fact that they are so far reduced as to be hardly able to obtain the necessities of life. This is indeed a hard lot, and we hope the friends and admirers of Mr. Poe will come promptly to his assistance in his bitterest hour of need."

2203 When Mark Twain was a young and struggling newspaper writer in San Francisco, a lady of his acquaintance saw him one day with a cigar-box under his arm looking in a shop window. "Mr. Clemens," she said, "I always see you with a cigar-box under your arm. I am afraid you are smoking too much." "It isn't that," said Mark. "I'm moving again."

2204 During his early newspaper days in Chicago, George Ade was accustomed to pawn a large old-fashioned gold watch every Monday morning, to tide him over that trying period between weekly pay checks.

Many years later, when he had become nationally known and had attained a certain degree of affluence, Ade met his old pawnbroker friend on the street.

"Why, George," asked the old pawnbroker, "what happened to you? I haven't seen you in years. Did you lose your watch?"

2205 C. R. W. Nevinson tells this story: "One day he (Henri Matisse) wanted to do a lithograph. I offered him all my chalk and stones, but he would have none of them. He got some lithographic paper, broke one of my lithographic chalks in half, and left himself with only about an inch and a quarter of grease to draw with. When I protested and pressed him to take a box, he assured me it was unnecessary and much too expensive a gift, a comment on the wonderful French economy and the appalling poverty he must have suffered in his early days."

2206 At one time Pablo Picasso was so poor that he and Max Jacob occupied the same bed in turns. Jacob, who besides being a cultivated poet, was an impoverished novelty-shop clerk, slept at night while Picasso worked. When Jacob got up in the morning to let Picasso go to bed, the floor would be carpeted with drawings, which Jacob had to walk on and from which his footprints later had to be cleaned by art experts, since every early Picasso fragment eventually became so valuable that it could be sold.

2207 Hogarth, the celebrated engraver, died, as he had for the greater part of his life lived, in the greatest poverty. Within a few days of his dissolution, bailiffs were sent to seize the bed on which he lay, for a small debt which he was unable to discharge. "Spare me," said the expiring artist, "my bed for a little while—only until I can find another in the grave."

2208 A New York firm applied to Lincoln, some years before he was President, for information as to the financial standing of one of his neighbors. Here was the answer:

"Yours of the 10th received. First of all he has a wife and baby; together they ought to be worth $500,000 to any man. Secondly, he has an office in which there is a table worth $1.50 and three chairs worth, say, $1.00. Last of all, there is in one corner a large rat hole, which will bear looking into.

Respectfully
A. Lincoln"

2209 A certain clergyman in charge of a poor church habitually suffered financial difficulties and was constantly appealing to his bishop for help. The bishop, losing patience, finally chided the man for making so many appeals. Not long after, the bishop received a wire from the clergyman, which said, "This is not an appeal. It is a report. I have no pants!"

2210 One of the saddest announcements ever seen, was that posted before the Negro church, saying, "Next Saturday night the annual Baptist strawberry festival will be held. On account of the depression, prunes will be served."

2211 On August 24, 1770, Chatterton's landlady, a Mrs. Angel, sack-maker, No. 4 Brook Street, Holborn, aware of his desperate condition, offered him a good dinner which he proudly refused. The following morning he failed to respond to a knock on the door of the garret where he lived. The door was broken down, the room was found strewn with bits of paper, fragments of Chatterton's manuscripts and letters which he had carefully destroyed, and himself dead, having taken arsenic, aged seventeen years, nine months and a few days.

RELATED SUBJECTS: *Debt* 2171-2174; *Wealth* 2181-2187; *Bankruptcy* 2196-2198; *Begging* 2216-2219; *Employment and Work* 2226-2228

SEE ALSO: *Pride* 457; *Inventors* 1126; *Painting* 1282; *Ministers* 1464; *Deathbed Scenes* 1775

BEGGING

2216 Thackeray tells of an Irishwoman begging alms from him, who, when she saw him put his hand in his pocket, cried out:
  "May the blessing of God follow you all your life!" But when he only pulled out his snuff box, immediately added: "and never overtake ye."

2217 A beggar, who was daily stationed near the office of a wealthy businessman, had received from him a dime a day over a long period of time. Business took the businessman out of town for a month. When he had returned he passed the beggar, who said to him with a slight tone of reproach, "You owe me $3.00."

2218 Boswell observing to Johnson that there was no instance of a beggar dying for want in the streets of Scotland, "I believe, sir, you are very right," says Johnson; "but this does not arise from the want of beggars, but the impossibility of starving a Scotsman."

2219 Leigh Richmond when traveling in Ireland, passed a man who was a painful spectacle of squalor and raggedness. His heart smote him, and he turned back and said to him:
  "If you are in want, my friend, why don't you beg?"
  "And sure, isn't it begging I am, your honor?"
  "You didn't say a word."
  "Ov coorse not, your honor; but see how the skin is speakin' through the holes of me trousers, and the bones crying out

through me skin! Look at me sunken cheeks, and the famine that is starin' in me eyes! Isn't it begging that I am with a hundred tongues?"

RELATED SUBJECTS: *Borrowing* 121-126; *Poverty* 2201-2211

SEE ALSO: *Generosity* 241; *Honesty* 286; *Shrewdness* 533

STATISTICS

2221 In the course of a Parliamentary debate, an opponent of Disraeli's government was supporting his arguments and charges with a ponderous and bewildering barrage of statistics. Instead of scurrying around for similar ammunition to refute these arguments, Disraeli rose and commented drily, "Gentlemen, there are three kinds of lies—lies, damned lies, and statistics."

2222 Louis Sterne of London tells this story of his father Simon Sterne who, while dining with Chauncey Depew and Edward Atkinson, was appealed to by the latter:

"Now, Sterne, you can bear me out in this; you know," (quoting certain statistics) "and that figures never lie."

"Never," said Mr. Sterne gravely, "except when liars figure."

RELATED SUBJECTS: *Accuracy* 91-92; *Mathematicians* 1146-1154; *Efficiency* 2266-2270

SEE ALSO: *Insurance* 2136

EMPLOYMENT AND WORK

2226 An enterprising American telephone engineer established somewhere in Panama a unique business, a four-leaf clover farm. The conditions were ideal and he raised fine, large clovers which he was able to market in a variety of ways for a variety of purposes, to florists, manufacturers of novelties, etc. At the height of his success, all of his employees, a group of Panamanian girls, confronted him with an unprecedented labor problem. They had no objections to the wages or the hours, they just seemed to have nothing to do with the money. Perplexed in the extreme, their employer racked his brains until he hit upon a brilliant solution. He sent for a Sears-Roebuck catalog and put it in the hands of the girls, explaining to them how they could come into possession of the many fabulous articles pictured therein. His problem was solved.

2227 A butter-fingered man who had been suffering from a long seige of unemployment at last found a job in a chinaware house. He had been at work only a few days when he smashed a large vase. He was summoned to the manager's office and told by that dignitary that he would have to have money deducted from his wages every week until the vase was paid for.

"How much did it cost?" asked the culprit.

"Three hundred dollars," said the manager.

"Oh, that's wonderful," he said, "I'm so happy. At last I've got a steady job!"

2228 In Paris a young man named Arsène hanged himself at his master's home. He left a memorandum bewailing his hard lot, and beseeching his parents to erect a simple tombstone to his memory with the inscription:

"Born to be a man—died a grocery clerk."

> RELATED SUBJECTS: *Bosses and Executives* 2231-2235; *Hiring and Firing* 2246-2249; *Salaries* 2251-2254; *Working Conditions* 2256; *Servants* 2276-2283; *Waiters* 2306-2308; *Farmers and Farming* 2311-2313

> SEE ALSO: *Lateness* 321; *Laziness* 326; *Learned Men* 1084; *Bishops* 1491; *Banks* 2153; *Machinery* 2271

BOSSES AND EXECUTIVES

2231 Ira Hirschmann, the department store executive, once visited a department store in a medium sized Mid-Western city. The manager of the store was a bustling little man filled with self-importance and a belief in himself as a modern high-pressure executive. "One of the things I pride myself on," he explained, "is the morale of the personnel in this store. I keep them up on their toes all the time with inspiring slogans. You'd be surprised how it works. Now the slogan this week is one I thought up myself. 'If a thing is worth doing, it's worth doing at all.'"

2232   That celebrated newspaper publisher, James Gordon Bennett, was a man of harsh principles; and most especially was he intolerant of drinking. One time one of his pressmen turned up, after a spree, with a conspicuous black eye. Bennett happened to enter the pressroom and, fearful of being spotted and asked for an explanation, the culprit hastily smeared printer's ink over his face, and applied himself to his tasks. "Who's that fellow?" Bennett demanded, noting the grimy workman. "What are you paying him?" he asked next. The foreman told him. "Double it!" ordered Bennett. "He's obviously doing more work than anyone else in the place."

2233   The owner of a fruit and vegetable store employed a boy whose duty it was to be on hand at 3 o'clock every morning to deal with the truck farmers. The proprietor did not arrive until opening time. For the sake of checking up he unexpectedly came to his shop one night, and at 3 o'clock the boy had not arrived; 3:05 and the boy had not yet come. A moment or so later the boy hastened in. "So," bellowed his employer, "Banker's hours!"

2234   Grover Whalen, during his administration of the World Fair, was known for his inaccessibility. The story is told of one man, who, after repeated rebuffs, stormed past the receptionist one morning. The astonished girl called out, "You can't speak to Mr. Whalen." The visitor paused in his advance long enough to say, "Young lady, I talk with God twice a day and He listens to me. I can certainly talk to Grover Whalen." He got his interview.

2235   Into the office of one of his subordinate executives came Edward H. Harriman, the railroad king. His unexpected entrance caught the man tilted back in his chair with his feet on his desk. The executive hastily straightened up, fearing a possible scene, and with visions of being fired on the spot. With relief he heard Harriman say, "I'm glad you take time to think."

RELATED SUBJECTS: *Employment and Work* 2226-2228; *Businessmen* 2236-2237; *Hiring and Firing* 2246-2249

BUSINESSMEN

2236   Soon after Colbert came into the management of the finances of France, he sent for the principal merchants of that kingdom; and in order to ingratiate himself with them, and to acquire their confidence, he asked what he could do for them. They unanimously answered:

"Pray, sir, do nothing! Laissez nous faire. Let us do for ourselves."

2237   Napoleon openly expressed his aversion to commerce and those engaged in it. When a deputation of businessmen came out from Antwerp to welcome him on his approach to that city, he met them with the words: "I don't like merchants! A merchant is a man who would sell his country for a shilling."

PARTNERSHIPS

2241   The father of the Marx Brothers was a tailor who operated, at one time, a business in Queens. Marx was a much liked and very nice man, but the suits he made did not always fit. He entered, therefore, into a partnership with a very skilful Negro tailor under the firm name of "Marx and Washington."

2242   "Oi, Sam," said one business man to his partner as they were about to enter the ocean at Coney Island on the afternoon they had decided to take off, "we forgot to close the safe!"

"What does it matter?" asked his partner. "We're both here, ain't we?"

RELATED SUBJECTS: *Businessmen* 2236-2237

HIRING AND FIRING

2246 The Irish foreman on the construction job was new to his post of dignity. One of his first acts was the discharge of one of his erstwhile fellow-workers. Asked why he had fired the man, he said, "I fired him not because I had anything against him, but because I had the authority."

2247 A personnel manager found himself confronted with a real problem. He had explained to the applicant that he could not place him because the firm was overstaffed. "That's all right," said the job seeker. "The little bit of work I would do wouldn't be noticed."

2248 So great has been the demand for typists in the many war bureaus of Washington, that the legend has come into existence that the following test is now the standard by which applicants for such positions are hired: the girl is shown into a room containing three objects, a washing machine, a typewriter and a machine-gun; if she can identify the typewriter, she's hired.

2249 Mark Twain was always impressed by the story of an industrious boy who became a millionaire. One of the things which remained in his mind was the fact that the boy had gotten his big chance by being noticed by a big business man while in the act of picking up a pin from the sidewalk.

When Mark Twain went to look for a job he deliberately went to the street in front of an office window and began to pick up some pins which he had surreptitiously strewn about. After a while he did succeed in attracting the attention of one of the men in the office. He came out into the street and, instead of the expected praise at such industry, Twain was astonished to hear the man say, "Here you, haven't you anything better to do than pick up pins in the street? You must be an utterly idle and worthless fool."

RELATED SUBJECTS: *Employment and Work* 2226-2228;

SALARIES

2251 A young man, employed at a very modest salary by a
bank, began conspicuously to lead a rather lavish life, dressing
flashily, buying a car, and otherwise giving evidence of sudden
wealth. Finally the personnel manager felt called upon to speak
about the matter and asked, "How is it that you, who are only
receiving a salary of $20 a week, can spend what must certainly
be $75 or more dollars a week." "Why, it's simple," the clerk re-
plied unabashed, "there are more than 200 employees here and
every payday I raffle off my salary at 50¢ a ticket."

2252 A group of newspapermen were talking about the various has-beens that they had known. One old-timer topped off
this session by telling them about a once prominent Chicago
newspaperman whom he had met just recently.

"I ran into him the other day and he looked fit to bust. I
asked him what the trouble was. 'Why,' says he, 'I've just been
offered a job in St. Joe, Mo. And am I insulted!'

" 'Insulted? Why should that be an insult?' I asked.

" 'It's the salary, it's the salary,' he shouts. 'They offered me
$12 a week.'

"Well I didn't want to insult him further by suggesting that
he hadn't earned even that much in a long time so I just said:
'Well, that's better than nothing.'

" 'The hell it is,' said the one time big shot. 'Why, I can
borrow more than that right here in Chicago.' "

2253 The colored sexton of a wealthy church had a very stylish mulatto wife. Finding his domestic income not quite equal
to his expenses, he decided to apply for an increase in salary.
So he wrote a letter to the committee in charge with this explanation at the close: "It's mighty hard to keep a sealskin wife
on a muskrat salary."

2254 At a meeting of the church board the minister announced that he had had a "call" to go to another parish.

After wishing him well in his new field, one of the deacons asked how much salary he was to get.

"Three hundred dollars," the minister replied.

"That's fine," said the deacon, "I don't blame you for going. But, Parson, don't you think you should be a bit more exact in your language. That isn't a 'call,' that's a 'raise.'"

RELATED SUBJECTS: *Employment and Work* 2226-2228; *Bosses and Executives* 2231-2235; *Working Conditions* 2256

SEE ALSO: *Quick Thinking* 472; *Shrewdness* 529; *Marriage* 888; *Singers* 1366; *Bosses* 2232; *Servants* 2279; *Farmers* 2312; *Soldiers* 2432

WORKING CONDITIONS

2256 A well-meaning employer desired to introduce a new spirit into his plant. He called his employees together, and said, "Whenever I come into the shop I want to see every man cheerfully at work. I am placing a box here and I should like anyone who has any suggestions as to how this may be brought about more efficiently to just put it in here."

The next day he saw a slip of paper in the box; took it out and looked at it. It said, "Take the rubber heels off your shoes."

RELATED SUBJECTS: *Employment and Work* 2226-2228; *Bosses and Executives* 2231-2235; *Hiring and Firing* 2246-2249; *Salaries* 2251-2254

SEE ALSO: *Kindness* 311; *Horses* 2288

MANUFACTURING

2261 Alfred O. Tate was riding one afternoon through central Jersey when Edison pointed from a ridge to a lovely valley through which a stream meandered.

"Tate," said Edison, "see that valley?"

"It's a beautiful valley," Tate replied.

"Well," said the inventor, "I'm going to make it more beautiful. I'm going to dot it with factories."

EFFICIENCY

2266 A New Yorker on one of the Ford Motor Company's tours of inspection for visitors lagged behind the party at one point and found himself alone with Henry Ford. Ford nodded to him; then, pointing to a completed automobile, said, "There are exactly 4719 parts in that car."

Greatly struck with Ford's grasp of affairs—and with his own —the visitor, talking subsequently with one of the company's engineers, asked him lightly if it were true that such-and-such a model had exactly 4719 parts. "I'm sure I don't know," the engineer said, "I can't think of a more useless piece of information."

2267 One of Chauncey Depew's stories:

Some years ago, a few days after I had sailed for Europe, a man went into my office and said:

"I want to see Chauncey Depew."

"He has gone to Europe," my colored porter told him.

"Well, I want to see his secretary."

"He has also gone to Europe."

"Then I want to see Cornelius Vanderbilt."

"He is in Newport."

"Oh, I guess I want to see W. K. Vanderbilt."

"He is also in Newport."

"You don't tell me. Well, may I see the first vice-president?"

"He is at Albany."

"How about the second vice-president?"

"He is out of town."

"Is the third vice-president in?"

"No, he is in Europe."

"Is the superintendent in?"

"No, he is up the road somewhere."

"How about the general passenger agent?"

"He has gone to Cape May."

"Who in thunder is running this road, anyway?"

"I guess it do be running itself."

2268 An assistant rushed into William S. Knudsen's office one day, very upset because a certain report was missing. How could they act?

"There are two kinds of reports," Knudsen said calmly. "One says you can't do it. The other says it has been done. The first kind is no good. The second kind you don't need."

2269 When Charles M. Schwab had not yet become a great man in his own right in the field of steel, he worked for Andrew Carnegie.

The little Scotchman taught him the hard lesson of the commercial world, that one day's laurels are of little use on the next.

"All records broken yesterday," Schwab wired to his chief.

In reply to which, Carnegie telegraphed, "What have you done today?"

2270 A sage bit of advice is contained in a rebuke delivered to no less a personage than William Jeffers, head of the Union Pacific Railway, by one of his employees.

Jeffers was traveling in his official car. At a certain stop, the engineer dismounted from his cab and came into the president's car and asked him a question concerning some details of their immediate route. Being preoccupied with some papers before him, Jeffers absently gave an obviously erroneous reply. Angrily the engineer snorted, "That doesn't make sense. Don't ever get so busy that you haven't time to think." Whereupon he turned and strode back to the cab.

RELATED SUBJECTS: *Diligence* 176-177; *Employment and Work* 2226-2228; *Bosses and Executives* 2231-2235; *Machinery* 2271-2272

SEE ALSO: *Procrastination* 461

MACHINERY

2271 The economic fallacy of unemployment arising from machinery is well illustrated by the two workmen who watched with awe the performance of a huge steam shovel which took up many tons of earth in one bite. Said one of them, "If it wasn't for that blasted scoop, five hundred of us might be working with shovels." "Yes," was the reply of the other, "and if it wasn't for our shovels, a million of us might be working with spoons."

2272 The value of specialized training is exemplified in this little episode.

The car simply would not run. The mechanic was called in, lifted the hood, reached inside, gave a twist of the wrist to a little mechanism—and all was well.

"What do I owe you?"

"One dollar and ten cents," said the mechanic.

"Great Heavens!" remonstrated the car owner. "It seems like an awful lot for just twisting a little gadget. How do you itemize it?"

"Well," said the mechanic, "for twisting the little gadget— 10¢. For knowing which little gadget to twist—$1.00."

RELATED SUBJECTS: *Inventors* 1126-1131; *Manufacturing* 2261; *Efficiency* 2266-2270

SERVANTS

2276 Lord St. John being some time ago in want of a servant, an Irishman offered his service, but being asked what countryman he was, answered: an Englishman.

"Where were you born?" said his Lordship.

"In Ireland an' plaze your worship," said the man.

"How then can you be an Englishman?" said his Lordship.

"My lord," replied the man, " 'sposen I was born in a stable, that's no razen I should be a horse."

2277 William K. Vanderbilt was fond of telling the following story on himself. He once observed to his valet that a towel which he was using did not seem clean. The man replied that the towels had been done by the regular laundry. "But," Vanderbilt said, "this one smells like dead fish."

"Well, sir," replied his man, "perhaps you have used it previously."

2278 Marshal Turenne had chosen for his valet the stoutest grenadier in the army, who frequently fought with another of his domestics, named Stephen. One day the marshal stooped down to look out of a window, with one of his hands upon his back. His valet, coming into the room, gave his master a furious blow upon his back. As the marshal turned, the valet fell upon his knees in despair, begging for mercy, for he "thought it was Stephen."

"Well," said the marshal, rubbing the pained part, "if it had been Stephen you ought not to have struck so hard," and he said no more on the subject.

2279 Mrs. William Dean Howells, wife of the noted novelist, had hired a girl to do the housework. Several weeks passed and from seeing her master constantly about the house, the girl received an erroneous impression.

"Excuse me, Mrs. Howells," she said to her mistress one day, "but I would like to say something."

"Well, Mary?"

The girl blushed and fumbled with her apron: "Well, you pay me four dollars a week——"

"I really can't pay you any more," interrupted Mrs. Howells apologetically.

"It's not that," hastily answered the girl, "but I am willing to take three till Mr. Howells lands a job."

2280 The hostess had the additional problem of breaking in a new maid just before a big party. She cautioned, winding up her instructions about dress, "Don't wear any jewelry."

"I don't have any, ma'am," answered the maid, "but thanks for the warning."

2281 A married couple, returning from Europe, became interested in an attractive red-cheeked Finnish girl in the steerage. They found that she was coming to America to look for work and decided to offer employment. "Can you cook?" they asked. "No," said the girl, "I can't cook. My mother always did the cooking."

"Well," they said, "then you can do the housework."

"No," said she, "I don't know how. My oldest sister always did the housework."

"Well, then we could let you take care of the children."

"No, I couldn't do that. My youngest sister always took care of the children."

"Well can you do the sewing?"

"No," said the girl, "my aunt always did the sewing."

"What can you do?" cried the despairing couple.

The girl was quite bright and cheerful as she volunteered, "I can milk reindeer."

2282 Entering the kitchen one evening the lady of the house was amazed to see her cook, who was going home for the night, packing some empty grapefruit hulls into her black bag. Completely mystified at this procedure and curious to find out the reason for it she asked, "Mandy, why in the world do you take the trouble to carry home those empty grapefruits?"

"Well, ma'am, Ah admit they ain't any use to me—but they sure does make my garbage look stylish."

2283 The Count de Mirabeau, brother of the celebrated orator, one morning called his valet to him: "You are faithful," said he, "you are zealous; in short—I am satisfied with your services, but I give you your dismissal."

"On what account?" naturally inquired the valet.

"Nothwithstanding our agreement, you get drunk on the same days as I do," said Mirabeau.

"It is not my fault," replied the valet, "you get drunk every day."

RELATED SUBJECTS: *Banquets and Dinners* 751-753; *Home Life* 996-1001; *Porters* 1806; *Employment and Work* 2226-2228; *Salaries* 2251-2254; *Working Conditions* 2256; *Waiters* 2306-2308

SEE ALSO: *Old Maids* 873; *Husband* 917; *Wife* 930; *Scientists* 1122; *Superstition* 1632; *Funerals* 1777; *Equality* 2046

PROPERTY

SEE ALSO: *Cheerfulness* 143; *Presidents* 1937; *Dictators* 2002

HORSES

2286 Abraham Lincoln, after a friendly contest of wits on the subject of horses, agreed to a horse trade with a certain judge, sealing the bargain by saying:

"Well, look here, Judge! I'll tell you what I'll do. I'll make a horse trade with you, only it must be upon these stipulations: neither party shall see the other's horse until it is produced here in the courtyard of the hotel and both parties must trade horses. If either party backs out of the agreement, he does so under a forfeiture of twenty-five dollars."

It was agreed. Lincoln and the judge parted to find their animals. The news of the trade got around and quite a crowd collected to see the fun. Great was the laughter when the judge appeared with an incredible looking animal; skinny, blind and scarcely able to walk. But the laughter turned to uproarious shouts when Lincoln strode upon the scene with a carpenter's saw-horse on his shoulders. Putting the saw-horse down, Lincoln surveyed the scene for a moment and, spying the judge's horse, said with a note of disgust, "Well, Judge, this is the first time I ever got the worst of it in a horse trade."

2287 Henry Ward Beecher, the famous preacher, was once contemplating buying a horse. After looking over many of them, the owner of the stables finally burst out into praise of one particularly fine animal.

"Now here's a horse that's really sound. He can go any gait. He stands without hitching; works any place you put him; goes when you want him to and stops the minute you say 'Whoa.' He is perfectly gentle, yet full of spirits. He has no bad traits, doesn't kick, doesn't bite. Comes when you call him and doesn't run off when he sees something strange."

With a wistful look in his eye, Mr. Beecher sighed, "If only that horse were a member of my church."

2288 Two staunch friends of a lifetime, Moe and Abe, were walking down the street. They discussed every phase of life together from politics to personal affairs. They were discussing the hereafter and made one of those agreements that whichever should die first should communicate with the other if possible.

Little more than a year later Abe passed away. Moe was downcast and had all but forgotten their agreement. It chanced that he was passing down the street one day when a sorrowful voice suddenly said, "Moe, Moe." He paused and looked around. There was no one in sight. He thought it must have been an illusion. He was about to move on when once again the voice cried, "Moe." He looked about once more. There was no living thing in sight except a horse hitched to an ice wagon.

He stared at the animal and the horse, to his astonishment, said, "Yes, Moe, it's me—Abe."

"Abe," cried Moe in horror, "a horse you come back?"

"Yes, Moe."

"But, Abe, what kind of a life is it? How are they treating you?"

"Oi, it's terrible," said the horse. "All day long pulling a heavy wagon in the hot sun and the driver he beats me. He doesn't give me water."

"This is terrible," said Moe, "I'll speak to the man. I'll tell him you're my friend. He shouldn't treat you so."

"Moe, Moe," said the horse in great alarm, "don't say nothing to him, please! He finds out I can talk, he'll make me yell 'Ice!'"

RELATED SUBJECTS: *Horse Racing* 1871-1872; *Farmers and Farming* 2311-2313

SEE ALSO: *Zanies* 643; *Civilians in War* 2346; *Officers* 2415; *Marches* 2456; *Hanging* 2566

PARROTS

2291   Pat was wandering around a pet shop one day. Coming to a cage which housed a large, green parrot, he put his hand in to pet it. The bird turned quickly and cackled, "Hello. Hello. Who are you?"

Startled, Pat drew back. Hastily he tipped his hat and said, "Excuse me, sor, I thought ye was a burrd."

2292   A certain old maid had a parrot which swore vigorously. She was used to the bird, but was in the habit of covering its cage every Sunday in order that it might remain silent on that day. It chanced on a Monday morning, after the cover had been removed, that the old lady saw the minister come up the walk to pay a call. Hastily she replaced the cover on the cage; hearing the parrot observe as she moved towards the door, "This has been a damn short week!"

2293   In the days of luxurious trans-Atlantic travel, shipboard entertainments frequently drew upon the professional talents to be found in the passenger list. On one occasion, the program followed up the performance of a remarkable parrot with a brief demonstration by a traveling magician. The parrot's cage had been shoved to one side of the stage when the magician came on for his act. Holding up a pack of cards, the man covered it with a handkerchief, waved his wand, and the cards disappeared. The parrot, looking on from the wings, cocked its head to one side. Next the magician took a book, covered it with a scarf, waved his wand, and the book disappeared. The parrot meditatively scratched its head with its claw. Taking a cloak, the magician threw it over a chair, waved his wand, and the chair disappeared. The parrot hopped up and down on its perch in the growing excitement. In the next moment the ship was struck by a submerged iceberg; split in two, the lights were extinguished, there were screams and cries, and shortly thereafter nothing was left on the black night sea save the parrot clinging to a piece of driftwood, bobbing up and down on the waters. The bird looked about at the dreary scene for a moment, and then said, "Marvelous! Marvelous!"

HOTELS AND RESTAURANTS

2296 A man walked into a hotel and asked for a room.
"On the American Plan or the Japanese Plan?" asked the clerk.
"What's the difference?"
"The American Plan is with cross ventilation. The Japanese Plan is with double-cross ventilation."

2297 A certain cafeteria in New York City caused much pleasure to many of its patrons by prominently displaying on its walls, the motto, "Courteous and Efficient Self-Service."

2298 A certain lodging-house in the south of Italy had the Russian writer Maxim Gorky as its guest some years ago. He complained to the landlady "the morning after the night before" that his bed was infested by vermin. The landlady indignantly remonstrated: "No, sir, we haven't one single bug in the house."
"No, madam," Gorky agreed amiably, "they are all married and have large families too."

2299 A game of poker at Delmonico's had lasted well into the night when one of the party, the late Colonel John R. Fellows, ordered a plate of sandwiches. The familiar dainty triangle variety was served and disappeared instantly. A hungry shout went up for more.

"More sandwiches, waiter," said Fellows.

"Yes, sir! How many, sir?" returned the waiter.

"Well," said Fellows, with a calculating air, "judging by the size of your sandwiches and the size of this bill, I should say about $2,000 worth."

2300   Mr. Disraeli said he did not remember a certain inn, upon which the owner assured him that he must be mistaken. "You must remember the house, sir; there was a very handsome bar-maid there—monstrous fine gal—you must have been in the King's Arms, sir."

"Perhaps," said Disraeli, "if I had been in her arms I might have remembered it."

2301   For a laconic philosophy it is hard to match the case of the man who checked into a hotel in a small Mid-Western city and went up to his room. Later in the evening he came down, his suitcase in his hand, and checked out.

"What's the trouble, sir?" asked the clerk, slightly puzzled. "Don't you find the room satisfactory?"

"The room is all right," said the man, "except for one thing. It's on fire."

2302   In a gloomy and depressed state Eugene Field wandered into a restaurant. A busy waiter hastened up and reeled off at high speed a long line of dishes on the present menu. Field gazed up in melancholy and said, "Friend, I want none of these things. All I want is an orange and a few kind words."

RELATED SUBJECTS: *Eating* 6-23; *Banquets and Dinners* 751-753; *Businessmen* 2236-2237; *Waiters* 2306-2308

SEE ALSO: *Eating* 17, 23; *Absent-Mindedness* 83; *Eccentricity* 196; *Prejudice* 448; *Shrewdness* 531; *Fatness* 684; *Authors* 1169; *Instrumentalists* 1354; *Politics* 1899; *Chiseling* 2121

WAITERS

2306   Robert Louis Stevenson, in the days of his residence in San Francisco, took a friend to a restaurant in which, he said, the waiters would never admit that there was anything lacking from the bill of fare. "They'll take your order for a slice of the moon," said he, "and go away as if to fetch it, and come back to tell you they're just out of it."

The two men seated themselves and the waiter came up. "A double order of broiled Behemoth," said Stevenson.

"Will you have it rare or well done?" asked the waiter.

"Rare," said Stevenson.

In a few moments, the waiter had returned: "I'm very sorry, sir," he began . . .

"What!" interrupted Stevenson in a tone of annoyance. "No more Behemoth?"

"Oh, no, sir," said the waiter hastily, then lowering his voice. "I have some more, sir," he explained, "but the truth is I would not bring it to you as it is not quite fresh."

2307 Bishop Brewster of Connecticut, while visiting some friends, tucked his napkin in his collar to avoid the juice of grapefruit at breakfast. He laughed as he did so, and said it reminded him of a man he knew who rushed into a restaurant and, seating himself at a table, proceeded to tuck his napkin under his chin. He called a waiter and said, "Can I get lunch here?"

"Yes," replied the waiter in a dignified manner, "but not a shampoo."

2308 Into a restaurant walked a wag in search of breakfast. The Negro girl who was waiting upon the tables came forward to take his order.

"I want ham and eggs," said the gentleman, "but I want the eggs eliminated."

"Yes, sir," said the waitress disappearing into the kitchen.

She was back again in due time with a plate of ham with regulation fried eggs.

"Waitress," said the customer, "I told you I wanted the eggs eliminated."

"Yassuh, boss," she said, "I'se sorry, but de truf is dat no-count cook has done drapped de eliminator and busted de handle right off."

RELATED SUBJECTS: *Eating* 6-23; *Banquets and Dinners* 751-753; *Servants* 2276-2283; *Hotels and Restaurants* 2296-2302

SEE ALSO: *Eating* 13; *Absent-Mindedness* 85; *Stealing* 2584

FARMERS AND FARMING

2311 "You have no complaint," a city man said to a farmer, "you have your own milk, butter, eggs, meat and vegetables. With enough to eat and a place to sleep what more do you want?"

"Well," said the farmer, "you come around a few months from now and you'll see the fattest, sleekest, nakedest farmer you ever saw."

2312 Ranches in some parts of the West are by no means always a paying proposition. At such a place a traveler stopped, seeking a night's lodging. Discussing with his host hard times in general, the stranger asked, "How in the world do you manage to make enough on this place to run it?" His host pointed toward his hired man at the far end of the table.

"You see that feller. Well, he works for me and I can't pay him. In two more years he gits the ranch. Then I'm goin' to work for him till I git it back!"

2313 The Department of Agriculture is the constant recipient of queries and pleas for advice from householders with small lawns and gardens as well as from farmers. The story is told about the man who had fought a losing battle against dandelions on his lawns. He wrote to the Department complaining how much he loved his lawn and begging them to help him save it. In due course, the Department of Agriculture replied with the practical suggestion that he learn to love the dandelions too.

RELATED SUBJECTS: *Employment and Work* 2226-2228; *Horses* 2286-2288

SEE ALSO: *Diligence* 176; *Endurance* 216; *Gratitude* 265; *Home Life* 997; *Hospitality* 1007; *Audiences* 1437; *Billiards* 1827; *Chiseling* 2128; *Loans* 2161

WAR AND THE MILITARY

WAR

2316 Jean Gabin, the film-actor, upon his arrival in New York recently, was asked what was the French attitude toward the British.

"We are both pro- and anti-British," he said. "Those who are pro-British say each night in their prayers, 'Please, God, let the gallant British win quickly.' Those who are anti-British say each night in their prayers, 'Please, God, let the dirty British win right away.'"

2317 According to one story, Marshal Foch's chauffeur was constantly besieged by journalists and plain information-seekers with the question, "When is the war going to end? What do you hear?"

The chauffeur put off his questioners, saying, "As soon as I hear the Marshal say anything, I will tell you." At last, he said, "The Marshal spoke today."

"Well," they demanded, "what did he say?"

"He said, 'Well, Pierre, what do you think? When is the war going to end?'"

2318 Mr. Pitt, speaking in the House of Commons of the glorious war preceding that in which England lost the colonies called it "The last war." Several members cried out: "The last but one!" He took no notice, and soon, after repeating the mistake, was interrupted by a general cry of "The last war but one!"

"I mean, sir," said Pitt, turning to the speaker, and raising his voice, "I mean, the last war that Britons would wish to remember."

2319 Bronislaw Malinowski says, "I once talked to an old cannibal who, hearing of the Great War raging then in Europe, was most curious to know how we Europeans managed to eat such enormous quantities of human flesh. When I told him that Europeans do not eat their slain foes, he looked at me in shocked horror and asked what sort of barbarians we were, to kill without any real object."

2320 In 1918 Premier Georges Clemenceau of France made the observation, "War is too important to leave to the Generals."

2321 In Italy it is whispered that a new technique for the fairy tale has come into existence. The old formula began, "Once upon a time." Now it begins, "The General Headquarters of the Armed Forces communicates."

2322 The Italians say among themselves, "In the First World War we prepared, fought, and made the Armistice. This time we made the Armistice (with France), fought, and now we are preparing."

2323 Lillah McCarthy went to stay with H. G. Wells in Essex. England also was now at war (1914).

"His face, generally so mobile, had become rigid and the playful look stern. I tried to distract him: 'No, Lillah,' he said, 'no, I can't get away from the war. The world is falling to pieces. I can do nothing but think, think.'"

CIVIL WAR

2326 During nullification in South Carolina, after President Jackson's proclamation, the governor of Virginia sent a request to the President, in case it became necessary to send United States troops down South, not to send them through that state. If he did they would have to pass over the Governor's dead body.

The President received the message and replied: "If it becomes necessary for the United States troops to go to South Carolina, I, as commander-in-chief of the army, will be at their

head. I will march them by the shortest route. They may pass
through Virginia; but if the governor makes it necessary to pass
over his dead body, it will be found that I will have previously
taken off both ears."

2327 Richmond fell. Lincoln himself entered the city on foot,
accompanied only by a few officers and a squad of sailors who
had rowed him ashore from the flotilla in the James River, a
Negro picked up on the way serving as a guide. Never had the
world seen a more modest conqueror and a less characteristic
triumphal procession—no army with banners and drums, only
a throng of those who had been slaves hastily run together, es-
corting the victorious chief into the capital of the vanquished
foe. We are told that they pressed around him, kissed his hands
and his garments and shouted and danced with joy, while tears
ran down the President's care-furrowed cheeks.

2328 Near the end of the Civil War, when the Confederate
forces were falling back on Richmond, an old Negro asked by
his mistress for encouraging news, replied:
  "Well, missy, due to de lie of de land where dey's fightin',
dem Yankees is retreatin' forward, while we is advancin' backwards."

2329 The prayer of a Unitarian preacher in Massachusetts
during the Civil War:
  "Oh, God, we pray thee to bless the rebels. Bless their hearts
with sincere repentance. Bless their armies with defeat. Bless
their social condition by emancipation."

  RELATED SUBJECTS: *Revolutions* 2061-2064; *War* 2316-
  2323

CIVILIANS IN WAR

2331 Louis Fischer, editor and correspondent, tells the story
that at a dinner-party in England, the guests were discussing
the fact that cigarettes were worse since the War started and
the transportation, food, and indeed everything was worse.
  "Only the people are better," someone observed.

2332 During a public "reception," a farmer from one of the
border counties of Virginia told President Lincoln, that the

Union soldiers, in passing his farm, had helped themselves not only to hay, but to his horse, and he hoped the President would urge the proper officer to consider his claim immediately.

Mr. Lincoln said that this reminded him of an old acquaintance of his, "Jack" Chase, a lumberman on the Illinois, a steady, sober man and the best raftsman on the river. It was quite a trick to take the logs over the rapids; but he was skilful with a raft and always kept her straight in the channel. Finally a steamer was put on, and Jack was made captain of her. He always used to take the wheel, going through the rapids. One day, when the boat was plunging and wallowing along the boiling current, and Jack's utmost vigilance was being exercised to keep her in the narrow channel, a boy pulled his coat-tail and hailed him with:

"Say, Mr. Captain! I wish you would stop your boat a minute —I've lost my apple overboard!"

2333 President Lincoln was bothered to death by those persons who boisterously demanded that the War be pushed vigorously; also, those who shouted their advice and opinions into his weary ears, but who never suggested anything practical. These fellows were not in the army, nor did they ever take any interest, in a personal way, in military affairs, except when engaged in dodging drafts.

"That reminds me," remarked Mr. Lincoln one day, "of a farmer who lost his way on the Western frontier. Night came on, and the embarrassments of his position were increased by a furious tempest which suddenly burst upon him. To add to his discomfort, his horse had given out, leaving him exposed to all the dangers of the pitiless storm.

"The peals of thunder were terrific, the frequent flashes of lightning afforded the only guide on the road as he resolutely trudged onward, leading his jaded steed. The earth seemed fairly to tremble beneath him in the war of elements. One bolt threw him suddenly upon his knees.

"Our traveler was not a prayerful man, but finding himself involuntarily brought to an attitude of devotion, he addressed himself to the Throne of Grace in the following prayer for his deliverance:

"'O God! hear my prayer this time, for Thou knowest it is not often that I call upon Thee. And, O Lord! if it is all the same to Thee, give us a little more light and a little less noise.'

"I wish," the President said, sadly, "there was a stronger disposition manifested on the part of our civilian warriors to unite in suppressing the rebellion, and a little less noise as to how and by whom the chief executive office shall be administered."

2334   At a particularly loud clap of thunder, a lady walking along a London street involuntarily and visibly started. "It's all right, Lidy," said a passing urchin.

"It ain't 'itler, it's Gawd."

2335   In occupied France a Frenchman, walking down the street in Paris, saw another Frenchman in altercation with a Storm Trooper. The Frenchman knocked the Trooper down and, as he got up again, the second Frenchman rushed over, joined the fray and knocked him down a second time. Reinforcements suddenly arrived and the two Frenchmen were overpowered and taken before a Military Judge. The first culprit explained the nature of his quarrel and the reason for his blow.

"But why," asked the judge of the second man, "did you get into this? It was no quarrel of yours."

"I know," he replied, "but when I saw him knock him down, for a moment I thought it was the beginning."

2336   When the disasters of the Franco-Prussian War were falling thickly, and the iron band was closing around Paris, word came that Victor Hugo was coming to the city. He came at the very moment that the investment was complete, with the last train, the last breath of free air. On the way he had seen the Germans, seen villages burned with petroleum, and he came to imprison himself in Paris. A memorable ovation was given him by the people, and they never forgot his voluntary sharing of their sufferings.

2337   Harvey Klemmer tells this story: "Just before leaving England, I met a Cockney who had been buried beneath the ruins of his fish-and-chip shop. Fish-and-chips are not my idea of the proper food for building morale. However, there was nothing wrong with the morale of this chap. When the rescue workers dug him out of the remains of his little business— which by now consisted of a potpourri of fish, fat, bricks and plaster—he dusted himself off, drew himself up to his full five feet seven and spat into the wreckage.

" 'To 'ell with 'itler.' "

2338 An old watchman in a London warehouse was a bit perturbed because his son wouldn't take cover in the air raids. He went into the street and gave the lad a cuff on the ear.

"Get the hell inside," he said, "and let that shrapnel fall down."

2339 At the outbreak of the Franco-Prussian War one patriotic Parisian cabman, after driving a Prussian attaché to the station to join his regiment, refused to take any fare. "A man does not pay for being driven to his own funeral. So, adieu, monsieur."

2340 One night, at the beginning of the World War, Picasso and Gertrude Stein were taking a walk when they saw a camouflaged truck for the first time. He was amazed by its resemblance to cubist art, and, in the tone of a man who has just been plagiarized, said, "Why, it is we who invented that!" Later, when a new field uniform for the French army was being discussed, he told Cocteau: "If they want to make an army invisible at a distance, all they have to do is dress the men as harlequins."

2341 The many persons who took First Aid courses in World War II will be interested in the case of an inquisitive elderly lady who bent solicitously over a wounded soldier whose head was swathed with bandages. "Are you wounded in the head, my boy?" she asked.

"No, ma'am," said the victim feebly, "I was shot in the foot and the bandages slipped up."

2342 Harvey Klemmer tells of how, "One of the London wardens, a slim, elderly man, directed the work of removing the bodies.

" 'They got my house last night,' he said simply.

"I heard from one of the other wardens that, while this man was working on a job, someone came running to tell him his own house, a few streets away, had been hit. The house and all of his belongings had been destroyed; his wife and children, fortunately, had gone to a nearby shelter. I asked the man what he would do if he could lay his hands on the airman who had dropped the bomb.

"He gulped a couple of times and I waited eagerly to hear what sort of punishment he would be prepared to mete out.

" 'Well,' he said slowly, 'I don't think I would give him a cup of tea.'

"That is the nearest thing to recrimination I have heard in England."

2343 An American, who had gone to England to carry out certain duties in connection with the War, was wearied by a seemingly interminable season of fog and rain. One day he glanced out of his window at the barrage balloons which could be seen mistily at their cable ends in the sky and asked, "Why don't they just cut the ropes on those things and let the place sink!"

2344 In Amsterdam, Nazi officers walking through the streets became conscious that many of the Dutch were hailing one another as they passed with the salute, "Heil, Rembrandt!" which they suspected to be a deeply subversive travesty of the required, "Heil, Hitler."

"Why do you say this?" demanded a German officer, accosting a Netherlander.

"You see," replied the man blandly, "we too have a great painter."

2345 During the First World War, the Germans entered and occupied a small Belgian town. Seeking to keep the occupants of the town under control, an officer of the German army called all the citizens to the town hall and insisted that they all take the oath of allegiance to the German Emperor.

One particularly truculent and obstinate inhabitant refused to be intimidated, and kept boasting of the brave defense the Belgians put up against the superior German force.

Finally, the German officer lost all patience:

"Take this oath of allegiance or you'll be shot!"

Faced with this alternative, the man gave in and took the oath.

"That's the spirit," said the German, "now you may come and go as you please. You are one of us."

With a sly grin on his face, the Belgian turned and said, "Say, didn't those Belgians give us a hell of a fight?"

2346 During the American Revolution, the soldiers sometimes had great difficulty getting horses. An officer was sent out to make the rounds in the Virginia countryside and confiscate all the horses he saw.

He came up to a fine, old mansion and, seeing a plow team down in the field, rang the bell and asked to see the mistress.

"Madam," he said to the dignified elderly woman who received him in the fine, old drawing-room, "I have come to claim your horses in the name of the government."

"Sir," was the answer, "you cannot have them. I need them for the spring plowing."

"I am sorry, madam. Those are the orders of my chief."

"And who is your chief?" she demanded.

"General George Washington, commander-in-chief of the American army."

"You go back and tell General George Washington that his mother says he cannot have her horses," replied the woman, a smile softening her hitherto stern features.

> RELATED SUBJECTS: *Courage* 151-153; *Patriotism* 396-407; *Censors* 2351-2355; *Rationing* 2356-2358; *Refugees* 2361
>
> SEE ALSO: *Patriotism* 398; *Hiring* 2248; *War* 2320

CENSORS

2351 According to John Gunther, an American journalist in Japan wrote to a friend and added the note, "Don't know if this will ever arrive because the Japanese censor may open it." A few days afterward, he received a note from the Japanese post office, saying, "The statement in your letter is not correct. We do not open letters."

2352 A young lady received a letter from her soldier sweetheart from "Somewhere in the Pacific Area." Upon opening the envelope she found, instead of a letter, a thin strip of paper bearing the brief message, "Your boy friend still loves you but he talks too much, (signed) Censor."

2353 The book of Helvetius "De l'Esprit" and Voltaire's poem of "La Pucelle d'Orleans" were prohibited in Switzerland at the same time. A magistrate of Berne, after a strict search for these two works, wrote the Senate: "We have not found in the whole province either wit or maid."

2354 The French Ambassador to Spain complimented Cervantes on the great reputation he had acquired by his "Don Quixote." Cervantes whispered in his ear, "Had it not been for the Inquisition, I should have made my book much more interesting."

2355 A grim lesson for the exponents of bigoted censorship is contained in the characteristic American-press-agent-story of how the famous picture "September Morn" was popularized.

An art dealer, stuck with a formidable surplus of this lithograph of a nude girl, consulted a well-known press agent, Harry Reichenbach. Reichenbach had many of the pictures placed in the shop window. He then hired a crowd of small children and grouped them around the front of the store. Next, he phoned to Anthony Comstock and hysterically demanded that he come and witness the sordid exhibition of vice and corruption. Comstock came and immediately opened one of his inimitable litigations. In consequence of the publicity resulting from this it might be said that Comstock "sold" 7,000,000 copies of this picture.

> RELATED SUBJECTS: *Prohibitions and Restrictions* 1641-1642; *Civilians in War* 2331-2346; *Laws* 2596-2599

> SEE ALSO: *Authors* 1199; *Painting* 1270

RATIONING

2356 A motorist driving through the back country of Vermont stopped at a little gas station and asked for a tankful. He remarked casually to the proprietor, "I guess you fellows are all pretty sore at Leon Henderson?" "Leon Henderson?" said the old timer. "Who's he?" The motorist, looking at him for a moment and then thinking quickly said, "Do you sell tires?" "Sure," the proprietor said, "you want some?" The motorist said, "I'll take four," paid his money and drove hastily away thanking Providence.

2357 A small boy, keenly aware of the transportation problems created by rationing, was looking at a book of Bible illustrations. One of these depicted the Prophet Elijah ascending to Heaven in a chariot of fire. He noted the halo above the

Prophet's head and cried, "Oh, Mother! Look, he's carrying an extra tire!"

2358 "Does anyone here," asked the teacher of the Night School for Adult Education, administering a vocabulary test, "know the meaning of ratiocination?"

"I know," said the young stenographer in the class. "It's what they're doing to sugar."

> RELATED SUBJECTS: *Patriotism* 396-407; *Civilians in War* 2331-2346; *Laws* 2596-2599

REFUGEES

2361 Many and devious have been the devices employed by refugees seeking to escape from occupied France. It is reported from hitherto unreliable sources, that such a man threw himself upon the mercy of the proprietor of a small traveling menagerie. "I am afraid to disguise you as an employee," said the man. "You might be discovered too easily. It happens that our gorilla died a little over a week ago and we preserved his hide, thinking that we might recoup the loss by having it stuffed some day. If you want to put it on, you can travel with us in the cage."

Faced by his desperate need, the refugee did so. And whenever the menagerie was on exhibition he put on as good a show as he could manage.

One night when no one was around, he was horror struck to discover that the bars had become loosened between his own and the adjoining cage on the same truck. One of them had fallen out, and through the opening came his neighbor, the lion. As the animal slunk toward him the "gorilla" cringed in the corner and began to cry, "Help! Help!" "Shut up, you damn fool!" growled the lion, "you aren't the only refugee."

> RELATED SUBJECTS: *Endurance* 216; *Poverty* 2201-2211; *Civilians in War* 2331-2346

PRISONERS

2366 Some of the Nazi airmen invite mistreatment by their belligerent attitude. There is the case of a wounded Nazi airman who panned English doctors, bemoaning the fact that he had no good German doctors to fix him up. In the middle of his tirade he had the misfortune to faint.

"Don't worry," the doctors told him when he came to. "You'll be all right. The chances are that you will have better manners, too, now that you've got a couple of pints of good Jewish blood in you."

RELATED SUBJECTS: *War* 2316-2323; *Battles* 2371-2385; *Soldiers and Sailors* 2430-2437

BATTLES

2371 During the Revolutionary War, an Irishman in the American service, having come by surprise on a small party of Hessians who were foraging, seized their arms which they had laid aside. He then presented his musket, and with threats drove them before him into the American camp, where the singularity of the exploit occasioning some wonder, he was brought with his prisoners before General Washington who asked him how he had taken them.

"By God, general," said he, "I surrounded them."

2372 General Winfield Scott said that during the War of 1812, before an action began between the two opposing armies, it was customary for the respective commanders to ride forward accompanied by their staffs, and formally salute each other. Each then returned to his own lines, and the battle opened.

This custom is well illustrated by the anecdote told by Fournier:

"Lord Hay at the Battle of Fontenay, 1745, called out: 'Gentlemen of the French Guard, fire first.'

"To which the Comte d'Auteroches replied:

" 'Monsieur, we never fire first; please to fire yourselves.' "

2373 A Confederate soldier was seen by General Lee, who met him retiring from the front with what Lee considered unbecoming haste. Lee said to him, "Why don't you go back to the front? That's the place where a soldier should be when a battle is going on."

The reply was, "General, I have been there, and I give you

my word of honor it is not a place where any self-respecting man would care to be."

2374   When General O'Kelly was introduced to Louis XVI soon after the Battle of Fontenay, his Majesty observed that Clare's regiment behaved very well in that engagement. "Sure," said the general, "they behaved well, it is true—many of them were wounded, but my regiment behaved better for we were all killed."

2375   This is Winston Churchill's story.
   "All was excitement and hustle at Abassiyeh Barracks (Cairo). Two squadrons of the 21st Lancers had already started up the Nile. The other two were to leave the next morning. Altogether seven additional officers from other cavalry regiments had been attached to the 21st to bring them up to full war-strength. . . . A troop had been reserved for me in one of the leading squadrons. But the delay and uncertainties about my coming had given this to another. Second Lieutenant Robert Grenfell had succeeded in obtaining this vacancy. He had gone off in the highest spirits. At the base everyone believed that we should be too late for the battle. Perhaps the first two squadrons might get up in time, but no one could tell. 'Fancy how lucky I am,' wrote Grenfell to his family. 'Here I have got the troop that would have been Winston's, and we are to be the first to start.' Chance is unceasingly at work in our lives, but we cannot always see its workings sharply and clearly defined. As it turned out, this troop was practically cut to pieces in the charge which the regiment made in the battle of September 2, and its brave young leader was killed."

2376   Almost everybody thought that Marshal Joffre had won the first battle of the Marne, but some refused to agree. One day a newspaperman appealed to Joffre: "Will you tell me who did win the battle of the Marne?"
   "I can't answer that," said the Marshal. "But I can tell you that if the battle of the Marne had been lost the blame would have been on me."

2377   It is notorious (says Marmontel in his incomparable biography) that with much nobleness and dignity of soul, Marshal Saxe was fond of mirth and jollity. By taste, as well as by system, he loved merriment in his armies, stating that the

French never did so well as when they were led on gayly, and what they most feared in war, was weary inactivity. He had always a comic opera in his camp. It was at the theatre that he gave the order of battle: and on these occasions, the principal actress used to come forward and say—"Gentlemen, tomorrow there will be no play on account of the battle the Marshal gives; after tomorrow the 'Cock of the Village, with the Merry Intrigues, etc.'"

2378 When Sir John Steel, the sculptor, had the Duke of Wellington sitting for a statue, he wanted to get him to look warlike. All his efforts were in vain, however, for Wellington seemed, judging by his face, never to have heard of Waterloo or Talavera.

At last Sir John lost patience, somewhat.

"As I am going to make the statue of Your Grace," he said, "can you not tell me what you were doing before, say, the battle of Salamanca? Were you not galloping about the fields, cheering on your men to deeds of valor by word and action?"

"Bah!" said the Duke scornfully. "If you really want to model me as I was on the morning of Salamanca, then do me crawling along a ditch on my stomach, with a telescope in my hand."

2379 One day Chauncey Depew met a soldier who had been wounded in the face. He was a Union Man and Depew asked him in which battle he had been injured.

"In the last battle of Bull Run, sir," he replied.

"But how could you get hit in the face at Bull Run?"

"Well, sir," said the man, half apologetically, "after I had run a mile or two I got careless and looked back."

2380 The Duke of Anjou, afterwards Henri III, besieged Rochelle, the bulwark of the Calvinists. Near the counterscarp was a mill which the besieged had no time to fortify. They threw in a handful of troops in the day, and at night commonly withdrew this small garrison, leaving behind only one man. The Duke made the necessary dispositions for carrying this post; and advanced by moonlight, with a small detachment and two culverins.

A single soldier had the guard this night and upon him the whole defence depended. This brave man remained firm and undismayed. He kept up, alone, a brisk fire upon the assailants; and varying continually the tones of his voice, he made them suppose that the besieged were in great numbers. From the ramparts of the town they called out to encourage this surprising commandant. They exhorted the garrison to remain firm, and assured them of immediate success; till at length the soldier, seeing his little post upon the point of being carried, asked quarter for himself and comrades which was instantly granted. He then laid down his arms, and revealed the whole garrison in his own person.

2381   The Duke of Marlborough, observing a soldier leaning pensively on the butt of his firelock, just after the battle of Blenheim, accosted him thus:

"Why so sad, my friend, after so glorious a victory?"

"It may be glorious, your grace, but I am thinking that all the blood I have spilt this day has only earned me fourpence."

2382   The Swiss always will honor the memory of their national hero Arnold von Winkelried. When at the battle of Sempach in 1397 he saw that his countrymen could not attack the Austrians because the latter, being completely armed and dismounted to form closed ranks, presented an iron front of lances and pikes, he addressed them as follows:

"Friends, I am going to lay down my life to procure you victory. All I have to recommend to you is to provide for my family. Follow me and imitate my example." With these words he arranged them in the form of a triangle, of which he himself occupied the point, and in this manner advanced towards the enemy. When close up to them, he seized as many of the pikes as he could lay hold of, and then falling on the ground, opened to those who followed him a way for piercing into this thick battalion. The Austrians, once broken, were defeated. The weight of their arms proved fatal to them.

2383   After a long period of inactivity among the Northern armies, a telegram came to President Lincoln informing him that General Burnside was believed to be in great peril at Cumberland Gap and that much firing had been heard in the vicinity of Knoxville. Great was the surprise of those about him when Lincoln calmly remarked that he was glad of it.

Seeing the astonishment in their faces, Lincoln said:

"Well, you see, it reminds me of Mistress Sallie Ward, a neighbor of mine, who had a very large family. Occasionally one of her numerous progeny would be heard crying in some out-of-the-way place, upon which Mrs. Ward would exclaim, 'There's one of my children not dead yet.' "

2384 A General rides forward. "I have the honor, your Imperial Highness, to announce a great victory."

"Very well. Go and congratulate your troops."

"There are none left."

2385 A Turkish pasha is surveying the field with his glass. An aide-de-camp rides up. "All our artillery has been captured."

The pasha strokes his beard philosophically and says, "Fortunately it was not paid for."

> RELATED SUBJECTS: *Courage* 151-153; *Cowardice* 156-160; *Death* 1746-1749; *War* 2316-2323; *Prisoners* 2366; *Strategy* 2386-2393; *Army and Navy* 2401-2404; *Officers* 2406-2427; *Soldiers and Sailors* 2430-2437

> SEE ALSO: *Cowardice* 156, 159; *Exaggeration* 226; *Officers* 2423, 2426, 2427

STRATEGY

2386 Toward the end of the Civil War, in 1865, fears were felt by the North that Johnson might break through to join General Lee and thereby crush the Northern Armies under Grant. A Congressman, representing the anxious House, was sent to discuss the matter with the President, whereupon the following conversation ensued:

"They are becoming anxious, some of them in the House, about the situation," said the Congressman. "Have you received anything lately? Aren't you afraid Grant is making a mistake by not moving?"

Seeming to move entirely away from the subject at hand the President asked, "Do you remember that Baptist revival in Springfield, in such a year?"

Puzzled, the Congressman said, "I do not recall it."

The President continued, "Well, Bill, a hardened sinner, was converted. Upon an appointed day the minister baptized the converts in a small stream. After Bill had been plunged under once, he asked the preacher to baptize him again; the latter replied it was unnecessary. Bill, however, urged the matter, and he was accordingly put under for the second time. As he came up, he again asked, as a particular favor, that he might be baptized just once more. The minister, a little angered, answered that he had already been under once more than the other converts. Still Bill pleaded, and the preacher put him under for the third time. As Bill came up puffing and blowing, he shook the water from his hair and exclaimed: 'There! I'll be blowed if the devil can get hold of me now.'"

The President went on in explanation of his story, "General Grant is very much like Bill. He is determined on making sure of the thing, and will not move until he has."

2387　After Lee had taken Harper's Ferry, the President, realizing how great a calamity it was to the Northern army, determined, if possible, to fix the responsibility. Halleck was summoned, but did not know where the blame lay. "Very well," said Lincoln, "I'll ask General Schenck." The latter could throw no light upon the question further than to say he was not to blame. Milroy was the next to be called to the presence of the commander-in-chief, and to enter a plea of "not guilty." Hooker was next given a hearing, and "Fighting Joe" made an emphatic disclaimer of all responsibility. Then the President assembled the four in his room, and said: "Gentlemen, Harper's Ferry was surrendered, and none of you, it seems, is responsible. I am very anxious to discover who is." After striding across the room several times, the President suddenly threw up his bowed head and exclaimed, "I have it! I know who is responsible." "Who, Mr. President; who is it?" anxiously inquired the distinguished quartet. "Gentlemen," said the President, "General Lee is the man."

2388　President Lincoln one day remarked to a number of personal friends who had called upon him at the White House:

"General McClellan's tardiness and unwillingness to fight the enemy or follow up advantages gained, reminds me of a man back in Illinois who knew a few law phrases but whose lawyer lacked aggressiveness. The man finally lost all patience and springing to his feet vociferated: 'Why don't you go at him with a fi. fa., a demurrer, a capias, a surrebutter, or a ne exeat, or something; or a nundam pactum or a non est?'

"I wish McClellan would go at the enemy with something —I don't care what. General McClellan is a pleasant and scholarly gentleman. He is an admirable engineer, but he seems to have a special talent for a stationary engine."

2389 In the first December of the first World War Admiral Beatty received a radiogram from Sir George Warrender from his ship: "Scarborough being shelled. I am proceeding toward Hull." Lord Beatty replied: "Are you? I am going to Scarborough."

2390 The Norwegian king, Harold Hardrada, who lost his life in the battle of Stamford Bridge in 1066, fought for some time under the banner of the Byzantine emperors. On one of his expeditions to Sicily, he came with his army to a populous town, to which he laid siege. The walls, however, were so strong, that he began to doubt whether it would be possible to make a breach in them; and the burghers had plenty of provisions, and everything which they needed for their defence. Harold, therefore, ordered his fowlers to catch the small birds that nested in the town, and flew to the forest during the day in quest of food. He then caused splinters of inflammable wood, smeared with wax and sulphur, to be fastened on their backs and enkindled. The birds, when set at liberty, flew immediately to the town to revisit their young and their nests on the roofs of the houses, which were thatched with reeds and straw. The fire fell from the birds on the thatch, and although each bore but a small quantity, their number was so great that one house after another began to burn, until the whole town was in flames. The inhabitants then came out and implored mercy, and Harold thus got possession of the town.

2391 When even the great patience of Lincoln had been exhausted by the "waiting campaign" of McClellan, he placed Hooker in command of the Army. In order to create the impression of immense and vigorous activity, General Hooker reported his movements in a dispatch headed "Headquarters in the Saddle." "The trouble with Hooker," Lincoln remarked, "is that he's got his headquarters where his hindquarters ought to be."

2392 Stories concerning the clashes between Lincoln and the inadequate General McClellan are common. Lincoln deemed it necessary for McClellan to report frequently and the General chaffed at this. One time he sent the President the following telegram from the field:

President Abraham Lincoln,
Washington, D. C.

Have just captured six cows. What shall we do with them?
                                    George B. McClellan

Lincoln promptly wired:
Gen. George B. McClellan
Army of the Potomac
As to six cows captured—milk them.

                                    A. Lincoln.

2393 President Lincoln once wrote to General McClellan, when the latter was in command of the army. General McClellan, as is well known, conducted a waiting campaign, being so careful not to make any mistakes that he made very little headway. President Lincoln sent this brief but exceedingly pertinent letter:

"My dear McClellan: If you don't want to use the army I should like to borrow it for a while.

                                    Yours respectfully,
                                    A. Lincoln."

> RELATED SUBJECTS: *Quick Thinking* 471-492; *Shrewdness* 526-541; *War* 2316-2323; *Battles* 2371-2385; *Officers* 2406-2427

ARMISTICE

2396 When the German delegation came to Marshal Foch at the end of the War to ask for armistice terms, the Frenchman picked up a paper from his desk and read a set of conditions. "But—there must be some mistake," the leader of the German officers stammered in dismay. "These are terms which no civilized nation could impose on another!"

"I am very glad to hear you say so," replied Foch gravely. "No, gentlemen, these are not our terms. They are the terms imposed on Lille by the German commander when that city surrendered."

2397 After the surrender of Lee to Grant at Appomatox Court House, the Union soldiers began, without orders, to salute the latter with cannon; but General Grant directed the firing to cease, lest it should wound the feelings of the prisoners, who, he said, were still their countrymen.

> RELATED SUBJECTS: *War* 2316-2323; *Battles* 2371-2385

ARMY AND NAVY

2401 Nearly all great scientific discoveries have been combated and misunderstood, even by great men. Admiral Sir Charles Napier fiercely opposed the introduction of steam power into the royal navy, and one day exclaimed in the House of Commons: "Mr. Speaker, when we enter her Majesty's naval service and face the chances of war, we go prepared to be hacked in pieces by cutlasses, to be riddled with bullets, or to be blown to bits by shot and shell; but, Mr. Speaker, we do not go prepared to be boiled alive!"

2402 General Washington seldom indulged in a joke or sarcasm, but when he did, he always made a decided hit. It is related that he was present in Congress during the debate on the establishment of the Federal Army, when a member offered a resolution limiting the army to three thousand men. Upon this Washington suggested to a member an amendment providing that no enemy should ever invade the country with more than two thousand soldiers. The laughter which ensued smothered the resolution completely.

2403 One day Lincoln and some of his friends were discussing the amount of manpower involved in the Civil War. Someone asked him how many men the Confederates had in the field. Lincoln astonished them by saying, "Twelve hundred thousand, according to the best authority."

"Yes, sir," repeated Lincoln, "twelve hundred thousand—no doubt of it. You see, all of our generals, when they get whipped, say the enemy outnumbers them from three or five to one, and I must believe them. We have four hundred thousand men in the field, and three times four make twelve. Don't you see it?"

2404 Following the battle of Antietam, the army under the command of McClellan lay unaccountably idle. President Lincoln accompanied by a friend, Mr. O. M. Hatch of Illinois, went to visit the camp.

They stood on a hill overlooking the vast army of tents. Turning to his friend, Lincoln said:

"Hatch, Hatch, what is all this?"

"Why," said Hatch, "that is the Army of the Potomac."

"No, Hatch, no," said Lincoln, "that is General McClellan's bodyguard."

RELATED SUBJECTS: *War* 2316-2323; *Battles* 2371-2385; *Officers* 2406-2427; *Soldiers and Sailors* 2430-2437; *Discipline* 2441-2442; *Regulations* 2446; *Camp* 2451; *Marches* 2456; *Drill* 2461-2462; *K. P.* 2466

SEE ALSO: *Discretion* 182; *Conversions* 1624

OFFICERS

2406 General Grant once expressed his contempt for a certain officer. Another General protested that the man in question had been through 10 campaigns. "General," said Grant, "so has that mule yonder, but he's still a jackass."

2407 Once, during the War, Barnum brought his show to Washington and invited President Lincoln to come and see its wonders.

The President noted all the exhibitions with appropriate remarks and, when shown the midgets, General Tom Thumb and Admiral Nut, remarked to Barnum, "You have some pretty small generals, but I think I can beat you."

2408 When George V was Prince of Wales, he held the rank of Lieutenant in the Marines. One day on the afterdeck of a battleship he was conducting drill under the supervision of a senior officer. The deck had been cleared even of its quadrails. The Prince was not well versed in drill and his superior was clearly put out at his awkwardness and slowness of command. At last the squad was marching full on for the stern and the unguarded edge and it seemed as though the Prince had either forgotten the command to stop, or face about, or else failed to realize the situation. Sputtering with wrath, the officer snapped, as the men neared the edge, "God Almighty, Sir, can't you at least say Good-bye to your men!"

2409 Stonewall Jackson sent the following telegram to the War Department at Richmond: "Send me more men and fewer questions."

2410 A French field-marshal who had attained that rank by court favor, not by valor, going one evening to the opera, forcibly took possession of the box of a respectable Abbé, who for this outrage brought a suit. The Abbé thus addressed the court: "I do not come here to complain of Admiral Suffrein who took so many ships in the East Indies; I do not come to complain of Count de Grasse who fought so nobly in the west; I do not come to complain of the Duke de Crébillon who took Minorca; but I come to complain of Marshal B——— who took my box at the Opera, and never took anything else."

2411   An officer, having had some trouble with General Sherman, being very angry, presented himself before Lincoln who was visiting the camp, and said: "Mr. President, I have a cause of grievance. This morning I went to General Sherman and he threatened to shoot me."

"Threatened to shoot you?" asked Lincoln. "Well," (in a stage whisper) "if I were you I would keep away from him; if he threatens to shoot, I would not trust him, for I believe he would do it."

2412   A group of high-ranking officers, on a tour of inspection, were being conducted through the trenches. They were led by a captain. He turned to the general behind him and said in a hoarse whisper, "We are now in the third line trenches."

The general turned to the officer behind him, repeated the information, which went in a whisper all the way down the line.

A moment later the captain turned again and said, "We are now in the second line trenches."

The general relayed the information again, and again the whisper went all the way down the line.

A moment later the captain said, "We are now in the front line trenches."

The whisper was sent backward.

"Now," whispered the general, "where is the enemy?"

"About a quarter of a mile away," said the captain.

"A quarter of a mile!" said the general. "Then why are we whispering?"

"Because I have laryngitis," said the captain.

2413   Napoleon often resorted to a species of charlatanism to augment the enthusiasm of his troops. He would say to one of his aides-de-camp, "Ascertain from the colonel of such a regiment, whether he has in his corps a man, who has served in the campaigns of Italy, or the campaigns of Egypt. Ascertain his name, where he was born, the particulars of his family, and what he has done. Learn his number in the ranks, and to what company he belongs, and furnish me with the information."

On the day of the review Napoleon, at a single glance, could spot the man who had been described to him. He would go up to him as if he recognized him, address him by his name, and say—"Oh! so you are here! You are a brave fellow—I saw you at Aboukir—How is your old father? What! Have you not got the cross? Stay, I will give it to you."

Then the delighted soldiers would say to each other, "You see the Emperor knows us all; he knows our families; he knows where we have served." What a stimulus this was to soldiers whom he succeeded in persuading that they would all, sooner or later, become marshals of the Empire.

2414 "Do you know General A——?" queried President Lincoln one day to a friend who had "dropped in" at the White House.

"Certainly; but you are not wasting any time thinking about him, are you?" was the rejoinder.

"You wrong him," responded the President, "he is a really great man—a philosopher."

"How do you make that out? He isn't worth the powder and ball necessary to kill him—so I have heard military men say," the friend remarked.

"He is a mighty thinker," the President returned, "because he has mastered that ancient and wise admonition, 'know thyself.' He has formed an intimate acquaintance with himself, knows as well for what he is fitted and unfitted as any man living. Without doubt he is a remarkable man. This War has not produced another like him. Greatly to my relief; and to the interests of the country, he has resigned. The country should express its gratitude in some substantial way."

2415 When President Lincoln heard of the Confederate raid at Fairfax, in which a brigadier-general and a number of valuable horses were captured, he gravely observed:

"Well, I am sorry for the horses."

"Sorry for the horses, Mr. President!" exclaimed the Secretary of War, raising his spectacles and throwing himself back in his chair in astonishment.

"Yes," replied Lincoln, "I can make a brigadier-general in five minutes, but it is not easy to replace a hundred and ten horses."

2416   "General Grant is a drunkard," asserted powerful and influential politicians to President Lincoln, "he is not himself half the time; he can't be relied upon, and it is a shame to have such a man in command of an army."

"So Grant gets drunk, does he?" queried Lincoln.

"Yes, he does, and I can prove it," was the reply.

"Well," returned Lincoln, with the faintest suspicion of a twinkle in his eyes, "you needn't waste your time getting proof; you just find out, to oblige me, what brand of whiskey Grant drinks because I want to send a barrel of it to each one of my generals."

2417   When in Washington Lieutenant de Tessan, aide to Marshal Joffre and Colonel Fabry, was approached by a pretty girl who said: "And did you kill a German soldier?"

"Yes."

"With what hand did you do it?"

"With this right hand."

The pretty American girl seized his right hand and kissed it. At this Colonel Fabry said: "Heavens, man, why didn't you tell her that you bit him to death?"

2418   A woman once approached Lincoln rather imperiously. "Mr. President," she said very theatrically, "you must give me a colonel's commission for my son. Sir, I demand it, not as a favor but as a right. Sir, my grandfather fought at Lexington. Sir, my uncle was the only man that did not run away at Bladensburg. Sir, my father fought at New Orleans, and my husband was killed at Monterey."

"I guess, madam," answered Lincoln dryly, "your family has done enough for the country. It is time to give someone else a chance."

2419   On one occasion a friend burst into Lincoln's room to tell him that a brigadier-general and twelve army mules had been carried off by a Confederate raid.

"How unfortunate! Those mules cost us two hundred dollars apiece!" was the President's reply.

2420   No figure of a popular hero in American public life probably was ever as much kissed as Richard Pearson Hobson who had distinguished himself in the Spanish American War. At a big function in Chicago, two pretty young cousins stood on tip-toe and kissed him. This started the ball rolling, and all the young ladies present, enamoured of the brave young Lieutenant, lined up to kiss him too. Count was kept up to one hundred and then given up. The audience stood by and rooted, calling out, "Good for number 76!" and other helpful comments. The kissing went on for 36 minutes with an average of five a minute. The publicity arising from this incident led to its repetition in every city to which the hero toured. He collected some 10,000 or more in all. A caramel was put on the market, called "Hobson's Kisses."

2421   Peter Heine, a Dutchman, from a cabin-boy rose to the rank of Admiral. He was killed in action at the moment his fleet triumphed over that of Spain.

The States-General sent a deputation to his mother, at Delft, to condole with her on the loss of her son. The simple old woman, who still remained in her original obscurity, answered:

"I always foretold that Peter would perish like the miserable wretch that he was. He loved nothing but rambling about from one country to another, and now he has received the reward of his folly!"

2422   At a council of Generals early in the Civil War one remarked that a certain Major was wounded and would not be able to perform a duty assigned to him.

"Wounded!" said Jackson. "If it really is so, I think it must have been by an accidental discharge of his duty."

2423   When the English fleet was bearing down upon the French off Trafalgar, a sailor who was devoutly kneeling at the side of a gun was asked by an officer if he was afraid. "Afraid!" replied the tar. "No! I was only praying that the enemy's shot might be distributed in the same proportion as the prize money, the greatest part among the officers."

2424   In camp, the soldiers were awaiting imminent transfer to the fighting front. In the dusk one of the soldiers called out to a khaki clad figure only dimly seen: "Hey, buddy, got a match?"

A lighted match was forthcoming, and by its light, as he started to thank the other for the courtesy, the private was horrified to see the markings of a general.

"I beg your pardon, sir," he said, saluting smartly, "I didn't see that you were a general."

"That's all right, son," said the general benignly. "Just thank God I wasn't a second lieutenant."

2425 During the First World War an American officer was reconnoitering in the war zone. A young pleasant-looking chap in the uniform of a British subaltern came toward him.

"Who are you?" the American challenged.

"The Prince of Wales," the young man said mildly, continuing on his way.

"Oh, yeah," was the sarcastic rejoinder of the American. "And I'm the King of England."

Several nights later at a Red Cross hut the two men met again. Great was the chagrin of the American to find that the young man was actually the Prince of Wales. He was still more embarrassed when the Prince, grinning widely, waved to him from across the room and called out cheerily, "Hello there, dad!"

2426 Major-Gen. Smedley Butler used to tell the story of a doughboy who, during a battle in Flanders, suffered shell shock. He started running towards the rear. After some time he was stopped by an officer.

"Here, don't you know that there's a big battle going on up at the front?" he asked.

"Y-y-yes, I-I-I know," stuttered the frightened soldier.

"Then what are you doing here?"

The doughboy did not answer and cast his eyes down abashed.

"Why don't you answer?" roared the officer. "Do you know who I am?"

The doughboy shook his head feebly.

"I am your general," snapped the officer.

"Great guns! Am I that far back?" exclaimed the soldier and fainted away.

2427 A soldier, telling his mother of the terrible fire, was asked by her why he did not get behind a tree.

"Tree?" said he. "Why, there weren't enough for the officers."

RELATED SUBJECTS: *War* 2316-2323; *Strategy* 2386-2393; *Army and Navy* 2401-2404; *Soldiers and Sailors* 2430-2437; *Discipline* 2441-2442

SOLDIERS AND SAILORS

2430 Vice-President Henry A. Wallace, in his famous speech on "The Century of the Common Man" told the following story of heroism and courage:

"The American people have always had guts and always will have. You know the story of bomber pilot Dixon and radioman Gene Aldrich and ordnanceman Tony Pastula—the story which Americans will be telling their children for generations to illustrate man's ability to master any fate. These men lived for 34 days on the open sea in a rubber life raft, 8 feet by 4 feet, with no food but that which they took from the sea and the air with one pocket knife and a pistol. And yet they lived it through and came at last to the beach of an island they did not know. In spite of their suffering and weakness, they stood like men, with no weapon left to protect themselves, and no shoes on their feet or clothes on their backs, and walked in military file because, they said, 'If there were Japs, we didn't want to be crawling.'"

2431 During the heroic defence of the Bataan Peninsula, one of the commanding officers lined up a company of his men and asked for a volunteer for a mission of the utmost peril. Anyone willing to serve was instructed to step forward two paces from the line.

He glanced for a second at a memorandum in his hand and, looking up, was shocked and disappointed to see the ranks unbroken.

"What," he said unbelievingly, "not a single man!"

"You do not understand, sir," said an aide at his elbow, "the whole line has stepped forward two paces."

2432 A profound philosophy of life is reflected in the reply of the sailor who, when asked what he had done with his pay, said, "Part went for liquor and part for women. The rest I spent foolishly."

2433 Shortly after the Revolutionary War Benedict Arnold was presented at Court in London. While the king was conversing with him, Lord Balcarass, a stately old nobleman, who had fought under Gen. Burgoyne in the campaigns of America, was presented. The King introduced them with: "Lord Balcarass—General Arnold."

"What, Sire," said the haughty old earl, drawing up his lofty form, "the traitor Arnold!" and refused to give him his hand.

The consequence was a challenge from Arnold. They met, and it was arranged that the parties should fire together. At the signal Arnold fired. Lord Balcarass, however, throwing down his pistol, turned on his heel, and was walking away, when Arnold called after him:

"Why don't you fire, my Lord?"

"Sir," said the Earl, "I will leave that to the executioner."

2434 Two young girls were watching a shipload of marines depart for places unknown. Wistfully they watched the ship as it rapidly disappeared from sight.

"Ain't it a shame," mourned one of them, "that those handsome marines have to go way off to China or somewhere. What will they ever do there?"

"What will they do?" rejoined the more worldly of the two. "Have you ever had a date with a marine?"

2435 A group of soldiers were discussing the many things they would do when they were discharged from the army.

"First thing I'm goin' to do when I get out of this army," said one disgruntled individual, "is bust that sergeant right on the nose."

"Oh, yeah," retorted a nearby comrade, "that's what you think. You're goin' to wait right in line and take your turn, just like all the rest of us."

2436 They tell the tale of an American lady of notable good works, much esteemed by the French, who, at the end of June, 1918, visited one of the field-hospitals behind Degoutte's Sixth French Army. Degoutte was fighting on the face of the Marne salient, and the 2d American Division, then in action around the Bois de Belleau, northwest of Chateau Thierry, was under his orders. It happened that occasional casualties of the Marine Brigade of the 2d American Division, wounded toward the flank where Degoutte's own horizon-blue infantry joined on, were picked up by French stretcher-bearers and evacuated to French hospitals. And this lady, looking down a long, crowded ward, saw on a pillow a face unlike the fiercely whiskered Gallic heads there displayed in rows. She went to it.

"Oh," she said, "surely you are an American!"

"No, ma'am," the casualty answered. "I'm a Marine."

2437 During the traitor Arnold's predatory operations in Virginia in 1781, he took an American captain prisoner. After some general conversation, he asked the captain "what he thought the Americans would do with him if they caught him." The captain declined at first giving him an answer, but upon being repeatedly urged, he said: "Why, sir, if I must answer the question, you will excuse my telling you the truth; if my countrymen should catch you, I believe they would first cut off your lame leg which was wounded in the cause of freedom and virtue at Quebec, and bury it with the honors of war, and afterwards hang the remainder of your body on a gibbet."

RELATED SUBJECTS: *Courage* 151-153; *Patriotism* 396-407; *Death* 1746-1749; *War* 2316-2323; *Prisoners* 2366; *Battles* 2371-2385; *Army and Navy* 2401-2404; *Officers* 2406-2427; *Discipline* 2441-2442

SEE ALSO: *Boners* 116; *Courage* 151; *Cowardice* 159; *Patriotism* 407; *Age* 678; *Sermons* 1556; *Medicines* 1727; *Deathbed Scenes* 1774; *Civilians in War* 2341; *Censors* 2352; *Battles* 2377, 2379, 2381; *Trials* 2479

DISCIPLINE

2441 A telegram from one of his generals was on Lincoln's desk while an old man was pleading for a pardon for his son. Lincoln turned to him gently but firmly, "I am sorry, I can do nothing for you," he said with finality. "Listen to this telegram I received from General Butler yesterday: 'President Lincoln, I pray you not to interfere with the courts-martial of the army. You will destroy all discipline among our soldiers.'"

Greatly affected by the hopeless despair on the old man's face, Lincoln said, "By jingo! Butler or no Butler, here goes!"

The old man read, "Job Smith is not to be shot until further orders from me—Abraham Lincoln." He expressed disappointment. "Why, I thought it was a pardon! You may order him to be shot next week."

"My old friend," the President replied, "I see you are not very well acquainted with me. If your son never dies till orders come from me to shoot him, he will live to be a great deal older than Methuselah."

2442 During the Black Hawk War, Captain Abe Lincoln was one of the first of his company to be arraigned for unmilitary conduct. Contrary to the rules he fired a gun "within the limits" and had his sword taken from him. The next infringement of rules was by some of the men who stole a quantity of liquor, drank it, and became unfit for duty, straggling out of the ranks the next day, and not getting together again until late at night.

For allowing this lawlessness the captain was condemned to wear a wooden sword for two days.

RELATED SUBJECTS: *Army and Navy* 2401-2404; *Officers* 2406-2427; *Soldiers and Sailors* 2430-2437; *Regulations* 2446; *Drill* 2461-2462; *K. P.* 2466

SEE ALSO: *Cowardice* 160

REGULATIONS

2446 Strange things happen in military circles. An army officer was given the task of preparing a factual report on heavy ordnance. Partly because he was pressed for time and partly because the facts were there, arranged in their best way, he copied pretty much verbatim the article on the subject in the Encyclopedia Britannica, and turned it over to his superiors. Not long thereafter, he received, along with all his other brother officers, a mimeographed copy of his report from the War Department in an envelope heavily sealed and labeled, "Extremely Confidential."

RELATED SUBJECTS: *Discipline* 2441-2442

CAMP

2451 A Negro sentry, but recently inducted into the service and slightly bewildered by the many formalities required to be learned in so short a time, startled a number of his superior officers while serving his sentry duty, by hailing them with the challenge, "Halt! Look who's here!"

RELATED SUBJECTS: *Army and Navy* 2401-2404; *Officers* 2406-2427; *Soldiers and Sailors* 2430-2437; *Discipline* 2441-2442; *Regulations* 2446; *Marches* 2456; *Drill* 2461-2462; *K. P.* 2466

MARCHES

2456 A green young lieutenant was assigned to a new detachment. He was a very small and helpless looking individual, and when he first appeared before his company there were many audible comments made about his apparent ineptness. From the rear of the ranks a voice boomed, "And a little child shall lead them." There was a roar of laughter.

Seemingly undisturbed the lieutenant finished the business of the day. Next day there appeared a notice on the bulletin board: "Company A will take a 25 mile hike today with full packs. And a little child shall lead them . . . on a damned big horse."

RELATED SUBJECTS: *Army and Navy* 2401-2404; *Officers* 2406-2427; *Soldiers and Sailors* 2430-2437; *Camp* 2451; *Drill* 2461-2462

DRILL

2461 In the course of the Black Hawk Indian War, Abraham Lincoln was Captain of a company. He was inexperienced in the formalities of drill and manoeuvre, and made many blunders in his orders. His native ingenuity often enabled him to get out of difficulties, as in the instance when, marching with a front of more than 20 men, he came to a fence with only a narrow gate offering passage into the next field. "I could not, for the life of me," he said, "remember the proper word of command for the getting my company endwise so that it could get through the gate. So as we came near I said, 'This company is dismissed for two minutes, when it will fall in again on the other side of the gate.'"

2462 A sergeant cannot always be blamed for his tough treatment of rookie soldiers. There is the story of the sergeant who was training a bunch of recruits on a rifle range. At a hundred yards the order to fire was given. After the smoke had cleared away, the target was revealed as smooth and untouched. The sergeant gave the order to move up to fifty yards. Again the firing order was given. And still the target was untouched. They moved up to twenty-five yards—with the same results.

Ordering the troops into closed ranks, the sergeant, red faced and seemingly about to burst, bellowed:

"Fix bayonets and charge!"

> RELATED SUBJECTS: *Army and Navy* 2401-2404; *Soldiers and Sailors* 2430-2437; *Camp* 2451; *Marches* 2456

K. P.

2466 The late Smedley D. Butler, always an impulsive man, was generally careful of the welfare of his men. One time in France he encountered two soldiers emerging from the kitchen with a large soup kettle. "Let me taste that," he ordered. "But Gen—. . . ." "No buts! Give me a spoon." Taking a taste, the General sputtered, "You don't call that soup, do you?" "No, sir," replied the soldier, "I was trying to tell you, sir, it's dishwater."

> RELATED SUBJECTS: *Army and Navy* 2401-2404; *Soldiers and Sailors* 2430-2437; *Discipline* 2441-2442; *Camp* 2451

COURTS

2471 Chief Justice Fuller was practicing before Judge MacArthur of the Supreme Court of Illinois in Chicago. In his speech before the Judge he pleaded his client's ignorance of an offense he had committed.

The Judge said, "Every man is supposed to know the law, Mr. Fuller."

"I am aware of that," responded Mr. Fuller. "Every shoemaker, tailor, mechanic and illiterate laborer is presumed to know the law. Yes, every man is presumed to know it, except the judges of the Supreme Court, and we have a Court of Appeals to correct their mistakes."

2472 The highly nervous young lawyer stepped up to plead his case before the Court. It was in New York City. He laid his coat and hat on the bench and stood before the Judge. "Is this the first time you've practiced in this Court?"

"Yes, your Honor," replied the lawyer, feeling nervous and afraid he had already committed some breach of precedent.

"Then get your hat and coat and put them where you can keep an eye on them."

2473 There seems to be enough evidence to prove that, even if Abe Lincoln had never been President of the United States, he still would have become immortal—as a story teller. Here is another example of his talents in that direction as related by a court clerk:

"I was never fined but once for contempt of court. Davis fined me five dollars. Mr. Lincoln had just come in, and leaning over my desk had told me a story so irresistibly funny that I broke out into a loud laugh. The Judge called me to order, saying, 'This must be stopped. Mr. Lincoln, you are constantly disturbing this court with your stories.' Then to me: 'You may fine yourself five dollars.' I apologized but told the Judge the story was worth the money. In a few minutes the Judge called me to him. 'What was that story Lincoln told you?' he asked. I told him, and he laughed aloud in spite of himself. 'Remit your fine,' he ordered."

TRIALS

2476 When Thaddeus Stevens was a young lawyer he once had a case before a bad-tempered judge of an obscure Pennsylvania court. Under what he considered a very erroneous ruling it was decided against him; thereupon he threw down his books and picked up his hat in a state of indignation, scattering imprecations all around him. The judge assumed an air of offended majesty, and asked Thaddeus Stevens if he meant to express his "contempt for this court?" Stevens turned to him very politely, made a respectful bow and feigned amazement. "Express my contempt for this court? No sir; I am trying to conceal it, your honor," adding as he turned to leave, "but I find it damned hard to do it."

2477 A Chinese thus describes a trial in the English law courts: "One man is quite silent, another talks all the time, and twelve men condemn the man who has not said a word."

2478 "I feel very strongly on this subject and must deal severely with you," began the Judge, in his address to Sam, who was in court on a charge of wife desertion.

"But, Boss, you don't understand," protested the Negro. "You don't know my old woman. I ain't no deserter. I'se a refugee!"

2479 A sentry near one of the army camps on Long Island was bitten by a valuable dog from one of the neighboring estates, and in self-defense drove his bayonet into the animal. The owner brought charges against him to retrieve its value and the evidence showed that the sentry had not been badly bitten.

"Why did you not knock the dog with the butt end of your rifle?" asked the judge.

The sentry clinched his case by replying, "Why didn't he bite me with his tail?"

2480 A deaf man went to law with another deaf man, and the judge was much deafer than either. One of them asserted that the other owed him five months' rent, and the other said that his opponent had been grinding corn at night to avoid the tax. The judge looked at them and said, "Why are you quarreling? She is your mother; you must both support her."

2481 One of Winston Churchill's favorite stories is of the Earl of Birkenhead as a young barrister. He had gotten into a heated controversy with the Judge over some aspect of a case. Their remarks grew more and more heated and personal. At last the Judge said, "Young man, you are extremely offensive." "Yes," said the Earl, "we both are. But I am trying to be, and you can't help it."

2482 When the celebrated Dunning, afterward Lord Ashburton, was "stating law" to a jury in court Lord Mansfield interrupted him by saying, "If that be law, I'll go home and burn my books."

"My lord," replied Dunning, "you had better go home and read them."

2483 Once opposing counsel objected to a juror on the ground that he knew Mr. Lincoln, and as this was a reflection upon the honor of a lawyer, Judge Davis promptly overruled the objection. But when Lincoln, following the example of his adversary examined two or three of the jury and found that they knew his opponent, the Judge, interfered. "Now, Mr. Lincoln," he observed severely, "you are wasting time. The mere fact that a juror knows your opponent does not disqualify him."

"No, Your Honor," responded Lincoln dryly, "but I am afraid some of the gentlemen may not know him which would place me at a disadvantage."

2484 Thelwall, about to be tried for treason, wrote to Lord Erskine, the following laconic epistle: "I shall plead my own cause."

To which Erskine as laconically replied: "You'll be hanged if you do."

Mr. Thelwall wittily rejoined: "Then if I do, I'll be hanged."

2485 Knowing his client to be innocent, the defense lawyer rested his case in the assurance that all would be well.

Great was his astonishment when the justice of the court

pronounced the man guilty, and imposed a fine of fifty dollars and a jail sentence.

The lawyer deliberately turned his chair so that his back was to the bench. "Fine me too," he said in a loud voice.

"Why?" asked the justice.

"For contempt."

Bewildered, the justice said, "Contempt? But you haven't said a word."

"Exactly. My contempt is silent."

> RELATED SUBJECTS: *Courts* 2471-2473; *Judges* 2486-2497; *Witnesses* 2501-2506; *Juries* 2511-2517; *Evidence* 2521-2523; *Lawyers* 2526-2537

> SEE ALSO: *Reputation* 78; *Absent-Mindedness* 89; *Laziness* 327; *Long-Windedness* 352, 355; *Wife* 933; *Erudition* 1072; *Stealing* 2589

JUDGES

2486   A certain judge in the mining territory of Nevada had a reputation for probity. In keeping with this opinion, he opened a mining claim case one morning with the following words to the court: "Gentlemen, this court has received from the plaintiff in this case a check for $10,000. He has received from the defendant a check for $15,000. The court has returned $5,000 to the defendant and will now try the case on its merits."

2487   The late Max Steuer, the prominent lawyer, was compelled to apologize to the court one day. With stately dignity he rose in his place and, bowing to the judge, said: "Your Honor is right and I am wrong, as your Honor generally is."

There was a dazed look in the judge's eyes. He hardly knew whether to feel pleased or fine the lawyer for contempt of court.

2488   "This hurts me more than it does you," remarked the Magistrate, as he fined his daughter $10.00 for speeding and $3.00 for running past a red light, and then dug into his pocket for the fines.

2489   Judge Jeffries, reprimanding a criminal, called him a scoundrel. The prisoner hotly retorted: "Sir, I am not as big a scoundrel as your honor—" here the culprit stopped to look at the apoplectic judge, but hurriedly added—"takes me to be."

"Put your words closer together," muttered the judge.

2490   Judge Jeffries, of notorious memory, pointing with his cane to a man who was about to be tried, said: "There is a rogue at the end of my cane."

The man to whom he pointed, looking at him, said: "At which end, my Lord?"

2491   Aristides being judge between two private persons, one of them declared that his adversary had greatly injured Aristides. "Relate rather," said he, "what wrong he has done you, for it is your cause not mine that I now sit judge of."

2492   Lord Mansfield chanced to be in one of the counties on the circuit when a poor woman was indicted for witchcraft. The inhabitants of the place were exasperated against her. Some witnesses deposed that they had seen her walk in the air; and with her feet upward and her head downward. Lord Mansfield heard the evidence with great tranquility, and perceiving the temper of the people, whom it would not have been prudent to irritate, he thus addressed them:

"I do not doubt that this woman has walked in the air with her feet upward, since you have all seen it; but she has the honor to be born in England as well as you and I, and consequently cannot be judged but by the laws of the country, nor punished but in proportion as she has violated them. Now, I know not one law that forbids walking in the air with the feet upward. We all have a right to it with impunity; I see no reason, therefore, for this prosecution, and this poor woman may return home when she pleases."

2493   Nobody was more witty or more biting than Lord Ellenborough. A young lawyer, trembling with fear, rose to make his first speech, and began: "My Lord, my unfortunate client—my Lord, my unfortunate client—my Lord——"

"Go on, sir, go on!" said Lord Ellenborough, "as far as you have proceeded hitherto, the court is entirely with you."

2494   In the traffic court of one of our large Mid-Western cities, a young lady was brought before the Judge to answer a ticket given her for driving through a red light. She explained to his Honor that she was a school teacher and requested an immediate disposal of her case in order that she might hasten away to her classes. A wild gleam came into the Judge's eye. "You're a school teacher, eh?" said he. "Madam, I shall realize my life-long ambition. I've waited years to have a school teacher in this court. Sit down at that table and write 'I went through a red light' five hundred times!"

2495 Lincoln's guileless exterior concealed a great fund of shrewdness and common sense about ordinary matters, as well as genius in the higher realms.

"I remember once," writes Whitney, "that while several of us lawyers were together, including Judge Davis, Lincoln suddenly asked a novel question regarding court practice, addressed to no one particularly, to which the judge, who was in the habit certainly of appropriating his full share of any conversation, replied, stating what he understood the practice should be. Lincoln thereat laughed and said: "I asked that question, hoping that you would answer. I have that very question to present to the court in the morning, and I am glad to find out that the court is on my side."

2496 Shortly after Charles Evans Hughes became Chief Justice of the Supreme Court in 1930, he was much acclaimed for the liberalism of his maiden opinion which confirmed the right of citizens in California to hoist a red flag. Shortly thereafter, F. W. Wile, the newspaper man, encountered Hughes at a garden party at the estate of Secretary Stimson. He inquired how Hughes was reacting to the plaudits received for having blossomed out as a liberal.

"Wile," said Hughes, "I blossomed out a long time ago. But the trouble is, it never bore fruit."

2497 A judge, noted for his gentleness to defendants, asked the contrite and broken man before him, "Have you ever been sentenced to imprisonment?"

"No, your Honor," said the prisoner and burst into tears.

"There, there, don't cry," said the judge kindly. "You're going to be now."

RELATED SUBJECTS: *Courts* 2471-2473; *Trials* 2476-2485

SEE ALSO: *Drinking* 40; *Long-Windedness* 353, 354; *Modesty* 385; *Bishops* 1492; *Banks* 2152; *Courts* 2472; *Lawyers* 2526; *Hanging* 2568

WITNESSES

2501 Two friendly enemies were involved in a lawsuit. The issue at stake was small, but each was determined to win.

The day of the trial arrived. Mr. Johnson, the party of the first part, came into the courtroom surrounded by a covey of witnesses for his side of the case.

A few minutes later, Logan, the other man involved, entered. Looking about, he spied Johnson with the witnesses.

"Good Lord, Johnson, are these your witnesses?"

"They certainly are."

"Well, in that case, I give up. You win! I've used these witnesses twice myself."

2502 It is extraordinary to watch the occasional results of the fact that the prisoner before the bar is concerned only and strictly with the question of his guilt on the count charged and none other.

A peculiarly brazen piece of testimony was once given by a defendant under the charge of Samuel Leibowitz. The issue at stake was the question of a frame-up. The great criminal lawyer was frank in his examination of the witness as to his general character.

He questioned him thus:

Q. What is your occupation?

A. Professional pickpocket.

Q. How long have you been a professional pickpocket?

A. Twenty-four years.

Q. If acquitted in this case, what will your occupation be in the future?

A. Professional pickpocket.

He was acquitted.

2503 This same character was one of Leibowitz's first cash clients. When he had come to the lawyer he had flashed a hundred dollar bill and handed it over as a retainer. He insisted that he had been framed.

"This guy says he felt my hand in his pocket. He's a liar. I've been a pickpocket for 24 years and no man ever felt my mitt in his kick."

When the client departed after this first interview, Leibowitz felt for the precious hundred dollar bill. No bill. He hunted through all his pockets, and was in the act of crawling under the desk when his client walked back in. "I told you it was a frame-up," said the man, "I wanted you to have your heart in this case. You can see for yourself the guy's a liar."

Wherewith he once again paid the hundred dollars.

2504 The Reverend Matthew Wilks, the celebrated London preacher, got caught in a shower in Billingsgate where there were a number of women dealing in fish; they were using the most profane and vulgar language.

"Don't you think," said Mr. Wilks with the greatest deliberation and solemnity, "I shall appear as a swift witness against you in the day of judgment?"

"I presume so," said one, "for the biggest rogue always turns State's evidence."

2505 In a Kansas court a witness, a tall awkward fellow, was called to testify. The counsel for the defense said to him, "Now, sir, stand up and tell your story like a preacher."

"No sir!" roared the judge. "None of that; I want you to tell the truth!"

2506 Samuel Leibowitz once discredited a witness whose testimony had a critical bearing on the case at hand. The person in question was a lug of the dese, dem, and dose variety. On two occasions, in the course of a long testimony, the witness popped out with most unusual phrases, one of them, "I heard a weird, uncanny sound, a gasp, a cackle," and the other, "He was all a-flutter."

Leibowitz insisted that nothing but the work of a coach or an animal trainer could have put such phrases in the witness's mouth. He was thus able to demonstrate perjury and the repeating of a prepared story.

RELATED SUBJECTS: *Courts* 2471-2473; *Trials* 2476-2485; *Evidence* 2521-2523

SEE ALSO: *Evidence* 2522

JURIES

2511 "It's a hundred dollars in your pocket," whispered the defendant's lawyer to the juror, "if you can bring about a verdict of manslaughter in the second degree." Such proved to be the verdict and the lawyer thanked the juror warmly as he paid him the money.

"Yes," said the juror, "it was tough work, but I got there after a while. All the rest wanted acquittal."

2512   The coroner's jury was pretty thoroughly baffled as to the cause of death in a certain case. Unable to come to any conclusion, they at last officially termed the case, "An act of God under very suspicious circumstances."

2513   The fifth day drew to its close with the twelfth juryman still unconvinced. The court was impatient.

"Well, gentlemen," said the court officer entering the jury room, "shall I, as usual, order twelve dinners?"

"Make it," said the foreman, "eleven dinners and one bale of hay."

2514   "Look here," said one of the jurymen, after they had retired, "if I understand aright, the plaintiff doesn't ask damages for blighted affections or anything of that sort, but only wants to get back what he's spent on presents, pleasure trips, and so forth."

"That is so," agreed the foreman.

"Well then, I vote we don't give him a penny," said the other hastily. "If all the fun he had with that girl didn't cover the amount he expended it must be his own fault. Gentlemen, I courted that girl once myself."

2515   John Scott Eldon, Lord Chancellor of England, was in court in York, one day when the Justice had spoken for over two hours and then observed, "there are only eleven jurymen in the box. Where is the twelfth?"

"Please you, my lord," said one of the jurors, "he had to go away on some business, but he has left his verdict with me."

2516   Annoyed by the long delay in settling what seemed to him to be a very plain case, the judge said, "I hereby discharge this jury."

One juryman, feeling that his personal integrity was at stake, exclaimed: "You can't do that."

"And why not?" asked the judge sternly.

"Because you didn't hire me," said the juror, pointing toward the defense lawyer. "I'm working for that man there."

2517 The community was shocked by a killing in its midst, doubly shocked because of the fact that the killer was one of the most popular and well-liked men in the town.

Realizing that the evidence against him was conclusive, the man entered his plea of guilty. No means of saving him from the electric chair could be seen.

But the jurors, all friends of his, determined to save him in spite of his plea of guilty. When, at the conclusion of the case, they were asked to give their verdict, it was "Not Guilty."

"Now how in the world," said the judge, "can you bring in such a verdict when the defendant pled guilty?"

"Well, your Honor," said the foreman of the jury, "the defendant is such a liar that we can't believe him, even under oath."

RELATED SUBJECTS: *Courts* 2471-2473; *Trials* 2476-2485

SEE ALSO: *Trials* 2483; *Hanging* 2567

EVIDENCE

2521 Justice John M. Harlan once explained the intricacies of evidence to a young man. "Usually in conflicting evidence one statement is far more probable than the other, so that we can decide easily which to believe. It is like the boy and the house-hunter. A house-hunter getting off the train at a suburban station, said to a lad, 'My boy, I'm looking for Mr. Smithson's new block of semi-detached cottages. How far are they from here?' 'About twenty minutes walk,' the boy replied. 'Twenty minutes!' exclaimed the house-hunter, 'nonsense, the advertisement says five.' 'Well,' said the boy, 'you can believe me or you can believe the advertisement, but I ain't trying to make a sale.' "

2522 In a case tried by the famous criminal lawyer, Samuel Leibowitz, the determining evidence was that of an alleged eye-witness to the crime, one Brecht, who claimed to have been at the scene in the legitimate capacity of a seller of Eskimo Pies. Shortly after this testimony had been given, Leibowitz sent out and had brought in to him some 20 Eskimo Pies, which he blandly distributed to the judge, the jurymen, and others before the bar. The ice cream was eaten with appreciation and pleasure by all in the presence of the witness who, still on the stand, was unaware of the significance of what was going on. By his failure to identify the objects being eaten, their wrappers; and his inability to explain how the pies had been kept from melting when he was selling them, Leibowitz proved the perjury and fraudulent pretensions of the witness and won his case.

2523 In a certain murder case the alibi of the defendant was that he had been working in a fish-market at 114th St. and Lexington Avenue. The prosecutor compelled the witness to identify a large number of fish which were brought in in a basket. The witness was wrong on every identification.

Samuel Leibowitz, however, summing up for the defense, obtained an acquittal by the following ingenious device.

Said he, addressing the jurors, "I want you, Mr. Rabinowitz, and you, Mr. Epstein, and you, Mr. Goldfogel, and you, Mr. Ginsberg, to explain to your fellow jurymen the fraud which has been perpetrated on my client. You see through it; they do not. Was there in all that array of fish a single pike, or pickerel, or any other fish that can be made into gefülte fish? There was not. My client told you that he worked in a store at 114th St. and Lexington Avenue. The prosecutor knows that is a Jewish neighborhood, and he did not show a single fish that makes gefülte fish. What a travesty on justice! My client is an Italian who works in a Jewish fish-market, and they try him on Christian fish!"

RELATED SUBJECTS: *Courts* 2471-2473; *Trials* 2476-2485; *Witnesses* 2501-2506

LAWYERS

2526 A lawyer from Wyoming, with the picturesqueness of a cowboy and an even more picturesque method of speech, was arguing a case before the Supreme Court while Justice Holmes still was on the bench, and despite a most impassioned appeal to the Court, full of the language of the frontier, he lost. As he concluded, Holmes, who sat on the right of Hughes, leaned over and in one of his loud, hoarse whispers said:

"Can't we hear that old bird again?"

The clerk of the Court heard the remark and afterward advised the cowboy that, if he applied for a rehearing, it might be granted. This was done. In the rehearing, the lawyer opened his appeal to the Court with these words.

"I come to you as John the Baptist saying: 'Repent ye, repent ye.'"

Whereupon Justice McReynolds, who was enjoying the performance almost as much as Justice Holmes, leaned forward and said: "But are you not aware of what happened to John the Baptist?"

"Yes, I am quite aware," was the immediate response. "He lost his head through the influence of a harlot. But I know the Supreme Court would not be so influenced."

2527 A man came to Newark, N. J. one day and asked a landlord to direct him to a first-rate lawyer.

"Well," said the landlord, "if, you have a good cause, go to Frelinghuysen; he is an honest lawyer and never undertakes any other kind: but if you want a keen, sharp lawyer, who sticks at nothing, go to lawyer So-and-so."

He watched the stranger and he went straight to So-and-so.

2528 A Dublin attorney died in poverty and many barristers of the city subscribed to a fund for his funeral. Toler, later Lord Chief Justice of Orbury, was approached for a shilling. "Only a shilling?" said Toler. "Only a shilling to bury an attorney? Here's a guinea; go and bury 20 of them."

2529 A blacksmith failed in business and a friend, to enable him to start once more, loaned him some iron which a creditor attached at the forge. The friend sued in trover for his iron. Rufus Choate, the well-known lawyer, appeared for him and pictured the cruelty of the sheriff's proceeding as follows: "He arrested the arm of industry as it fell towards the anvil; he put out the breath of his bellows. Like pirates in a gale at sea, his enemies swept everything by the board, leaving him, gentlemen of the jury, not so much as a horseshoe to nail upon his door post to keep the witches off."

The tears came into the blacksmith's eyes at this affecting description. One of his friends, noticing them, said to him, "Why, Tom, what's the matter with you? What are you crying about?"

"I had no idea I had been so much abused," said the blacksmith, weeping bitterly.

2530 A certain lawyer had his portrait done in his favorite attitude, standing with one hand in his pocket. His friends thought it was an excellent picture of him. An old farmer remarked that the portrait would have looked much more like the lawyer if it had represented him with his hand in another man's pocket instead of his own.

2531   A lawyer and physician having a dispute about precedence, referred it to Diogenes, who gave it in favor of the lawyer in these terms: "Let the thief go before and the executioner follow."

2532   A lawyer, when pleading the cause of an infant, took the child in his arms and presented it to the jury suffused with tears. This had a great effect, but the opposing counsel asked the child what made him cry. "He pinched me," said the little innocent.

2533   Joseph Choate was one of the most accomplished lawyers who ever practiced in this country. At one time in the New York courts, his opponent was a Westchester County attorney, representing a client from White Plains. Having a weak case, the latter fell back in his plea to the jury upon the effort to belittle the opposing attorney, and cautioned the jury not to be hoodwinked by Choate's "Chesterfieldian urbanity."

Choate, in due time, acknowledged this by briefly admonishing the jury not to be too greatly influenced by "my opponent's Westchesterfieldian suburbanity."

2534   When Samuel Leibowitz graduated from Cornell Law School he consulted the Dean as to whether or not he should become a criminal lawyer.

"Not that, Sam. Anything but that," said the Dean.

2535   A stranger, arriving in a small New England town, approached the first native he saw and asked:

"Have you a criminal lawyer in this town?"

"Well," replied the native cautiously, "we think we have, but so far we can't prove it on him."

2536   When Lincoln was practicing law, with his partner, Mr. Herndon, in Springfield, Ill., he was approached by a would-be client who wished to press a claim which involved several hundred dollars.

Before taking the case Lincoln investigated and found that

if his client won it would ruin a widow and her six children.
He wrote the following letter refusing to take up the case:
"We shall not take your case, though we can doubtless gain
it for you. Some things that are right legally are not right mor-
ally. But we will give you some advice for which we will charge
nothing. We advise a sprightly, energetic man like you to try
your hand at making six hundred dollars in some other way."

2537 Justice Benjamin Cardozo did not like Washington and
frequently lamented, during the sessions of the Supreme Court,
that he could not return to New York.

At a dinner party where he had been expressing this sentiment the discussion later turned to fur coats. "I won a fur coat
case in New York once," said Cardozo. "My client was so over-
joyed when we won that she threw her arms around my neck
and kissed me."

Seth Richardson, Assistant Attorney General, retorted,
"Well, Mr. Justice, in view of the type of practice you had, I
don't wonder you want to return to New York."

> RELATED SUBJECTS: *Speeches* 756-782; *Courts* 2471-
> 2473; *Trials* 2476-2485; *Witnesses* 2501-2506; *Juries*
> 2511-2517; *Evidence* 2521-2523; *Lawyers' Fees* 2541-
> 2545; *Criminals* 2571; *Laws* 2596-2599

> SEE ALSO: *Honesty* 294; *Long-Windedness* 353, 354,
> 356; *Memory* 371; *Shrewdness* 528; *Tolerance* 601;
> *Erudition* 1074; *Doctors* 1676; *Office Seekers* 1970;
> *Courts* 2472; *Judges* 2493; *Evidence* 2523

LAWYERS' FEES

2541 "How can I ever show my appreciation?" gushed a
woman to Clarence Darrow, after he had solved her legal
troubles.

"My dear woman," replied Darrow, "ever since the Phoeni-
cians invented money there has been only one answer to that
question."

2542 Lincoln was a poor money-maker. Daniel Webster, who
sent him a case, was amazed at the smallness of his bill, and his
fellow-lawyers looked upon his charges as very low. This was

his only fault in their eyes. Once, when another lawyer collected $250 for their joint services he refused to accept his share until the fee had been reduced to what he considered fair proportions and the overcharge had been returned to the client. When the presiding judge of the circuit heard of this, he indignantly exclaimed, "Lincoln, your picayune charges will impoverish the bar."

2543   One of the best trust stories I know had the late John G. Johnson, Philadelphia corporation lawyer, for its hero. Johnson was retained, among others, by E. H. Harriman, one of those "malefactors of great wealth" whom T. R. was fond of berating. There came a time when Johnson's counsel was urgently required in connection with one of the Napoleonic railroad mergers which Harriman specialized in sponsoring. So a cable of prodigious length was dispatched to Johnson, narrating in minutest detail exactly what the project was. The point on which the railroad magnate and his associates needed guidance was whether the merger could be accomplished without subjecting its authors to Federal prosecution under the Sherman Anti-Trust Act. Harriman requested Johnson to spare no words or expense in cabling his opinion, as the deal depended on it. An answer came within twenty-four hours. It was four words long. It read "Merger possible; conviction certain." Someone told me that Johnson rendered Harriman a bill of $100,000 for that opinion—$25,000 a word.

2544   It was a common thing for Lincoln to discourage unnecessary lawsuits, and consequently he was continually sacrificing opportunities to make money. One man who asked him to bring suit for $2.50 against a debtor would not be put off in his passion for revenge. His counsel therefore gravely demanded ten dollars as a retainer. Half of this he gave to the poor defendant, who therefore confessed judgment and paid the $2.50. Thus the suit was ended to the entire satisfaction of the angry creditor.

2545   A young Jewish lawyer asked the eminent Joseph Choate if he thought $500 would be too large a fee in his first important case.
   "You should make it $5,000, young man," said Choate, "in view of the great amount of effort and the importance of the issues involved."

"Almost thou persuadeth me to be a Christian!" the young Hebrew exclaimed.

RELATED SUBJECTS: *Lawyers* 2526-2537

SEE ALSO: *Quick Thinking* 486

LAW ENFORCEMENT

2546   The story is told of Bill MacDonald, an early Captain of the Texas Rangers. He received a request that a company of Rangers come to a nearby town to suppress a riot. He showed up himself, unaccompanied. The citizens' committee were disappointed and said, "We wanted a company, not one Ranger."

"Well, you ain't got but one mob, have you?"

2547   Robert Burns had a collie named Thurlow. When he was a Revenue officer he used to encourage Thurlow, who was well known throughout the countryside, to run a quarter of a mile or so ahead of him, that the moonshiners might be warned of his approach.

2548   During Prohibition a malicious person directed the Revenue officers to a man in whose cellar, they said, would be found a large cache of liquor. Swooping down upon the residence, they found nothing except the slightly incriminating presence of a hundred or more empty whiskey bottles.

"How did these get here?" they demanded of the owner.

"I certainly don't know," replied the man innocently, "I never bought an empty whiskey bottle in my life."

RELATED SUBJECTS: *Prohibitions and Restrictions* 1641-1642; *Courts* 2471-2473; *Police* 2551-2552; *Detectives* 2556-2557; *Jail* 2561-2563; *Hanging* 2566-2568; *Criminals* 2571; *Laws* 2596-2599; *Justice* 2601

SEE ALSO: *Shrewdness* 535; *Vanity* 625; *Credit* 2167

POLICE

2551   A policeman's life is sometimes a happy one. This is indicated by the floor-walker who threw up his job and entered the police force. When asked why, he said, "Well, the pay and the hours are all right, but the best thing is that the customer is always wrong."

2552   In New York City recently a Police car cruising along the street received the following radio call.

"Calling Car 13. Car 13. Go to Third Avenue and 14th Street. Nude woman running down the street. That is all."

There was a pause. Then came the afterthought. "All other cars stay on your beats. That is all."

RELATED SUBJECTS: *Law Enforcement* 2546-2548; *Detectives* 2556-2557; *Jail* 2561-2563; *Criminals* 2571

SEE ALSO: *Prejudice* 447; *Shrewdness* 537

DETECTIVES

2556   The French are lovers of ratiocination. Accordingly there are to be found in that nation, many admirers of the works of Conan Doyle. Sir Arthur had once taxied from the station to his hotel in Paris, and as he left the cab the driver said, "Merci, Monsieur Conan Doyle."

"How did you know who I am?" asked Doyle curiously.

The taximan explained, "There was a notice in the paper that you were arriving in Paris from the South of France. I knew from your general appearance that you were an Englishman. It is evident that your hair was last cut by a barber of the South of France. By these indications I knew you." "This is extraordinary. You had no other evidence to go upon?" asked Doyle. "Nothing except," said the driver, "the fact that your name is on your luggage."

2557   Edith Bolling Wilson tells the following story: "Writing the words 'Secret Service' recalls the funny idea of my colored Susan when the President (Woodrow Wilson) used to come to see me before we were married. She always announced the ceremony: 'The President and his Silver Service.' But when I told her it was not 'Silver' Service but 'Secret' Service, she amended it to 'The President and his Secretive Servants,' and beyond that she refused to budge!"

RELATED SUBJECTS: *Police* 2551-2552; *Criminals* 2571

JAIL

2561 In the first days of his governorship of the State of New York, Al Smith spoke to the assembled inmates of Sing Sing. Not until he had already risen to his feet did he realize that he did not know how to address this particular audience. "My fellow citizens," he said, almost without thinking, but then stopped, remembering that the citizenship of those there imprisoned was forfeited. Embarrassed he said, "My fellow convicts," and that too did not seem to be the mot juste. Giving the thing up as hopeless he launched once and for all into the sentence, "Well, in any case, I'm glad to see so many of you here."

2562 In an English act of Parliament there was a law passed for rebuilding Chelmsford jail. By one part of the law the new jail was to be built from the material of the old one; by another part of the law, the prisoners were to be kept in the old jail until the new jail was finished.

2563 John Bunyan, while in Bedford jail, was called upon by a Quaker desirous of making a convert of him.

"Friend John," said he, "I come to thee with a message from the Lord; and after having searched for thee in all the prisons in England, I am glad I have found thee at last."

"If the Lord has sent you," answered Bunyan, "you need not have had so much pains to find me out, for the Lord knows I have been here for twelve years."

> RELATED SUBJECTS: *Courts* 2471-2473; *Law Enforcement* 2546-2548; *Police* 2551-2552; *Criminals* 2571; *Stealing* 2581-2590

> SEE ALSO: *Drinking* 53; *Honesty* 293; *Speeches* 771; *Authors* 1215; *Woman's Suffrage* 2051; *Insurance* 2138; *Criminals* 2571; *Stealing* 2590

HANGING

2566 "It is very hard, my lord," said a convicted felon at the bar to Judge Barnet, "to hang a poor man for stealing a horse."

"You are not to be hanged, sir," answered the judge, "for

stealing a horse; but you are to be hanged that horses may not be stolen."

2567 Allen, the Quaker, waited upon the Duke of Sussex to remind him of his promise to present a petition to abolish capital punishment. The Duke did not seem to like the job, and observed that Scripture has declared,

"Whoso sheddeth man's blood, by man shall his blood be shed."

"But please note," replied the Quaker, "that when Cain killed Abel he was not hung for it."

"That's true," rejoined the Duke, "but remember, Allen, there were not twelve men in the world then to make a jury."

2568 When Lord Bacon was Chancellor of England, a witty criminal was brought before him. "Your Honor should let me go," he observed. "We're kin. My name is Hogg, and Hogg is kin to bacon."

"Not until it's hung," said Bacon.

RELATED SUBJECTS: *Death* 1746-1749; *Courts* 2471-2473; *Law Enforcement* 2546-2548; *Criminals* 2571; *Murder* 2576; *Justice* 2601

SEE ALSO: *Lateness* 324; *Courtship* 855; *Family* 950; *Bishops* 1492; *Trials* 2484

CRIMINALS

2571 A young criminal in Samuel Leibowitz's charge entered a plea of guilty. When the judge, on the set day, some days later, pronounced sentence dispatching the prisoner to Elmira, the latter spoke up unexpectedly, saying, "I don't see why I should go to jail, I am innocent."

"How about it?" demanded the judge.

Leibowitz replied, "He's guilty all right, your Honor, but since he entered his plea of guilty, he has been in the Raymond Street jail and the boys there have given him a post-graduate course in law. They tell him it is lovely at Sing Sing and terrible at Elmira. And now that you've sentenced him to Elmira, he wants to get out of it."

MURDER

2576 In France the Comte de Charolais shot a tiler on the roof of a house for the pleasure of seeing him fall off. Louis XV pardoned him, saying, "Understand me well. I will likewise pardon any one who shoots you."

STEALING

2581 Lord Chatham rebuked a dishonest Chancellor of the Exchequer by finishing a quotation the latter had commenced. The debate turned upon some grant of money for the encouragement of art, which was opposed by the Chancellor who finished his speech against Lord Chatham's motion by saying, "Why was not this ointmnt sold, and the money given to the poor?"

Chatham rose and said, "Why did not the noble lord complete the quotation, the application being so striking? As he has shrunk from it, I will finish the verse for him:

" 'This Judas said, not because he cared for the poor, but because he was a thief and carried the bag!' "

2582 Dr. Whipple, long Bishop of Minnesota, was about to hold religious services at an Indian village in one of the Western states, and before going to the place of meeting asked the chief, who was his host, whether it was safe for him to leave his effects in the lodge.

"There is no white man within a hundred miles of here," answered the chief.

2583   A man was once attending a formal dinner party. Finding himself next to a banker with whom he had very little acquaintanceship, he attempted to establish a friendly footing by remarking:

"I used to know Mr. Jones, who was with your firm. I understand he is a tried and trusted employee—"

The banker immediately assumed an air of cold unfriendliness.

"He was trusted, yes; and he will be tried, if we're fortunate enough to catch him."

2584   A certain celebrated New York night club proprietor is known for his laxness in the disciplining of his waiters on the point of honesty. It is in effect an extension of the tipping principle. Said he, on one occasion, "Most of the stealing they do is from the customers, so what do I care?"

2585   Balzac was once lying awake in bed when he saw a man enter his room cautiously and attempt to pick the lock of his writing desk. The rogue was not a little disconcerted at hearing a loud laugh from the occupant of the apartment whom he supposed asleep.

"Why do you laugh?" asked the thief.

"I am laughing, my good fellow," said Balzac, "to think what pains and risks you are taking in the hope of finding money by night in a desk where the lawful owner can never find any by day."

2586   President Lincoln had not forgotten some of the gossip once heard from Thad Stevens. Stevens and Simon Cameron had come into the Republican party from opposite sides. In conversation the Representative (Stevens) had relieved himself of some unkind expressions.

"You don't mean he'd (Cameron) steal!" exclaimed Lincoln, who had formed an accurate estimate of his aide's probity and knew that common theft was not one of his failings.

"He wouldn't steal a red-hot stove," retorted old Thad bitterly.

It was the sort of joke that helped make Lincoln's task bearable. He thought the Secretary of War should have a little fun, too, but the gentle Simon was not amused. He raged, and in his rage sent off an impulsive demand for a retraction. Unfortunately he found Stevens only too ready to oblige.

"I said you would not steal a red-hot stove," the apology ran. "I now take that back."

2587 The motto which was inserted under the arms of William, Prince of Orange, on his accession to the English crown, was, Non rapui sed recepi, ("I did not steal but I received").

This being shown to Dean Swift, he said with a sarcastic smile, "The receiver's as bad as the thief."

2588 Brahms' gold watch was stolen one day from his rooms which he never locked. When the police came and urged him to take the matter up officially, he simply said: "Leave me in peace! The watch was probably carried away by some poor devil who needs it more than I do."

2589 One of the most celebrated courts-martial during the Civil War was that of Franklin W. Smith and his brother, charged with defrauding the government. These men bore a high character for integrity. At this time, however, courts-martial were seldom invoked for any other purpose than to convict the accused, and the Smiths shared the usual fate of persons whose cases were submitted to such arbitrament. They were kept in prison, their papers seized, their business destroyed, and their reputations ruined, all of which was followed by a conviction.

The finding of the court was submitted to President Lincoln who, after a careful investigation, disapproved the judgment and wrote the following endorsement upon the papers:

"Whereas, Franklin W. Smith had transactions with the Navy Department to the amount of a million and quarter of dollars; and

"Whereas, he had a chance to steal at least a quarter of a million and was only charged with stealing twenty-two hundred dollars and the question now is about his stealing one hundred, I don't believe he stole anything at all.

"Therefore, the record and findings are disapproved, declared null and void and the defendants are fully discharged."

2590 Floyd Odlum, prominent authority on securities and exchange, once had a couple of Gainsboroughs and Watteaus stolen from him by a butler. The culprit ultimately landed in Sing Sing, and was there occupied in writing a novel. His former employer sent him pocket money and he, in turn, would forward to Odlum portions of his manuscript for his opinion.

"You write very well," Odlum once wrote to him, "but your style is a trifle stilted."

RELATED SUBJECTS: *Honesty* 286-294; *Police* 2551-2552; *Jail* 2561-2563; *Criminals* 2571

SEE ALSO: *Long-Windedness* 344; *Quick Thinking* 487; *Clothing* 716; *Authors* 1188, 1190, 1205; *Buying and Selling* 2066; *Chiseling* 2128; *Debt* 2172; *Wealth* 2182; *Witnesses* 2503; *Hanging* 2566

STOOL PIGEONS

2591 A disciple came to Mohammed and said:

"Master, my six brethren are all asleep, and I alone have remained awake to worship Allah."

Mohammed replied:

"And you too had better been asleep, if your worship of Allah consists of accusations against your brethren."

2592 One day M. Villemain, the Secretary of the French Academy, was declaiming in the library in a vigorous manner against Napoleon III. Leverrier, who was an ardent imperialist, chanced to overhear some of his remarks, and demanded:

"How dare you speak in this manner of the emperor in a public building?"

Villemain looked up carefully and replied:

"And who are you?"

"You know me, sir," said the astronomer.

"Your face may be familiar to me, but I don't exactly recall your name."

"Leverrier is my name."

"Oh, yes, Leverrier. Astronomer, I think. In his day I was intimately acquainted with Laplace; he was an astronomer too, and a gentleman."

"Sir," said Leverrier, "I despise wit, but if you continue speaking thus I warn you that I shall report your words to the proper authorities."

"Well," said Villemain, shrugging his shoulders, "every one has his way of making a living."

RELATED SUBJECTS: *Cowardice* 156-160; *Honor* 296-298; *Witnesses* 2501-2506; *Evidence* 2521-2523; *Police* 2551-2552; *Criminals* 2571

SEE ALSO: *Honor* 298

LAWS

2596 Lord John Russell said to David Hume, the philosopher: "What do you consider the object of legislation?"
"The greatest good to the greatest number."
"What do you consider the greatest number?"
"Number one," replied Hume.

2597 Mayor Frank Hague of Jersey City was one of America's more notorious characters for many years. He was noted for his peculiar interpretations of the law, beginning with his insistent, "I am the law" policy. He pursued his legal interpretations into more specialized channels however. He cut down Jersey City's murder statistics at the expense of manslaughter by rigidly classifying all inter-marital killings as manslaughter. "When a man kills his wife that's not murder, that's manslaughter," says Hague.

2598 Lincoln was once arguing a case against an opponent who tried to convince the jury that precedent is superior to law, and that custom makes things legal in all cases. Lincoln's reply was one of his many effective analogies in the form of a story. He told the jury that he would argue the case in the same way as his opponent, and began: "Old Squire Bagley came into my office one day and said: 'Lincoln, I want your advice as a lawyer. Has a man what's been elected justice of the peace a right to issue a marriage license?'

"I told him no. Whereupon the old squire threw himself back in his chair very indignantly and said, 'Lincoln, I thought you was a lawyer. Now Bob Thomas and me had a bet on this thing, and we agreed to let you decide, but if this is your opinion I don't want it, for I know a thunderin' sight better. I've been a squire eight years, and I've issued marriage licenses all that time.'"

2599 A rather celebrated case tried by the Supreme Court involved a decision upholding the Virginia statute providing for the sterilization of imbeciles. The majority opinion was written by Justice Oliver Wendell Holmes and O.K.'d by all except Justice Pierce Butler, who was a Roman Catholic.

Speculating about this, Holmes is said to have remarked to a colleague, "He knows the law is the way I have written it. But he is afraid of the Church. I'll lay you a bet the Church beats the law."

Professor Powell of Harvard was in the habit of reading Holmes' opinions to his Law classes, " 'Three generations of imbeciles are enough,' " he would read, adding, "Mr. Justice Butler dissenting."

> RELATED SUBJECTS: *Congress* 1941-1948; *Courts* 2471-2473; *Judges* 2486-2497; *Lawyers* 2526-2537; *Law Enforcement* 2546-2548; *Justice* 2601; *Wills and Testaments* 2606-2607

> SEE ALSO: *Behavior* 1; *Drinking* 42; *Endurance* 216; *Honesty* 289; *Vanity* 625; *Gossip* 823; *United States* 2031; *Chiseling* 2132; *Courts* 2471; *Trials* 2482; *Judges* 2492; *Jail* 2562

JUSTICE

2601 A French nobleman had been satirized by Voltaire and meeting the author soon after gave him a severe caning. Voltaire immediately complained to the Duke of Orleans and begged him to do him justice. "Sir," replied the duke, "you have had it done you already."

> RELATED SUBJECTS: *Freedom* 2036-2042; *Equality* 2046; *Courts* 2471-2473; *Laws* 2596-2599

> SEE ALSO: *Murder* 2576

WILLS AND TESTAMENTS

2606 The merchant Guyot lived and died in the town of Marseilles in France. He amassed a large fortune by the most laborious industry and by habits of the severest abstinence and privation. His neighbors considered him a miser and thought he was hoarding up money from mean and avaricious motives. The populace, whenever he appeared, pursued him with hootings and execrations, and the boys sometimes threw stones at him. At length he died and in his will were found the following words:

"Having observed from my infancy that the poor of Marseilles are badly supplied with water which they can only purchase at a high price, I have cheerfully labored the whole of my life to procure for them this great blessing, and I direct that the whole of my property be laid out in building an aqueduct for their use."

2607　The will of Stephen Girard, endowing Girard College in Philadelphia, prohibits clergymen from coming onto the premises. Horace Greeley one day approached the campus in his customary, somewhat clerical-looking garb. The gatekeeper challenged him, calling out, "You can't enter here."

"The hell I can't!" retorted Greeley.

"I beg your pardon, sir," replied the guard. "Pass right in."

RELATED SUBJECTS: *Death* 1746-1749; *Wealth* 2181-2187; *Taxes* 2191-2194; *Lawyers* 2526-2537; *Laws* 2596-2599

SEE ALSO: *Extravagance* 232; *Playwrights* 1380; *Bankruptcy* 2196

INDEX OF NAMES

INDEX OF SUBJECTS